TARAS SHEVCHENKO: A LIFE

Self-portrait, 1840

PAVLO ZAITSEV

Taras Shevchenko

A LIFE

Edited, abridged, and translated
with an introduction by
GEORGE S.N. LUCKYJ

Published for the Shevchenko Scientific Society by
UNIVERSITY OF TORONTO PRESS
Toronto Buffalo London

© University of Toronto Press 1988
Toronto Buffalo London
Printed in Canada
Reprinted in 2018
ISBN 0-8020-3450-0
ISBN 978-1-4875-7328-7 (paper)

Printed on acid-free paper

Canadian Cataloguing in Publication Data

Zaĭt͡sev, Pavlo, 1886–1965.
   Taras Shevchenko, a life

   Translation of: Z͡hyttî͡a Tarasa Shevchenka.
   Includes index.
   ISBN 0-8020-3450-0

   1. Shevchenko, T.H. (Taras Hryhorovych), 1814–1861 – Biography.
   2. Poets, Ukrainian – 19th century – Biography.
   I. Luckyj, George, 1919–
   II. Naukove tovarystvo imeny Shevchenka. III. Title.

   PG3948.S51Z3413 1988   891.7'912   C88-093324-0

Contents

Illustrations / vi

Introduction / vii

PART ONE
Childhood and Youth 1814–38 / 1

PART TWO
The Maturing Artist 1838–43 / 39

PART THREE
The Ukrainian Journeys 1843–47 / 77

PART FOUR
Arrest and Exile 1847–57 / 137

PART FIVE
Back to Freedom 1858–61 / 221

Glossary / 269

Selected Bibliography / 271

Index / 273

Illustrations

Frontispiece Self-portrait, 1840

FOLLOWING PAGE xi

A drawing by Shevchenko of his childhood home
Briullov's portrait of Zhukovsky, which bought Shevchenko's freedom
A portrait of Briullov by Shevchenko
A drawing of a blind minstrel by Shevchenko
Princess Barbara Repnina, by Shevchenko
Vasyl Tarnovsky
Panteleimon Kulish
Facsimile of the manuscript of Shevchenko's poem 'Testament'
The Third Section's file on Shevchenko
The gaol in St Petersburg where members of the Cyrilo-Methodian Brotherhood were interrogated in 1847
The 'bootleg' notebooks
The house in Orenburg where Shevchenko lived in 1849–50
Yakiv Kukharenko
A drawing of Count Fiodor Tolstoy by Shevchenko
Marko Vovchok
A portrait of Ira Aldridge by Shevchenko
Shevchenko's portrait of Lykera Polusmakivna
Self-portrait, 1860
Monument to Shevchenko at Kaniv

COLOUR PLATES

Portrait of Keikuatova, 1847; oil *facing page 28*
Catherine, 1842; illustration to a poem; oil *facing page 60*
Fire in the steppes, 1848; watercolour *facing page 188*
Moonlit night at Kos Aral, 1848; watercolour *facing page 188*

Introduction

*The history of my life is a part
of the history of my homeland.*   TARAS SHEVCHENKO

Taras Shevchenko, the greatest poet of Ukraine, occupies a very special place in the hearts and minds of his fellow-countrymen. He is not only a great literary genius whose poetry possesses unsurpassed beauty but a national prophet who definitively expressed the quintessence of Ukraine's existence as a nation. In fact it may be said that he created modern Ukraine, for without Shevchenko it might still be what it had been earlier – Little Russia. The real meaning of this statement, which is a truism for Ukrainians, is revealed not only through the study of his poetry (most of it known by heart in his native country) but in the story of his life. The bare bones of his biography are also well known to the public. His deprived childhood and youth as a serf, his liberation from serfdom and his success as an art student in St Petersburg, the two extended journeys to Ukraine and the writing of revolutionary poetry, the arrest in 1847, the hardships of exile until 1857, and finally, the return to St Petersburg, the final trip to Ukraine, and his untimely death in Russia – all are familiar events in the life of a man who is regarded as a national martyr. Yet the full, detailed story of his life is little known. The exact unfolding of his life-story was not accomplished until Pavlo Zaitsev published his *Life of Taras Shevchenko (Zhyttia Tarasa Shevchenka)* in 1955.

It might be appropriate to cast a quick look at the attempts to produce a biography of Shevchenko both before and after that date. No mention will be made of biographical fragments but only of complete biographies. The first attempt was made by Mykhailo Chaly, a man who knew Shevchenko personally. In 1882 he published *The Life and Works of Taras Shevchenko (Zhizn i proizvedeniia Tarasa Shevchenko)*. Chaly, who spent twenty years writing his book, regarded it as merely a compilation of facts for the use of future biographers. Many important facts of the poet's life and many more of his poems, unpublished during the tsarist regime, were unknown to Chaly. The next important attempt to produce a comprehensive story of Shevchenko's life was made by the well-known writer Oleksander

Konysky, who published *Taras Shevchenko-Hrushivsky: The Chronicle of His Life* (*Taras Shevchenko-Hrushivsky: Khronika yoho zhyttia*) in two parts in Lviv in 1898 and 1901. This extensive study goes well beyond being a simple collection of documents and attempts to interpret the development of the poet's outlook, based on his life-story.

The revolution of 1917 gave fresh impetus to Shevchenko studies, primarily because a great deal of material relating to his life and work was published for the first time. Yet curiously enough, for decades no new biography of the poet was forthcoming. This was because the Soviet regime had great difficulty interpreting Shevchenko's life and work according to a new ideology. The so-called struggle for Shevchenko began, and lasted well into the late 1930s. Finally, Shevchenko's heritage was accepted as that of a 'revolutionary democrat' (following the 'Theses' issued by the Central Committee of the Ukrainian Communist Party in 1934), but there was still no new biography of him. The gains made by Shevchenko scholarship in the relatively liberal 1920s were wiped out, and yet no comprehensive new study of his life was produced. According to a Soviet source, 'The problem of a political biography and the outlook of Shevchenko became the centre of biographical studies.'*

It was outside the Soviet Ukraine, in western Ukraine and in Poland, that an attempt was made. The Ukrainian Scientific Institute in Warsaw began, in the mid-1930s, to publish the collected works of Shevchenko in thirteen volumes under the editorship of Pavlo Zaitsev. The first volume of this edition was to be a new biography of the poet, written by Zaitsev. The volume was indeed finished and was in print when the Soviet Union annexed western Ukraine in 1939. The book never appeared, but the proofs were saved and the author was able to revise and publish it in Munich in 1955. This is the volume that has been edited and translated here. Its chief merit is that it was produced outside the sphere of Soviet political control by one of the most reputable Shevchenko scholars. Pavlo Zaitsev (1886–1965) was born in the district of Sumy in eastern Ukraine. During the brief period of Ukrainian independence in 1917–18 he was an official in the ministry of education. He emigrated in 1921 and became a lecturer at Warsaw University and a member of the Ukrainian Scientific Institute in that city. He began his work as a scholar in the field of Shevchenko studies before the revolution, publishing valuable materials, until then unknown. From 1934 to 1939 he edited the thirteen-volume edition of Shevchenko's works and wrote a monograph on Shevchenko and the Poles. His major work was this biography of Schevchenko.

* *Shevchenkoznavstvo; pidsumky i problemy* (Kiev 1975), 254

After the end of the Second World War it took a long time for Soviet Ukrainian scholarship to produce a comprehensive biography of Shevchenko. Some short biographical sketches appeared, and a great deal of valuable biographical research was published. Finally, Yevhen Kyryliuk published *T.H. Shevchenko: Life and Work* (*T.H. Shevchenko: zhyttia i tvorchist*) in 1959. The book was republished in 1964 and received a Lenin prize. In the same year a new, most comprehensive (633 pages) biography of the poet was published by a 'collective' of three scholars, Yevhen Kyryliuk, Yevhen Shabliovsky, and Vasyl Shubravsky – *T.H. Shevchenko: A Biography* (*T.H. Shevchenko: Biohrafiia*). It is the most up-to-date account of Shevchenko's life, with, needless to say, the required official emphasis.

Under the circumstances, Zaitsev's biography remains the most balanced and scholarly. It does not make Shevchenko more of a nationalist than he actually was. Shevchenko's love for his country is the central, undeniable fact of his entire life. It is this love which makes it difficult for the English, Canadian, or American reader of non-Ukrainian descent to appreciate him fully. For in their literatures such deep sentiments, so directly and forcefully expressed, are unknown and may be regarded as obsessive. This brings me to the consideration of some of the difficulties encountered in this translation. Zaitsev's narrative, like Shevchenko's life itself, is tinged with passion and sentiment that, literally translated, may be unpalatable to the English reader. Language has a great deal to do with it. It is possible to say certain things in Ukrainian without sounding sentimental, while in English a different form of expression is required if the reader is not to be put off. Bearing this in mind, a translator has to become an editor at the same time. The factual and intentional structure of Zaitsev's work has been preserved, but his prose has on occasion been condensed and abridged. Further, as a guide for the English reader to the major stages of Shevchenko's life, the original sixteen chapters of the book have been grouped into five parts.

A striking example of the difficulties encountered during the translation was the decision to give prose translations of the quotations from Shevchenko's poems. Shevchenko's poetry is untranslatable, and all the existing English translations are in one way or another unsatisfactory. It was decided, therefore, to render the quotations in literal prose, borrowing occasionally from the translations made by Vera Rich, Watson Kirkconnell, and John Weir. The result may be disappointing, and non-Ukrainian readers may wonder about the greatness of Shevchenko's poetry, which is totally missing. Yet this is not a book about his poetry but the story of his life, where quotations of poems are always merely illustrations of his state of mind at a given place and time. Each quotation of more than two lines is footnoted, with an indication of its Ukrainian source.

Another problem the editor faced was deciding which of the collected works of Shevchenko should be used as a source of references. It might appear logical to use the collected works (Warsaw edition) edited by Zaitsev himself. However, in order to bring Shevchenko closer to readers who knew no Russian, Zaitsev had all Shevchenko's works in Russian, including his letters and the journal, translated into Ukrainian. This makes his edition defective, and it was decided to use for reference the six-volume Soviet edition of Shevchenko's works unless there was a good reason to refer to Zaitsev's edition. In preparing his edition Zaitsev had no direct access to manuscripts of Shevchenko's Ukrainian poems, another severe drawback. In prose quotations in the text itself it was decided to supply footnotes only for any quotation longer than two sentences, so as not to overburden the book with footnotes. The 1955 edition of Zaitsev's book contained a bibliography, which this editor has supplemented, but no footnotes, which had to be added. A modified Library of Congress transliteration of Ukrainian and Russian has been used, with titles of works appearing first in translation and then in parentheses in the original, on first mention (with the exception of *Kobzar*).

In this post-Freudian age, when Carlyle's dictum that 'the history of the world is but the biography of great men' is once more being taken seriously, it is redundant to stress the importance of a knowledge of Shevchenko's biography. It is a most dramatic and readable story of a great Ukrainian, whose specific achievement is unique in world literature. No other example comes to mind of a poet conjuring up through his work the very basis of a national existence. His nationalism, however, is tempered by universal concerns of human love and brotherhood. Indeed, his is a millenarian vision in which not only his oppressed countrymen but all men one day will be free. His life-story is not merely a backdrop to his works but a telling example of human frailty overcome by will and the creative urge. It is told here in great detail, and it is in the detail that both the frailty and the will are revealed. For a student of Ukrainian and Russian intellectual history the story is also instructive concerning nineteenth-century Russia. Although it tells of great oppression, serfdom, injustice, and censorship (including the tsar's own attempt to prohibit Shevchenko from writing and painting) the poet's biography also demonstrates the great affection, humanity, and kindness shown to him by friends and oppressors alike. The conditions of his arrest and exile would compare very favourably to today's GULAG. The fact that so many minute details of his hard life have been preserved for posterity shows that, in spite of the cruel regime, people in Russia and Ukraine were aware that Shevchenko was an extraordinary human being whose life-story would always be remembered. It is, of course, not only his own personal story but a symbolic history of Ukraine. The intense suffering is overshadowed by an even more intense yearning for freedom, the long humiliation and deprivation by the frantic search for marital happiness (in the end denied to him, just as complete self-realization was denied to his people). Yet the final message of Shevchenko's life-story is one of confidence and hope.

The Shevchenko Scientific Society, which has also published the biography by Konysky, deserves praise for completing this project. I wish to thank Susan Kent for her expert editing. My greatest debt is to my wife, Moira.

George S.N. Luckyj

A drawing by Shevchenko of his childhood home

A drawing of a blind minstrel by Shevchenko

A portrait of Briullov
by Shevchenko

Princess Barbara Repnina,
by Shevchenko

Briullov's portrait
of Zhukovsky,
which bought
Shevchenko's freedom

Vasyl Tarnovsky

Panteleimon Kulish

Як умру то поховайте
Мене на могилі
Серед стелу широкого
На вкраїні милій,
Щоб лани широкополі,
И Дніпро, и кручі
Було видно, було чути
Як реве ревучий,
Як понесе въ Украины
У синье море
Кровъ ворожу.... отойди я
И ланы и горы
Все покину, и полыну
До самого Бога

Facsimile of
the manuscript of
Shevchenko's poem
'Testament'

The Third Section's
file on Shevchenko

The gaol in St Petersburg where members of the
Cyrilo-Methodian Brotherhood were interrogated in 1847

The 'bootleg' notebooks

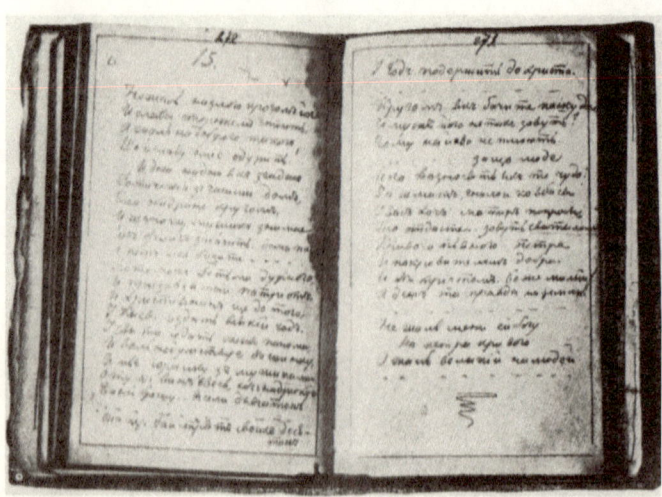

The house in Orenburg where Shevchenko lived in 1849–50

Monument to Shevchenko
at Kaniv

Yakiv Kukharenko

Shevchenko's portrait of Lykera Polusmakivna

A portrait of Ira Aldridge by Shevchenko

A drawing of
Count Fiodor Tolstoy
by Shevchenko

Marko Vovchok

Self-portrait, 1860

PART ONE

Childhood and Youth

1814-38

I

On the steppe borderlands of ancient Kiev, in the southern region of princely Zvenyhorod, between the high and rolling hills, in the valleys full of green groves, there spread the large and picturesque village of Kerelivka[1] hiding its white houses among luscious orchards. It is not known when the village came into being, but by 1741 its 130 serf households were subject to Princess Jabłonowski, the wife of the later Polish Grand Crown Hetman.[2] Later Kerelivka came into the domain of another Crown Hetman, Count Ksawery Branicki, and only at the very end of the eighteenth century did it become the property of the Russian magnate Vasiliy Engelhardt. Having obtained several villages in this region as a bequest after the death of his uncle, the mighty favourite of Tsarina Catherine II, His Excellency the Prince of Tauria, Grigoriy Potemkin, Engelhardt added to these possessions some neighbouring villages, including Kerelivka. Himself a descendant of Livonian barons, a general in the Russian army and decorated many times, later a privy councillor and senator, in the 1820s and 1830s Vasiliy Engelhardt owned in Zvenyhorod district alone one town and twelve villages with 8,500 Ukrainian serfs, but his spacious estates formed only a small wedge in the huge territory that belonged to his sister, Countess Alexandra Branicki. Those Branicki holdings comprised parts of Bila Tserkva, Kaniv, Uman, and Chyhyryn districts and totalled 300,000 *desiatinas*.[3] Most of this land the countess received either as a bequest or as a dowry from her beloved uncle, whose mistress she was when Potemkin, with the permission of the tsarina, married her off to the aging Count Ksawery Branicki, the Crown

---

1 This is how Shevchenko and all the local people pronounced the name of the village. Its official name was Kyrylivka.
2 Grand Crown Hetman was the title of the Polish military leaders. The title Hetman was later given by the Ukrainian Cossacks to their leaders.
3 A *desiatina* equalled 2.7 acres.

Hetman and one of the instigators of the confederacy of Targowica.[4] Her brother, Senator Vasiliy Engelhardt, after leaving the service, settled in the 1820s in the small town of Vilshana, which was the administrative centre of his estates. Here he lived in retirement, managing his vast possessions, which stretched as far as the Katerynoslav and Kherson districts, which Potemkin had seized from the Zaporozhians.[5] In addition he owned estates in Yaroslav, Smolensk, and Chernihiv provinces. His possessions amounted to over 160,000 *desiatinas*, with 50,000 serfs of both sexes. Kerelivka was only six *versts*[6] away from Engelhardt's main residence.

On 25 February old style (9 March new style)[7] 1814, in the household of one of Engelhardt's serfs, a son, Taras, was born to Hryhoriy Hrushivsky-Shevchenko and his wife Kateryna. He was born in the neighbouring village of Moryntsi, the birthplace of his mother, where his parents then lived. Two years later Hryhoriy Shevchenko returned with his family to his native Kerelivka, where Taras's grandfather, Ivan, also lived. It was in Kerelivka that Taras grew up.

Shevchenko's house was poor and dilapidated and its inhabitants poverty-stricken. The entire family, like the majority of Engelhardt's serfs, led a destitute existence. As early as 1795 Kerelivka largely consisted of landless servants, labourers, and menial workers, and the impoverishment of the peasants intensified. As in the rest of Ukraine, here too the number of 'wandering' serfs increased. These were peasants without livestock, who were ready to work, without pay, for board alone at the landlord's farms or at the distilleries, mills, and smithies. The entire clan of Taras's mother, the Boikos,[8] consisted of hired labourers such as these. Taras's father did not sink to such a level because of his innate intelligence, diligence, and shrewdness. He was literate and well known in his village for his practical knowledge. Having learned the wheelwright's trade, he had a certain local fame in the craft; in addition, during

---

4 The confederacy of Polish nobles at Targowica in 1792 was directed against the constitution of 1791. Catherine II made use of the confederacy to justify Russian intervention in Poland.
5 Zaporozhian Cossacks – literally, 'living beyond the Dnieper rapids'
6 A *verst* equalled 3,500 feet.
7 'Old style' refers to the Julian calendar in use in the Russian empire before the 1917 revolution and, in the nineteenth century, twelve days behind the Gregorian calendar now in use.
8 The Boikos are a Ukrainian tribe in the central Carpathians. Like the Hutsuls and the Lemkos they have retained their tribal characteristics. Inclined to be traders, the Boikos often travelled to distant Ukrainian lands. Taras's mother's maiden name was Boiko, which indicated that her ancestors came from the Boiko region.

5   Childhood and Youth 1814–38

the summer he became a *chumak* (itinerant salt-vendor), taking the various products by cart to Kiev or even to the seaport of Odessa. Only through hard work did Hryhoriy and Kateryna keep their heads above water and care for their six children. Taras was their third child. Mykyta his brother and his sister Kateryna preceded him, and after him came Yosyp and the blind Maria. When later remembering his family, the poet wrote

> bondage,
> hard work. No
> time is granted to pray[9]

he did not exaggerate. In the light of documentary and historical evidence, the life of the Kerelivka serfs was indeed a hell, as Shevchenko described it in his poems:

> I dread remembering
> The small cottage at the end of the village
> ...
> My mother bore me there,
> And she sang as she nursed me,
> Pouring out her sorrow
> Into her child. In that grove,
> In this cottage, in this paradise
> I saw hell.[10]

The serfs had no right to inherit land, which was allotted to them in repartitional holding. They had no access to forests, and in return for each cartful of wood they had to labour for their master. This labour for the landlord was theoretically limited to three days a week, but in fact they had to work to fill the quotas of tied sheafs, loaded wagons, measures of grain, and so on. These quotas were high, and the peasants had to work full time to fulfil them. As well as the labour in the fields, they were obliged to render other services to their master. Shevchenko's parents had little time to work on the plot that supplied them with produce. In addition to everything else they had to buy clothes for themselves and their children and pay taxes to the state. Their lives were hard and joyless, and there was scarcely a ray of hope.

The hardships of life in Kerelivka are amply documented in the

9 'Yak by vy znaly panychi,' T. Shevchenko, *Povne zibrannia tvoriv v shesty tomakh* (Kiev 1963–64), II, 252, hereinafter referred to as *Povne*
10 Ibid, II, 252, 253

archives. There are records stating that the serfs of Potemkin's nephew frequently ran away from the village and did not return home for years. In addition, the farm managers and supervisors used cruel and excessive punishment, sometimes flogging the peasants to death. This was true until the 1840s, when relations between masters and serfs were formalized and when some protection was offered to the latter. Times were much harder during Shevchenko's childhood, when the landlords' licence was the only law.

Yet before the stark reality of life registered in Taras's mind, the boy had his years of carefree childhood. The house in which he lived with his parents stood at the edge of the village. It was dingy and old, with a thatched roof and a black chimney. It was painted white on the outside. In front of the house was a flower garden, tended by Taras's older sister Kateryna; next to the gate there grew an old ramose willow withered at the crown, and beyond that was a shed. Beyond the shed was an orchard, and a path through the orchard led to a meadow where a stream meandered, surrounded by willows, guelder rose, and broad-leaved dark green burdocks. Taras bathed in the little stream, and in the orchard, as he later wrote, he 'fell asleep in carefree dreams.' His sister Kateryna looked after him and was 'his tender nurse.' She was eight years older than he. The boy was active and restless. He was difficult to care for and would occasionally eat earth or disappear. Kateryna's nursing duties came to an end when Taras was five. His sister, Maria, was born blind, and from then on she demanded Kateryna's undivided attention.

One episode stood out in Taras's memories of his childhood. It was accentuated by later memories and experiences and found a place in his poetry. This was his tender friendship with a neighbour's young girl of similar age, the curly-haired Oksana Kovalenko. They played together as small children, and this play led to a youthful love. We shall see this love story a little later, but while they were both eight years old we can see their mothers observing their children's love, looking forward, jokingly perhaps, to their later marriage.

> We grew up together
> And loved one another,
> Small as we were,
> And our mothers looked on
> And said that later
> They would see us married.[11]

11 'My vkupochtsi kolys rosly,' ibid, 229

Childhood and Youth 1814-38

Taras grew, like most village children, protected only by Divine Providence. Even as a small boy he distinguished himself by his talent. He learned how to make clay whistles and 'nightingales'; he knew how to fashion toys from reeds, and above all he drew with coal or chalk, on fences, walls, and wherever he could. He was a curious child, always asking questions, and began, quite early, to live in a world of fantasy. In order to satisfy his curiosity he went out into the fields to find the pillars that prop up the sky. After leaving the village he reached a high gravemound,[12] climbed it, but all he could see from there was another village. He lost his way, and the itinerant *chumaks* brought him home to Kerelivka. But the next day he was still thinking of how to reach these pillars. He loved listening to stories told by grown-ups and to their songs. He had an excellent musical memory and soon was able to remember countless songs. His deep sensitivity and good memory opened the mysterious world of make-believe for him, full of unusual images.

Taras's father was a wise and literate man. On holidays, especially during the winter-time, he read aloud *The Lives of the Saints* (*Minea*). This was a very popular book. The young boy listened to stories of the Christian martyrs, told in ringing and solemn Old Church Slavonic, about men who gave their lives for the Christian faith, about biblical events, adorned with popular apocryphal motifs, and he saw a different world, distant but full of terrible happenings, miracles, and heroic strivings. But apart from this printed book, which was so full of wonders, there was also another, unprinted book open to Taras. This was the account of those recent bloody times which had also touched his native Kerelivka. The story, told by Taras's grandfather, Ivan, was about the peasant rebellion known in history as 'Koliivshchyna,' a bloody uprising of the peasants against their Polish landlords in 1768. Grandpa Ivan had himself been a participant. He was of powerful physique, and when Taras was six years old, grandpa Ivan married, for the third time, at the age of eighty. His grandfather's tales were later mentioned by Shevchenko in the epilogue to his long poem 'The Haidamaks' ('Haidamaky'), the popular appellation of the peasant rebels:

> It happened that on a Sunday,
> After closing the *Minea*
> And after drinking a glass with the neighbour,
> My father would ask grandfather to tell

---

12 A gravemound (*mohyla*) was a tall mound of earth over the burial places of the Cossacks.

> About Kolii, in the days of yore,
> How Zalizniak and Honta punished the Poles.
> The eyes of the nearly hundred-year-old man
> Would shine like stars,
> And his words flowed one after another.
> Not once did I cry over the sexton's fate,
> And no one noticed that a small child
> Was crying in the corner.[13]

At a very tender age Taras could empathize with these tragic stories. The seeds of feeling for the injured were even then planted in his heart. He soaked up the tales of the past of his own people, their sufferings and the injustices they had endured. The third source of the boy's inspiration and reflection, after his father's books and his grandfather's stories, was the rich heritage of Ukrainian folksongs. Deprived of national leadership and betrayed by its elite, which for the sake of privilege became Russified, the Ukrainian people, enslaved and denied any possibility of normal cultural development, retained the ancient heritage of their culture in folksongs. These were songs about the distant and not so distant past and about the dismal present. The political and ethical ideals of the people were preserved in these songs. They were sung during the hated working days, expressed popular grievances and sorrows, and also were a consolation and a means of celebrating holidays. The songs re-created and resurrected the Cossack state, abolished a hundred years earlier; they of course idealized it fondly. The peasant masses had tied their hopes of liberation to these Cossack wars, and now their political dreams were attached to the imaginary return of the Cossack era. This longing was often heard by the little Taras, who also listened to songs describing the peasant yoke under the Polish magnates and later under the aristocratic rule of imperial Russia: 'A black cloud has gathered, and a grey one too, / There was Poland and now Russia new.'[14]

People sang about Tsarina Catherine, the 'hostile old hag' who had enslaved Ukraine, 'the wide and merry land.' They remembered the destruction of the Zaporozhian Sich by the Russians in 1775 and how life became unbearable under the 'damned landlords.' The old lands of the Cossacks, of which they had been deprived half a century earlier, began only a dozen *versts* beyond Kerelivka. After abolishing the Sich, Catherine II, with a stroke of a pen, gave twenty thousand *desiatinas* of this land

13 'Haidamaky,' *Povne*, I, 139
14 Lines from a famous folksong. M. Drahomanov, *Novi ukrainski pisni pro hromadski spravy* (Geneva 1881), 25

to Countess Branicki. As a small boy Taras must have seen old Cossacks who had fled to the Zaporozhian Sich from their masters. The Crown Hetman Branicki had at one time commanded the main street in Kerelivka to be 'decorated' with impaled serfs, peasants who had tried to set his stored grain on fire. This had happened not so long before; people still talked about it, and Taras must have heard about these tragic events, which seemed to confirm the words of a song: 'There is no truth in this world and it cannot be found.' No wonder these vivid impressions in the boy's mind led him later to write about truth, which had been stolen from the people.

Taras was of slender build, smaller than other boys of his age. He was more attached to his mother and his sister than to his father, who, when the boy was eight and a half, sent him to school. Literacy was highly valued in the Shevchenko household. The school building was next to the church, dilapidated and bereft of trees or fences. The cantor (*diak*), who was also a teacher, lived in one room; the other one was a classroom, with a long table in the middle. Pupils sat around the table and often on the floor. The instruction consisted of reading, arithmetic, and readings in the psalter. In truth the instruction was very hard, since the entire primer had to be learned by heart. An additional difficulty was the quaint Old Church Slavonic language. Later, Shevchenko often recalled how he could not master it. His teacher, the cantor, was cross-eyed[15] and short, thickset like a Zaporozhian.

Shevchenko has left us a detailed description of his school-days in the introductory pages to his long story 'The Princess' ('Kniaginia'), written in Russian. The cantor-teacher, nicknamed Sovhyr, was, according to him, 'of stern disposition rather than kind, and in matters of daily comfort he was a true Spartan.'[16] This Spartan, in accordance with the old pedagogical tradition, gave all his students, without exception, a sound thrashing every Saturday. The twigs needed for this execution had to be gathered by the pupils themselves, after they stole them from the neighbouring orchard of Hrytsko Piany (Gregory the Drunkard). 'We were used to these beatings,' writes Shevchenko, 'but the worst of it was that while being thrashed one was asked to recite the commandments. A true Spartan! ... When my turn came I begged him to spare me ... but sometimes he would beat me so severely that it was better not to ask for favours.'[17] However, Shevchenko had a kind word to say of the cantor.

---

15 According to documentary evidence, he was probably Cantor Hubsky.
16 'Kniaginia,' *Povne*, III, 178
17 Ibid

'May you rest in peace,' he continued, 'you, poor man, did not know what you were doing. They beat you, so you beat others and saw no sin in it ... Sometimes I would go out of school into the street and would see other boys playing in the straw around the shed without knowing anything about the school. I would feel so miserable and wonder why I was tormented in school. Without further ado I would join the carefree lads in the warm straw, but then two pupils would fetch me back to school, and one knows what they did there to boys who ran away.'[18]

Taras, who was a bright pupil, suffered a great deal not only through the beatings he received but because of the stultifying instruction. He learned to read very quickly. He then began reading prayers and the psalter, thus reaching an advanced level. The occasion was, as usual, celebrated in a special way, by offering other pupils a bowl of gruel and some copper coins. After that he gained the status of a scribe, and to prove it he drew letters with chalk on the blackboard. He recalled his school-days as an 'almost happy period' shattered only by the death of his mother, an event that left a deep scar in his psyche. His mother died on 20 August 1823, when Taras was nine and a half years old: 'Still young, she was laid in the grave / by hardship and work.'[19]

His mother was thirty-seven years old and on her death left six children, from the eldest, Mykyta, who was thirteen, to the youngest, Marusia, four years old. The Shevchenko household, bereft of the mother, was filled with sorrow and hopelessness. The father, who continued to work, could not look after all the children. The eldest daughter, Kateryna, Taras's nurse, had earlier that year married a boy in the village of Zelena Dibrova. The younger, Yaryna, was only eight years old and could not look after the house. There was no other solution than for Taras's father to marry again: early the next year he married Oksana Tereshchenko, a widow with three small children. Grandfather Ivan was the matchmaker. Thus Shevchenko's tiny house accepted four more people. Of all the children Taras missed his mother most. He later recalled how on Christmas Eve that year he and his brother Mykyta and sister Yaryna in sorrow brought the holy supper to Grandpa Ivan and how they could not repeat the traditional formula without crying that their 'father and mother had sent us.' Very soon Taras's life at home became hell. The stepmother was quarrelsome and took a particular dislike to Taras – perhaps, Taras confessed, 'because I often tormented her weakly son, Stepan.'

18 Ibid, 177
19 'Yak by vy znaly panychi,' *Povne*, II, 252

Childhood and Youth 1814-38

The year 1824, marked by such turmoil and tragedy in Taras's family, brought reform to the Kerelivka school. Following the state reform of the Ukrainian church schools in 1820, a new cantor, with higher paper qualifications, was sent to Kerelivka. He was one of many among the new breed of cantor-teachers who were given the position because they were unsuited to become priests and incapable of further education. The new cantors replaced the old ones, like Sovhyr, whom the parishioners of Kerelivka liked for his attractive voice. The new reform abrogated the old rights in Ukraine, according to which self-governing parishes had the right to select their own cantors. The new cantor, parachuted into the church consistory from above, turned out to be a drunkard and did not get a warm reception in Kerelivka. Many pupils, including Taras, decided to leave the school, 'like lambs fleeing the wolf.' Sovhyr tried to resist his dismissal but had to give in to the law. The new cantor, Bohorsky, took possession of the school, and Sovhyr, after packing his few belongings, went off in search of a new job in one of those schools that had not yet received the new type of cantor.

Probably in the summer of that year, perhaps in May or June, Taras experienced something new – he joined his father's *chumak* expedition. Before, only his older brother, Mykyta, had gone with their father on these trips, but this time, perhaps to save Taras from his stepmother's ire, his father took him along. The landscape with which Taras was familiar was rather hilly. Kerelivka and the neighbouring villages of Tarasivka, Pedynivka, and Budyshcha were spread on the uplands, which were quite mountainous, and the entire region was bisected by valleys and forests. There was no wide horizon open to the inhabitants, and their world seemed narrow and closed. Now for the first time Taras saw the steppe, and it impressed him with all its wide mystery. At Huliay-Pole it seemed limitless. The young, sensitive boy did not look at the village of Novomyrhorod tucked away along the stream but gazed into the boundless expanse of the steppe. As they drove along Taras asked his father about the Arakcheev military settlements,[20] numbered according to the military companies that inhabited them. Near Yelysavet he saw a Gypsy camp. The boy's poetic soul was filled with these vivid impressions, which stirred in him cosmic feelings – 'when there is a desire to comprehend the entire world in time and space.' There was an extraordinary stillness in the air, especially during the moonlit nights, when he was overcome by fear:

---

20 Count Aleksey Arakcheev (1769–1834), a tsarist minister, was the creator and director (from 1817) of military settlements throughout the country.

> Around you – the steppe, like a sea,
> Wide and blue.
> Gravemound beyond gravemound
> Shimmers in the distance.[21]

As he listened to the creaking wheels of the *chumak* cart and looked at the moonlight flooding the wide steppes, the presence of the universe made itself felt within him. The seeds of his later poems, full of cosmic awareness, were planted here, when he was travelling across the steppe. In particular, the famous invocation to the long poem 'The Haidamaks' (1842) shows traces of these childhood memories, when the 'white-faced moon' whispered to him in a friendly conversation 'like a brother or a sister.'

The trips with his father twice removed him from the hellish home where the stepmother nagged her stepchildren. At one time she even expelled little Marusia. Full of special hatred for Taras, in order to get rid of him she sent him to tend the calves and swine. With a piece of bread as a packed lunch, Taras spent hours as a swineherd in the leafy valleys between Kerelivka and Tarasivka, sitting on high gravemounds and gazing into the blue sky above. Sometimes his orphan life was brightened by a pilgrimage that he and his sister Kateryna made on foot to the Motronyn monastery. There in the graveyard were buried some of the leaders of the Koliivshchyna. The boy could read to some of the pilgrims, who remembered those bloody days, the names on the gravestones. Tales were told of bygone years, and tears were shed, too. They added to the knowledge that Taras had gained from his grandfather.

A new tragedy was soon to descend on the Shevchenko family. In the late fall of 1824 Taras's father came back from a trip to Kiev. On the way home he caught a chill and, after an illness, died on 21 March 1825, in his forty-seventh year. The oldest son, Mykyta, was fifteen; Taras, eleven. The stepmother became the head of the household. Before his death, making his last bequests, Hryhoriy Shevchenko said these words: 'My son Taras does not need anything from my estate. He will not be an ordinary man. He will be either someone very good or a good-for-nothing; in either case my bequest will be of little help to him.'[22] This wise and observant peasant knew his son very well. He saw how easily Taras had learnt at school, what a good memory he had, how curious he was about everything, what a sensitive nature he had, unwilling to perform dull tasks, how restless he was and given to sudden urges and impulses. He

21 'Perebendia,' *Povne*, I, 53
22 A.M. Lazarevsky, 'Detstvo Shevchenko,' *T.G. Shevchenko v vospominaniiakh sovremennikov* (Moscow 1962), 19, hereinafter referred to as *Vospominaniia*

realized his son's unusual talents but was not sure whether conditions would be favourable for their development. In any case he was convinced that Taras would not till the soil and would not be an ordinary man.

Grandfather Ivan often thought about his orphaned grandchildren. He tried to tame Taras's stepmother and eventually expelled her from their house. But for the time being she ruled supreme, and frequently Taras would run away to his sister Kateryna, to avoid his stepmother's blows. Kateryna, in her old age, remembered Taras's visits very well. He would come to her house after walking across the fields and village cemeteries. Once, on reaching his sister's house, he was so exhausted that he dropped down on to a bench and fell asleep. His hair was unkempt and full of lice. He could not say whether he had been expelled, denied food, or beaten. His sister knew, however, that all three guesses were correct.

One violent incident in particular enraged Taras. A Russian soldier was staying at the Shevchenko house, and some of his money was stolen. As it turned out later, the thief was Stepan, the little son of the stepmother. When the soldier demanded that the money be returned, the stepmother accused Taras. The helpless boy ran away and hid in some bushes. He stayed in his hiding place for four days. There he made himself a dugout, with paths all around it, covered with sand, and improvised a target pinned on a tree, at which he shot from a sling. Nobody knew where he was except his sister Yaryna, who brought him food. On the fifth day his hiding place was discovered by the stepmother's children. Taras was caught and interrogated. The chief inquisitor was his uncle Pavlo, who was known for his cruelty. Not being able to stand torture, the boy, prompted by his sister, confessed to a crime he had not committed. When he was untied he was asked to show them the place where the money was hidden. This he could not do, because he was innocent. The torture began again, but they could not get anything out of the boy, who was finally released, half-dead.

This was the worst physical abuse Shevchenko experienced in his entire life. His chief tormentor, his uncle, decided to take the boy to his household to 'make a man' out of him. For food and lodging Taras had to tend a herd of swine in the summer and help the groom in the winter. Uncle Pavlo lived together with grandfather Ivan. Pavlo was much better off than his dead older brother had been. He had servants and many horses. His son Petro remembered Taras's work on his father's farm when, during the ploughing, he became so fed up with the work that he would escape into the bushes. No one could force him to do something he did not want to do. His constant running away was the only form of protest available to him.

While working for his uncle, Taras conceived of a bold project – to begin an independent life. He decided to return as a student-assistant to cantor Bohorsky, probably in the fall of the year his father died. No one could complain about Taras's step: uncle Pavlo and Taras's stepmother approved because it relieved them of the responsibility of looking after the disobedient boy. Also, the cantor needed an assistant. Bohorsky was a well-known drunkard and for days did not leave the tavern. He appointed Taras his 'consul.' Included among Taras's new duties was the supervision of the Saturday thrashing of all the pupils, though this did not prevent the cantor from beating his new assistant. And Bohorsky was more violent than Sovhyr.

The twelve-year-old consul helped out with teaching and checked the pupils' homework. Apart from these tasks, as he wrote in his short autobiography, 'the cantor, having assured himself of his assistant's ability, sent him, as a deputy, to read the psalter at the funerals of dead peasants, rewarding him with every tenth *kopek*.'[23] In his story 'The Princess' Shevchenko tells us more about how he earned the 'tenth *kopek*.' 'I knew the entire psalter by heart and read it out loud, so my hearers told me. There was not one burial in the village without my reading the psalter. For this I received some bread and a handful of money, which I gave to the cantor, who then gave me five kopeks for doughnuts. And this was my only source of income.'[24] In spite of the fact that Taras swept the house, started the fire, and took out the garbage, in addition to his duties as consul, he often went hungry, as did the drunken cantor. 'It was lucky,' he went on, 'that people died in the village (God forgive me) – then we managed somehow; when there were no burials we were hungry for days. In the evening I would take a satchel and the cantor a long walking stick and we would go singing religious songs under the windows of houses. Sometimes we would bring something to the school, but sometimes we would come back with empty hands, but not hungry.'[25]

Taras could have told many more such stories, but they were so sad. Soon after Taras went to help the cantor, his stepmother became the cantor's mistress. They would go drinking and dancing together, and, perhaps on the stepmother's urging, the cantor beat Taras more often. Once again Taras had to flee, and this time he was helped by his blind sister, Marusia, who brought him food. Fleeing from the cantor's blows, Taras found refuge in the orchard of the peasant Zhelekh. There he made himself a bed from twigs and lived for a while, nourished by his sisters. It

23 'Avtobiohrafiia,' *Povne*, v, 255
24 Ibid, III, 180
25 Ibid

was there that, as he wrote later, he compiled booklets with verses and illustrations just like those he had seen in school:

> It happened long ago. In school,
> at the cantor-teacher's.
> I would steal five *kopeks*
> (since I was almost naked
> and poor) and would buy
> a sheet of paper, from which
> I made a booklet. With crosses
> and flowers I adorned it,
> surrounding it with
> drawings of leaves.
> I would then copy Skovoroda
> or *The Three Magi with Gifts*.
> While doing this I would
> sit alone in the burdocks,
> singing and crying.[26]

In February 1827 Taras was thirteen. His stay with the cantor Bohorsky ended with unexpected abruptness. One day he found the cantor and his bosom friend, Yona Lymar, blind drunk. Taras took their pants down and whipped them both hard, 'repaying him for all the cruelties.' He did not hesitate to steal an illustrated book besides. Immediately afterwards he fled. This time he went to the neighbouring town of Lysianka, where he found himself a painting teacher, a deacon, who was also someting of a Spartan. For a long time the young boy had had the desire to draw, and while he was at school he drew not on fences but on paper. A former pupil in Kerelivka, Honcharenko, had stuck Taras's drawings on the walls of his house – drawn on coarse grey paper, they depicted horses and soldiers. The desire to draw was not merely a hobby but a persistent urge to communicate visual impressions of life. In the course of time he must have realized himself that he had talent. This was reinforced by the praise he received from his peers and from the older villagers, who long remembered his work. With this favourable reception he was encouraged to think of the next step in his artistic development – painting. But he needed a teacher, different materials, and equipment – brushes and paints – of which he was totally ignorant. Having found refuge with the Lysianka deacon, Taras hoped to start painting. Instead he was asked to carry pails of water from the Tykych River and to thin out powdered paints

26 'A.O. Kozachkovskomu,' *Povne*, II, 63

spread on a tin. In his brief autobiography Shevchenko tells how, on the fourth day, he fled from the deacon.[27]

Taras's next stop was the village of Tarasivka, where he tried to apprentice himself to a painter-cantor who was famous for painting an icon of St Nicetas and of Ivan the Warrior. But the cantor refused to hire Taras. After carefully examining his left palm he declared that Taras was unfit to be not only a painter but a cobbler or a cooper as well. The boy was thoroughly disheartened, ready to give up his dreams of becoming an artist. He returned to his native village, resigned to being a swineherd again and to looking from time to time through a newly acquired illustrated book. But even this was denied him. The new master, Pavel Vasilievich Engelhardt, who had just inherited his father's estate (he was an illegitimate son), wanted a page-boy, and Taras was chosen as the master's *kozachok*.

Shevchenko's own account of these events, written more than thirty years later, is concise and straight forward. There is no reason to doubt its veracity, but there is evidence from other sources that, before becoming Engelhardt's page-boy, Taras had experienced other adventures. There is good reason to believe that before his career as a *kozachok* began, he had learned the wheelwright's trade from his elder brother, Mykyta, and that he had been a servant at the house of Kerelivka's priest, Father Hryhoriy Koshyts, or, as the villagers called him, Koshytsia. We know that his brother beat him severely, conceivably for disobedience and restlessness. We know more about his life with Father Koshyts. Here, after many years of the vagrant and miserable life of an orphan, for the first time he found a warm niche. He was well fed and dressed, and no one beat or nagged him. His duties included caring for the cattle and the priest's light bay mare, which was well known to everyone in the neighbourhood. Apart from this he washed the dishes and, during the winter, laid fires in two small rooms. The other part of the priest's house consisted of a large kitchen, where the patriarchal Koshyts family spent most of the day with their servants.

Father Hryhoriy had two orchards and a fine farm. The Koshytses had two children, a son, Yas, and a daughter, Fedosia. Yas was at a boarding-school in Bohuslav, and Taras drove him there after the holidays. Later he took the priest's son to Kiev, when he had finished school at Bohuslav. Taras also carted plums, apples, and melons to the marketplaces of the neighbouring small towns of Burty and Shpola. He drove the horses when the priest and his wife went on visits to Tarasivka

---

27 'Avtobiohrafiia,' *Povne*, v, 256

and to Zelena where Taras's sister, Kateryna Krasytska, also lived. Later, remembering their servant Taras, the Koshytses had nothing bad to say about him except that he was an idler, not suited for farm work. During the long winter evenings Taras would usually read, and the priest's wife recalled that he also learned by heart verses from the psalter. This information comes from Father Lebedyntsev,[28] who was a friend of the young Koshyts. We also know that in the stables Taras drew with coal figures of cockerels, people, outlines of churches, and even of the Kiev belfry. Although there was plenty of work on the Koshyts's farm, the priest did not burden his servants unduly, and his wife was a warm-hearted woman who saw to it that everybody had enough to eat. It is hard to estimate how long Taras stayed with the Koshytses. Some believe it was as long as two years, but it seems more likely that he was there for almost a year. It would be natural, after his earlier experiences, that the boy would want to stay put, but sometime around the fall of 1823 he left the place and found himself in Engelhardt's household. There is reason to believe that before that he had tried to apprentice himself to another painter.

Before we describe his life there, and later on Engelhardt's estate, it is necessary to dwell a little longer on the period from 1825 to 1828. While still with the cantor Bohorsky Taras often went hungry and was ill clad. Only the Koshytses took real care of him. Ordinarily, as he wrote in his poetry, he was 'an orphan in rags, so poor, almost naked ... wandering in the world, trying to find people to teach me some good.' In the 1840s he told A. Kozachkovsky[29] that he had sometimes been so hungry that he would steal chickens and young pigs and roast them in a cave on the outskirts of the village, the smoke of the fire frightening the superstitious peasants, who thought the devil himself lived in the cave. The hungry, bedraggled boy often drew the attention of the villagers, and he had the reputation of being an eccentric who cut his hair in adult fashion and wore a homemade cap, like those worn by the Polish confederate army.

When he was thirteen an emotional episode occurred in Taras's life which he has described in the poem 'My Thirteenth Year Was Passing' ('Meni trynadtsiaty mynalo').[30] He was tending sheep beyond the village when his heart was overcome by a devout feeling and a strange presentiment of happiness. The mood was shared, it seemed, by 'God's sky, the village,' and the sheep. Yet at the same time another feeling surfaced – that of loneliness, alienation, and homelessness, and he began to cry bitterly. At that moment there suddenly appeared a girl, who was

28 P.G. Lebedintsev, 'Taras Grigorievich Shevchenko,' *Vospominaniia*, 41
29 A.O. Kozachkovsky, 'Iz vospominanii o T.G. Shevchenko,' *Vospominaniia*, 104–5
30 'Meni trynadtsiaty mynalo,' *Povne*, II, 38–9

sorting hemp nearby and who wiped away his tears with her kisses. Once more he felt happy, and they drove the sheep to water together.

The heroine of this poem is not identified. There are strong reasons to believe that she was Oksana Kovalenko, a childhood playmate, to whom he later dedicated his poem 'Mariana the Nun' ('Mariana Chernytsia'). The dedication reads: 'To Oksana K[ovalenk]o, in memory of what happened long ago,' which testifies that Shevchenko's first love occurred when he was between thirteen and fifteen years old. The lines of the dedication confirm it:

> It is true, Oksana, alien and black-browed,
> That you will not remember the orphan
> Who, in a grey jacket, was so happy
> To see a wonder – your beauty,
> Whom you taught, without talk or words,
> How to speak with the eyes, soul and heart,
> With whom you smiled, cried, and worried,
> To whom you loved to sing a song about Petrus.
> You will recall ... Oksana, Oksana!
> But I still cry today and I still worry,
> I pour out my tears for the little Mariana
> While I look at you and pray for you.
> Remember, Oksana, alien and black-browed,
> And deck sister Mariana with flowers.
> Sometimes smile happily at Petrus
> And, even jokingly, remember what happened.[31]

There is little to add to this evocation of common joys, sorrows, meetings, and partings between two young lovers – a testament of Taras's first love. Later, Oksana would become Shevchenko's Beatrice. Her name will decorate his poems, and her tragic fate will, as we shall later learn, become his own tragedy. In the joyless life of a poor orphan this episode was a ray of sunshine, a source of encouragement to a young dreamer, and led to the awakening of new personal feelings.

Vasiliy Engelhardt, the landowner, privy councillor, recipient of the Maltese cross, and a senator of the Russian Empire, died on 12 May 1828 in Vilshana. On 29 October of that year three of his illegitimate sons, Colonels Vasiliy and Andrey and Guards Lieutenant Pavel, divided among them the estate of 160,000 *desiatinas* of land, around fifty thousand serfs,

---

31 'Mariana chernytsia,' ibid, I, 145–6

both male and female, houses in the capital, and many family heirlooms. Lieutenant Pavel received the Zvenyhorod estates. In the spring of 1829 the body of the old Engelhardt was transferred from Vilshana to the family crypt in the village of Chizhov in Smolensk province, where it was laid to rest on 12 March.

The new landlord, Pavel Engelhardt, sometime between November 1828 and March 1829 ordered 'about a dozen boys' to be recruited for his service. They were to be coachmen, cooks, lackeys, accountants, and even one painter-decorator. Shevchenko recorded that he himself was conscripted into the kitchen as an aide, but there is reason to believe that this was his second assignment and that he served at first as a servant boy. According to Taras's sister Yaryna, the manager of the Vilshana estate, Dmytrenko, took Taras into service. This came about when Taras attempted to apprentice himself to a painter in the village of Khlypnivka. The painter examined Taras, who stayed with him for two weeks, and, recognizing the boy's talent, was ready to hire him. However, he was afraid of keeping a serf without permission, and this written permission Taras was trying to obtain from Vilshana. It was on this occasion that he was spotted by Dmytrenko, who was so impressed with him that he decided to keep him. According to still another account there was an intermediary between Taras and Dmytrenko – a Pole, Jan Dymowski. It may be that this well-educated, kindly Pole, was the first to teach Taras some manners, such as how to serve and how to address ladies and gentlemen. Dymowski and Dmytrenko could have been confused in these accounts. Taras remained grateful to Dymowski all his life and later corresponded with him. It might have been Dymowski who left a note in Engelhardt's household register about Shevchenko's suitability for a job as a house painter. Taras entered the master's kitchen only after being trained by Dymowski, and later, when the new young landlord arrived at Vilshana, Taras became his *kozachok*.

In the kitchen Taras washed the dishes, brought in firewood, and took out garbage. He disliked the monotonous routine. The restless boy got out whenever he could into the leafy park surrounding the palace, and there, on the trees, he hung the collection of illustrated drawings that he had amassed. This desire to display his art collection did not flourish without repercussions. The chef, to whom Taras's absences from the kitchen were far too long, beat the boy, something to which Taras was quite well used. When he graduated to being his master's page-boy, Taras spent whole days without any actual work. He then began to copy secretly the pictures, hanging on the walls, of the 'Suzdal School,' which was a high-sounding euphemism for the inferior but popular art of the period. This raises an important question: what was there of novelty and interest for Taras to find in his master's palace? Was there anything that might feed the imagination of an aspiring young artist? Unfortunately, the palace at Vilshana contained only inferior art. The best of Engelhardt's art collection adorned the walls of his house in St Petersburg, his ancestral home in Chizhov, and his estate in Lialychi, in Chernihiv province, where the buildings had been designed by the Italian architect Guarengi. Engelhardt acquired Lialychi from Count Zavadovsky. True, the Vilshana estate had an orchestra, consisting of serfs, but because of the mourning for Pavel's father, it was inactive. So much for the new artistic milieu, or, rather, the lack of it.

As far as other impressions that the palace must have left on Taras, we can be sure of the following. The young, sensitive boy was struck by the contrast between the poverty of the peasants and cantors that he knew so well and the luxuries of the proud landowning class. He was able to see with his own eyes one of the centres of the complex feudal order – life on an estate, where the landlord wielded absolute power and controlled a hierarchy of managers at the top and helpless servants like Taras at the bottom. He could not miss the fact that thousands of people, the subject serfs of the master, laboured in the sweat of their brow and lived in squalour only to enable the upper classes to live so well, in such luxury. He also learned here for the first time that some people did not use Ukrainian. Taras heard Russian at the cantor's and at the priest's house. It is uncertain whether Russian was the dominant language in the palace. The Engelhardts had accepted the Orthodox faith and been Russified in the second half of the eighteenth century. But it is uncertain what language prevailed at their palace in Vilshana. The former owner, with whom Potemkin's cousin had three sons, was a Polish princess, a Catholic, who had been freed by this Orthodox knight from a nunnery. Some local people thought she was German, but in all probability she was Polish. Although all her sons were educated in the Russian culture, they knew Polish. It is thus uncertain whether the young landlord in his 'Polish estate' used Russian or Polish. In any case, everything Ukrainian was foreign to him. Among his managers there were some Ukrainians (Dmytrenko) and some Poles (Dymowski, Prechtel). It is possible that Taras had to learn how to read Polish since he had to accompany his master to Warsaw, where he served in the Life Guards regiment of *Uhlans* and where the servants needed to use Polish. Apart from this conjecture, one can only say that Taras probably felt in the palace like a bird in a gilded cage – he dreamt of freedom and the art of painting. In his new post Taras served his master at least six months and at the most one year.

His master took Taras to Kiev several times, but in the fall of 1829 a distant trip beckoned him to Vilno[32] and Warsaw. On that trip his stern master had in his possession a register that specified that Taras had the ability to become a house painter. Thus, in Engelhardt's large retinue travelled this stubborn and restless boy of fifteen who had experienced many hardships and tribulations in his life, including Cupid's arrow in his heart. He was an ordinary serf whose duty it was to clean his master's boots and to light his pipe. But this young man was already consumed by an ambition to become an artist, and his soul was filled with the images and sounds of nature, real and imagined life, folksongs, the *dumy*[33] sung by the minstrels, historical tales, the verses of Skovoroda, and the psalms of David.

---

32 The Ukrainian form, Vilno, is used here for the Lithuanian Vilnius.
33 The *dumy* were epic-lyric songs about the Cossacks, chanted by the *kobzars* to the accompaniment of a *bandura*.

II

The Life Guards regiment in which Pavel Engelhardt served was stationed in Warsaw, but on the way there Shevchenko's young master stopped in the ancient Lithuanian capital of Vilno. Taras rode there together with the other servants. Earlier he had visited Yelysavet and Kiev, but now he looked out on to the monotonous forest landscapes of a new land – the 'land of sorrow and weeping' of the 'forever hungry Belorussia.' Later he recalled that he saw there 'moving scenes, hunger, poverty, debauchery, and its sad participants.' The convoy with the servants moved slowly, and Taras had plenty of time to see the country, which he was never to see again.

We do not know exactly when Taras arrived in Vilno, but it could not have been earlier than in the late fall. On 6 December 1829 an incident occurred during his brief stay in Vilno that was most memorable. In his own words,

> while staying at the inns with the master, [he] stole the portraits of various historical heroes ... intending to copy them later. An opportunity to do this occurred in Vilno. It was on 6 December. The master and mistress went to a ball. The house was quiet; everybody was asleep. Then he took out the stolen treasures and selecting [the portrait of] Cossack Platov he began with religious diligence to copy it. He had reached the place where the small Cossacks prance around the mighty hooves of Platov's horse when suddenly the door opened: the master and his wife had come back from the ball. The enraged master tweaked his ears and gave him a spanking, saying that he could have set on fire not only the house but the entire city. The next day the master ordered the coachman Sidorka to whip him, an order which was carried out immediately.[1]

In the second version of this autobiography, edited by Kulish, there is

---

1 'Avtobiohrafiia,' *Povne*, v, 250

an addition that recounts that at the critical moment, when the master seized Taras's copy, he 'paid no attention to his art.'[2] This is Kulish's own opinion. There is reason to think that, despite the cruel treatment of Taras, his master realized that the boy had real talent. In any case, soon, when they reached Warsaw, Engelhardt apprenticed Shevchenko to a painter.

In his short autobiography, written in 1860, Shevchenko's intention was to illustrate his hard life as a serf. That is why he mentioned the Vilno episode when, as Konysky later aptly wrote, 'the master wrote on Shevchenko's back the charter of lordly despotism.' There are other later echoes of the stay in Vilno in the letters and diaries of Shevchenko. In a letter to his friend Bronisław Zaleski, written on the eve of liberation from exile, twenty-eight years after the Vilno episode, the poet described the following dream: 'I am taking you from the arms of your happy mother and on a fine morning we both pray in front of the picture of the Mother of God from Ostra Brama. Vilno with its memories is as dear to my heart as it is to yours.'[3] On 5 September 1857 he wrote in his diary: 'In my dreams I saw the church of St Ann in Vilno and my dear, blackbrowed Dunia Husikowska, who prayed in the church.'[4] He explained the dream by the fact that the previous day he had been reading a book about Queen Barbara Radziwiłł, in which Vilno was often mentioned. Yet this mention makes it plausible to assume that something did occur between the poet and the black-browed Dunia. The church of St Ann was Catholic, and Dunia, or more likely Dziunia, was Polish. From Soshenko's memoirs we know that Shevchenko told him about a romance with a Polish girl in Warsaw. It is impossible to be certain that the evocation of a dream about Vilno was confused with the memory of the girl from Warsaw. At the same time, Soshenko might have been mistaken in referring to a Warsaw, rather than a Vilno, romance. No matter what happened, there are other indications that Shevchenko had friends or at least knew people who sympathized with him in Vilno. It was in that city that a portrait of Shevchenko's father by the fifteen-year-old Taras was miraculously preserved until 1920 in a beautiful contemporary frame. Notwithstanding the harsh punishment which he had received from Engelhardt, Taras did draw in Vilno and perhaps attracted someone's attention. In another letter to Bronisław Zaleski, Shevchenko refers to the view of art held by the Vilno professor Jan Rustem that a student must draw for six years and paint for six months before becoming a master. Some scholars have

2 Ibid, 258
3 Ibid, VI, 151
4 Ibid, 118

concluded from this that Shevchenko was a pupil of Rustem's, but the poet might have heard this pronouncement from someone else, not necessarily in Vilno.

In any case the brief Vilno sojourn brought some light to Shevchenko's life, and even if we do not know many details about it, the whole episode left a trace in the poet's artistic imagination. That after twenty-eight years he remembered so well the interior of one of the finest Gothic monuments of Vilno architecture – the church of St Ann – confirms this. Vilno was at that time a small town that was being slowly rebuilt after the disastrous fire of 1812. It was a lively centre of Polish culture, and its university was well known. Shevchenko could have heard many interesting things there, since he was not always waiting in his master's antechamber. It was after all the city of the Polish Philarets and Philomats.[5] One other reference to Vilno concerns a bloody love affair, which Shevchenko mentions in the poem beginning with the lines 'In Vilno, the most famous city.'[6]

From Vilno the Engelhardts went to Warsaw. There Taras was apprenticed, on his master's orders, to a painter-decorator. This guildmaster, whose name we do not know, told Engelhardt, as he collected the fee, that Taras was so gifted that he ought to be apprenticed to Franz Lampi Junior, who was the best painter in Warsaw. Engelhardt asked Lampi to accept Shevchenko as a boarder, but he only agreed to give Taras lessons. The boy received better clothes, since he was to be taught together with the burghers' children, even perhaps with the landlords' sons. His page boy uniform was exchanged for a suit with cuffs and a tie. This is how Taras started his first classes with a professional painter. It is possible that while still in Warsaw he finished a drawing of St Mary Magdalene (1833), a copy of a well-known lithograph by the Vilno artist Moszczynski.

Soshenko refers to Shevchenko's romance with a pretty Polish seamstress during his apprenticeship with Lampi. It is possible that this seamstress was Dziunia Husikowska. She looked after the boy's clothes and underwear and pressed his ties and shirtfronts. Shevchenko spoke to her in Polish, since this was the only language she knew. The acquaintance of Dziunia was also a social education for Taras: Dziunia was not a serf but was free. 'It was the first time,' Shevchenko told Soshenko, 'that I began to wonder why we unlucky serfs are not free people like the other classes.'[7] Even if in this third-hand account the words 'for the first time' were added, it is obvious that this relationship must have inspired some

---

5 A secret Polish literary society in Vilno (1817–23)
6 'U Vilni, horodi preslavnim,' *Povne*, II, 178–80
7 M.K. Chaly, 'Vospominaniia I.M. Soshenko,' *Vospominaniia*, 49

new thoughts in him. The human dignity of the modest seamstress could not be abused, but he, who was in love with her, could be whipped by his master like a dog. The social gap was too obvious to escape notice. This young love was one of the brightest and warmest moments in the life of a sixteen-year-old boy.

We do not know how long Taras studied with Lampi – probably not very long. On 29 November 1830 an uprising broke out in Warsaw, and this must have interrupted the usual classes, which consisted of copying clay models and engravings. To be sure, Shevchenko could have observed the work of more advanced students and studied examples of good art, as well as heard some discussions that would further develop his own artistic talent. It is possible that in Lampi's studio Shevchenko appreciated classical art for the first time.

As soon as the uprising began, Engelhardt and his regiment left the city. Retreating quickly into the countryside, he had no time to collect all his servants, and some of them, including Taras, were left in Warsaw. He could see a great deal with his own eyes. There is an account of unknown origin that during the first military operations Taras 'climbed into the attic and from there looked on to the street and the fights that were going on between the Polish insurgents and the Russian army.'[8] At the beginning of the uprising Warsaw's inhabitants displayed open hatred of the Russian occupiers, and this fact must have been clear to Shevchenko, who pondered over it. He, as a serf, was a Russian subject, but he must have read the Polish revolutionary proclamation, calling on the subjugated Russians to rise along with the Poles against the tsar. He could not have missed the proclamation dethroning Tsar Nicholas I, who, only a year earlier, had been crowned in Warsaw as king of Poland. If Shevchenko could feel the social injustice of serfs not being free, he could easily begin thinking of the national injustice as he watched the Polish insurgents fighting Russian rule. It is doubtful whether Shevchenko continued to attend classes after the outbreak of the rebellion. Engelhardt had in Warsaw a 'commissar' who was entrusted with all the business of his estates. It was this person who took charge of Shevchenko and the other servants, who, as Russian subjects, were now being ejected from Warsaw by the Polish revolutionary government.

Several of Shevchenko's later friends, M. Kostomarov, I. Soshenko, and V. Zabila, remembered what Shevchenko told them about leaving Warsaw. Shevchenko told Kostomarov that when he was expelled from

---

8 Professor Fedir Vovk narrated it at a meeting of *Hromada* in 1876. It might have been his own invention.

the city by the revolutionary government he also received from that government a sum of money in banknotes put out by the revolutionaries. The reports by Soshenko and Zabila have come down to us second-hand and, bereft of commentaries and speculation, tell us little about the flight from Warsaw. We know that Engelhardt's 'commissar' dispatched to St Petersburg (where Shevchenko's master had fled) the staff of servants, all of whom had to travel in one cart, since there was not enough transport or horses because of the rebellion. It was at the end of February 1831 and the road was hard, so the servants, including Shevchenko, had to walk part of the way. Because of this Shevchenko's footwear was torn, one of his boots lost a sole, and he had to change his boots to avoid frostbite. This, apparently, annoyed the escorting soldiers, and one of them struck Shevchenko across the neck. The whole journey was an *étape*, as Shevchenko himself called it. It is understandable why this was so. The Polish revolutionary government, having expelled Engelhardt's entourage, had linked them with other unhappy expellees and sent them off under military guard. Engelhardt's 'commissar' made sure that they were well provided for the journey. The Polish guards could only take them to a point near the Russian front, perhaps somewhere in Lithuania. At that point the expellees had to report to the Russian authorities. Men of free estate could continue the journey on their own, but the serfs were sent on together as an 'étape' – that is, as a convoy of prisoners. On the way they had to spend their nights in local gaols. Shevchenko tasted all the pleasures of this convoy. He travelled hungry, as he later recorded in his poem 'Catherine':

> the path to Muscovy.
> It's a long path, gentlemen!
> I know it very well!
> I measured it once
> And I wish I had not!
> I would tell you about this plight
> But who would believe it?[9]

The trip from Lithuania to the banks of the Neva was a long one – it might have lasted a month or more. But finally the day arrived when the miserable wagon filled with the many servants of the master of Kerelivka stopped at the gate of his palace on Mokhova Street, in the very centre of misty St Petersburg.

---

9 'Kateryna,' *Povne*, I, 30

Childhood and Youth 1814-38

A year and a half had passed since Taras left Kerelivka. He had seen other countries, learned Polish, witnessed momentous political events, started to study art, met many new people, and had experienced a great deal and thought about it all. He began his eighteenth year in this inhospitable northern capital surrounded by granite and fog. The memories of Vilno and Warsaw, the studio of Franz Lampi, became a distant fantastic dream for Taras. The real world consisted of the antechamber of the lord's apartment. His master made him a page-boy once more.

In 1831 Pavel Engelhardt was promoted to the rank of captain of cavalry and appointed an aide-de-camp to His Royal Highness the Duke Alexander of Wurtemberg, at that time in charge of communications. These were not onerous duties for an aristocrat who was very slowly making his career. For his first twelve years of service Engelhardt remained a mere lieutenant and did not distinguish himself in any way. His older brothers, Vasiliy and Andrey, were colonels in the Guards regiment and were much more talented. They belonged to the social élite of St Petersburg, especially Vasiliy, a well-known card-player, snob, and bon vivant, a close friend of the poet Pushkin. He owned a big house, built on the Nevsky Prospekt, where various masquerades, balls, and concerts were held. His brilliant anecdotes circulated around the capital. Andrey, the hero of the 1812 campaign, was a prominent front-line officer. But Shevchenko's master, Pavel Engelhardt, could lay claim to no such achievements. He was married to Baroness Sophia Engelhardt, the daughter of Lieutenant-General Baron Gotthardt Gerard von Engelhardt, a distant relative from the German line of Engelhardts. His career consisted almost entirely of being aide-de-camp to various high dignitaries. His service record stated that he took no part in any campaigns, but he had a good knowledge of French and German and he did find himself a beautiful wife. This was all he could boast about. Still, as a grandson of Potemkin's sister, as the son of the general and senator Vasiliy Engelhardt, and finally as the brother of his brothers, the husband of a pretty woman, and later, as of 1832, as colonel on leaving the service, he found all the palaces and aristocratic salons of St Petersburg open to him. Educated in the Imperial Corps of Pages, this thirty-two-year-old colonel could live in his luxurious ancestral palace the normal carefree life of leisure of his class, without bothering too much about the duties imposed by the service. Like many people without deeper interests or spiritual urges, he was simply born and educated in order to live like a lord.

It is not known why Engelhardt delayed for a year Shevchenko's education as an artist, though it would have been easy to continue it in St

Petersburg. The dreamy youth with wise, sad eyes became once more his master's slave. But in the soul of this slave, carrying out the duties of a page-boy, there grew a strong desire to study the 'divine art' that he had already tasted. The boy was also probably conscious of his own talent. He thus began to implore his master to allow him to study art again. At long last his appeals bore fruit: Engelhardt signed a contract for four years, allowing Shevchenko to be apprenticed to the painter and guildmaster Shiriaev.

One can only speculate as to why Shevchenko was sent to a guildmaster and not to a real painter. One might surmise that Engelhardt did not want to spend much money, which he would have had to do if Taras, who as a serf was unable to enter the Academy of Fine Arts, had gone to study with one of the well-known artists. That is why Taras himself, anxious to study, persuaded his master to send him to a painter-decorator. Having agreed to this, Engelhardt could hope, in time, to reap some benefit from this arrangement, since he would receive some of the money Taras earned. Shevchenko's plan, in accepting the arrangement, might have been to become a master-painter himself and then one day to be able to pay Engelhardt the amount necessary to buy his freedom. That is why his appeals to Engelhardt were so insistent. His master must have realized, too, that Taras would never make a perfect page-boy, and he may have been attracted by the possibility of reaping material advantages. It is possible that as soon as Shevchenko was apprenticed to Shiriaev, Engelhardt began receiving some money from him, since Taras was by no means a beginner but, after his Warsaw training, was able to use not only a paintbrush but the pencil as well. For Shiriaev, Shevchenko was already a highly qualified worker, and he demonstrated this by passing the necessary tests.

Taking off his page-boy's jacket, Taras put on a painter's smock. His new life was a great deal harder than serving in the palace. It was full of humiliations. The editorial comment that Kulish furnished for Shevchenko's autobiography is an apt description. Mentioning the young apprentices, he wrote: 'Their master's rights over them have no prescribed limits. The apprentices are totally their masters' slaves. Their unquestioned duty is to carry out all the domestic work and all the possible whims of the master and the members of his family.'[10] According to Shevchenko himself, Shiriaev 'kept three or more ruffians, whom he called his pupils, in multicoloured smocks, and in addition hired on a daily or monthly basis up to ten peasants from Kostroma as painters and glaziers. Thus he did

10 'Avtobiohrafiia,' ibid, v, 255

Portrait of Keikuatova, 1847; oil

well for himself as a businessman as well as an artist.'[11] He was tight-fisted, uncultured, and cruel. His youth had been spent in poverty, which he now considered the normal path to fortune, which he himself had reached with difficulty. He showed no kindness to his pupils, and on occasion, when they made mistakes, he beat them. When the painting season was over, Shiriaev forbade his pupils to leave his house even for a holiday, though they were allowed to go to church. When Shevchenko was late for dinner, he knew that he could be whipped. Shiriaev's philosophy with regard to his pupils was very simple: he had not been stroked on the head when he was young, so why should he stroke anyone? In Shevchenko's words, his master was harsher than the 'Spartan cantor.' Perhaps Taras had been hoping that here, as at the painter's in Warsaw, he would find a quiet life. But his former master had been a humane and kind man, in the tradition of the European guildmasters, while in St Petersburg Taras found himself a slave, subject to a man who, after climbing out of darkness and poverty, condemned to that state everyone who worked for him.

It was impossible for Taras to run away from Shiriaev, as he once had from the painter in Lysianka. He was under contract to Shiriaev for four years. It was better to become reconciled to his fate and to learn as much as possible from this painter-decorator, who, after all, knew his craft well. At that time it was fashionable to paint rooms with classical ornaments and compositions. Borders and medallions with Cupids and mythological or bucolic scenes were used on walls, more complicated motifs on ceilings. For this Taras needed, above all, to learn the technique of mixing colours and the ability to use his brush. He was, in other words, learning more than mere decorating; he was learning true painting. There was no escape from this situation, and he had to realize that rebellion would be counter-productive. His master kept him busy decorating, and only occasionally was better work available. Shevchenko recalled how dull his work was, how he mixed the paints and then spread them on floors, roofs, and fences. Not much creativity was needed, and Taras kept reminding himself of an old Ukrainian proverb: 'Suffer, Cossack, and you will be an *otaman.*'

While he was at his master's palace on Mokhova Street he had had the congenial company of his countrymen, all servants like himself, and one of them, Ivan Nechyporenko, had become a real friend. At Shiriaev's the atmosphere was foreign, except for one compatriot, Khtodot Tkachenko, who wore the same painter's smock. Tkachenko was a phlegmatic man of

11 'Khudozhnik,' ibid, IV, 147

few words, but he was still a kindred soul. Shevchenko slowly learnt to speak Russian, a language he had heard spoken only by his master and the noble guests in the palace. His Russian vocabulary was limited. Still, in Kerelivka he used to read, especially when serving at Father Koshyts's. Here he seized every opportunity to read, but it was difficult to do so because Shiriaev regarded reading as a waste of time and did not allow any lights to be burnt. To circumvent this Taras needed a candle, which he could ill afford. Shiriaev did have some books in his house, among them the six-volume Russian translation of an encyclopaedia of the ancient world, the work of Prior Barthelemy. Shevchenko could only look through it during the holidays, when the master was not at home. On the walls there hung reproductions of Raphael, Odran, Poussin, and other masters, and there was also an album of other art, which Shevchenko was forbidden to copy. Yet this stultifying atmosphere was disturbed from time to time by a fresh breath from the world of art. A distant cousin of Shiriaev's was a student at the Academy of Fine Arts, and although he did not live at Shiriaev's house, he visited it often. Another student, I.K. Zaitsev, was also a frequent visitor. On rare occasions literary evenings were held: Zaitsev read aloud from the poems of Pushkin and Zhukovsky. Taras and Tkachenko listened to the reading through half-closed doors, with great delight.

Summer and early fall were the seasons for house decoration, renovation, and construction. Taras was busy in the city from morning till night. He slept in the attic. We do not know whether it was an attic which could only be used in the summer or a proper mansard. In any case it was possible to enter and leave it without opening the door to the living quarters. So during the so-called 'white nights' in St Petersburg, when it was so light outside that it was possible to read outdoors, Shevchenko would leave his attic very early in the morning, before going to work, and would go to the Summer Gardens to copy the statues of gods and goddesses that adorned the park. He knew that all artists had to master the human figure. He had already practised this at Lampi's in Warsaw and had heard from Shiriaev's visitors that this was what they did at the academy, and so now he discovered an opportunity for free classes in figure drawing, minus a teacher, in the alleys of the Summer Garden. He would sit on a pail of paint and draw the smiling goddesses and stern-looking gods. Although his drawings were quite good copies, there were no shadows, since these did not exist in the sharp moonlight. He had to be satisfied with contours alone.

In the summer of 1835 an event occurred that brought great joy to Shevchenko's heart. It encouraged him to hope for better things, but it also brought new doubts and worries. During one of his copying sessions in the Summer Gardens he attracted the attention of an unknown gentleman, who was anxious to see the boy's drawings. In the conversation that followed it appeared that the gentleman, whose name was Soshenko, was a painter himself, a student at the Academy of Fine Arts. Moreover, Soshenko came from Bohuslav, close to Taras's Kerelivka. For a while he had even lived in Vilshana, where he had studied with the painter S. Prevlotsky. Soshenko took a real interest in the unkempt young apprentice and, after examining his drawings, at once recognized Taras's talent. He invited Shevchenko to visit him on Sundays. For his first visit Shevchenko wore a dirty, paint-smudged smock, trousers of thick cloth, and no shoes or cap. He was withdrawn and low-spirited. Soshenko took the boy's fate to heart.

Throughout the entire summer of 1836 Taras was working at the Great Theatre, which was then being renovated by the well-known architect Kavos. Shiriaev was allotted a large share of the decorative work. According to Kavos's instructions Taras executed a series of projects for the motifs and arabesques that were to decorate the theatre's ceiling. The actual painting of the ceiling took Taras a great deal of time. His work was watched by a young mechanic on the staff, Kartashov, who made him a cup of tea every morning. Shiriaev finally realized that Shevchenko possessed unusual ablities, but he was still unwilling to promote this excellent worker.

On Sundays Shevchenko visited Soshenko at his student lodgings in the basement on the fourth line of Vasilievsky Island. Soshenko had, in the meantime, met Shiriaev and was doing everything he could to improve the lot of his new protégé. At Soshenko's request Shiriaev had agreed that Shevchenko might visit his friend not only on Sundays but on weekdays when there was no work to be done. Soshenko undertook to educate Taras, showing him how to copy and draw. He supplied him with the necessary materials. Seeing Shevchenko's rapid progress, he encouraged him to try his hand at water-colours. Soshenko himself and Ivan Nechyporenko posed for him frequently. Nechyporenko was still in Engelhardt's service and one day showed his master a drawing by Shevchenko. Engelhardt liked it so much that he asked Taras to draw the portraits of his favourite mistresses and from time to time rewarded him with a 'silver rouble, but no more,' as Shevchenko wrote in his autobiography. In 1834 Shevchenko drew a portrait of his master. A comparison of this work with those Shevchenko was painting in 1836–37 demonstrates the great progress made by the artist. Not only was Soshenko's advice valuable, but so was the fact that Soshenko took him to art galleries where he could see world masterpieces. Now, on Sundays, Shevchenko spent his time at the famous Hermitage museum. Back in 1835 Taras had also begun to attend the drawing classes offered by the Society for the Promotion of Artists, and the committee of this organization singled him out as a promising student. Although he did not visit these classes regularly, he learned a great deal from the instructors there. In the winter of 1836–37 he could certainly be proud of his achievements. The best evidence for this is a series of water-colour portraits painted in 1837 and a composition in sepia in 1836 entitled *Alexander of Macedon expressing confidence in his physician*. They show not only a very skilled draughtsman but a master of composition and colour who knows how to solve the problems of light and shadow. Transferred on to cloth, the composition of Alexander of Macedon could have gained diploma standing for any student in the academy.

While visiting Soshenko, Taras told him the story of his life and usually ended by blaming his unlucky fate. Soshenko soon started thinking about the possibility of freeing the young artist. Another friend of Shevchenko's, Apollon Mokrytsky, attests that moves were under way as early as 1835. Soshenko was a close friend of the Ukrainian writer Yevhen Hrebinka, and he told him of his plans for Shevchenko, who later met Hrebinka. Having taken to heart Shevchenko's plight, Hrebinka invited him to visit.

Hrebinka was a graduate of the Nizhyn Lyceum, of which Gogol was an alumnus, and came from a family of impoverished gentry of Cossack stock in Pyriatyn. A gentle, kind-hearted man, he was already a popular writer, especially among his countrymen, as the author of a book of Ukrainian fables. In 1834 he settled in St Petersburg, where he obtained a teaching post and later an administrative position in the directorate of church schools. Having a bent for humour, he began to imitate Gogol and write, in Russian, stories on Ukrainian topics, which gained him a certain degree of popularity. In St Petersburg he was also known in literary circles as good company and a 'hospitable Little Russian.' His view of Ukrainian national affairs was on the same level as that of most of his countrymen, especially those writers who wrote in both Ukrainian and Russian. He believed in what might be called the 'Provençal' status of Ukrainian culture: he was a regional patriot, closely tied to his native land and to the customs and language of his people. His dream was to have a quiet, self-contained existence in the Epicurean stillness of the Ukrainian *khutir*, (homestead), with its succulent dishes and brandies, interspersed with jaunty anecdotes and sometimes with a sad song or a good book. He took little interest in politics, but he had the open heart of an honest and sensitive man and he hated every kind of violence. After he met Shevchenko, as a teacher he concentrated on his education, giving him books to read and expanding his intellectual horizons. It is almost certain that it was Hrebinka, whom Shevchenko met in the spring of 1837, who introduced him to the very few Ukrainian literary works of Kotliarevsky, Hulak-Artemovsky, Kvitka-Osnovianenko, Borovykovsky, Bodiansky, and his own. He must also have shown Shevchenko the published collections of Ukrainian songs and the *History of Little Russia* (*Istoriia Maloi Rossii*) by Bantysh-Kamensky. Hrebinka also supplied his friend with the Russian works of Pushkin and Gogol. Returning to his attic after visiting Hrebinka, Shevchenko devoured all these books in the summer of 1837. Soshenko supplied him with the candles he could not afford.

That summer Shevchenko once again showed his rebellious nature. Soshenko was living for a while in Engelhardt's house, where he painted the portrait of the wife of Engelhardt's manager, Prekhtel. While visiting him, Taras began to discuss politics with the servants, who demanded more rights for themselves. Prekhtel was enraged, and one Sunday when Shevchenko visited, he had him apprehended and wanted to whip him. It was only through the intervention of Soshenko and Prekhtel's wife that this punishment was not carried out. Taras was forbidden to visit the servants in future. This incident deepened Soshenko's anxiety about Taras's fate.

Having introduced Shevchenko to Hrebinka, Soshenko also made him meet Vasyl Hryhorovych, professor of aesthetics and secretary of the Academy of Fine Arts. Hryhorovych was also from Pyriatyn and knew Hrebinka well. He was married to the daughter of the famous Ukrainian sculptor Ivan Martos. The doors of this happily married couple were always open to young visitors. As the secretary of the academy and of the Society for the Promotion of Artists, Hryhorovych did a great deal to support impoverished young artists. He was a Ukrainian patriot and had 'not renounced his mother tongue,' as Shevchenko wrote in his dedication to the poem 'The Haidamaks.' A wise, experienced man, Hryhorovych knew at once whose influence would be decisive in seeking help for Shevchenko. Through Hrebinka, Shevchenko met the well-known artist and academician Venetsianov, who was born in Nizhyn, where Hrebinka had attended school. Venetsianov was a 'court painter' and knew the poet Zhukovsky, who was a tutor to the heir to the throne, Tsarevich Alexander. Venetsianov and Hryhorovych decided to introduce Shevchenko to Zhukovsky.

Vasiliy Zhukovsky was the illegitimate son of a Turkish serf and a Russian landowner. As a romantic poet he could reconcile his devotion to the tsar and his family with his humane conscience and outlook. Often, he used his high position at court to help someone, to correct an injustice, or to save someone from trouble. His own deep and genuine interest in art could only increase his interest in this Ukrainian 'jewel in a sheepskin coat.' Before deciding to help Shevchenko, he tried to observe him closely and find out his abilities as well as his sad life-story. He even asked Shevchenko to write an account of the artist's life, which was duly delivered to him but has not been preserved. After reading it, Zhukovsky, impressed, decided to use all his influence to arrange for the purchase of Shevchenko's freedom from Engelhardt.

Apart from Zhukovsky, the man who contributed the lion's share to the liberation of Shevchenko was Karl Briullov, the Russified descendant of French Huguenots, who was a distinguished painter and a professor at the academy. In the fall of 1836 he returned in triumph from Italy, where he had lived and worked for a long time. He had started his artistic career as a ten-year-old prodigy in St Petersburg. After a series of successes he reached the apogee of fame after painting on a huge canvas *The Last Days of Pompeii*. Few other contemporary painters could compete with Briullov. Gogol called his great picture 'the resurrection of painting.' Sir Walter Scott, who made a special journey to Italy to view it, said that this 'was not a picture, but an entire epic.' Italian and German art critics, led by Cornelius, praised it to the skies, and the Academy of Florence made Briullov an honorary professor.

Briullov's return to Russia, from Odessa to St Petersburg, was a triumphal procession. In Moscow banquets were held in his honour. Artists in Moscow and St Petersburg vied with each other in painting portraits of Briullov; poets wrote panegyrics to him, and composers produced musical works dedicated to him. The academy in St Petersburg elected him a member and professor of historical art, and he was crowned with a wreath of laurels, accompanied by festive music. The poet Zhukovsky named him 'Charles the Great,' and his old teacher, Professor Yegorov, turning to his former pupil, pronounced, 'You praise God himself with your brush, Karl Pavlovich.'

When *The Last Days of Pompeii* was exhibited at the academy, Shevchenko had an opportunity to see the famous picture, and a little later, in May or June 1837, he met Briullov personally. He owed the introduction to Soshenko. After meeting Shevchenko Briullov noticed the 'unserflike' face of the boy, and after seeing his drawings and hearing about his life, he took an interest in him. At Briullov's request Soshenko brought Shevchenko to see him, and the great master 'kindly and condescendingly praised his drawing.' Shevchenko was overjoyed – Briullov's praise and

Childhood and Youth 1814-38

kindness overwhelmed him. He also noticed the furnishings of the great master's study. It was a 'red room, decorated chiefly with oriental weaponry, sunlit through transparent curtains, with the master himself in a red smock against this background.'[12] All this left an indelible mark on Taras's memory.

When Taras returned home he told Shiriaev all about it. Shiriaev not only did not believe him but doubted that Taras had seen Briullov at all and dismissed him as a fool. One day at Briullov's Soshenko met Zhukovsky and Count Velgorsky. All three went to the adjoining room and, on returning, Briullov told Soshenko that their preparations were ready, hinting that both Zhukovsky and Velgorsky had agreed to help in the liberation of Shevchenko. Soon afterwards Briullov himself went to see Engelhardt and asked him to free the talented serf. But his mission ended in failure: Engelhardt was not interested in philanthropy. Briullov felt insulted and upon his return home raged, and called Engelhardt a 'feudal dog-trader' and 'a swine in slippers,' but this outburst from a man who was not used to rebuffs was ineffective. The whole matter had to be handled differently. A new mission was undertaken, this time by Soshenko's old teacher, Professor Venetsianov. This son of a Nizhyn Greek and a Ukrainian mother willingly undertook the role of honest broker in this matter of the liberation of his countryman. He had some experience in these dealings. When Venetsianov saw Engelhardt and impressed on him the importance of education and philanthropy, the latter interrupted him and asked for more concrete terms. Later on, he asked for the sum of 2,500 roubles as the final price for his 'indispensable worker.' He dismissed all the talk of philanthropy, and recalling his interview with Briullov, he called the latter 'a real American madman.' It became clear that somehow the sum of 2,500 roubles had to be raised.

Shevchenko described Briullov's role in his liberation in the novel *The Artist* (*Khudozhnik*). It is clear from this story that the initiative in this matter belonged to Briullov and that it was he who made the first contact with Engelhardt. Yet in his autobiography Shevchenko does not mention Briullov's central role. He also omits any reference to Venetsianov's mission. He reports briefly that Soshenko introduced him to Hryhorovych, who in turn contacted Zhukovsky. The latter found out the price from Engelhardt and asked Briullov to paint his portrait, which was then sold at a lottery that produced the necessary sum of 2,500 roubles from the tickets bought by the imperial family. According to this version, the initiative for Shevchenko's liberation came not from Briullov but from

12 Ibid, 154

Zhukovsky. This contradiction of the earlier account cannot be resolved by assuming that the first version occurs in a work of fiction, where real situations are interspersed with imaginary ones, because it is difficult to imagine that in describing these important events of his life Shevchenko would confuse the names of his benefactors. The fact that in the autobiography Shevchenko omitted the scene of Briullov's visit to Engelhardt may be explained by the failure of the visit. But the contradiction between the earlier version, of which the hero is Briullov, and the later one, in which Zhukovsky plays the principal role, will remain unresolved.

Regardless of which story is true, one fine day Briullov and Zhukovsky agreed on the painting of the latter's portrait. A third person who knew of this confidential arrangement was Count Velgorsky, who was close to the imperial family and a good friend of Zhukovsky. He was a well-known patron of the arts and a virtuoso violinist who was always ready to assist an unfortunate devotee of the muses. His task was to organize the lottery in which Zhukovsky's portrait was sold to those members of the imperial family who bought the tickets.

Apparently neither Shevchenko nor Soshenko was told anything about the plan at first. Shevchenko soon learnt, however, that his liberation, which was supported by such influential men as Venetsianov, Zhukovsky, and Velgorsky, was not making much progress. According to Soshenko, Taras grew very depressed and at one time became very angry. He cursed his fate, swore at the landlord who would not set him free, and threatened to take revenge. Shevchenko himself later told Princess Repnina that he had been close to committing suicide and only a brief note from Zhukovsky calmed him a little. Zhukovsky must have learned from the frightened Soshenko about Taras's mental anguish. Taras's state of mind was understandable. It was already April 1838. For the past winter, whenever there was no work, he had spent his time away from home. Soshenko, with the help of Hryhorovych, gained permission for Taras to work in the studios of the Society for the Promotion of Artists, which were open to members of the society and which were well equipped for drawing. Taras made great strides in drawing, dreamt about the academy, and grew daily more depressed about the prospects of entry there. Freedom beckoned but was out of reach. Once, after a few hours in Briullov's company, he came home and cried the rest of the day. He was beginning to feel at home in the halls of the society, and in March he moved to Soshenko's for the whole month in order to paint a portrait of Shiriaev. The month of relative freedom was finally drawing to a close and the prospect of more work for Shiriaev, painting roofs and fences, living in the same old attic, and doing odd jobs around Shiriaev's house, including sweeping the floor, did not appeal to him. The very thought of it made him depressed.

In the meantime things were progressing to a happy solution. Zhukovsky's portrait had been painted. The lottery had been organized and a new member of the committee was found – the Countess Baranov, nee Adlerberg, governess to the tsar's daughters and a lady-in-waiting to the tsarina. The winning ticket was drawn by the tsarina Alexandra Fedorovna herself. At the beginning of May Zhukovsky was scheduled to leave on a trip to Europe to accompany the young tsarevich Alexander. Everyone was in a hurry. Zhukovsky asked Countess Baranov to send the money as soon as possible. His letters to her were very humorous and illustrated by his own drawings, which showed how deeply he was involved in this affair. The captions for the drawings were:

This is Mr Shevchenko. He is talking to himself:
'I would like to paint a picture, but my master has ordered me to sweep the floor.'
He is holding his paintbrush in one hand and a broom in the other. He is very upset.
Here Briullov is painting Zhukovsky's portrait.
In the distance Shevchenko is sweeping the floor. For the last time.
These are Shevchenko and Zhukovsky. Both are turning somersaults out of joy.[13]

At last the day of liberation arrived. On 22 April 1838 Taras Shevchenko received his 'release' – that is, a document signed by Engelhardt, testifying that he had received his freedom. Shortly before, Soshenko had received an order to paint a picture of the four evangelists, and on that day he was working on it in his studio. Suddenly, Taras jumped into the room through the window, knocked the picture down from the easel, and flung his arms around Soshenko's neck, yelling 'freedom, freedom.' Soshenko was overjoyed, and embraced and kissed Taras. The scene ended with both of them 'crying like children.'

The doors of Sesame opened for Shevchenko. The very next day he became a 'free' student of drawing at the Academy of Fine Arts. Reality exceeded all his expectations; not only was he free to study all the secrets of 'divine art' but at once he became the student of 'Charles the Great,' the 'immortal' Briullov, whom he regarded as the 'greatest painter of the nineteenth century' and 'the greatest living artist.'[14] Filled with a feeling

13 V.A. Zhukovsky, *Sobranie sochinenii* (Moscow, Leningrad 1960), IV, 635–7
14 'Khudozhnik,' *Povne*, IV, 173ff

of gratitude to his benefactors, the twenty-four-year-old youth, whose freedom had been purchased as if he were an object being redeemed in a pawnshop, was so happy he did not know what to do.

He took his 'release' out of his pocket again and again and kissed all the signatures on it, especially those of Briullov, Zhukovsky, and Velgorsky, who had stretched out helping hands to liberate this self-taught artist, a son of the open Ukrainian steppes.

Quickly, Taras moved from Shiriaev's attic to Briullov's sumptuous studio. Twenty years later he still could not believe that all this had happened, that an unknown, grubby boy could win the confidence of the greatest artist in the world. His slavery in his master's antechamber and Shiriaev's attic receded like a bad dream. He was now placed in the studios of the painter of *The Last Days of Pompeii* himself. What more could he wish?

PART TWO

The Maturing Artist

1838-43

III

At his entrance to the academy Shevchenko received a scholarship from the Society for the Promotion of Artists. The society was headed by men from the reign of Alexander I: P. Kikin, the head, and F. Prianishnikov, his deputy, who was also a freemason and a member of the Bible Society. They were idealists, even mystics, men of sincerity and truly humane values who kept alive the philanthropic and masonic traditions of their generation. They both loved art passionately. Prianishnikov was one of the most active Russian collectors and had a wonderful private art gallery. There were very few students of noble birth in the Academy of Fine Arts; most came from the families of burghers and artisans, occasionally from among the peasants and even serfs. Kikin and Prianishnikov assisted these talented young artists, especially those with a serf background. Sapozhnikov, a gifted painter, who did not come from the upper strata of society and who was also a military engineer, was the treasurer of the society. Shevchenko's scholarship was easily arranged by Hryhorovych, the secretary of the society. In the eyes of Hryhorovych, as well as of Briullov and Venetsianov, Shevchenko was a most promising student and his material security had to be safeguarded.

Slowly, the state of euphoria after the liberation subsided. After buying himself new clothes and completing all the formalities connected with his new status, Taras began to attend classes and get used to a milieu familiar to him only as an occasional visitor but which had now become his own. Soon the summer holiday approached. It is not known where and how he spent it. It is certain that during the vacation he read and worked a great deal on his education, which had been very sporadic and, as he himself admitted, was deficient in arithmetic. By the autumn of 1838 he was beginning to feel at home in his new environment, to which he 'had flown as if on wings' from his old attic. Classes began again at the academy, but so did the theatrical and social season.

Briullov took a great liking to his new pupil, and Shevchenko worshipped his teacher. In Briullov's lavishly furnished studio Shevchenko met romantics who talked of 'divine art,' swore by the Venus of Milo, and called themselves 'priests of Apollo.' Among these Karl Briullov was elevated to semi-divine status, and his studio was for them a temple of creative mysteries. Shevchenko knew that his master was venerated by Sir Walter Scott and Pushkin and saw how Zhukovsky showered him with kisses. Briullov himself did nothing to discourage this adulation and believed in his own artistic mission. In his relationships with others he developed a theatrical, grandiloquent style and played the part of the anointed prophet of art. He rarely spoke but declaimed, did not teach but preached, turning even the most ordinary observations into philosophical verities and aphorisms. His own career had been that of a spoilt *Wunderkind*, and that, together with his latest successes, undoubtedly affected the entire personality of this gifted artist. He was a poseur, but although he sometimes declined to do a small favour for Pushkin or even for Nicholas I himself, he sometimes stepped down from his Olympus and could be sincere and unaffected among his friends and pupils. Shevchenko knew him in both roles and grew very close to him in St Petersburg. His teacher, too, could sense his pupil's honesty and devotion and could appreciate his genuine gratitude, which came from the heart. He also valued Shevchenko's talent and enthusiasm. This close relationship between teacher and pupil was particularly evident when Shevchenko read aloud to him from Walter Scott or Dickens. This was a favourite habit of Briullov's – to have someone read to him while he was painting in his studio. The lonely demigod felt the warm companionship of the ex-serf. Briullov had a splendid library, and he also borrowed books from the bookseller Smirdin. Shevchenko had free access to all these books and journals.

From October 1838 Shevchenko shared rooms with Soshenko on the fourth line of Vasilievsky Island, near the academy. They shared expenses. Soshenko was Taras's real benefactor, one who had contributed a great deal of time and effort to his liberation. Although Shevchenko was grateful, he found that he and Soshenko were incompatible. Their characters were very different. Soshenko, who was six years older than Taras, was a good and sensitive man but, lacking great talent, concentrated all his attention on his work. After fulfilling his dream of becoming a student at the academy, he directed all his energies to one goal: his studies. He was modest and sensible, and he did not nurture great aspirations. His life was that of an ascetic artist and hard worker. He had got to know Shevchenko when Taras was apprenticed to Shiriaev. Then Shevchenko had been depressed about his fate and yearned to give himself entirely to art should he become free. Now Soshenko saw a different man – a carefree youth who was attracted to the temptations of the capital and who was ready to enjoy himself. Later Soshenko recalled that 'at that time he changed entirely. Introduced by Briullov to the best St Petersburg families, he frequently went out in the evenings, dressed smartly, even with some pretensions to elegance. In a word, he became possessed, for a while, by the social demon. I was saddened to see this gay life, unsuitable for a brother artist, who should live for art alone. So this, I thought to myself, is how he understood freedom, which had taken such effort to win.'[1]

Shevchenko bought himself a fur coat, a watch with a chain, and other luxuries, used coaches for transportation, visited people, and returned home late. Soshenko admonished him for all this and begged him to devote all his time to his profession. But Taras did not listen to his friend's admonitions and instead began to read him some of his poems. Soshenko refused to listen and advised him again and again to mend his ways. It is curious that the language of the poem 'Catherine,' which Shevchenko read to him, made no great impression on Taras's fellow-countryman.

What Soshenko failed to understand was something which, for a man of such great vitality as Shevchenko, was very natural, especially in his new environment. Taras was delighted with the many new experiences that had been inaccessible to him as a serf, and life itself seemed to offer many new joys. Briullov's and Hrebinka's introductions were helpful, but it was Taras's own spontaneous personality that opened the doors to many houses. How could he listen to Soshenko's admonitions when the lifestyles of so many artists, especially the bohemian attitudes of Briullov himself, pulled him in another direction? Having entered, with Briullov's help, the circle of people around the 'triumvirate of frenzied romantics' – Briullov, the composer Glinka, and the writer Kukolnik – Shevchenko came to believe that the way of moderation was the very worst for an artist and that the life of the tavern might be preferable. His new friends had long ago declared war on the grey, conventional bourgeois existence. He was not experienced enough to see that often the brilliant entertainment, the high-flown gestures, and the rhetoric merely served to fill the spiritual emptiness of these people. His own conscience was clear, and he did not find that his new social life interfered with his work or education. He attended classes regularly, continued reading books, and often what he learned in society widened his intellectual horizons and stimulated original thoughts. His young soul, free at last, bubbled like new wine. To

1 M.K. Chaly, 'Vospominaniia I.M. Soshenko,' *Vospominaniia*, 54

his brother Mykyta he wrote: 'It is a great happiness to be a free man. You do what you want; no one can stop you.' He was solicitous about his family, sent money to his brother, and asked him to write 'in his own language, not in Russian.'[2]

His work at the academy was quite successful. A year after his entry, on 3 May 1839, he received a silver medal as a prize for his drawings. Although his life was a little boisterous, with his unusual ability he found the time to concentrate on his work and to broaden his education. He read a great deal, not only fiction and poetry but scholarly literature as well, especially in the field of history. Even at Shiriaev's he had read, on Soshenko's advice, a two-volume history of ancient Greece by John Gillies and, later, the multi-volume *Journey of Anakharsis* by Abbot Barthelemy. During his first year at the academy he read Plutarch's *Lives* and the *History of the Crusades* by Michaud, the multi-volumed classic work on the masters of the Renaissance by Vasari, and some critical works on art history and aesthetics. As to the literary classics, he read some in Polish and others chiefly in Russian translation. These included Dante's *Inferno*, Goldsmith, Byron, Richardson, Macpherson, Shakespeare, Defoe, Scott, Dickens, Rousseau, Chateaubriand, Hugo, Sue, Goethe, Schiller, Heine, and others. He also read travel sketches by Arago, Dumont d'Urville, and Washington Irving. He had a good grasp of Russian literature, beginning with Trediakovsky, Lomonosov, and Derzhavin and ending with contemporary authors. He was an avid reader of Russian journals. Polish authors with whom he was familiar were Mickiewicz, Krasiński, Czajkowski, Zaleski, Goszczyński, and others. His curriculum at the academy included courses in physics, anatomy, zoology, and aesthetics.

In the fall of 1838 Wilhelm Schternberg, a talented painter, returned from Ukraine to St Petersburg. He had been the guest of the Ukrainian magnate Hryhoriy Tarnovsky, owner of the Kachanivka estate in the Chernihiv district. Shevchenko had already heard a great deal about Schternberg, who was a typical romantic idealist. He was modest, gentle, sentimental, and sincere in his relations with others, a man with high moral standards. In spite of his puritanism he enjoyed parties and friendly chats over a glass of wine or beer. He was full of life, very active, and very good company. 'What a good and gentle being he is,' Shevchenko wrote, 'a true artist. Everything smiles at him and he smiles at everything. A happy, enviable character.'[3] Shevchenko was particularly drawn to people like Schternberg, people full of energy yet level-headed and rational. The two men quickly became close friends.

2 *Povne*, VI, 10
3 'Khudozhnik,' ibid, IV, 182

The Maturing Artist 1838–43

This friendship brought some stability into Taras's life. Having been left an orphan and later burdened by his page-boy's duties and his apprentice's worries, he was inclined to be withdrawn and showed a certain distrust of people he met. Now, the chains of serfdom shed, in the new milieu of intelligent, humane people, he went to the other extreme and bared his soul to his new friends and acquaintances. With his spontaneous, energetic nature he had a great need to share his thoughts and feelings. From the day of his arrival in St Petersburg until he gained his freedom he had had no close friends to sympathize with his aspirations and understand his artistic temperament. Neither Ivan Nechyporenko nor the phlegmatic Khtodot Tkachenko, both peasant boys, whom Taras dearly loved, could be true friends. Soshenko became a real friend, but this good and honest man, despite the artistic vocation that had driven him from the distant Ukrainian Bohuslav to St Petersburg, had his limitations and showed no great imagination. Taras, with his grateful heart and enthusiastic nature, was not understood by his honourable and hard-working fellow-countryman. Having gained Briullov's friendship, Taras could not but be aware of the distance separating him from the teacher whom he worshipped and who, while very approachable, remained a distant ideal, to be placed on a pedestal of fame and perfection. Taras was, in fact, rather lonely and he searched for friends with whom he could share not only his thoughts and emotions but his doubts and disappointments as well. Schternberg became this friend, the first in his life. They soon began to share an apartment. This happened after Shevchenko had quarrelled with Soshenko at the end of January 1839. Soshenko was not prepared to have Taras as his roommate. The real reason for this was Soshenko's jealousy, for Taras began to pay too much attention to the German girl Masha, the landlord's cousin, with whom Soshenko was in love but who preferred the carefree Taras.

Shevchenko shared rooms with Schternberg for four months, until, in the early summer of 1839, the latter left for Orenburg to take part in a military expedition to Khiva led by General Count V. Perovsky. Schternberg introduced Shevchenko to several German families – the Schmidts, the Vitzthums, and the Joachims. After seven in the evening Taras was usually free, after study, and along with Schternberg he either visited his friends or went to the theatre. He had attended the theatre even before his liberation. He had met the technical personnel of the Great Theatre in 1836, when he had helped to decorate the ceilings, and he used these connections to obtain free tickets. Early in 1837, together with Briullov and his friends, he went to see a guest appearance by the famous ballerina Maria Taglioni. He could now afford to buy theatre tickets since, apart from the scholarship, he was earning some money by painting portraits in water-colours and by illustrating books. Opera, ballet, and drama fascinated him equally. He did not miss a single important play, even though the repertory of the Russian theatre in those days was rather poor. It was sustained by adaptations of cheap, sentimental French melodramas and vaudevilles or mediocre imitations of them like the plays of Kukolnik, Polevoy, or Rosen. Exceptions were the famous play *Woe from Wit* by Griboedov and Gogol's immortal *Inspector General*. Even Schiller's *Robbers* was staged as an adaptation, not as a faithful translation. Opera and music were a little better, and here Shevchenko could listen with relish to his favourite composers. The 'bewitching opera' remained a source of pleasure throughout his life. He heard concerts by famous European virtuosi – cellists, violinists, and pianists.

Accepted as a regular guest by the Schmidt, Vitzthum, and Joachim families, Shevchenko came to know the lives of these bourgeois German families, which were more restrained and methodical than those of Russian or Ukrainian families. This new milieu was very different from the bohemian literary atmosphere that he was used to. At the Schmidts', where young ladies were present, Shevchenko was asked to organize literary soirées. The Vitzthums held musical evenings. Vitzthum himself was a university inspector, and through him Shevchenko got to know some influential people. Schternberg introduced Shevchenko to the Ukrainian magnate Hryhoriy Tarnovsky, owner of the fabulous Kachanivka. Tarnovsky was a rather limited person with little education, but he knew how to play the role of benefactor, art patron, and protector of artists. During the winter season he appeared in St Petersburg with large supplies of Ukrainian brandy and held receptions for painters and writers, entertaining them with much lavish dining and wining. His visitors on these occasions would ingratiate themselves with this rich man. Shevchenko disliked this, and he also disliked Tarnovsky's patronizing tone. However, the acquaintance with Tarnovsky turned out to be useful since through him he met the Kiev branch of the family, who later inherited Kachanivka.

Schternberg fell in love with one of Tarnovsky's cousins, who at first reciprocated his feelings but eventually became engaged to someone else. Schternberg was heartbroken and confided his sorrow in Shevchenko. A few years later, writing from faraway Rome, Schternberg praised Taras's goodness: 'One can be good for a specific reason, but to be a friend and share another's woes and joys – that requires a good and sensitive soul.'[4]

4 *Lysty do T.H. Shevchenka* (Kiev 1962), 19

What cemented their friendship was their affinity of artistic interests. Schternberg, having visited Ukraine, sensed all the beauty of Shevchenko's homeland and re-created with great expressiveness in his paintings features of both the Ukrainian landscape and life. It was nine years since Taras had seen Ukraine. Now Schternberg's paintings resurrected in his imagination familiar scenes of his picturesque homeland. They lived and worked in the same room. Schternberg painted his pictures from sketches he had brought with him. It is clear that Ukraine was the central topic of their conversations, with Schternberg contributing his fresh impressions of the country. Where Soshenko had regarded Shevchenko's literary attempts as unnecessary and a waste of precious time, the romantic Schternberg eagerly listened to Taras's first poetic attempts.

During Schternberg's stay in St Petersburg two events occurred in the life of his and Shevchenko's great teacher – his 'senseless marriage and a sensible parting,' as Shevchenko described them. Briullov had married Emilia Timm, the daughter of a German from Riga, who was a great beauty. On 8 January 1839 Shevchenko and Schternberg attended the wedding ceremony at an evangelical church. There was no traditional wedding reception. During their brief marriage Shevchenko often visited the Briullovs and shared his master's admiration for Emilia's beauty. Suddenly, after less than two months, Emilia left Briullov and never came back to him. Apparently, he had gravely offended her. Briullov disintegrated under the impact of this drama and became ill. For a time Shevchenko even moved to his studio and helped to look after him. He was one of the few to know of Briullov's tragedy, which also left its mark on Shevchenko's own life. The reason for the failure of Briullov's marriage was Tsar Nicholas himself, who chose the beautiful Emilia as his mistress. There is no reason to believe that before that time Shevchenko had known anything about the tsar's intimate life, but he now learned a great deal about it from his beloved teacher.

As early as the fall of 1838 some of Shevchenko's friends learned that he was not only a talented painter but a poet as well. Hrebinka received some poems from him for the almanac he was planning to publish. At first it was to be called *Spring* (*Vesna*) but later it became *The Swallow* (*Lastivka*). On 18 November 1838 Hrebinka wrote to the old writer Hryhoriy Kvitka-Osnovianenko in Kharkiv: 'I have here a countryman of ours, Shevchenko who is more determined to write verse than anyone I know. What he has written is so good that you can smack your lips and clap your hands. He has given me some of his verses for my collection.'[5] And in a letter in

5 Ye. P. Hrebinka, *Tvory v triokh tomakh* (Kiev 1981), III, 594–5

January 1839 he added, 'I have a wonderful helper – Shevchenko, a remarkable man.'[6]

As Shevchenko himself said, he started writing poetry in 1837, while still at Shiriaev's, though only one poem has been preserved from these early attempts, the ballad 'The Bewitched Woman' ('Prychynna'), written in the Summer Gardens, a romantic work composed in romantic surroundings. Shevchenko started to write poetry soon after he met Hrebinka. It was to him that he first confessed his poetic ambitions, and it was Hrebinka who supervised Taras's literary education, giving him some Ukrainian literary works to read, of which there were not many in circulation. Shevchenko had read Russian, and possibly Polish, poetry before. Hrebinka told him that there were not only Ukrainian folksongs that had been written down but some original poetry as well. Taras learned that the folksongs, many of which he knew and sang either at work or in his spare time, were now highly regarded and valued by scholars and poets as true poetry and that some people regarded them as being of the highest poetic order, which other poets should emulate.

Shevchenko was overjoyed when he saw some of the songs he knew printed in collections by Tsertelev and Maksymovych.[7] In a mood of deep nostalgia for his native land and a yearning for freedom, befriended by some good people and disappointed in others, Taras was full of longing. His lyrical talent found expression for this longing in the words of his native language. His outpouring was finer and more accomplished than a simple Ukrainian folksong. The two genres, folksong and models from Russian and Polish poetry, blended under his pen into a new Ukrainian lyrical poetry.

We do not know whether he wrote any other poems in 1837, though Hrebinka did secure the poem 'The Bewitched Woman' for his almanac. This ballad derived from Zhukovsky's translation of Buerger's 'Lenora,' which was also adapted by Zhukovsky into the poem 'Svetlana' and was later adapted further in Borovykovsky's poem 'Marusia.' Using all three poems, Shevchenko, treating the same theme of a girl's experiences after parting with her lover, created a work of great individual power and distinctiveness. While his predecessors were preoccupied with romantic horrors, he concentrated on a re-creation of the psychology of the unfortunate heroine. Buerger's fantasy appears to be real and Zhukovsky's is a dream, while Shevchenko's is a vision of a bewitched, insane

---

6 Ibid, 597

7 Prince Nikolay Tsertelev published his *Opyt sobraniia malorosiiskikh pesnei* in St Petersburg in 1819. Maksymovych's first collection, *Malorossiiskie pesni*, appeared in 1827. The second, expanded edition, *Ukrainskie narodnye pesni*, came out in Moscow in 1834.

woman. He portrays her and her death as a psychiatrist might. A detailed account of somnambulism and psychic illness is masterfully dramatized. The intense feeling in this work springs from the author's exceptional sensitivity and his great ability to enter into someone else's state of mind. It is a work of true poetic genius.

It is possible that Shevchenko told Hrebinka about the poetry he was writing because of the death, in 1838, of the great Ukrainian poet Ivan Kotliarevsky. Saddened by the news, Shevchenko wrote an elegy on Kotliarevsky's death, a loss which was widely discussed among the Ukrainians in St Petersburg. Perhaps Shevchenko read this elegy to Hrebinka and, with his encouragement, confessed to writing other poems. That this was how it may have happened we can see from Hrebinka's letter to Kvitka on 18 November, soon after the news of Kotliarevsky's death had reached St Petersburg.

Hrebinka's praise of Shevchenko's poetry is understandable. Never before had Ukrainian poetry shown so much power, purity, and richness of language as well as great formal perfection. The elegy on Kotliarevsky's death shows one source of Shevchenko's growing national consciousness. In the poem Shevchenko wrote that it was Kotliarevsky who

> All the Cossack glory, with a single word,
> Transferred to the orphan's wretched house.[8]

In the classicist travesty of the *Aeneid* by Kotliarevsky, Shevchenko saw a reflection of national history and a psychological re-creation of the 'Cossack nation.' He discerned this beneath the shell of the burlesque genre, with its formal devices and acid humour. Encouraged by Hrebinka's praise and perhaps by others as well, Shevchenko began a longer poem, 'Catherine' ('Kateryna'). Taking the unoriginal, well-worn tale of the seduced and abandoned woman, he made a masterpiece of it in which the tragedy of the Ukrainian girl seduced by a Russian soldier grew into the larger dimensions of Ukraine's fate under Russia.

Ever since the autumn of 1838 Hrebinka had planned to publish a quarterly Ukrainian almanac, and he was trying to persuade Kraevsky, the editor of the Russian journal *Notes of the Fatherland* (*Otechestvennye zapiski*), to publish four Ukrainian supplements annually. It is possible that he was counting on the help of his 'marvellous assistant' Shevchenko. But only a few of these plans were realized: in 1841 the almanac *The Swallow* (*Lastivka*) appeared, to which, in addition to the 'Bewitched

8 'Na vichnu pamiat Kotliarevskomu,' *Povne*, I, 19

Woman' and two *dumky*, Shevchenko also contributed a segment from his long poem 'The Haidamaks' ('Haidamaky'), which he had composed in 1840–41.

'Catherine' was probably written at the very end of 1838 or even in January 1839. During 1839 Shevchenko wrote 'Perebendia,' the ballad 'Poplar' ('Topola'), 'To Osnovianenko' ('Do Osnovianenko'), 'Ivan Pidkova,' and 'The Night of Taras' ('Tarasova nich'), which he was still polishing in 1840. During this time he also wrote three songs, which he called *dumky*: 'The Water Flows into the Blue Sea' ('Teche voda v synie more'), 'The Wild Wind' ('Vitre buiny'), both published in *The Swallow*, and 'What Use Are My Black Brows?' ('Nashcho meni chorni brovy'). These pure lyrics and his lyrical ballads were the most successful of his works.

> My heart was torn, it laughed –
> It poured out in words
> As well as it could –
> About the dark nights
> About the green cherry orchard
> About the girls' favours.[9]

Later came the narrative lyrical poems, and still later the historical, romantic poems. The latter were influenced by the historical poems of Walter Scott, Macpherson's 'Ossian,' Pushkin's 'Poltava,' and Ryleev's 'Nalyvaiko's Death' and 'Voinarovsky.' He himself has described how difficult it was to write on historical themes:

> My heart fainted and did not want
> To sing in a foreign land ...
> It did not want in the steppe, in the forest
> To gather the Cossack host,
> With its maces and horse-tails,
> For a council.[10]

In the meantime this Cossack host, the steppes, and the gravemounds strongly attracted his imagination. The Ukraine of cherry orchards and dark nights was replaced by the Ukraine of national stirrings striving to be heard. Seventeen or eighteen years later he recalled how, in Briullov's

9 'Dumy moi, dumy moi,' ibid, 48
10 Ibid

The Maturing Artist 1838-43

luxurious studio, as if 'on the hot steppes along the Dnieper,' there arose before him 'the martyred shadows of our hapless hetmans'; the 'steppe was strewn with gravemounds,' and 'the ill-starred beautiful Ukraine preened herself in her entire immaculate, melancholy beauty.' He grew pensive and 'could not tear his eyes from this native, compelling beauty.'[11]

In the fall of 1839 Shevchenko started corresponding with Kvitka-Osnovianenko and sent the old writer his 'epistle' under the pseudonym 'Perebendia.' The epistle was strongly influenced by a reading of Kvitka's sketch of the Zaporozhian *otaman* Antin Holovaty. This historical figure had been well delineated by Kvitka, and the portrait captivated Shevchenko. In re-creating history he placed great emphasis on documentary evidence. He regarded himself as inadequately equipped for such a task and therefore begged Kvitka to sing

> About the Sich, about the gravemounds,
> Which, at what time, were erected,
> And who was buried there within.
> About the old days, the marvels
> Which once were and which have passed ...
> Let us hear you sing, father!
> So that the entire world may hear,
> What happened in Ukraine,
> Why the land was oppressed,
> Why the Cossack glory
> Came to ring across the world![12]

Later, in the introduction to his first collection of poems, Shevchenko once again mentioned his inadequacy, but stressed his lyrical temperament. He wrote of the minstrels (*kobzars*):

> They always sing about the past
> These poor blind men
> Because they are wise.
> But I, but I
> Can only weep
> And shed tears for Ukraine,
> I lack the words.[13]

---

11 'Shchodennyk,' ibid, v, 43
12 'Do Osnovianenka,' ibid, I, 64
13 'Dumy moi, dumy moi,' ibid, 48-50

As far as historical material was concerned, Shevchenko's knowledge of Ukrainian history, up to this point based on folk legends, the *dumy* that the *kobzars* sang, and historical songs, began to assume much sharper contours. In the winter of 1839 the Ukrainian historian Mykola Markevych appeared in St Petersburg. He had failed to steer his *History of Little Russia (Istoriia Malorossii)* through the censorship in Moscow, and now he attempted to do so in St Petersburg. Markevych was a friend of Hrebinka. Suddenly, Shevchenko found himself in a circle where Ukrainian history was the subject of animated discussions. He was already familiar with the *History of Little Russia (Istoriia Maloi Rossii)* by Bantysh-Kamensky, and now he read, in manuscript, *History of the Rus People (Istoriia Rusov)* and Markevych's large, unpublished history. All these works were saturated with the spirit of Ukrainian Cossack patriotism. They contained a great deal of poetical and legendary material. They were no less romantic than the legends and songs with which Shevchenko was already familiar. These three histories, as well as Sreznevsky's collection *Zaporozhian Antiquity (Zaporozhskaia starina)*, became the sources of Shevchenko's historical imagination. They transported him back to a glorious and colourful past that was in stark contrast to the country's present hardships, which seemed to him like a bad dream. It was enough for him to read the *duma* about the sea voyage of *otaman* Ivan Serpiaha (whom Sreznevsky wrongly identified with the historical figure of Ivan Pidkova) in order to create a masterful and dynamic portrayal of a Cossack national leader, an able psychologist, and his faithful military company. He had only to read Bantysh-Kamensky's short description of the battle of Pereiaslav of 1638 in order to create 'The Night of Taras,' a poem full of bloody mirages from the past and permeated with the spirit of struggle that had now disappeared among the descendants of the Cossacks.

From October 1838 to the end of January 1839 Shevchenko had shared his quarters with Soshenko on the fourth line of Vasilievsky Island, where the building of the Academy of Fine Arts stood. From January until the summer of 1839 Shevchenko lived with Schternberg in Arens's or Arnst's house on the ninth line of the island. That summer Schternberg left for Orenburg. After his departure Shevchenko found a new roommate, a poor Polish student, Leonard Demski, who was recommended to him by the university inspector, Vitzthum. Shevchenko mentions that Demski gave him lessons in French. In his novel *The Artist (Khudozhnik)* Shevchenko recalls how they read Paul de Kock together, as well as a French translation of Gibbon's history of Byzantium. Together they attended lectures on zoology, given by Professor Kutorga. Shevchenko remembered Demski as a 'very modest, well-educated young man,' an idealistic dreamer, who saw himself pursuing a brilliant scholarly career. Demski had among his books Mickiewicz's works as well as Lelewel's historical studies. Shevchenko must have read these and other Polish books, since he had no difficulty with the language. It is possible that Demski introduced him to some of his Polish friends and that he received Polish émigré newspapers, which were banned in Russia because of their anti-Russian and anti-serfdom attitudes. These journals were steeped in the ideas of European thinkers, the creators of social (Fourier) or Christian (Lamennais) utopias. Shevchenko learned from these journals about the ideologies of the 'New Europe,' – the Europe of Garibaldi, Mazzini, and Worcell – and perhaps like them began to have visions of a future revolutionary order that would bring liberation to captive nations.

On 16 December 1839 Schternberg returned unexpectedly from Orenburg, and Demski had to vacate his room. Much later, in his journal written in exile, Shevchenko reminisced fondly about life with Schternberg:

I could visualize the room on the ninth line, in the house of the baker Donnerberg[14] – the room with all its paraphernalia (I do not say furnishings, since this would not be true). Alongside a wall, over the desk, there were two shelves. The upper shelf was crowded with statuettes and little horses by Baron Klodt; the lower was crammed with books. The wall opposite the only half-closed window was covered with statues and casts of feet and hands, including Laocoon's mask and the famous nude Fortunata. This décor would not be comprehensible to a non-painter. To crown it all, I remembered the day when the late Schternberg and I spent our last pennies on a simple lamp, put it in our studio, and lit it in broad daylight. We put it on the table and were as pleased with it as small children. After his enthusiasm had subsided a little, Schternberg took a book and sat on one side of the lamp, while I took up some work and sat on the other side. We sat like this, with the lamp lit in the middle of the day, until five o'clock in the evening. At five we went to the academy and told everybody in the class about our precious acquisition. We invited some friends to come and see our marvel; in fact we gave a party: tea with biscuits. We were very poor, but as innocent as children.[15]

For Shevchenko these memories were 'golden days,' and he fondly recalled 'the enchanted world of the most enticing and graceful images.' The modest room in Arens's house, where Shevchenko had lived earlier,

14 Shevchenko's mistake. The firm was called Donnenberg and remained at that location until the 1917 revolution.
15 'Progulka,' *Povne*, IV, 293–4

from the end of 1839 to the beginning of 1840, has been described by the landowner P. Martos, whose portrait Shevchenko painted then in water-colour:

His apartment was on Vasilievsky Island, not far from the Academy of Fine Arts, somewhere high up near the sky. It consisted of a small, empty anteroom and a small room with a bay window. There was a bed, some kind of table, strewn picturesquely and chaotically with various objects of the inmates' art studies, and various half-torn papers and sketches, and an easel and a half-broken chair were squeezed with some difficulty into the room. Propped against the walls were framed canvases, some showing the beginnings of portraits and other paintings.[16]

These were the modest studios where Shevchenko worked. Here he was visited by people whose portraits he painted, mostly in water-colour. He had quite a few orders, but Shevchenko was not very practical in dealing with his clients, who sometimes did not pay him for his work. He later recalled how a rich landowner, the guards officer Demidov, forgot to pay for the portrait of his fiancée and how the captain of cavalry Aprelev, a 'Sybarite and glutton' who brought his own breakfast to the studio, along with gin and wine and sometimes champagne, also did not pay him for his portrait, since he considered that to give the painter a treat occasionally was quite enough.

When he read the scraps of Shevchenko's poem 'The Night of Taras' that he found on the floor, Martos liked them so much that he offered to publish them. This was early in 1840, probably at the end of January. Shevchenko entitled his collection *Kobzar (The Minstrel)*. Schternberg drew a frontispiece for it, depicting a blind *kobzar* with a youthful guide. On 12 February the censor P. Korsakov, who was himself a minor writer and valued Ukrainian poetry since he had visited Ukraine, signed the permission to print the book. Although Korsakov was a very mild censor, he did delete some passages from the poems by Shevchenko, who also made some cuts himself. It was impossible, for instance, to hope that the Russian censor would allow a passage from the 'Night of Taras' like 'Over the Cossack children / There rule the evil ones,' or the description of Ukraine from the poem 'To Osnovianenko' as 'A ragged orphan / Crying along the Dnieper.'

Before the appearance of the *Kobzar* Shevchenko's life was uneventful. He was busy with his studies, but he did not neglect his writing. This was only his second year of study, but he was already allowed to use oil-

---

16 P.I. Martos, 'Epizody iz zhizni Shevchenko,' *Vospominaniia*, 70

paints, earlier than some of his classmates. He had to complete his program before the summer vacation and he chose a composition called *A Beggar Boy Sharing Bread with a Dog*. This was to bring him, in the fall, not only a silver medal, the second in a row, but a special testimonial from the council of the academy. The Society for the Promotion of Artists, which had awarded Shevchenko a scholarship, sent him a special letter of congratulation and assured him of further assistance, provided he continued to show the same 'dedication and industry.' In the same year Shevchenko painted a self-portrait in a very romantic manner, trying his hand at oil painting. His work left him some spare time to fill private orders. Slowly he 'came into money,' as Martos wrote later. In March he could afford to send fifty roubles to his brother Mykyta. He spent money freely, went to theatres, where he bought good seats and sometimes bought himself expensive objects, and was as pleased as a child. Remembering those times he later wrote:

You know what interested me then most? – I am at a loss to confess ... I was like a child then: I was most interested in my waterproof raincoat ... When you think about it, this was not so strange. Looking at the skirts of this shining coat, I thought to myself: was it so long ago that, wearing a dirty smock, I did not even dare to think about such shining clothes? But now I spend a hundred roubles on a coat ... Truly the metamorphoses of Ovid! Once, when I managed to get a miserable half-rouble, I would go to a theatre, into the upper gallery, and would laugh and cry so much more than anyone else in his entire life for this half a rouble. Was it so long ago? But now whenever I go to the theatre, I take a seat and only rarely do I sit at the back. I go to see not just anything, but try to get tickets for the benefit performance, and even if the play is old I always select the best.[17]

Shevchenko's material well-being was uneven: sometimes he was short of money and sometimes he lived like a lord. He had many friends and acquaintances, and there was never a dull moment in his life. When he was not working he enjoyed himself. Apart from the German families to whom Schternberg had introduced him, he continued to visit Hrebinka, Hryhorovych, Tarnovsky, and Markevych, all of whom spent the winter of 1839–40 in St Petersburg. He sometimes went to *jours fixes* held by Kukolnik and often went to receptions and banquets given by writers, artists, editors, and publishers. The memoirs of the Russian writers of that era frequently mention Shevchenko as a participant in literary soirées. There he met the whole of literary and artistic St Petersburg. At Hrebinka's he met the writers Vladislavlev, Strugovshchikov, Panaev,

---

17 'Khudozhnik,' *Povne*, IV, 205

Dal, Yershov, D. Grigorovich, and Benediktov. Kukolnik and Markevych were also present, though they held receptions of their own, where 'wine flowed abundantly.' Shevchenko also attended Briullov's parties. Sometimes he met writers who were outside these circles. At Strugovshchikov's he met Prince Odoevsky, the son-in-law of Prince Velgorsky, Count Sologub, and even Vissarion Belinsky. All these soirées were attended by prominent artists and Shevchenko's fellow students from the academy.

Shevchenko's circle of friends also included young government officials and officers born in Ukraine. A close Russian friend was Grigoriy Mikhailov, a well-known bon vivant and a student of Briullov's. He also knew the Ukrainian painters Petrovsky, Boryshpolets, Mokrytsky, and the sculptor Ponomarev.

Throughout his student life Shevchenko took part in various escapades and masquerades organized by students. These often lasted past midnight and ended up in Kley's restaurant. During the summer there were boat trips with Briullov to one of the islands on the Neva. There they drew, read, and talked as well as sang and drank. One of these boat trips lasted two days and two nights, and not until the third day did the revellers return home. In the spring and summer of 1840 Shevchenko and Schternberg would start off at dawn to sketch at the Smolensk cemetery. Some student discussions also went on in their studios, with Briullov participating. 'The brilliant, heartfelt talk was like the playful sea,' Shevchenko reminisced later: 'it sparkled with golden reflections; it echoed and gurgled – that is how we spent our time, in animated discussion.'

Outside the academy Shevchenko met some Ukrainian friends –Dziubyn, Yezuchevsky, Trotsyna, Haluzevsky, Kandyba, and Soshalsky – and some he remembered all his life. These grandsons of Ukrainian Cossacks, now members of the nobility, were serving in various government offices in the capital but retained their local patriotism. Among them were some who recognized and appreciated Shevchenko's talents. On the whole he welcomed contacts with people, but sometimes he was disappointed in them. He did not like to talk about others, but there are occasional comments that reflect some bitterness, such as one in a letter to H. Tarnovsky: 'To hell with them! I have tasted that honey, let it go sour!' Describing later his student life in the novel *The Artist*, Shevchenko wrote: 'I do not have the good fortune to be able to size up people, but I have the unlucky disposition to strike up friendships with them.' This was, possibly, the true reason for disappointment.

All the revelry, the visits to friends, and the excursions occurred on weekends and holidays, mostly in the evenings. Attendance at classes at the academy was compulsory, and it was impossible to miss lectures or studios. On weekdays students were free after seven o'clock in the evening. Shevchenko usually breakfasted at home and ate whatever was available. For dinner he frequently went to the restaurant of Madame Jurgens, a German woman, where most of the art students and carefree bohemians ate their meals. On occasion Shevchenko and Schternberg were joined there by Briullov, who declined an 'aristocratic dinner' to partake of a 'democratic soup' and good company. The modest restaurant was known to Shevchenko while he was still at Shiriaev's. At Madame Jurgens's one could see 'a poor clerk from a government office in his only, shabby uniform,' as well as 'a university student, pale and thin, who dined there on the money earned by copying out lecture notes for a rich colleague.' The largest group of Madame Jurgens's guests was made up of painters and sculptors. They could be recognized by their beards and their long hair down to their shoulders, their eccentric dress, their carefully cultivated carelessness, and their wide-brimmed hats.

At that time the appearance of the capital was changing rapidly. A new stratum of 'declassed' intellectuals was appearing, forming an ever-growing body between the nobility and other citizens. This stratum came to be called *raznochintsy* (men of different ranks) and included artists and littérateurs of all kinds, with their bohemian life-style. This was the only milieu Shevchenko knew well.

In the summer of 1840 Shevchenko bade farewell forever to his dear friend Schternberg. Willi departed for Rome. Shevchenko missed him and was at a loss as to what he should do. Fortunately his attention was occupied by the wide echo that the publication of his *Kobzar* had evoked in the Russian press and among the Ukrainian intelligentsia. Shevchenko's book became the subject of heated discussion, the object of praise but of reservations as well about his use of the Ukrainian language and the very existence of Ukrainian literature. His countrymen received the work with great enthusiasm. All this could not but fill Shevchenko with excitement.

Kobzar appeared sometime in March or early April. Like all young authors Shevchenko was probably anxiously awaiting the critical response to his first book. He did not have to wait long – the first reviews began to appear in May. There were several, and they must have led to lively discussions among Shevchenko's circle of friends. Some reviews pleased him; others annoyed, even enraged him. To be sure, all the reviewers recognized the author's poetic gifts, most of them praising him very highly. At the same time many of them denied Ukrainian literature any right to exist, ridiculed the Ukrainian language, and regretted that such a gifted poet was wasting his talent.

The most hostile response came, it is believed, from a renegade Ukrainian, Professor Nikitenko, in the *Son of the Fatherland* (*Syn otechestva*),[18] and from a renegade Pole, Senkovsky, in the *Library for Reading* (*Biblioteka dlia chteniia*).[19] Nikitenko, the probable author of the first review, considered Ukrainian poetry to be 'artificial,' a 'joke and a whim,' and could not understand how talented people could 'occupy themselves with such stupidities.' He was not sorry that some second-rate writers, like Hrebinka, wrote in Ukrainian, for then the Russian reader was relieved of the duty of reading them. He deplored, however, the same attempt by a talented poet who had 'a soul and feeling' and could enrich Russian poetry. Instead, he was 'badly perverting Russian thought and language' by trying to write in Ukrainian. To Shevchenko the recognition of his talent in this context could only be an insult.

Senkovsky's attack on the Ukrainian language and Ukrainian literature was even stronger. Like Nikitenko, Senkovsky deplored the fact that Shevchenko wrote in an 'artificial' language, but praised him as a poet. He contradicted those who maintained that after Pushkin's death there were no more talented poets. The *Kobzar*, for Senkovsky, was evidence of a great new talent. He considered its 'marvellous songs' a sign of 'undoubted talent.' No matter what language Shevchenko wrote in, 'each of his works has the stamp of poetry on it.' However, Senkovsky simultaneously lashed out against the Ukrainian language, which he considered 'a dialect which does not even exist in Russia,' for no part of Russia, 'neither the great nor the small, neither black nor white, nor red, nor new, nor old,' could recognize it as its own. He also, without any foundation, accused all Ukrainian writers of 'transforming Russian words into Ukrainian.' Shevchenko's poetry, for Senkovsky, was closer to Russian poetry in its verse form than to the folk poetry of Ukraine.

The aristocratic *Contemporary* (*Sovremennik*),[20] which, after Pushkin's death, was edited by Professor Pletnev, evaluated *Kobzar* as a remarkable appearance in contemporary poetry, full of 'living, lyrical folk poetry,' and expressed the hope that those who understood Ukrainian would read the collection with gratitude. At the same time this positive response was coupled with a warning that the book was written in a 'local dialect' and might, therefore, tend to be treated as a 'parody or a literary joke.' The author of the review in Bulgarin's and Grech's *Northern Bee* (*Severnaia*

18 *Syn otechestva* II, 4 (1840)
19 *Biblioteka dlia chteniia*, no 39 (1840)
20 *Sovremennik* XIX (1840)

pchela),²¹ a very reactionary journal, surprisingly accurately fathomed the characteristic features of Shevchenko's muse and showed a deep aesthetic sensitivity. The image of Perebendia was evaluated as 'masterful, strong, and full of unadulterated poetry.' 'Catherine' was a moving poem that, despite the familiarity of the topic, 'penetrated deeply into the soul.' The reviewer, who greeted the new author 'with sincere joy,' ended his piece with these prophetic words: 'If these are his first attempts, we must place great hopes in Mr Shevchenko's talents.' Yet even this critic advised Shevchenko to write in Russian. 'It is sad,' he wrote, 'to behold the literature of those Slavic dialects that are doomed to wither in their creators, to die in the archives, losing the words and sounds with which they were adorned, and even sadder to see these dialects used by people who might adorn the all-consuming Slavic literature [that is, Russian].' The last two reviewers, laying all their cards on the table, did not, at least, mock Ukrainian literature by calling it 'artificial,' as did Nikitenko and Senkovsky.

Only three reviewers wrote positively about Shevchenko's work and grudgingly admitted Ukrainian literature the right to exist – as a 'regional' literature, to be sure. These reviews appeared in the *Notes of the Fatherland* (*Otechestvennye zapiski*),²² the *Literary Gazette* (*Literaturnaia gazeta*),²³ of A. Krasovsky, and the conservative and Slavophil the *Beacon* (*Maiak*).²⁴ The latter review was written by the *Kobzar's* censor, P. Korsakov, himself a writer and translator. The author, who was familiar with Ukraine and Ukrainian folk poetry as well as with the works of Shevchenko's Ukrainian predecessors, praised the collection very highly and thought that Shevchenko's poems 'would do honour to any name in any literature.' He maintained that the poems were written in the 'national spirit' and that they were 'full of feeling, reason, simplicity, grace, and honest truth.' He welcomed them with 'an open heart.'

Although forty years had passed since Ivan Kotliarevsky had revived modern Ukrainian literature, no single author in this literature had produced such artistically powerful works as those included in the

---

21 *Severnaia pchela*, no 101 (1840)
22 *Otechestvennye zapiski*, no. 5 (1840). In 1939 the Soviet critic Spiridonov tried unsuccessfully to ascribe this favourable review to Belinsky. This conjecture, avidly supported by other Soviet scholars, has been definitely disproved by V. Swoboda and R. Martin in 'Schevchenko and Belinsky Revisited,' *Slavonic and East European Review* LVI, 4 (Oct. 1978).
23 *Literaturnaia gazeta*, no 36 (1840)
24 *Maiak*, no 6 (1840)

Kobzar. No one had aroused in the reader similar thoughts and feelings. Shevchenko was the first to represent Ukraine as oppressed by her enemies, a country over which 'a black eagle / Circles like a guard.' Although most of the passages describing Ukraine's subjugation were censored, the images of struggle in such poems as 'The Night of Taras' and 'Ivan Pidkova' were permeated with a fervent patriotism, which inspired a yearning for the independence lost by the ancestors of the Ukrainian people. Among these images perhaps the most striking was that of the enslaved farm-hand, the mower who humbly takes his scythe to work past the gravemounds of his ancestors who had been knights and conquerors, who

> knew how to rule.
> They ruled and conquered
> Glory and freedom.[25]

Not all Shevchenko's countrymen absorbed the full impact of this small, 114-page volume, but most received the book with enthusiasm as a real literary treasure. After Korsun and Kostomarov, two young poets in Kharkiv, bought *Kobzar*, they sat down on the street and did not move until they had finished reading it. Old Kvitka wrote to Shevchenko that his hair had stood on end when he read the *Kobzar*.

In that same year, 1840, Shevchenko began writing a long poem, 'The Haidamaks' ('Haidamaky'). We do not know when he conceived the idea of this poem. There was very little historical literature about the so-called Koliivshchyna or Haidamachchyna, a peasant rebellion in Ukraine in 1768, but Shevchenko knew many legends about it. The subject had been used by some Polish poets. Now the descendant of an eyewitness of the famous and bloody rebellion began an epic work himself. Early in April 1841 'The Haidamaks' was finished, and on 7 April Shevchenko dedicated the poem to his beloved benefactor, Hryhorovych.

In the dedication Shevchenko gave a sharp reply to all those enemies of the Ukrainian language who regarded it as 'artificial' or 'dying' or even 'non-existent.' As early as 1839, in the epistle to Osnovianenko, Shevchenko had anticipated a hostile response to his 'psalms' on Ukrainian history:

> They will laugh at this psalm,
> Which I'll pour out in tears;

---

25 'Ivan Pidkova,' *Povne*, I, 65

Catherine, 1842; illustration to a poem; oil

> They will laugh at it. It is hard, father,
> To live among enemies.[26]

And yet he did not hesitate to publish his psalm. After finishing 'The Haidamaks' he met, head on, a new enemy of the Ukrainian national and cultural revival, an enemy armed with great talent and temperament – the 'furious'[27] Vissarion Belinsky. In 1839 the critic left Moscow and moved to St Petersburg. He was invited to collaborate on the monthly *Notes of the Fatherland* by the publisher, the sly, commercially minded Kraevsky. In 1840 Hrebinka's almanac the *Swallow*, on which Shevchenko had collaborated, fell into the hands of the reviewer Belinsky. The *Swallow* appeared in the second half of March 1841, and Belinsky was asked to review it for the May issue of *Notes of the Fatherland*. Hrebinka, who knew Kraevsky well, was given the text or the proofs of the review in advance. Both he and Shevchenko were anxious about what the new critic would say about their 'child.' Belinsky was famous both for his aesthetic judgment and for his sharp, abrupt attacks on literature he did not like, and that included the poetry of Mickiewicz.

What did Shevchenko find in Belinsky's review? It was closer to being a pamphlet arguing against Ukrainian literature in general, and against its preoccupation with folk subjects in particular. It contained no real criticism but demonstrated only the reviewer's ignorance and prejudice. It was a tract on the subjects 'Does the Ukrainian language exist or is it only a regional dialect?' and 'Is Ukrainian literature possible?' After praising Ukrainian folk poetry and making a bold foray into the Ukrainian past, Belinsky concluded that the Ukrainian language did not yet exist but was only a regional folk dialect. Education and culture had flourished in Muscovy and Ukraine only since the times of Peter I, and a division into estates had occurred in which the Ukrainian gentry, having accepted Russian and European customs, had also accepted the Russian language. The Ukrainian folk language had begun to deteriorate (when and how?), and there remained in Ukraine only a regional dialect. Thus, there could be no Ukrainian literature, since writers write for the educated class and produce poetry in the idealization of truth. The educated class of Ukrainian society had 'outgrown' the Ukrainian language, argued Belinsky, because it spoke Russian, and Ukrainian had become a peasant dialect. Peasant life, however, was of no interest to an educated person, and extraordinary talent was required to idealize this life and to depict it

---

26 'Do Osnovianenka,' ibid, I, 63
27 The nickname 'Furious' was given to Belinsky because of his first name, which once belonged to a Cardinal Vissarione, also known as 'Furioso.'

poetically. This had only been achieved by great writers like Gogol, but even he, while passionately in love with Ukraine, wrote in Russian. Therefore Belinsky was 'sorry to see' meagre talents 'waste their gifts' by writing in Ukrainian for Ukrainian peasants. Citing two short examples from Kvitka and Hrebinka that were supposed to illustrate the 'naïveté' of Ukrainian topics that bored the critics, he ironically declared that 'this must be beautiful literature which breathes the coarse peasant language and the woodenness of the *muzhik* mind.' Here the ignorance of the self-taught *raznochinets* was mixed with the impudence with which he discussed authoritatively matters he knew nothing about. In his review Belinsky exceeded the attacks by Nikitenko and Senkovsky, who were simply abusive. In order to find a basis for his chauvinistic and dicriminatory theories, which ruled out all provincial separatism and any views he held to be reactionary, he used false historical arguments.

Apart from this, Belinsky's article contained no critical analysis of the works included in the *Swallow*. He refused to evaluate them because he understood the Ukrainian text very imperfectly. Certainly in Hrebinka's writing some attempt had been made to create artificially simple peasant language and thought, but here he was only trying to emulate the style of Rudy Panko in Gogol's Ukrainian tales. While stressing that Gogol could find universal motifs in Ukrainian peasant life, Belinsky failed to find any universality in Shevchenko's works, even though the *Swallow* contained such masterpieces as the elegy on Kotliarevsky's death, the ballad 'The Bewitched Woman,' and part of 'The Haidamaks.' Belinsky ignored them completely. Instead he used the appearance of the *Swallow* as an excuse to attack Ukrainian cultural separatism.

What hurt Shevchenko most in Belinsky's article was the scorn with which he treated the '*muzhik* themes' in Ukrainian literature. Therefore, he decided to rebuff the views of Belinsky and other Russian critics in his dedication of 'The Haidamaks' to Hryhorovych. He wrote the dedication hastily, in one night, probably after reading the proofs of Belinsky's article. He introduced the rebuttal by illustrating the imagined response of the Russian critics to his new work:

> They will mock and sneer
> And throw it under the bench.
> 'Let it stay there,' they will say,
> 'Until our father will arise,
> And tell in our language
> About their hetmans.
> For now this is a fool

The Maturing Artist 1838–43

> Telling a tale in a dead language,
> Who shows off before us
> Some Yarema in bast shoes.
> He is a fool, indeed!
> They were beaten, yet they were not taught.
> Only the gravemounds have remained
> From Cossack and hetman times,
> Nothing more.
> And even these gravemounds
> Are ransacked.
> And yet he wants us
> To hear an old man sing!
> It is in vain! A waste of time,
> My friend! If you want to sing
> For money and for glory,
> Then you must sing about Matriosha
> And Parasha and subjects
> Like the sultans, parquet floors, spurs,
> That's where glory lies. But
> He sings – "The blue sea is playing ... "
> While he himself is crying. Behind
> Him stands a whole crowd,
> All in peasant coats.'[28]

Shevchenko's attack on the popular repertoire of themes and motifs in Russian literature, which brought money and glory to their authors, was a sharp satirical response directed particularly against Belinsky, who praised in his reviews such mediocre patriotic stuff as Polevoy's 'Parasha, the Siberian' and all sorts of military heroes. In opposition to these 'noble' and 'worthy' subjects, Shevchenko offered his peasant, Cossack muse in these defiant terms:

> Thanks for the advice!
> It is a warm coat, but, alas,
> Not made for me.
> And your wise words
> Are laced with lies.
> Sorry! You may rant and rave,
> But I will not listen![29]

28 'Haidamaky,' *Povne*, I, 72–3
29 Ibid, 73

Belinsky's charge that Ukrainian was an 'artificial,' 'dead' language hurt Shevchenko so much because he wrote in a language 'that his mother had sung to him when he was a baby,' in a language used by millions of his countrymen, the language of his poetic imagination. So he wrote with bitter irony, 'It will suffice, so long as I shall live, / [To write] in a dead language.' In Shevchenko's defence of the Ukrainian language, the main thrust of the argument rested not on his ironic and sarcastic sally against the Ukrainophobic critics but on a highly artistic presentation of his own creative process, the spontaneous creation of a genius enticed by his own imagination. How ridiculous the charges of these petty critics about *'muzhik* language' and *'muzhik* topics' must have seemed to Ukrainian readers when they learned how Shevchenko introduced them to the 'limitless steppes' of his fantasy.

> I alone
> In my little hut
> Will sing and cry
> Like a small child!
> I will sing – the sea will play
> The wind blow
> The steppe darken
> And the mound talk to the wind.
> As I sing – the high mound
> Has opened up
> And the Zaporozhians
> Have filled the steppes as far as the sea.
> Their *otamans* on raven black horses
> Prance before the horse-tailed banners
> And the [Dnieper] rapids
> Between the reedy banks
> Are groaning, they are angry
> And sing of dreadful deeds.
> I will listen and grieve
> And ask the old people:
> 'Why are you sad, fathers?'
> 'It is sad, my son!
> The Dnieper is angry with us,
> Ukraine is in tears ...'
> And so I cry, too.
> In the meantime,

The Maturing Artist 1838-43

> In glittering rows
> The *otamans* come forward,
> The captains and the hetmans
> All covered in gold,
> Come into my hut.
> They come and sit beside me
> And tell me about Ukraine,
> How they built the Sich,
> How the Cossacks in their boats
> Passed through the rapids,
> How they roamed the blue seas
> And warmed themselves in Skutari
> And how they smoked their pipes
> After the fires in Poland
> And came back to Ukraine.[30]

Even before the scene of the Homeric Cossack banquet, the poet confesses his inability to bury his poetic talent in the ground.

> I have children – where shall I put them?
> To hug them to myself – it is a sin, for their souls are alive!

This is followed once more by a graphic account of his creative experiences:

> And I look on
> While I cry,
> I look, I laugh, and wipe away my tears –
> I am not alone – I have company in this world!
> In my little hut the steppe is limitless,
> The Cossacks dance, the valley echoes,
> In my little hut the blue sea is playing,
> The gravemound is grieving,
> The poplar rustles,
> A girl sings a ballad quietly –
> I am not alone – I have company in this world!
> That is where my wealth, my money is,
> That is where my glory lies.[31]

30 Ibid, 73-4
31 Ibid, 76

It is uncertain when 'The Haidamaks' was sent to the censor, but a decision was long in coming, and Shevchenko had many problems with the publication. An epic poem about a peasant rebellion was something the censors were afraid to pass. Shevchenko wrote about it to Tarnovsky: 'I have had trouble with them; the censors passed it with difficulty. They said it was 'inciting to rebellion' and that is all. At last I managed to persuade them that I am no rebel. Now I have to send copies out quickly before they change their minds.'[32] The censors allowed publication of the poem on 29 November 1841. Shevchenko's worries were not over. He had published the poem at his own expense, but he wanted to recover some costs through subscription, and this proceeded very slowly. Shevchenko was unable to pay all the printing costs, and the book remained with the printers. In Kharkiv, the centre of Ukrainian literary life, the subscriptions were handled by Kvitka-Osnovianenko himself, but the response, as in the case of the *Swallow*, was very slow. Some people did not trust subscriptions and preferred to wait and buy the book in the bookstore. Kvitka wrote to Shevchenko about it. Not until March 1842 did Shevchenko succeed in getting the book released from the printers.

The latter part of 1841 was a productive period for Shevchenko. At the end of November he finished a new long poem, 'Mariana the Nun' ('Chernytsia Mariana'), to which he added an interesting introduction, directed to his former playmate, Oksana Kovalenko, who was his first true love. On 8 December, in one day, he composed the ballad 'The Drowned Woman' ('Utoplena') for the new Kharkiv almanac the *New Moon* (*Molodyk*), on which Kvitka had asked him to collaborate. During 1841, after finishing 'The Haidamaks,' he managed to write, in Russian, a tragedy, *Nikita Gaiday*, which he then reworked as a play, *The Young Bride* (*Nevesta*). In December he was working on another play, which he wanted to call *The Blind Beauty* (*Slepaia krasavitsa*). In 1841 a Ukrainian almanac, the *Sheaf* (*Snip*), appeared in Kharkiv under the editorship of Oleksander Korsun. In November of that year Korsun asked Shevchenko to contribute to a new issue of the *Sheaf* for 1842. Shevchenko sent him 'Mariana the Nun' but not the entire poem, since he had lost some of the drafts.

In the same year Shevchenko corresponded with Kvitka-Osnovianenko. The elderly writer showed great interest in the works of the young poet and greeted them with enthusiasm. Early in 1841 he received from Shevchenko part of 'The Haidamaks' in manuscript form. In March he wrote to the author that this was a 'wonderful piece' and that those Ukrainians to whom he had read it 'smacked their lips' in approval.

32 Ibid, VI, 17

He urged that the poem be printed immediately and told Shevchenko that another writer, Petro Hulak-Artemovsky, admired *Kobzar*. In November Kvitka expressed his satisfaction that Shevchenko had ignored the Russian critics' attacks and continued to write in Ukrainian. 'Thank you,' he wrote, 'for not looking into the eyes of the stupid Russians [katsapam],[33] who, ignorant of our language and not understanding anything about it, are screaming like Jews on the Sabbath: what is all this writing? – We do not understand anything. Thank God, you spit on it all and do not stop writing. Write, write, may God help you!'[34]

Shevchenko also sent Kvitka some of his drawings, illustrated Kvitka's works, and in December 1841 he drew Kvitka's *Captain's Daughter* (*Sotnykivna*), complaining in his letters that the winter daylight in St Petersburg was very short. He asked Kvitka to send him some women's national costumes and shared his future plans with him. Kvitka, for his part, read everything that was written about Shevchenko and reacted quickly to it. Shevchenko expressed his admiration and love for the author of 'Marusia': 'Do not hold back,' he wrote, 'love me the way I love you, although I have never seen you in my life. I have not seen you, but I see your soul and heart better than anyone in the world. Your 'Marusia' told me all about you.'[35] Shevchenko dreamt about visiting Kvitka in Kharkiv when, in two years, as he expected, he would be awarded a prize and would travel to Italy.

Shevchenko's studies at the academy and his painting continued normally. Early in 1841 he planned a painting 'depicting a black-browed girl praying before going to sleep,' but later he chose another topic: a gypsy fortune-teller, for which he received, for the third time, a silver medal.

The first three months of 1842 were taken up by his worry over the publication of 'The Haidamaks.' Not until April of that year did the book appear in the bookstores. The first reviews appeared in the summer. Belinsky picked up the gauntlet Shevchenko had thrown at him and other critics hostile to Ukrainian literature and attacked not only 'so-called Little Russian literature' but the author personally. Two years earlier he had castigated Ukrainian writers for writing for the peasants and not for the educated class. Now he maintained that the poems of 'mister *kobzars*' were unintelligible to the people even though they were full of vulgarisms. He advised Shevchenko to 'refuse any claims to the title of poet' and write in

33 *Katsap* (nanny-goat) is a Ukrainian pejorative appellation for the Russians. The Russian *khokhol* (tuft of hair) indicates the same Russian condescension towards Ukrainians.
34 *Lysty do T.H. Schevchenka*, 14
35 *Povne*, VI, 13

Ukrainian popular brochures for the people on social and family topics, in the style of Kvitka's 'Letters to My Dear Countrymen.' He called Shevchenko 'a privileged, perhaps, Little Russian poet,' hinting at his great popularity in Ukrainian circles, of which Belinsky was well aware. Specifically about 'The Haidamaks' Belinsky wrote as follows: 'There is everything here which can be found in every Ukrainian poem: the Poles, the Jews, the Cossacks; here they swear a lot, drink, fight, set things on fire, and butcher each other; in the intervals, of course, there is a *kobzar* (for which Ukrainian poem can be without one?) who sings his elevated songs without much sense, and a girl who weeps in a raging storm.' Further on, Belinsky discussed one scene, in which the Polish confederates beat up the Jews, only in order to ridicule Shevchenko's portrayal, and followed that with a completely false interpretation of the love scene between Yarema and Oksana, calling it pornographic. These were cheap efforts worthy of an enraged clown rather than a literary critic. Shevchenko's charge that Belinsky approved 'fashionable' subjects despite his lofty literary theories must have hurt the Russian critic very deeply. Now he was getting his own back. The universality of some of the finest passages in the poem was completely ignored by a man whose malice caused him to forget his aesthetics.

Belinsky's review appeared in the *Notes of the Fatherland*. Only two Slavophil journals, Burachek's *Beacon* and Pogodin's *Muscovite*, published favourable reviews, both by Ukrainian authors. The other periodicals were silent. The *Muscovite's* reviewer, Fedir Kytchenko, called 'The Haidamaks' a 'precious gift' and stressed that it was a 'national' work and therefore could only be written in Ukrainian. Mykola Tykhorsky was the reviewer for the *Beacon*. His long article (nineteen pages) was very uneven, since the author was wrapped up in mystical philosophy and idealist aesthetics, but it contained some real insights. He was the first critic to acknowledge Shevchenko's genius, though, out of sheer cautiousness, he did not actually use this word. He called Shevchenko an extraordinary talent, and identified the source of the poet's genius by pointing out that the 'The Haidamaks' 'was not a product of cool reflection but the deep, inner song of the heart, embodied in living sounds.' Tykhorsky underlined the national form of the poem, the close links to folk poetry, especially in its rhythm, and said that while reading it aloud, he could not help singing it. Commenting on the introduction to the poem, in which Shevchenko wrote ironically about his unwillingness to depict peasant topics, Tykhorsky assured the author that not everybody followed German or French literary models. He stressed that in the poem there were scenes of bloody revenge which the author depicted truthfully without either toning down or excusing them. To him the important element in the poem was its subjectivity and emotion. He thought that great possibilities were opening for Shevchenko and ended the article with a warning that the poet should not listen to Russian advice. He even hoped that 'some intelligent Russians may begin to study our language.'

Shevchenko read all this in the summer of 1842. A year before he had announced, with irony, that he was satisfied to write in a 'dead language.' While determined to continue writing in Ukrainian, he had also written several pieces in Russian. Why did he begin writing in Russian and with what purpose? He started to write in Russian after Belinsky's review of the *Swallow* which, as we know, had enraged him. Belinsky maintained that only a genius could write about Ukrainian life. Shevchenko's friends must have urged him to do this in Russian so that he could become even more famous. Lastly, Shevchenko himself must have had the feeling that his Russian was not very good. He expressed this in a later letter to H. Tarnovsky, promising to send him a poem, 'The Blind Woman' ('Slepaia'), 'written in Russian, so that the Russians cannot say that I do not know their language.' In pursuing this ambition to show that he could write in Russian, he might have tried to satisfy his friends' urging in order to gain a higher reputation both for himself and for Ukrainian literature. Perhaps his Russian friends, too, were trying to persuade him to stop writing in a language that they could not understand. In any case, Shevchenko's own explanation, that he wanted to show that he knew Russian, must be taken at face value. This did not mean that he intended to give up writing in Ukrainian or that he was trying to be a bilingual poet. However, after writing some poems in Russian, he wrote to Yakiv Kukharenko: 'Some devil must have met me, and for my sins I am confessing to the Russians [katsapam] in dry Russian [katsapskym] words.' Shevchenko always emphasized that his Russian works were written in a 'foreign' language. This was a clear rejection of the theory, popular at that time, of a 'common Russian' (*obshcherussky*) language, which held that Ukrainian literature was also part of a common Russian literature.

Both of his first attempts to write in Russian were in the field of drama. The first play, *Nikita Gaiday* (transformed into *The Bride*), was set in the era of Khmelnytsky. The drama contained fiery patriotic, revolutionary speeches:

> The Cossack is languishing in captivity,
> The glorious field of battle is overgrown
> With sparse grass.

> The sound and memory of the past is dying.
> No! We shall sing a song of glory
> On the lethal, scorched places.
> We will break the chains of slavery,
> Bringing fire and blood
> Into the enemy camp.
> Our howls and wails
> Will die along with their greedy rage.
> And our free laws
> Will quicken in the wide steppes.[36]

It is also possible that in his Russian works Shevchenko wanted to persuade the Russians of his deep patriotic feelings. The stage offered greater possibilities for this, and perhaps that was why he attempted to write plays. In contrast to the saccharine patriotism of the plays of Kukolnik, Polevoy, or Rosen, Shevchenko might have wanted to display in his dramas a spontaneous and sincere love of his country. The excerpt quoted above, printed in the *Beacon* in 1842, was excised by the censor, and this demonstrated to the poet that, under Nicholas I, the censors were not naïve enough not to understand that the captain's speech could refer to contemporary Russia.

The play *The Blind Beauty* Shevchenko reworked into a poem with a peasant subject. He did not expect it to be a success and was afraid that the Russian critics would view it as a *mauvais sujet*. Behind the scenes there lurked the figure of a landowner, perhaps one of those 'enlightened ones' who, according to Belinsky, became known in Ukraine only after the civilizing reign of Peter I. The two victims of this bestial landowner were the female serf whom he seduced and their daughter, also ravished by her degenerate father. Perhaps this deeply tragic story of Ukrainian peasant women was served up by Shevchenko to Belinsky and his ilk as an ironic present to those who were bored by Ukrainian *paysan* subjects. In spite of its sentimentality, stylistic faults, and metrical mistakes in Russian, the poem contained strong passages and was liked by those who read the manuscript, who urged Shevchenko to publish it. At the end of September someone bought it from Shevchenko, but it did not appear in print until 1886.

Meanwhile, Shevchenko's fame as a Ukrainian poet grew steadily. Tykhorsky in his review of 'The Haidamaks' wrote about the enthusiasm with which Shevchenko's works were greeted, and Kvitka gave high praise to his most recently published poem. 'You have pleased us

---

36 'Nikita Gaiday,' ibid, III, 57–8

enormously with your "Haidamaks," he wrote. 'Readers smack their lips ... Mr [Hulak] Artemovsky jumps for joy and is full of praise ... Write my boy, as much as possible. Write something for us and let us have a respite from Muscovite lies.'[37]

The experience that Shevchenko had gained from writing in Russian taught him that this was not where his creative genius lay. He could not master the 'dry' foreign language. It took him almost a year to write and rewrite 'The Blind Woman,' while he composed Ukrainian works spontaneously and quickly. Several months after finishing 'The Blind Woman,' he wrote to Tarnovsky, recalling how the Russians had ridiculed 'The Haidamaks': 'They call me an enthusiast, almost a fool. May God forgive them. Let me be a peasant poet, but still a poet. I ask for nothing more. Let the dogs bark; the wind will scatter the noise.'[38]

While he was finishing 'The Blind Woman' and reacting to the various responses to 'The Haidamaks,' during the summer holidays of 1842, Shevchenko found great pleasure in the company of some new friends. Two of them were striking personalities – the singer Semen Hulak-Artemovsky and Yakiv Kukharenko, a writer from the Black Sea Cossack area. At that time Shevchenko was sharing his rooms with two other students of the academy, Khtodot Tkachenko and Kindrat Yezhov, both Ukrainians. Shevchenko had met Semen Hulak-Artemovsky for the first time in 1839, when the composer Glinka brought him from Ukraine along with an entire group of singers chosen for the tsar's choral ensemble. Soon afterwards Hulak-Artemovsky left for Italy to study singing, but three years later, after a successful début at the Milan Opera, he had returned to St Petersburg to become a soloist in the imperial opera house. He was a genial and lively man, a great raconteur, a gifted actor in both comedy and tragedy, and a bass baritone with a phenomenal range and great beauty of tone. He was a Ukrainian patriot and immediately struck up a friendship with Shevchenko, who was not only gifted as a painter but had an excellent musical ear and a beautiful, though small, voice that was especially expressive in the interpretation of Ukrainian folksongs. The district *otaman* (though the tsar had abolished that office) Yakiv Kukharenko was a connoisseur of the life-style of the Black Sea Zaporozhian Cossacks, and a Ukrainian writer. He was a high-minded, good, and simple man. This relic of the Zaporozhian tradition became the object of adulation of Shevchenko and his Ukrainian friends, and he himself liked the poet so much that, as he wrote to him later, he was ready 'to send him his soul.'

37 *Lysty do T.H. Shevchenka*, 16
38 *Povne*, VI, 23

The student apartment on Vasilievsky Island was soon turned into a self-styled literary 'outpost' of true Sich eccentricity and Zaporozhian fashion. The *otaman* was raised to the rank of Sich leader (*batko koshovy*). The 'comrades-in-arms' prepared national dishes and were overjoyed when Hulak-Artemovsky one day brought a roasted pig with dumplings in a basket. The small, inadequately furnished apartment did not hinder this group of romantic and patriotic students from merry-making, singing, dancing, and story-telling or from more serious discussions about Ukrainian literature and theatre and what was required of them. Like Hulak-Artemovsky and Shevchenko, Kukharenko knew dozens of Ukrainian songs. He brought with him his play *Life in the Land of the Black Sea* (*Chornomorsky pobyt*), which contained many songs from that region. For all these romantics the folksong was the most effective sign of the right of a people to cultural self-determination. The group was joined from time to time by the critic of 'The Haidamaks,' Tykhorsky, the publisher Semenenko-Kramarevsky, a relative of Hulak-Artemovsky who was a violinist and a writer, and by the polyglot Elkan. When Kukharenko left St Petersburg, around 20 September, all the members of this inspired circle were sorry to see him go. Kindrat Yezhov, anticipating Kukharenko's return, told Shevchenko that this would be the time 'not to leave the house, to talk, to cook all kinds of dishes, and to sing and dance.' Everybody, and above all Shevchenko, was swept up with enthusiasm and high spirits. Recalling this episode of his youth, Shevchenko wrote to Hulak-Artemovsky many years later that he could see the entire company vividly, and called it a 'happy time.' In a letter to Kukharenko on 22 April 1857 he recalled his own 'faith and hope,' which were then as pure and immaculate 'as a baby fresh from the bath, shining and strong as a cut jewel.' Then, nothing seemed to shake Shevchenko's hope in Ukraine's bright future. That is why he was known to everyone as 'the enthusiast.'

One of the results of the discussions in Shevchenko's circle during Kukharenko's visit was the writing of a play in three acts, *Danylo Reva*. This, we can surmise, was the first version of what later became *Nazar Stodolia*. Shevchenko wrote it in a few days, and on 30 September he mentioned in a letter to Kukharenko that he had finished it. During the same period he transcribed and reworked the poem 'The Blind Woman,' which he read to Kukharenko; he interceded with the censor, Korsakov, on behalf of Kukharenko's play, said goodbye to Khtodot Tkachenko, who was leaving St Petersburg, and last, though not least, attended his classes at the academy.

The Ukrainian theatrical repertoire in those days was very limited. There were very few plays, and these were mostly vaudevilles, if one ignores the unsuccessful tragedy by Kostomarov, *The Night of Pereiaslav* (*Pereiaslavska nich*). Kukharenko's play inspired Shevchenko to create a drama set in Cossack times. He realized that his *Nikita Gaiday* (or *The Bride*) was a literary work unsuited to the stage. The future *Nazar Stodolia* was his first attempt to write a successful Ukrainian play. It required genius to compose such a work, full of historical and ethnographic detail, in only a few days. In the play Shevchenko did not forget to respond to Belinsky's claim that there was no educated class in Ukraine before Peter I. He twice put into the mouth of his character Hnat Kary a description of the Kiev brotherhood school, the Mohyla Academy.

All this merry camaraderie took up a lot of Shevchenko's time. Yet that summer was also very productive for him. He painted two oils, *Catherine* and *Family beside the House*, and in order to earn some money he illustrated *The History of Suvorov* for the publisher Isakov. Soon after Kukharenko left, he was penniless once more.

When Kukharenko was in St Petersburg he heard Shevchenko talking of visiting foreign countries 'across the sea.' Sometime late in October or in early November 1842 Shevchenko went on a trip to Sweden and Denmark. The voyage made a vivid impression on him and stirred his creative energy. Up to that point he had only visited the dreamy waters of the Bay of Finland in St Petersburg, and Kronstadt. Now, under circumstances we know very little about, he undertook the long sea voyage to Copenhagen and Stockholm. It is not known whether he had some definite plans or if he was merely satisfying a desire to see foreign lands. Perhaps an opportunity had arisen that he could not decline. He travelled with his friend from the academy, Boryshpolets. The voyage ended badly because Shevchenko fell ill, but it inspired the poet to write one of his masterpieces, 'Hamaliia,' a dynamic poem that brought a brilliant end to this period of Shevchenko's creative life. On his return to St Petersburg the poet wrote on November 18 to his friend Korolev:

The cursed boat carried me to Sweden and Denmark. On the way to Stockholm I composed 'Hamaliia,' a small poem, and then fell ill, and it was only with difficulty that I was brought to Revel, where I recovered a little. Now I am back in this cursed swamp and do not know when I'll recover fully. The doctor says it is 'nothing,' but he shakes his head so much it makes me sad. Today I feel a little better – I can hold a pen in my hand. Oh, my dear, how reluctant one is to leave this earth, although it is so bad! And yet leave we must – but it is still early. I pray to almighty God to help me to wait for spring so that I can die in Ukraine.[39]

39 Ibid, 21

Shevchenko never suffered from seasickness and did not complain of it later during his long voyage on the stormy Aral Sea. The start of this serious illness was a severe cold. Eager for new impressions, he wanted to observe the sea, and stayed on deck too long. He remembered the sea voyages of the Cossacks and relived the feelings of courage and bravery they must have felt during their crossings of the Black Sea in small boats to Turkey, where, on landing, they fought pitched battles with the well-armed Turks. It was the furious sea, with its stormy waves, that dictated 'Hamaliia' to him, that hymn to the human will and courage. The symphonic poem blends elemental energy with multi-dimensional sounds and colours into one monumental whole.

At the end of January 1843 Shevchenko wrote to Tarnovsky that he would like to visit Ukraine early in the spring. 'If I could arrive,' he wrote, 'at the time of the nightingales, it would be such a joy.' But he doubted whether this would be possible: 'The cursed Russians have so beset me that I don't know how to get away. But I will get away somehow, even if it is after Easter, and I will go straight to your place and then travel farther.'[40] We do not know precisely what difficulties he was encountering with the 'cursed Russians,' but he might have been referring to the negotiations over the sale of the rights to his publications. In the letter to Korolev, Shevchenko complained that 'hard times' had forced him to sell all his work, both printed and in manuscript, and that, beginning in December, the buyer would print them. Whether this was a written or a verbal agreement with a publisher is unknown, but the hard times were real enough to Shevchenko because he sold all the works he had written, even the unprinted 'Mariana the Nun' and 'The Blind Woman.' We know that he did succeed in getting out of this agreement in the end, because on 8 February 1843 he signed an agreement with the publisher Lisenkov, selling him only the eight poems printed in *Kobzar* and 'The Haidamaks.' The other works, those printed in the *New Moon*, the *Swallow*, and 'Hamaliia' and other pieces, remained his property, and he had the right to publish the second edition of *Kobzar* or to sell these works to someone else. Lisenkov paid him a very small sum of money. Later, Shevchenko complained that no one had paid him a cent for his works and warned Marko Vovchok in a letter not to trust publishers who 'can smell our hard times.' To say that he did not receive 'a cent' was hyperbole, but it proves that the honorarium he received was a mere pittance. It could not have been large, because eight hundred copies of 'The Haidamaks' were waiting at the printer's, and Lisenkov, exploiting this fact, offered the author only a very low price. Shevchenko's *Kobzar* sold fairly well in the

---

40 Ibid, 22–3

second edition. Lisenkov, a sly countryman of the poet, realized and exploited Shevchenko's lack of practical sense and his desire to see his works on sale.

The small sum received from Lisenkov was supplemented by Shevchenko with money he earned or hoped to earn through painting. In February he wrote to Kukharenko that in March he was planning to go abroad. An incorrigible optimist and enthusiast, he tended to exaggerate future possibilities. We do not know what exactly inspired this hope of travel abroad, except that as early as 1838–39 he had 'dreamt about that marvellous land, about the capital of the world, crowned with Buonarotti's dome' – Italy and Rome, with their 'immortal miracles.' It was the cradle of world art, a place where his great teacher had completed his masterpiece, where his friend Willie Schternberg lived and worked, to which another of his friends, Apollon Mokrytsky, was going to travel, and from which Shevchenko received enthusiastic letters from his older friends.

Yet this dream was not to be fulfilled. Instead Shevchenko travelled to Ukraine, even though, writing to Kukharenko about his proposed trip abroad, he declared, 'I will not go to Little Russia, the devil take it, since there I'll hear nothing but crying.' In Ukraine, he continued, 'there are no people, only cursed Germans.'[41] Both sentences were underlined. Either the projected trip to Italy was unrealistic, or Shevchenko's hopes were dashed through his own or someone else's action. Perhaps a clue is contained in a letter that may refer to the events of the spring of 1843, in which he wrote that as soon as he passed his exams, he had done something that he was ashamed to remember. As a result of this (whatever it was) he was once more in debt, an obligation that he was able to pay off only because he received an advance from the writer Polevoy, who commissioned twelve portraits of Russian military leaders to accompany their biographies.

And so Shevchenko had no choice but to visit the 'cursed Germans' and the Russified Ukrainian landowners who served the tsar as faithfully as his Prussian generals and bureaucrats. He went to the land where he would hear 'nothing but weeping' but where, apart from those Little Russians who had sold themselves to Moscow, he would find some 'living souls' and 'the Dnieper with its sacred hills,' golden-domed Kiev, the 'limitless steppe,' and, above all, plenty of sunshine. There was also the definite possibility of earning some money by painting portraits in the homes of the gentry.

41 Ibid, 25. By Germans, Shevchenko meant Russian bureaucrats, who were often of German stock.

PART THREE

The Ukrainian Journeys

1843-47

IV

It is not known exactly when Shevchenko left St Petersburg, probably not earlier than May 1843. He went straight to the Chernihiv region to visit Tarnovsky on his estate in Kachanivka. In advance he sent him the oil painting *Catherine* and some unprinted poems. In the luxurious park surrounding the palace he could certainly hear the nightingales he dreamt of. Yet the poet disliked the atmosphere of Kachanivka. The lord of the manor was not only tight-fisted but pretentious and pompous, his wealth in stark contrast to the surrounding lawlessness and poverty. Although in St Petersburg Shevchenko had planned to make Kachanivka his Ukrainian headquarters, he now decided to leave soon after his arrival. He met many Ukrainian landowners there and a man for whom he felt some liking, Viktor Zabila, a minor Ukrainian poet who had been discharged from the army in connection with the Decembrist conspiracy. This elderly gentleman lived on his *khutir*, Kukurivshchyna, near Borzna, and treated his few serfs well. He wore national costume and lived simply and modestly. He sang well to the accompaniment of the *bandura* and was a famous story-teller. His simple lyrical poems, often imitations of folksongs and set to music by Glinka, could not but appeal to Shevchenko, who visited him. They became very friendly. Zabila was no great intellectual, but Shevchenko liked honest, unpretentious people who were of strong moral character. Zabila was also very hospitable.

From Kukurivshchyna, Shevchenko went to Kiev. From Hrebinka, Tarnovsky, or Zabila he could have obtained the address of Panteleimon Kulish, who was a teacher there. Kulish was born of Cossack stock in Voronizh, Chernihiv region, and was an ambitious young man, very hard-working and dedicated to scholarly pursuits. Shevchenko knew his published works, and he had also heard that Kulish was an enthusiastic Ukrainian, with an encyclopaedic knowledge of the country's history and culture. Their meeting was quite unusual, and was described in Kulish's short autobiography, written in the third person:

Someone came up to Kulish, wearing a canvas coat.
'Greetings,' [he said], 'and guess who this is?'
'None other than Shevchenko' (I had not seen a picture of him). 'Yes, it's him! Don't you have a glass of *horilka*? ... After that, truly Sich-like desultory talk followed, and soon they started singing. Later they began to take trips around Kiev, sketching and catching fish on the other side of the Dnieper.[1]

This must all have happened no later than the first half of June. Both writers went together to visit the burnt-out eighteenth-century ruins of the Zaporozhian monastery, Mezhyhirsky Spas. This romantic visit to 'the poor ruins' left an indelible mark on Shevchenko's memory, and echoes of it reappeared in a later poem, 'The Monk' ('Chernets'), dedicated to Kulish, as well as in 'The Great Vault' ('Velyky liokh'), full of hatred for the Russians.

In Kulish Shevchenko met for the first time a modern Ukrainian, the kind of man he had dreamt about and searched for, a true patriot, and an intellectual who always kept in his mind's eye a clear vision of the development of Ukrainian culture and of the national consciousness. At that time Kulish was, ideologically, a kindred soul to Shevchenko. Kulish then still idealized the Cossack past, which was for him, as it was for Shevchenko, a source of political concepts for the future and an arsenal of national and educational ideas. Their trips together must have been most stimulating to each of them. Shevchenko surpassed Kulish in his imagination and in the vividness of the impressions which always coloured his thoughts. Kulish surpassed Shevchenko in his forceful, critical argument, since, as a man with a more rounded education, he was more knowledgeable and confident. The pattern of their relationship was already set then: there was some protectiveness and encouragement from the self-confident Kulish, who both privately and publicly had a high opinion of Shevchenko's talent, and on the part of the latter there was an open admission of Kulish's intelligence and judiciousness. Yet Shevchenko still remained critical of Kulish's great ambition and conceit; he could always set limits to Kulish's role as mentor and to his overbearing manner. 'The truly Sich-like gossip' did not lead to a true Sich comradeship between them. The differing psychological make-up of these two giants of the Ukrainian revival formed a wall between them, through which they reached to each other whenever it was necessary. Shevchenko always did so openly, Kulish sometimes deviously. At their first meeting Shevchenko

1 'Zhyzn Kulisha,' *Pravda* (Lviv 1868), 285

admired Kulish's intellectual power and his scholarly plans. Kulish was about to set out on a prolonged study-tour of Right Bank Ukraine on behalf of the Kiev Archeographic Commission. It was most likely at that time that Shevchenko painted an unfinished portrait in oil of Kulish's head, strongly emphasizing the romantic dreaminess of his new friend, captivated by the music of the Ukrainian past and future. Shevchenko also met at Kiev at that time Mykhailo Maksymovych, the well-known scholar of Ukrainian ethnography and antiquity with whose publications of Ukrainian folksongs[2] he was also familiar.

From Kiev Shevchenko went straight to the Poltava region. First of all he wanted to visit his old friend and benefactor Hrebinka on his secluded *khutir* 'Ubezhishche' near Pyriatyn, where, sitting under his plum and pear trees, Hrebinka rested after his government, pedagogical, and literary labours in St Petersburg. Together they visited Hrebinka's neighbours, and on 29 June, the feast of St Peter and St Paul, they drove in a modest carriage to the 'Ukrainian Versailles' – the estate of Moisivka, belonging to Mrs Tetiana Vilkhivska. This splendid empire-style palace was the gathering place for hundreds of the nobility descended from the Cossacks; they came there to attend the extravagantly lavish balls given by the old widow, who was very fond of playing cards and acting as hostess at receptions, on which all her fortune was spent. Especially on her birthday (12 January) and the birthday of her late husband, the general (29 June), the balls were indeed memorable occasions.

Shevchenko and Hrebinka were met on the veranda by the poet Afanasiev-Chuzhbynsky, who had recently praised Shevchenko and had dedicated some poems to him. Both visitors were covered with dust after travelling in an open carriage and went to freshen up. In the meantime the news that Shevchenko had arrived spread like lightning. When, accompanied by Hrebinka and Chuzhbynsky, he entered the ballroom, 'all the guests crowded together at the entrance, and even well-dressed ladies who only spoke in French eagerly awaited Shevchenko's appearance.' Shevchenko was overwhelmed by the reception, was introduced to his hostess, and took his place beside a young writer, the debutante Sophia Zakrevska. 'Throughout the day he was the object of undivided attention,'[3] and he soon overcame his emotion and felt at home. Many pretty ladies read some of his poems to him, and he praised their pure Poltavan intonation. Shevchenko was delighted by it all and spoke only in

2 See part two, n 7.
3 A.S. Afanasev-Chuzhbynsky, 'Vospominanie o T.G. Shevchenko,' *Vospominaniia*, 76–7

Ukrainian. After dinner, finding himself in jovial male company, Shevchenko told Chuzhbynsky that he had not expected to be so well received by the landowners and that he liked some of the young ladies.

The group that gathered round Shevchenko and applauded him so enthusiastically was in fact a 'tight circle of wise and benevolent men' who, because they could not find an appropriate channel for their energies, or because they still wanted to live as they had in their youth, found an escape in an old Latin adage, *in vino veritas*. The circle was known as 'the society of wet mugs' (*mochemordy*) and was a kind of order that resembled the Polish *balaguly* societies in Right Bank Ukraine. The 'wet mugs' had a set of statutes and held various titles. The leader of this group, which included some interesting people, was the 'Grand Magister,' Viktor Zakrevsky, whose supreme title was 'the Tipsiest.' He was a former Hussar officer. He was clever, witty, and very good at telling drinking stories. He treated his serfs extremely well, always joking with them. After spending the entire night with this company, Shevchenko struck up some new friendships. The most fascinating figure among them was Count Yakiv de Balmen, the scion of an old Scottish family and the owner of a splendid palace at Lynovtsi. He was an accomplished draughtsman, specializing in illustrations of contemporary Ukrainian life. As one who followed the true cult of the Cossacks, he was a great admirer of Shevchenko's *Kobzar*. After five years of Bohemian St Petersburg, the energetic and temperamental Shevchenko, in moments when it was possible to forget the torments of his soul, enjoyed a circle in which witty anecdotes were told, where discussions of liberal thought and even political satire thrived, and where there was no room for what he most disliked – 'the lackeys of His Majesty.' There was also another factor in the enjoyment of this milieu – the friendly company of the women relatives and wives of these men. Viktor Zakrevsky had two sisters, Maria, an excellent pianist, and Sophia, a great raconteuse and talented writer. The wife of Viktor's brother Platon, Hanna, was a woman of exceptional beauty. This charming young woman, a daughter of the *otaman* from Lebedyn, cast her spell on the poet.[4]

After two days in Moisivka, Shevchenko visited the de Balmens and the Zakrevskys and late in July went to Kovalivka to visit Count Oleksa

---

4 There is good reason to believe that the relationship between Shevchenko and Hanna Zakrevska during this encounter and in subsequent visits to her home was a short but full-blown love affair; see Marietta Shaginian, *Taras Shevchenko* (Moscow 1946), 171–83. Later, in exile, Shevchenko testified in several of his poems to the profound affection he felt for Hanna.

Kapnist, son of the writer Vasyl Kapnist, the author of 'Ode to Serfdom' ('Oda na rabstvo'). One of the Kapnists at one time had visited King Frederick of Prussia to plead Ukraine's case against Russia.[5] Oleksa Kapnist was a former Decembrist and a freemason. He was a typical representative of those Ukrainian patriots who fostered national, masonic, and libertarian ideas in Ukraine in the first quarter of the nineteenth century, ideas that connected with the new Ukrainian political plans. Echoes of the Decembrist rebellion and of the Ukrainian political societies during the reign of Alexander I, such as the United Slavs, the Little Russian Society of V. Lukashevych in the Poltava region, and the circle of A. Oleksiev in the Katerynoslav area, were still audible in Ukraine. There were those still living who remembered how the country had borne those times of unrest and who had hoped for changes during Napoleon's invasion. Oleksa Kapnist had at one time been a member of the masonic lodge in Poltava, where, according to one ritual, the question 'where does the sun rise?' required the answer 'In Chyhyryn.'[6]

Shevchenko accompanied Kapnist twice on a visit to the palace of Prince Nikolay Repnin-Volkonsky in Yahotyn. On the first occasion, in July, he went to survey the prince's art collection; the second visit, soon after, was to see the prince's portrait by the Swiss artist Hornung. Tarnovsky and Kapnist commissioned Shevchenko to copy this portrait.

Knowledge of Shevchenko's whereabouts during August is scanty, but at the end of the month he visited the Ukrainian ethnographer Platon Lukashevych on his estate of Berezan in the Pereiaslav district, not far from Kovalivka, Yahotyn, and the Zakrevskys' Berezova Rudka. He attempted to see as many Ukrainian writers and scholars as possible. He had already met Zabila and Kulish, who had published some works in the *Swallow*, and he also made the acquaintance of Maksymovych and Afanasiev-Chuzhbynsky. He anticipated a great deal from his meeting with Lukashevych, who was not only the collector and publisher of Ukrainian songs but one of the few scholars, apart from Sreznevsky and Bodiansky, to have visited Galicia, where he made friends among the young activists in the Ukrainian revival there. He had added to his collection of Ukrainian songs the entire collection of Galician songs

---

5 See Georg Sacke, 'V.V. Kapnist und seine Ode "Na rabstvo,"' *Zeitschrift für slavische Philologie* 17 (1941), 300. For a different interpretation see W.B. Edgerton, 'Laying a Legend to Rest: The Poet Kapnist and Ukraino-German Intrigue,' *Slavic Review* 30, no 3 (1971). See also the reply by O. Ohloblyn, 'Berlinska misiia Kapnista 1791 roku,' *Ukrainsky istoryk* 11, no 1–3 (1974).

6 Chyhyryn was the capital of the hetman state.

published by Wacław Zaleski. In his library he had a rare edition of Shashkevych's *The Maid of Dniester* (*Rusalka Dnistrovaia*).[7] During his stay with Lukashevych Shevchenko read the *Rusalka*, containing Vahylevych's poem 'Madey,' one of the finest Galician works. About this time a letter from Vahylevych arrived, and Lukashevych, in his reply, mentioned Shevchenko's visit. He also told Vahylevych that he had asked Shevchenko to use some of Vahylevych's Galician vocabulary and that the poet had agreed. One can imagine the lively conversations in Berezan between Lukashevych and Shevchenko, who was eager to learn about events in Galicia. His decision to use Western Ukrainian words was a sign of his feeling for a united Ukrainian literary language. This is the more understandable because, ever since he had started to write, Shevchenko had avoided over-use of his own local dialect, learning other Ukrainian dialects from his compatriots in St Petersburg and thus creating a literary language that was understandable throughout the country.

In August or early September Shevchenko left Berezan in order to visit his native village, Kerelivka. He also went to Chyhyryn and to the Dnieper island of Khortytsia, the site of the former Sich. On 18 September he was in Kerelivka, but by the end of the month he was back in Kachanivka. It must, then, be concluded that the trip to the Sich, along the Dnieper, was undertaken in the first half of September. It is possible, however, that he made the trip as early as August and travelled later to the Poltavan region and to his native village. It is not certain when he was in the Chyhyryn district, on his return from the Sich or on his way there.

The visit home, after a fourteen-year absence, and the trips to Chyhyryn and to the Sich were great experiences in Shevchenko's life and in his creative process. They left deep wounds in his heart, and his pen has left a vivid record of them. He had visited Chyhyryn for the first time as a small boy, when he went on a pilgrimage. In his poem 'The Haidamaks' he recalled the ruins of the hetman state and wrote:

> Hetmans, oh hetmans, if only you were to rise,
> Rise and see the Chyhyryn
> Which you had built, and where you reigned!
> You would cry bitterly, for you would not recognize
> The Cossack glory in these derelict ruins.[8]

Now, drawing in his sketchbook the Chyhyryn hills, formerly the site of

---

7 This work, published in 1837 in Budapest, is usually regarded as the beginning of the Galician revival.
8 'Haidamaky,' *Povne*, I, 93

the mighty Cossack fortress, the inaccessible domain of the hetmans Khmelnytsky and Doroshenko, he experienced deep emotions as he recalled the ancient glory. He heard the bitter accusations hurled by the ancestors to their worthless grandsons:

> Great days and great nights,
> Great men rise from the ruins
> And declare to the world
> With terrible words ... The hills are weeping
> And so is the heart.[9]

In Subotiv, the former residence of Khmelnytsky, Shevchenko sketched Cossack crosses in the fields, the church that the Hetman built, and the foundations, ravaged by the Russians, of the palace of the hetmans. Amid the ruins of Subotiv and Chyhyryn he felt poignantly the eclipse of that ancient glory and the existence of a shameful national servitude, the consequence of betrayal by whole generations of Ukrainians:

> Ukraine fell asleep,
> It is covered with weeds,
> Blossoming with mould.
> Its heart is sunk in a mire,
> And the hollow of a rotten tree
> Is full of cold snakes.[10]

He felt bitterly lonely, knowing that no one cared about the future of the nation:

> Only I, accursed,
> Cry day and night
> At the crowded crossroads.
> And no one sees,
> Neither sees nor knows,
> They are deaf, they do not hear.[11]

In such a solitude without hope all faith may be lost, leaving madness as the only way out:

9 This passage is from an early version of the poem 'The Princess' (Kniazhna), written in 1847 (ibid, II, 462).
10 'Chyhyryne, Chyhyryne,' ibid, I, 223–4
11 'I mertvym i zhyvym,' ibid, 329

> And I, God's fool,
> Shed my tears in vain
> On your ruins.[12]

But the poet's soul was not only 'weeping' – it cried out 'for sacred truth upon this earth' and was ready to fight. It can be said with certainty that it was at the ruins of Subotiv and Chyhyryn that Shevchenko decided to sound the alarm, to waken his 'countrymen, both living and dead,' to call out punishment upon them, implore and curse them. Here, Shevchenko the prophet was born. His finest poems, 'The Ransacked Grave' ('Rozryta mohyla') and 'The Great Vault' ('Velyky liokh'), had their origin here. Possibly some passages from these poems were first composed here, on the ruins of a desecrated glory.

The poet's explicitly anti-Russian political stance was also formed here. Thinking of Ukraine, 'plundered' and 'besmirched' by Russians, gazing at Bohdan Khmelnytsky's church, that symbol of national ruin, he cursed the great Bohdan's decision to form a union with Moscow. His recent experiences, pain, and suffering engendered the belief he was to proclaim in his poems, a belief that from this awareness of past injustice and from the betrayal of the national interest by the nation's élite

> There will spring and grow
> Sharp swords
> Which will cut to pieces
> The bad and rotten heart,
> Will remove the canker,
> Replenishing it
> With Cossack blood,
> Pure and sacred.[13]

In a moment of exaltation he prophesied the resurrection of his country:

> Ukraine will rise,
> Dispel the dark servitude,
> A light of truth will shine,
> And slave children
> Will pray in freedom.[14]

As for the visit to the Sich, Shevchenko himself commented a year later

12 'Chyhyryne, Chyhyryne,' ibid, 223
13 Ibid, 224–5
14 'Stoit v seli Subotovi,' ibid, 307

in a letter to Kukharenko: 'Last year I was in Ukraine, visiting the Mezhyhirsky Spas and Khortytsia. I went everywhere and I cried all the time: our Ukraine has been plundered by the goddam Germans and Russians, confound them.'[15] Seeing the German colonies in Khortytsia, he remarked that 'on the Sich the clever Germans plant potatoes.' The Zaporozhian steppes were 'sold to the Jews and Germans' – a reference to the German colonies and the large estates of the Jewish magnate Count Stieglitz, spreading out over the ancient Cossack lands. He upbraided those of his countrymen who were able to reconcile Russian patriotism with pictures of Cossack romanticism. He asked them:

> Whose blood
> Soaks the land
> Which bears the potatoes?[16]

The trip to Kerelivka also evoked in Shevchenko a whole gamut of painful emotions. In distant St Petersburg he had longed for his native land. Only a few years earlier he had written to his brother Mykyta, 'Every night I see in my dreams you, Kerelivka, and my family, and the weeds (in which I hid when playing hookey), I rejoice, then awake and start crying.' Now he stood, at last, before the poor cottage of his birth. It was exactly the same as when he left it, like the village, where 'nothing new / Grew or rotted.' Yet now the 'once-bright village' seemed to him 'dark and deaf.' Now, free, educated and nationally conscious, he had come face to face with the bleak existence of the serfs, so near and dear to him. Yet he was utterly helpless.

Shevchenko's heart was heavy with sorrow, and he was stricken by yet another piece of news, which came while he was visiting the graves of his parents, with 'their bent oak crosses, and words worn away by the rain.' His brother told him then that Taras's childhood sweetheart, Oksana Kovalenko, had been seduced by a Russian soldier, had borne him a child, and, abandoned, had become insane. This tragedy overwhelmed Shevchenko. Only three years earlier, writing in 'The Haidamaks' about the union of two pure hearts – Oksana and Yarema – he had remembered his own first love for Oksana Kovalenko. He confirmed the memory by identifying himself with the happy Yarema. Two years earlier he had written 'Mariana the Nun,' in which his love for Oksana had served as a model for the love story in the poem. In his dedication to the poem he

---

15 Ibid, VI, 34
16 'I mertvym i zhyvym,' ibid, I, 333

proclaimed that 'While I weep over my Mariana / I look at you and pray for you.'

While he had not cherished any hope that Oksana would remain free and unmarried so that one day they might reunite, all the same Shevchenko carried with him the memory of his first love as something sacred. He even wrote that it all 'has passed ... without a trace,' yet the trace remained, and it was very deep. The girl who had 'taught him the language of the heart' had suddenly become a tragic figure in a horrible tale:

> Oksana wandered off
> After the departing *moskals*
> And vanished.
> True, after a year
> She returned with a bastard.
> Her hair was cropped.
> At night she would sit
> Under the fence, like a cuckoo,
> And call and shriek,
> Or sing quietly,
> Trying to unplait her [vanished] braids.
> Then she would go somewhere,
> No one knows where she is.
> She has wasted and gone mad.[17]

The tenderest flower in the poet's heart had been brutally trampled and sullied. He could not understand why this should have happened to his Oksana. The terrible image of the seduced woman depicted in 'Catherine' was to haunt him from that moment on, to be endlessly repeated, in, for example, the portrayal of the insane Oksana in 'The Blind Woman.'

It is not known how long Shevchenko remained in Kerelivka where, on 18 September, he was a guest at the christening of his brother Yosyp's child. In September he returned to Kachanivka and on 9 October revisited Platon Lukashevych in Berezan and wrote his poem 'The Ransacked Grave' ('Rozryta mohyla'). Sometime in the middle of October he left for Yahotyn to carry out a commission to copy the portrait of Prince Repnin. The prince and princess had a married son, Vasiliy, and an unmarried daughter, Varvara, who was then thirty-five. Princess Varvara had heard a great deal about Shevchenko, his unusual early history, and the view that

---

17 'My vkupochtsi kolys rosly,' ibid, II, 230

'he was more a poet than a painter.' When her brother introduced Shevchenko to her, the poet appeared to her to be 'simple and unpretentious' and at once became a welcome guest in their house, 'one of those who are so congenial in the country, who is well received in a salon, and whom one can leave alone without any fear that some trifle will offend him.'[18]

In Yahotyn Shevchenko made a very good impression. He was appreciated for his 'tact, his goodness and his respect for all sacred things. He was polite to everyone, respectful to the old, and loved by all.' He wore a stylish, long grey fitted coat with a velvet collar, and a fashionable cravat, tied high under his chin. He paid no special attention to his hair. He had shaved his moustache, but left slight side-whiskers. He was of medium height, but well proportioned and strong. His broad shoulders, hips, and general bearing gave his figure a distinctive character, which the Russians call 'angularity' (*uglovatost*) and the French *raideur des manières* or *absence de grâce*. His movements were neither elegant nor graceful. His hair was a reddish colour. At first sight his face seemed ordinary enough, but anyone inspecting it carefully was struck by his small, prominent eyes, which shone with intelligence and kindness. It was his eyes which appealed to so many people. 'He was relaxed and tactful in society and never used clichés.'

This is how he appeared to the Repnins and their guests at Yahotyn, where everyone knew about the poet's childhood and youth. Princess Varvara wrote to Einar that Shevchenko, 'has suffered a great deal and these terrible experiences have bought him the right to castigate the powerful.' However, she added that the poet did not like to discuss it. Everyone liked him and wished him luck and success. The princess saw him as the poet of Ukrainian independence, and she was convinced that he was born in Chyhyryn.

The elder Princess Repnina's eyesight was failing. The proud granddaughter of Hetman Rozumovsky was kind to her guests but preferred to remain secluded in her own part of the palace. The old prince spent most of his time in his study, reading books. He was very well educated, a wise and hospitable man. Varvara was the soul of this ancient home. She was thin, with large, expressive eyes, and possessed a great deal of

---

18 Princess Repnina left many accounts of Shevchenko, primarily in her letters to her former Swiss teacher, Charles Einar. These documents were collected and published by M. Gershenzon in *Russkie propilei*, vol. II (Moscow 1916). Most of the quotations are from that book. A separate study of the relationship between the Princess and Shevchenko was published by M. Vozniak, *Shevchenko i kniazhna Repnina* (Lviv 1925).

energy, even enthusiasm. 'She was witty, kind, and good to people, cared for the poor and the unfortunate, gave her possessions away, and helped all those who needed her advice.' She despised the institution of serfdom. She had inherited her views, her openness and simplicity, from her father and her passionate nature from her mother. Radiating goodness and charity, the princess compensated for her lack of personal happiness. Her despotic mother would not allow her to marry the younger brother of the poet Baratynsky, who was the prince's aide-de-camp and with whom Varvara had fallen in love. This unhappy episode made her even more sensitive and highly strung. Her personal life was joyless. Brought up in the intellectual atmosphere of the first quarter of the nineteenth century, she fell under the influence of mystical literature, which held sway in the 1840s in Russia and Ukraine in an atmosphere of forced political passivity.

From his first appearance in Yahotyn Shevchenko rescued the princess from her joyless existence. The restraints she placed on her emotions were suddenly removed, and 'her soul floated on a sea of impressions, fantasy and exaltation,' until she told herself that Shevchenko was 'the choice of her heart' and that 'if he had shown one sign of love, she would have responded with passion.' In an autobiographical novel about her love for the poet, the princess painted a good picture of herself and her Parnassian choice. The novel is permeated with a heady romantic aroma, but it nevertheless reveals the characters of both hero and heroine. The heroine is 'neither beautiful nor young, but her face shines with true goodness, clouded at times by contempt, rage and anger ... Her emotions are fiery; her eyes shine with intelligence, but more often they express deep sorrow, like two bright stars in a cloudy sky; they shine in that pale, tired face, not bereft of attraction for those who are unafraid of autumnal storms, cemeteries, and skeletons.'

The psychological portrait of Shevchenko as man and poet is drawn with great mastery. Shevchenko, 'ate and drank like everyone else, and anyone entering a room where the poet was among young people – so many, alas – would not have singled him out. He could indulge in frivolous, banal conversation for hours, and even gave the appearance of being fascinated by it. His goodness bordered on weakness, his gaiety on cruelty; he was both indecisive and rash, capable of impulsive actions. It was difficult not to love him, but for those who did love him he was a source of worry, with his constant transitions from enthusiasm to rage, from sympathy to indifference.' Shevchenko was also 'a poet in every sense of the word. He captivated everybody with his verse and brought gentle tears to the eyes of his listeners. He played on people's hearts with his wide-ranging lyre, enchanting everyone; he attracted both old and young, the cold and the passionate. When he read from his marvellous works he became an enchanter: his musical voice reverberated with deep emotion, which dominated him at such moments. He had more than a talent; it was genius, and his good and sensitive heart tuned his lyre to the lofty and sacred.' In his inspired moments Shevchenko seemed to Varvara to be the embodiment of poetic genius as described by Pushkin.

A few days after Shevchenko's arrival Princess Varvara fell ill and was confined to her bedroom. During the day Shevchenko painted, and in the evening he mingled with the guests in the drawing-room. The palace itself was an enormous wooden structure in the Empire style and had served at one time as the residence of Hetman Rozumovsky in the Pechersk district of Kiev. During one of the wars with Turkey, when accommodation was needed by the army, the hetman requested that it should be dismantled and transferred to Yahotyn. This was speedily done. The palace was moved on three thousand wagons to its new site and faithfully reconstructed there. It was surrounded by a great park of 150 *desiatinas* and the River Supiy encircled the property.

The palace had been bequeathed to Rozumovsky's granddaughter, Princess Varvara Alekseevna, the wife of Prince Repnin-Volkonsky, on her father's death. There was never a shortage of guests at Yahotyn, and Shevchenko became the centre of attention, especially among the ladies. He was attracted to one of them, Hlafira Psiol, an orphan who was brought up by the Repnins and was the sister of a talented Ukrainian poet and painter, Oleksandra Psiol. The old Princess Repnina, before her eyes started troubling her, noticed that 'Hlafira had captivated Shevchenko, who, although not in love, might fall in love should an opportunity be offered.' On her recovery the young princess noticed that Hlafira 'was his sun, as she herself had been.' Hlafira was no beauty, but her open, intelligent face and dark auburn hair attracted everyone. She was pretty and 'endowed with a feeling for the beautiful.' When Shevchenko began to pay too much attention to the young painter, Princess Varvara became jealous.

On one of the literary evenings Shevchenko elected to read his poem 'The Blind Woman.' Although the story behind the poem was invented, Shevchenko was still feeling the impact of Oksana Kovalenko's tragedy and when reading it grew carried away by the coincidences in the poem, whose heroine was also named Oksana, who was also seduced by a landlord, and who became insane. 'If I could only tell you,' wrote Princess Varvara, 'what I experienced during this recitation. What feelings and thoughts, what beauty, enchantment, and pain I felt. My face was wet with tears, and I felt happy, for I would have had to cry had I not felt as I did. I felt an immense pain in my chest ... And with what a charming manner it was recited. It was like music.' When Shevchenko had finished his recitation, Varvara was at first speechless, but later told him: 'When Hlafira sells her first painting, she has promised to give me the money, and I will buy you a golden pen.' The princess was falling in love. 'Before falling asleep,' she wrote, 'I prayed ardently, I loved the whole world so much.' Although this was the second time in her life that she had fallen in love, in her heart, yearning for happiness, this feeling blossomed like a flower and filled her with the shared desire of lovers – to pray and embrace the entire world. As in all those with passionate natures, this feeling turned in Varvara into an urge to dominate the poet's entire being. She grew exceedingly jealous, especially of Hlafira. She wanted him to be 'eternally bright and radiant' and through herself (she revealed her own insatiable ego) to manifest the destiny of his incomparable talent. She wanted to 'see him be great,' and when he sometimes joked with her, she scolded him for debasing his high calling. On one occasion, after such a scolding, when the poet kissed her hand, she was so overjoyed that, as she said, 'her boat glided more swiftly.'

Once, at a wedding, Shevchenko was enjoying himself hugely, and for the princess this was like 'a stab in the heart.' She composed and gave him an allegory in which, brought up as she was on the novels of Richardson, she revealed the depths of her soul. For 'gold from the lyre of the inspired poet' she paid with mysterious prayers and promises to improve herself. 'Poor Oksana,' she wrote, 'has perished, and your poet is forgetting you.' This was the introduction. In the allegory itself the princess depicted the poet's guardian angel over his head, heavy with sinful dreams. The angel 'prays for the vessel entrusted to him, into which the Creator has poured so much beauty.' The vessel is threatened by 'sin and temptation; the pure fluid with which it is filled may spill, and be swallowed by filthy debauchery ... A hot tear falls from the angel's eyes on the poet's heart – it burned the heart through and revived it: the poet will not perish. His penitence is clothed in a white shroud of innocence.'

After another literary evening, when the princess asked Shevchenko what he thought of her allegory and whether he was angry with her, Shevchenko denied that he was angry, but his tone did not convince her. Yet the poet was not angry. He was deeply moved. For a few days he disappeared from society and, as a reply to Varvara's allegory, began to write a poem about himself that he called 'The Unfortunate One' ('Beztalanny'). He wrote it in Russian, since the princess knew no Ukrainian. He had never told her much about his personal life. The stereotypes of Russian romantic poetry flowed involuntarily from his pen. He knew Russian poetry too well to be able to avoid this, but here and there, through the mass of what to him was foreign verse, shone real pearls of poetry. He wrote, as he always did, from the innermost recesses of his being. He wrote about his loneliness and alienation, his disenchantment with people, his lack of personal happiness and love, the inability to realize his revolutionary dreams.

The princess, who had noticed Shevchenko's temporary absence, inquired what had happened to him. Other guests at the palace had also noticed that Shevchenko had 'taken a place' in Varvara's heart, something she herself confessed to. A few days later the poet reappeared. He was merry and mischievous. The princess once more upbraided him. A silence followed. Shevchenko said: 'The quiet angel has flown.' 'You can talk to angels?' asked the princess. 'Tell me what they told you.' Shevchenko dashed to the table, took pen and paper, wrote out a poem, and handed it to Varvara. This was the introduction to the poem he was writing. When she read it, the princess's heart 'was filled with pure, sweet joy.' This is what she read:

> I cast off joyfully for you
> My life's fetters.
> I acted solemnly once more,
> My tears transformed to sounds.
> Your good angel shadowed me
> With immortal wings
> And with tender speech
> Awakened dreams of paradise.[19]

He wrote this with sincerity, responding to the impression of the last few days, firmly believing that he had succeeded in 'casting off the burden of life,' that he was once more 'an angel in paradise 'who would resist petty temptations. While reading these lines the princess felt that if she were to follow her true feelings she would 'embrace Shevchenko,' but she controlled herself. After a second reading of what seemed to her to be a hymn to her victory, she said, 'Give me your forehead,' and, in the presence of her friends Tania and Hlafira Psiol, she gave the poet a kiss. This happened on 13 or 14 November.

The next few days passed quietly. The princess and the poet appeared to find the right tone for their relationship. It was a tone of simple, open friendship, far from the sentimental. The poet left Yahotyn for ten days,

---

19 'Trizna,' *Povne*, I, 204

but as soon as he returned, the princess could no longer control herself and became quite emotional. When he entered the salon she alone stood up, although the poet greeted everyone there. In an exalted mood, the princess wanted her beloved poet to appear in the solemn pose of an emissary of Apollo, but instead he joked with Prince Vasiliy and talked a great deal of nonsense. The princess was beside herself, jumped up and down on a sofa which stood near the door, and disappeared. She did not realize that her behaviour had attracted everybody's attention. In the evening the princess was present when Shevchenko read the poem he had dedicated to her. On this occasion he did appear as the high priest of Apollo and captivated Varvara, who confessed afterwards that she was deeply moved, 'could not hold back her tears,' while 'her face was flushed' and her eyes 'gleaming.' Shevchenko offered her the manuscript of the poem and promised to give her his portrait the next day.

The next evening the princess gave Shevchenko a copy of her novel, entitled *The Girl (Devochka)*. In it, in highly sentimental style, she described the four stages of her spiritual life. She began by describing the dreams of love of a twelve-year-old girl, whose heart is filled with anticipation of future happiness as well as with presentiments of sinful pleasures. Later, between the ages of eighteen and twenty-five, the girl faces the staidness of those who surround her and try to protect her from crying out for love. Varvara analysed the education of an aristocrat, which 'extinguished the pure fire of enthusiasm for everything beautiful' and instilled false concepts of morality. She told the story of her first love and of the disappointment that followed and her realization that life was full of falsehood. The last period of her life began when true love appeared in the shape of the poet, but the rules of social respectability once more deprived her of happiness. Her wounded heart was exhausted, and she found refuge in religion. Finally, she compared herself, 'a middle-aged woman,' to a 'lyre with broken strings' with only one string remaining – that of Christian love. She hoped that she would fare better in the next world and imagined her gravestone inscribed with the words, 'Come to me all ye that labour and are heavy-laden, and I will give you rest.'

In her confessions the princess did not hesitate to reveal the most intimate details of her experiences. Shevchenko's poem had stirred her imagination, and she too felt 'like a stranger' among those who knew her. Sometimes she rephrased the poet's own words, opening her heart to him in the hope that he would reciprocate and tell her that he was ready to fulfil her happiness. But the poet remained silent. Varvara's confession made a great impact on Shevchenko. A very sensitive human being, he was shattered by it. The story of her life as related by the princess amounted to a great tragedy. We can see how deeply he was moved by his reply to the author of *The Girl*. 'The very stones would groan,' he wrote, 'and bleed if they could hear the weeping of this "girl."' He took the princess's patience and heroism as a model for himself. He ended with these words: 'O my good angel. You have confirmed in me a shaky belief in the existence of holy people on this earth.'

However, the princess did not want to be canonized and had hoped for a different reply. Princess Lizaveta Keikuatova, the daughter of Platon Lukashevych, told Varvara's mother about the novel her daughter had written. The old princess asked for a copy so that she might read it. Princess Varvara read it to her mother and included Shevchenko's reply. The old princess sternly remarked that her daughter 'exposed her heartfelt confessions too easily.' When her daughter replied that Shevchenko was not a stranger and that she trusted him completely, her mother's comment was that this was simply 'shameful.' To the old princess the daughter's confession, full of accusations against the customs of the world in which she lived, customs accepted by her mother without question, was blasphemous. Some passages in this confession where her daughter, without naming anyone, described her love for Baratynsky, whom the old princess had refused to accept as her son-in-law, were personally offensive to her. Princess Varvara wept after this confrontation with her mother and only calmed down after reading passages from the Bible to her.

During the next few days Shevchenko and the princess appeared to the other guests 'like two lovers who had quarrelled.' The poet withdrew into himself and remained silent. He was embarrassed by Varvara's confessions. He had surrounded her with an aura of sanctity and was ready to pray to this strange, aristocratic girl who had such great spiritual beauty. But was this feeling of gratitude and sincere friendship accompanied by the deeper feeling of a man for a woman? Probably not. If it had been so, his passionate nature could not have been restrained by arguments about the hopelessness of the situation because of the presumably negative attitude of Varvara's parents, especially that of her mother, or of the difficulties that both might encounter. Whenever any strong feeling gripped him, it would engulf him entirely. The poet's sombre mood had a different cause: he was convinced that Varvara was in love with him. He had never met a woman who had shown so much sympathy and enthusiasm towards him, but he could not reciprocate these feelings. He realized that she was suffering, and, fearing the dramatic consequences of this unexpected romance, he was at a loss. The princess was unable to divine his mood and, at last, requested a meeting.

'Why have you stopped talking to me?' she asked when they were alone.
'I cannot, I cannot,' the poet answered.

The princess began to talk about her confessional mood. She told him that in writing this 'weak' story, she had followed his example, but 'had been overturned, since the sleigh she chose was not for her.'

'No, no,' protested Shevchenko. 'This is poetry, true poetry.' He said that he had never experienced what he was feeling now as he read her work, that he had never met a more kindred soul.

This represented the climax of the tension in their entire relationship. Shevchenko did not open his arms wide to embrace her, did not hug her. The princess understood it all. She controlled herself, began to talk of her friendship for him, and asked him to look on her as a sister. Then she said that faith was a great support in her life. Taking his leave, Shevchenko said 'Good-bye, sister.'

The next day the poet was calm, even merry. What he was most afraid of had dissipated. He hoped that the princess would overcome her feelings. For a few days their relationship was free and easy, full of mutual trust. However, the poet once more noticed something disturbing in Varvara's behaviour, and he grew more reserved and aloof. Seeing this 'coldness,' the princess tormented herself, and in a few days, as the poet grew even more reserved, she fell ill. She did not eat for eight days and became very weak. When she got up, she believed that Shevchenko had not noticed the change in her. On 4 December, the princess's name-day, they all attended a church service. When Shevchenko extended his best wishes to her after the service and kissed her hand, the princess was overjoyed.

Soon, Kapnist came to Yahotyn to celebrate her name-day and had several conversations with the princess. For some time he had been playing the role of mentor, a role to which he believed himself entitled because of the respect shown to him by the entire Repnin family. This time Kapnist struck a tone more intimate than he had ever used before in talking to the princess. In spite of his libertarian views, he had obviously ruled out any possibility of a real liaison between the princess and the poet that might end in marriage. He criticized the princess for going too far in expressing her feelings to the poet and warned her that she might make him unhappy because all this might go to his head. Kapnist maintained that the princess could not correct or transform the poet's behaviour and that in trying to do so she was acting selfishly. He did not say that he believed she was in love with the poet, but the next day he heard her say: 'I think that at the age of thirty-five I have the right to do something I could not do in my youth ... I want to be Shevchenko's friend and sister.' Kapnist's answer was that 'age does not prove anything, and when a woman and a young man call each other sister and brother, there is always danger in this.' Shevchenko, Kapnist argued, might fall in love with her, and this would be a misfortune for him. If Varvara's attention flattered him, the Princess must be doubly careful. He concluded that Shevchenko must leave Yahotyn. He promised to persuade the poet to do so. The princess's heart sank, and she became depressed. Seeing this, Kapnist remarked that he had never thought things were 'so serious.'

Around 8 December he departed, taking Shevchenko with him. The poet left a letter addressed to the princess in which, using the familiar 'Thou,' he, as her brother, asked her to 'keep alive the treasures which God had placed in one of his loveliest creatures.' A few days later Kapnist returned and told the princess that he was certain that Shevchenko believed that the princess was in love with him. However, he and Varvara decided that Shevchenko should return to Yahotyn for a few days so that his sudden departure would not evoke further comment.

The renewed meeting between Shevchenko and the princess was very warm. She was in full control of herself. In her talk to him she even said that she would love his wife, should he marry. Shevchenko remained very reserved and 'cold.' One episode in Yahotyn infuriated the poet. Platon Lukashevych had sent a serf from Berezan to Yahotyn with a letter to Shevchenko. The messenger had to walk for twenty-five *versts* in frosty, wintry weather. This enraged Shevchenko, and he wrote a sharp letter to the landowner, who replied derisively that he 'had three hundred fools like Shevchenko.' While reporting this cruel incident to the princess, Shevchenko 'cried with pain.' The princess did not know what to say to comfort him. 'I drew his head on to my chest,' she wrote later, 'embraced him, kissed his hands, and would have kissed his feet. I wanted to show him that if a scoundrel existed who, instead of being glad to see the genius of his people freed from serfdom, identified himself with it, there was also someone else who valued noble feelings and the sacred fire higher than any accident of birth.' Shevchenko calmed down and 'quickly passed from sorrow to gaiety.'

At the end of December Shevchenko left Yahotyn for a few days, but upon his return he noticed that the princess was once more paying him special attention. She herself admitted to being even more drawn to him. They celebrated the New Year together. Every change in the poet's mood tormented the princess. The time of the poet's departure from Yahotyn drew near. He spent two full days with the princess while he was painting the portrait of Prince Vasiliy's children. The princess was there to see that the children behaved themselves during the sittings. While he was working, Shevchenko was silent and withdrawn. The last three days of his stay in Yahotyn were marked by his friendliness and kindness to Varvara. Finally, on 10 January, when the time for departure came, the princess 'threw her arms around his neck, crossed his forehead, and he ran out of the room.' Leaving Yahotyn, the poet was confident that he was leaving a friend who would never betray him.

During his three-month-long stay in Yahotyn, Shevchenko frequently visited the neighbouring landlords. He often went to Berezova Rudka, to visit the Zakrevskys. His friendship with the head of the 'society of wet mugs' was a deep disappointment to his 'sister' Varvara. She tried desperately and persistently to draw Shevchenko away from that group. She transferred her dislike of Viktor Zakrevsky to his entire family, including his brother Platon, with whom Shevchenko liked to spend many a happy hour. Maria Zakrevska was a talented pianist, and Sophia was a writer who attempted to follow in Gogol's footsteps, depicting in her 'The Fair' ('Yarmarok') the life of the Poltava gentry. The entire Zakrevsky family was known for their 'oppositionist' views. What attracted Shevchenko most to that milieu was the presence of Hanna Zakrevska, a striking Ukrainian beauty with 'dark blue eyes' and 'a sinuous waist.' In her company he forgot about the stern admonitions of the princess, who would have preferred him to be a knight of a monastic order. Here he could relax in the presence of a woman he really loved and ignore the sentimentality of high society.

Among those he met at Yahotyn were many striking personalities. Princess Varvara has written about the special attention he devoted to Hlafira Psiol, who made several successful sketches of Shevchenko's head. Another guest, Roman Schtrandmann, was a learned economist and a student of French Utopian socialism. He was an intellectual, and from talks with him Shevchenko learned about the social utopias of Saint Simon and Fourier. Schtrandmann called Shevchenko 'the last of the Cossacks,' since the poet fascinated him with his 'Cossack' love of freedom and his hopes for, if not an ideal, then at least a renewed Ukrainian social structure. Yet another guest, Doctor Fischer, Repnin's personal physician, came from Saxony and was a well-educated man.

The Repnin family preserved Ukrainian autonomist traditions as well as a passive but clear opposition to the regime of Nicholas 1. The old prince throughout his life fought against abuses of the law of serfdom by the Left Bank landowners and was always on the side of the enlightened gentry, who were not utterly debauched and who defended justice and decency. As a result he became a target of abuse, which culminated in charges that he had defrauded the state of monies. His estate was placed under surveillance, and he himself came under lengthy police investigation.

Two of the Cossack volunteer regiments that he had formed in 1831 were sent on the tsar's orders to the northern Caucasus, despite his plea that this would separate them from their native land and their families. He was removed from the office of governor general of Little Russia because of his pro-Ukrainian sympathies and alleged 'separatist' ideas.

Now, living in retirement, the old prince could demonstrate his displeasure only by openly giving away portraits of the tsars, symbols of the hated regime, from his art gallery. Shevchenko was full of respect for the prince, and during the New Year celebrations kissed his hand and said that he venerated old men like him. At the palace of Yahotyn there was a good deal that was good and noble, the antithesis of Muscovite tyranny. The two-year-old son of the Prince's brother, the Decembrist Sergey Volkonsky, had been left there by his mother, the heroic wife of Sergey, who shared her husband's exile in Siberia, and he died in Yahotyn. The memory of another Decembrist whom the prince knew well, the poet Kondratiy Ryleev, was kept alive among the Repnins. Ryleev, who was hanged on the orders of Nicholas I, was the author of several poems on Ukrainian themes which captivated Shevchenko. Another friend of the Repnins was Ivan Kotliarevsky, the Ukrainian writer, whom Shevchenko depicted in his novel *The Twins* (*Bliznetsy*), probably relying on stories he had heard about him at Yahotyn. Shevchenko could also have learnt there about Ukrainian freemasonry, abolished twenty years earlier. Its last members, Oleksa Kapnist, the Lyzohubs, and Ivan Kotliarevsky, were friends of the Repnins. Many freemasons were exponents of Ukrainian autonomism in the first quarter of the nineteenth century. Although the old Repnins did not often mix with their guests, Shevchenko came to know the old prince, who was habitually reading in his study, where they could have talked a great deal. Princess Varvara reported that Shevchenko gained the affection of this 'old candidate for hetman,' as he was sometimes regarded by the Ukrainian autonomists. The old princess, the granddaughter of Rozumovsky, the 'hetman who was once a shepherd,' could not but like the poet who was also once a shepherd.

Apart from literary soirées (the record of four of them has been preserved) at which Shevchenko recited his own or others' poems, Yahotyn was well known for its free-wheeling discussions, with many brilliant participants. Sometimes particular projects were started, one of them, of which some details are known, being of particular interest. This was a plan to stage a new opera at Yahotyn. The libretto, which satisfied everyone with its rich dramatic action, was chosen – 'Mazepa.' Shevchenko was to write the libretto, while P. Seletsky, the marshal of the nobility from Poltava, was to supply the music. Seletsky was known to be a very reactionary man and a Russian patriot. Whereas 'everybody else voted for Mazepa and wanted to see him as the defender of freedom in the struggle with the despotic tsar, Peter,' Seletsky 'did not find in Mazepa's actions anything heroic and wanted to depict him as he really was.' When he called Mazepa 'a traitor,' the rest of the group quarrelled and split up.[20] In addition, Princess Varvara and Shevchenko wanted the libretto to be written in Ukrainian, but Seletsky objected and declared that the opera must be in Russian. The entire project collapsed. Shevchenko, the princess, and their followers looked at Mazepa in the same way as Pushkin did, through the words of the hero of his long poem 'Poltava':

> Without dear freedom and glory
> We long bent down our heads
> Under the protection of Warsaw
> And under Moscow's autocracy.
> But it is time for Ukraine
> To be an independent state,
> And I raise the banner
> Of bloody liberty against Peter.[21]

The quarrel with Seletsky and the incident with Lukashevych were dissonant sounds in the harmony of the palace at Yahotyn. The poet's personal experiences in his relationship with the princess, although painful at times, did not touch his convictions or debase his national dignity. That is why, on 10 December, he wrote to Hryhorovych that he felt extremely well.

After leaving Yahotyn the poet stayed at various estates over the next month. He visited the Zakrevskys, the de Balmens, and, possibly, Markevych. It was carnival time, and dances and receptions were being held everywhere. From Yakiv de Balmen Shevchenko received a rare gift – the illustrated *Kobzar*, with the addition of 'Hamaliia.' Some of the illustrations were by de Balmen himself, others by his brother-in-law, Bashylov. Facing the title-page was Shevchenko's portrait, painted by Bashylov. One remnant of this merry season was the 'universal,'[22] sent by 'Hetman' Shevchenko to the 'quartermaster-general,' Mykola Marke-

---

20 'Zapiski P.D. Seletskogo,' *Kievskaia starina*, no. 9 (1884), 621
21 A.S. Pushkin, *Sobranie sochinenii* (Moscow 1960), III, 209
22 The 'universals' were proclamations by Cossack hetmans.

vych, requesting his immediate attendance on the hetman in Bezbukhivka. Aside from the hetman, the document was signed by 'the company colonel' Korba, 'the general secretary' Mochemordenko, the 'wet mug' Viktor Zakrevsky, and the 'army captain' Dybailo (Yakiv de Balmen). The hetman had deleted from the statute of the fraternity all the Muscovite terminology and replaced it with Cossack usage. The witty sybarite and snob Markevych. replied to the 'universal' with a rhymed ditty in which he advised the hetman not 'to swing his Mazepa's mace' too much or else he would be beaten 'by a Muscovite' fist and would not even be allowed to cry. It is possible that the reference to Mazepa's mace was an echo of Shevchenko's bold anti-Muscovite conversations as they were reported to Markevych. There is no doubt that those conversations took place, for two years later, recalling with deep sorrow de Balmen's death in the Caucasus, Shevchenko wrote:

> Not for Ukraine, but for her executioner
> You had to shed good blood.

After taking leave of the Zakrevskys and his other friends from the Pyriatyn and Pryluky districts, Shevchenko went to Kachanivka to say goodbye to Tarnovsky, to whom he delivered a copy of Hornung's portrait of Prince Repnin. He must have been paid for it, as he was by Kapnist for another copy. In December he had written to Hryhorovych that he 'was making money,' adding that he was surprised 'that it was coming into my hands.' Two portraits of Repnin, the group portrait of his grandchildren, the portrait of Mrs Maevska, portraits of the Zakrevskys (husband and wife), the portrait of Lukomsky – all were painted by Shevchenko in 1843; others from the same period must have been lost. He had no living expenses since he was visiting friends, and thus he was able to take back with him a tidy sum of money, which, after the lean winter of 1842–43, was a pleasant surprise.

Shevchenko did not travel north when he left the Chernihiv district but went to Kiev to attend the famous fair (the so-called *kontrakty*). It was held between the sixth and the thirteenth of February. The decision to go there might have been made because one of his friends, possibly Tarnovsky, had asked him to accompany them. All the wealthy landowners from both Right and Left Bank Ukraine were there to finalize many different business deals. In one of his letters Vasyl Bilozersky testified that he met Shevchenko at the fair. Unfortunately, we do not know what impression the fair made on the poet. It was a great social occasion, with champagne flowing at the receptions, bands playing, and amateur theatres presenting cabaret-type performances. Some estates changed hands as a result of victories or losses at cards, and some landowners lost fortunes while others made new ones.

From Kiev, Shevchenko hurried to Moscow and St Petersburg, without looking up, as he had promised his friend Viktor Zabila on his *khutir*. Zabila was quite dismayed and sent Shevchenko an epistle in verse in which he castigated him for making friends with the landlords and neglecting his humble friends. He hoped that Shevchenko would be punished by being denied good Ukrainian food for six months.

In the middle of February Shevchenko reached Moscow. On 19 February he gave an autographed copy of the poem 'Chyhyryn' to the famous actor M. Shchepkin, about whom he had heard so much at Yahotyn. Prince Nikolay, who had helped to buy Shchepkin's freedom from serfdom, was a great admirer of his art. Another fellow-countryman whom Shevchenko met in Moscow was Professor Osyp Bodiansky, who had published a great deal in the field of Ukrainian history. Bodiansky was also an ethnographer and was aware of all the latest developments in other Slavic countries. He helped Shevchenko to emend his text of 'Hamaliia.' It is possible that both Shchepkin and Bodiansky introduced Shevchenko, of whom they were very proud, to various prominent Moscow Slavophils. Ivan Kireevsky was possibly one of these. Unfortunately, we have only indirect testimony about these meetings. Both Bodiansky and Shchepkin loved and respected the poet, and the former, in one of his letters, called Shevchenko 'the leader of all of us.' Later correspondence between Bodiansky and Shevchenko demonstrates great mutual admiration. Shevchenko's dedication of some of his poems to Shchepkin (particularly 'Chyhyryn') shows how deeply attached he had become to the famous actor, who complained that all his life he had worked 'in a foreign land.' Shchepkin later became famous for his masterful recitations of Shevchenko's poems.

After five days in Moscow Shevchenko left for St Petersburg. He took with him the most vivid impressions of his Ukrainian journey. He had seen what he had expected to see. His country was subjugated and poverty-stricken. He saw how it was 'plundered by the Germans and the Russians,' how it was being ruined by Russian bureaucrats (Germans), and that his own countrymen were only too ready to serve Moscow. Against the backdrop of a larger picture, Dantean in proportion, demonstrating the moral and cultural decay of the ruling class and the deprivations of the peasants, there remained the image of his Beatrice, Oksana, and the memory of the tumbledown houses in his native village as his brothers and sisters continued in serfdom. True, the impressions were not entirely disheartening. Here and there he had met some attractive people: his 'angel' Varvara, the honest though dull mystic Kapnist, the comic figures of Zabila and Zakrevsky, the enthusiastic Kulish, and others, but these were merely golden ears of corn in the heap of dead, stale chaff. The poet carved in his heart the tragic image of the 'ransacked grave.'

V

Shevchenko returned to St Petersburg in late February. He had been away for almost ten months and had missed the entire academic year. Had he not stayed so long in Ukraine he would have finished his studies at the academy in the spring of 1844, six years after he had enrolled as a student. Now he had to spend an additional year studying. All he needed was a diploma. The portraits completed in Ukraine in 1843 were the proof of a mature artist. He enjoyed a deserved reputation as an excellent portrait painter and illustrator.

For two or three weeks after his return he did not work but visited his old friends. A young Ukrainian landowner, Hryhoriy Halahan, was visiting the capital. He gave a reception for all Ukrainian expatriates and invited Shevchenko. It was one party after another. In a letter to Bodiansky the Ukrainian Lytvyniv gave a vivid description of how he, Halahan, and Shevchenko amused themselves 'like brothers.' He also described an evening spent in the home of Hryhorovych, where Shevchenko entertained the guests with lively stories.

Once more Shevchenko found rooms on Vasilievsky Island, close to a group of fellow-countrymen: Ivan Hudovsky from Kiev, Mykhailo Karpo and Khyvrych from Slobidska Ukraine. The Zaporozhian 'camp' was re-established, with Shevchenko as *otaman*. The poem 'Hamaliia' was printed. Bodiansky's emendation of the poem turned out to be futile, since the Russian publisher was slapdash and the printing was fuzzy. A drawing of a drum and a clown adorned the frontispiece. Another poem, 'The Unfortunate One' ('Beztalanny'), which Shevchenko had sent to *The Beacon*, had also been printed in that journal. Because no offprints were available, Shevchenko published it separately under the new title 'The Funeral Feast' ('Trizna'). Bodiansky offered to help with the sale of the publication in Moscow, and Princess Varvara and Maria Seletska were to promote it in Ukraine. The critics' responses were not very serious. The Slavophil publications had ceased to be interested in Ukrainian literature, and other journals treated it with contempt. The fine poem 'Hamaliia' was reviewed by the *Library for Reading* (*Biblioteka dlia chteniia*), which characterized it as the story of a Ukrainian Achilles or Ajax who beat the Jews, the Turks, and the Poles. The illiterate review was probably written by a reactionary Ukrainian who was poking fun at Ukrainian history. Shevchenko could find some solace in the critical review of modern Ukrainian literature written by a young scholar, Mykola Kostomarov, and published in the Kharkiv almanac *The New Moon* (*Molodyk*) for 1844.

While still travelling in Ukraine Shevchenko had conceived of a project that would raise national consciousness among those of his countrymen who were literate. A romantic and an idealist, he was deeply convinced that art had a beneficent influence on people and made them morally better. From the impressions he had gathered while inspecting the ruins of Chyhyryn and Subotiv, he made up his mind to publish some albums, entitled *Picturesque Ukraine* (*Zhivopisnaia Ukraina*), that would illustrate the political history of Ukraine, starting with the princely era, as well as survey its art, national customs, and folklore. The project was intended, in his mind, to buy freedom for his brothers and sisters from the proceeds. This idea received warm support from Princess Repnina.

Shevchenko brought various sketches with him from his Ukrainian travels. He had amassed a great deal of rich material that had to be shaped by a plan. We know only of those illustrations that he announced. The choice was very interesting. Among the historical monuments we see, apart from the Vydubytsky monastery, Chyhyryn, Subotiv, and Baturyn, the witnesses of 'ancient glory,' places connected with the Ukrainian struggle for liberation, and homes of national heroes. Among the finished sketches for a historical series there are scenes to arouse a feeling of national pride ('*The Gifts to Bohdan and the Ukrainian People*) or scenes illustrating the deep sacrifices made by Ukrainians in the struggle with their enemies (the execution of Ivan Pidkova, Pavlo Polubotok in St Petersburg, Semen Paliy in Siberia), or else portraits of traitors (Sava Chaly). In the series depicting life in Ukraine there are scenes of poetic intensity (*The Funeral of a Young Bride*), folk humour (*The Tale of the Soldier and Death*), or some ancient traditions (*The Matchmakers*), or ways of life (*Chumaky*). Shevchenko planned a publication, then, that would reveal a complete picture of the characteristic, distinguishing features of his country. The primary goal was national and patriotic, though arousing love for things Ukrainian went hand in hand with his own artistic ambitions.

The problems of mass reproduction of art had begun to interest Shevchenko a few years earlier, when he had started work as an illustrator. Two methods were known at that time: lithography and engraving. He preferred engraving as the more artistic means of reproducing an original, but the usual woodcuts and linocuts did not satisfy him. In 1842 he took part in researching a new method of 'galvanographics' and used this in his illustrations of *King Lear*, made for his benefactor Sapozhnikov, treasurer of the Society for the Promotion of Artists. But experience told him that the most satisfactory method was engraving with acid on copper, known as etching, an old method used by Rembrandt which produced the best possible results. It reproduced all the finer shades of the original sketch, and the best results were achieved when the artist himself did all the work. Thus he chose etching as his favourite method.

He worked furiously, and between March and May he completed three etchings. He learned as he worked and showed a special talent for etching, which was not taught at the academy. He must have used the advice and direction of people he knew, especially Professor Klodt von Jurgensburg, who etched and engraved as a hobby. Before beginning an etching he produced the pictures in sepia, which he always used for illustrations. All this required a great deal of time and patience.

As soon as the first three pictures were ready, Shevchenko started to organize the publication. He thought of choosing appropriate texts to accompany the illustrations. At first he intended to put out ten illustrations annually, in three separate issues, including explanatory texts. He informed Bodiansky and Princess Repnina of this plan. Then, in an advertisement, he announced that twelve pictures would appear annually. The price he wanted to charge for them kept changing. When Princess Repnina and other friends collected subscriptions for the publication, they collected, in fact, more money than was needed. There were fewer etchings than promised. In all his dealings Shevchenko showed a great deal of premature optimism and little practical business skill. He behaved like a 'true poet.' Yuzefovych agreed to promote *Picturesque Ukraine* in Kiev, but Shevchenko failed to give him his address, so that Yuzefovych was unable to send him the money. Princess Varvara waited several months for the printed program and subscription tickets, and when the first three etchings finally appeared, she received only thirty tickets, although she needed a hundred. Yet matters were improving. The Society for the Promotion of Artists assigned three hundred roubles to the project. This was not a large sum, but it made it possible to start printing. Subscriptions increased the capital needed for the enterprise. Princess Repnina was very energetic in promoting the publication, and, had it not been for Shevchenko's ineptness, she would have been more successful.

Governor General Dolgorukov officially recommended that the gentry of the three provinces subscribe to *Picturesque Ukraine*.

In the meantime Shevchenko, though lacking a clear plan of action, spent a great deal of energy on the project. He corresponded with many influential people who could assist him in promoting the publication. He was also in touch with the bookstores. The enthusiasm with which he pursued this plan is obvious in a letter he wrote to Prince Tsertelev, who was an outstanding ethnographer. 'If God helps me,' he wrote, 'to complete the task that I have begun, I shall be ready to fold my hands and be buried. I will have achieved something, and my Ukraine will not forget me – miserable creature.'[1] The publication became the mirror of his all-consuming ambition to stir up national feelings in any fellow-countrymen who looked through it.

Apart from art, this publication contained literary texts – explanatory notes that Shevchenko wanted to place with the illustrations. Here again he showed little common sense. At first he wanted to invite Bodiansky to write the historical commentaries; other texts were to be written by Kulish or himself. He invited Kulish to do this, but his friend replied that he did not quite understand what exactly he was to write. Shevchenko failed to supply him with further information, and although he did not yet have Kulish's consent, he wrote to Bodiansky that Kulish had agreed to compose the texts. What was merely a desire became an accomplished fact. When work on the etchings was proceeding well and was admired by those who saw them, he began to alter and expand his plans and, in thought, to attract other scholars (Budkov and Storozhenko) as his collaborators. He held the unfounded notion that the Polish writer Michał Grabowski would assist him with the Polish texts and wrote about it to Bodiansky as if it had already been agreed upon. He told the Polish writer Romuald Podberezki that *Picturesque Ukraine* would contain illustrations of the most important historical events, beginning with the founding of Kiev, but soon afterwards he told a Russian journalist who was preparing an advertisement for the publication to appear in the *Northern Bee* (*Severnaia Pchela*) that plans had been changed and the illustrations would begin with the era of Gedymin. All this was the result of quicksilver changes in his mood when he envisaged different plans and, finding them difficult to realize, made constant changes. What was essential was to ask each author to write the text to accompany a particular etching. Shevchenko, however, asked Bodiansky to suggest a text to him after reading something interesting in the chronicles, or even to write historical

1 *Povne*, VI, 30

explanations for illustrations that did not yet exist. In the end, because of his own capriciousness in dealing with other people, only one possibility remained for Shevchenko: to write the texts himself. They were brief, and would have been much better had he proceeded in a more organized way by inviting experts to help him.

At the end of December *Picturesque Ukraine* was ready to be sent to subscribers. Almost an entire year had been spent on this publication, and Shevchenko had written poetry only sporadically. This time he wrote not about an idealized Ukraine but about the living country that he had seen with his own eyes not so long before. Although before his Ukrainian journey he had expected to see a dark reality there, what he had seen was much worse than he had imagined or could recall from his childhood. In the village church registers of those days the most common cause of death recorded for a serf was 'died after a beating by the overseer' or 'died after punishment by flogging.' In his own Kerelivka the peasants were beaten down by the landlord's henchmen. Oppression continued everywhere. The peasants lived stagnant lives in material and moral squalour. Scarcely any education was available to them, for village schools were rare. On the Left Bank, where over a thousand village schools had been active in the hetman state, none was left. The calling up of young men to the army was, in fact, a violation of law and justice. It was always the poorest boys who had to join the army, boys who were often the sole support of their families. After travelling through the Chernihiv, Poltava, and Kiev regions and visiting the distant Zaporozhian steppes, Shevchenko could see all this with his own eyes and hear the complaints and grievances of the weeping peasants. All traces of the old Ukrainian liberties had been destroyed by Nicholas I. Administrators like Prince Repnin, who defended the peasants from landlords and high taxes, were replaced by reactionaries of the worst type. The Slobidska Ukraine and the lands of the Hetmanate were governed by Prince Dolgorukov, with a reputation for embezzlement, high living, and drinking. Right Bank Ukraine was under the direct rule of General Dmitriy Bibikov, a self-satisfied egoist and careerist. Later, in his poem 'God's Fool' ('Yurodyvy'), Shevchenko satirized both of them.

The university of Kiev had recently reopened after being closed for a few years following the Polish uprising. General Traskin, a man who knew nothing about science or scholarship, was in charge. Young men who were not of the nobility had difficulty in receiving a secondary education and were barred from entering the university altogether. While many noblemen in Russia tried, in spite of obstacles, to improve the lot of the common people, in Ukraine serfdom existed in its worst form, and there was almost no one among the upper classes who wanted to alleviate the peasants' suffering or gave any thought to their education. Even the few whom Shevchenko met in his travels did little for their serfs. Their only virtue was a certain reluctance to exploit the peasants unduly and thus abuse the social and political system that prevailed in the feudal state. That Ukraine 'reeked of mould and let the snakes into the hollow tree' was only too true. The national elite were living evidence of a dreadful moral decay. One of the finest Russian intellectuals of the time, Yuriy Samarin, in his treatise on serfdom maintained that the reality of serfdom was far worse in Ukraine than in Russia. When Shevchenko visited the land of the peasants, he heard 'crying everywhere,' and thus he too cried everywhere. He could see how the Ukrainian people, although betrayed by their upper classes, still exhibited high moral standards, deep spirituality, a love of art, and a desire to preserve through their conservatism the national identity. As a former serf himself Shevchenko could not but respond deeply to their grievances. He also heard a great deal about peasant rebellions that were erupting all over the country. Like all spontaneous rebellions they were doomed to fail, but they showed the great potential for revolution among the peasant masses.

Shevchenko's new cycle of poems, which were written under the impression of this terrible reality, was started, as we saw, in the fall of 1843 in Ukraine, in his poem 'The Ransacked Grave.' It was followed by 'Chyhyryn.' In May 1844 he wrote in St Petersburg the poem 'The Owl' ('Sova'), depicting the tragedy of a widowed mother whose only son had been drafted into the army. She was unable to bear the pain and went mad. In June he composed 'The Dream' ('Son'), a poem that is difficult to classify and that, after Dante, he called a 'comedy.' Notwithstanding the strong influence of Mickiewicz's 'Ancestors' Eve' ('Dziady'), the poem was the highly original expression of a soul tormented by the national anguish. Drawing sharp satirical vignettes of Imperial Russia, Shevchenko re-created the sufferings of the Ukrainian nation and surpassed everything written by the poets of other subjugated peoples in speaking out against the Russian imperial yoke. The grotesque, satirical portrayal of Nicholas I and his wife was reminiscent of the folk puppet theatre (*vertep*), saturated as it was in venom and brutal sarcasm. Shevchenko was striking blindly at the enemy, just as the peasants beat a horsethief.

In the fall Shchepkin made his debut in St Petersburg. It was meetings with him, and his splendid acting, that prompted Shevchenko to turn to drama. He tried to translate into Ukrainian *Danilo Reva, or Nazar Stodolia*, a play he had written in Russian. He had hoped to see it staged by Easter of 1843. On 23 November he asked Kukharenko to send him his play about life in Chornomoria (*Chornomorsky pobyt*), which he wanted to stage. He reported that other plays (*Moskal the Sorcerer* by Kotliarevsky, *Shelmenko* and *Wedding at Honcharivka* by Kvitka, and his own *Nazar Stodolia*) were to be performed during the Christmas holiday at the medical academy. Shevchenko was quite enthusiastic about these productions and wrote again to Kukharenko that 'the Cossacks have come to life again.' His plans, as usual exaggerated by fantasy, were not fully realized, and it is doubtful whether *Nazar Stodolia* had actually been performed.

The end of 1844 was full of vivid, contrasting experiences. An echo of his loneliness may be found in the lyric poem 'Why am I depressed, why am I bored?' ('Choho meni tiazhko, choho meni nudno'), which ends with these ringing words:

> Fall asleep, my heart, sleep for ever,
> Uncovered and broken ... Let the mad
> Rave ... Cover your eyes, my heart.[2]

Although he spent his time with friends and admirers, he continually felt lonely. He opened his heart only to those whom he regarded as the best and purest. In an 'epistle' to Shchepkin he asked for advice:

> Be my brother, even by pretending!
> Tell me what to do:
> To pray, or to worry,
> Or to dash my brains out![3]

While deeply in tune with art and artists, this 'grey-haired friend' of Shevchenko could scarcely provide him with an answer, since 'his own heart was sealed,' and having become a professional actor, he felt very differently from the younger Shevchenko about Ukrainian affairs. To whom should Shevchenko turn for the advice he so ardently desired? In utter desolation he turned, in a tragic epistle, to Gogol, though the poem was probably never sent to the addressee:

> *Duma* flies out, swarming after *duma*,
> One oppresses the heart, the other tears it,
> A third is crying very quietly
> In my very heart, perhaps even unseen by God.[4]

2 'Choho meni tiazhko,' ibid, I, 255
3 'Zavorozhy meni, vokhve,' ibid, 256
4 'Hoholiu,' ibid, 257. In Ukrainian *duma* may mean all of 'thought,' 'poem,' and 'song.'

It seemed to Shevchenko that Gogol, this man with 'knowledge of the human heart,' would recognize Shevchenko's intention. In this he was mistaken. Shevchenko's great countryman was full of admiration for Russia and was very distant in his outlook from the former serf, who sang of the 'ill fate of the Cossack land.' Shevchenko seems to have forgotten that Gogol was in the same category of fellow-countrymen about whom he wrote in the 'Dream'

> They are smothered by
> Muscovite henbane
> And German hothouses.[5]

In vain the poet searched for kindred spirits, not realizing that great spirits are always alone.

At the beginning of 1845 the time had come to finish his studies at the academy. On 22 March the academy's council conferred on Shevchenko the title of artist. In order to be sent abroad to Italy, the candidate had to be awarded a gold medal. It is not known why Shevchenko failed to qualify for the gold medal. Less talented students had received it and thus travelled to Italy. The seven years of academic study had finally come to an end.

---

5 'Son,' ibid, 250

VI

On 25 March 1845, having secured a document from the academy that testified that he was proceeding to 'the Little Russian provinces on an artistic assignment,' Shevchenko left St Petersburg. Before his departure he left a forwarding address at the village of Mariinske in the Myrhorod district, where he was to be the guest of the landowner, O. Lukianovych, who had commissioned him to paint several portraits. Shevchenko also planned to visit Korsun in Tahanrih and Kukharenko in Chornomoria. On 13 April he was in the neighbourhood of Yahotyn and called on his 'sister,' Princess Varvara, who was in deep mourning for her father's death on 7 January. How welcome Shevchenko's sympathy and friendship were may be seen from the fact that the princess wrote him a letter during a terrible snowstorm on the way to Pryluky, to which city she was taking her father's body, for he had wished to be buried in the monastery of Hustyn. She asked the poet to 'sing a song in memory of the man whom you loved and respected so much.' This letter as well as others the princess wrote remained unanswered, perhaps because Shevchenko was planning a trip to Ukraine. He now hurried to revisit Yahotyn. From the princess's letter he knew that the peasants in Pryluky had mounted a great demonstration in honour of the dead prince, carrying their defender's coffin in procession through the town. It is not known how long Shevchenko stayed at Yahotyn. It is difficult to establish the exact chronology or itinerary of his journey through the Poltava region in the spring and summer of 1845. Only a couple of dates are known. While at Yahotyn he must have visited Hustyn, to pay his last respects to the prince, but from the drawings he made of what he called 'this Ukrainian St Clair abbey' we can see that he was there in the summer. It is certain that in the spring he must have visited friends in the Pyriatyn and Pereiaslav regions. Very likely he called on the Zakrevskys, despite Varvara's warnings to avoid them.

One can assume that from the very beginning of his journey through the Poltava region Shevchenko began to study and sketch the local antiquities and historical monuments systematically. It is possible that he was still thinking of continuing to publish *Picturesque Ukraine* and that he was collecting material for this book. It is also possible that his work was related to the plan to study Ukrainian antiquities contemplated by the newly founded Kievan Archaeographic Commission. Shevchenko must also have visited Kiev at that time, and it was there that his services were engaged by the commission. Although not yet official, in fact his participation began then. One could surmise that M. Yuzefovych, the assistant curator of the Kiev school district and deputy chairman of the commission, was instrumental in this. His sister was the wife of Vasyl Tarnovsky, a cousin of the owner of Kachanivka, Hryhoriy Tarnovsky. Vasyl and Yakiv Tarnovsky had a small estate in Potoky, in the Kiev region, but they were expecting to inherit some of the wealth of their childless uncle from Kachanivka. In 1843, with the help of the Tarnovskys and Kulish, Shevchenko met Yuzefovych, who then enticed the poet to work for the commission.

In the spring and summer of 1845 Shevchenko visited places around Pyriatyn, Myrhorod, Pryluky, Romny, Khorol, Lubny, and Poltava. The landscapes sketched at that time include Hustyn, Reshetylivka, Gogol's Vasylivka, Ivan Kotliarevsky's house in Poltava, and the Zdvyzhensky monastery in Poltava. How deeply he was preoccupied with the study of the old hetman state lands may be seen from the scores of localities he visited. He studied his native land with insatiable zeal and enthusiasm.

In Hustyn he was deeply disturbed by the 'barbarous restoration' of the famous monastery by the Russian archimandrite Paisiy, which removed all traces of the old Ukrainian architecture. On 29 June Shevchenko visited the Halahans on their estates in the Pryluky and Chernihiv regions. His impressions of this visit were later eloquently described in his story 'The Musician' ('Muzykant'). He had met Hryhoriy Halahan before. The latter was a very liberal-minded gentleman who, as a young man, had been a great Ukrainophil, while his uncle Petro, the owner of Dekhtiari, was a reactionary magnate. A trip to Irzhavets, also owned by the Halahans, gave the poet some material for a later poem with that title. On 20 July Shevchenko was at a fair in Romny, where, as he later noted in his diary in exile, he spent three days in the hospitable tent of the merrymaker Lev Svichka. In Romny Shevchenko had an opportunity to enjoy a performance by the famous Ukrainian actor Karpo Solenyk, playing the part of Chuprun in Kotliarevsky's *Moskal, the Sorcerer*. To visit the fair at Romny meant meeting nearly all the Poltavan gentry, who had travelled there from their secluded *khutirs*. He could observe all the different

Ukrainian types, reminiscent of Gogol's Sobakeviches, Manilovs, and Nozdrevs. That summer he visited Lubny and the neighbouring Mharsky monastery. Later reminiscences of this precious monument of Ukrainian architecture indicate that it left a lasting impression on the poet. In the Poltava region he also saw old ruins, the remains of old fortifications and towers, and historic gravemounds. He carefully noted down everything that people told him about these relics.

The middle of August was spent with A. Kozachkovsky, a physician and friend in Pereiaslav. They had first met in 1842 in St Petersburg, when Kozachkovsky, then in the Russian navy, returned from a voyage around the world. After leaving the service in 1844, he practised medicine in Pereiaslav. He was a man of high moral principle, a Ukrainian patriot, and was very interested in Ukrainian poetry. While studying local antiquities in Pereiaslav, Shevchenko became a close friend of Kozachkovsky. Both were waiting for the arrival of Professor Bodiansky, who had promised the previous spring to visit Kozachkovsky but then cancelled his visit. Both friends were very disappointed. One of Shevchenko's most vivid impressions of the stay in Pereiaslav was the day spent on Kozachkovsky's *khutir*, Hyrsky, where all the guests walked on the bank of the Dnieper. The poet was enchanted by the views of Pereiaslav, Trakhtemyriv, and Monastyryshche on the hilly right bank of the Dnieper and with the view on to the left bank. This magnificent panorama was later recalled in a poem written in exile, full of nostalgia for Ukraine, beginning with the lines 'My steep hills' ('Hory moi vysokii').

On 19 August Kozachkovsky gave a reception at his home that was attended by many guests, a number of them young. Shevchenko was in a good mood, recited his poems, and charmed everyone with his witty conversation. He stayed at Pereiaslav for nine days. Before leaving he told Kozachkovsky that he was planning to spend the fall in Kharkiv and then pass the winter in Kiev and call again at Pereiaslav on the way. As it happened, he never went to Kharkiv, but at the end of September he revisited Kerelivka. Before visiting his native village he went to see Tarnovsky in Potoky. The Tarnovsky family was one of the few enlightened and patriotic gentry families in Ukraine, and they appreciated Shevchenko's talent. Vasyl Tarnovsky paid close attention to the development of Ukrainian literature and Ukrainian studies, and he had brought up his little son, Vasyl, in this patriotic spirit. Vasyl's sister Nadia was a cultured and pious woman. Simplicity and openness characterized their modest household, run by Maria Tarnovsky, who also admired Shevchenko. What might be called a cult of the poet reigned in that household, even while Shevchenko was alive. There the poet met sympathetic people who shared his interest in Ukrainian life and history. Later, Vasyl Tarnovsky the younger was to donate his rich collection of Ukrainian antiquities, particularly the Shevchenko memorabilia, towards the establishment of the first historical museum to be named after Shevchenko. The poet also struck up a friendship with Vasyl's brother Yakiv, the co-owner of Potoky.

On 26 September Shevchenko participated in a religious festival in his native village. He talked to the villagers and met some of his old schoolfriends. It appears that his arrival in Kerelivka was connected with a plan to get married. As recently as 1843, during an earlier visit there, Shevchenko had noticed Fedosia, the young daughter of Father Hryhoriy Koshyts. His attraction to the girl had grown stronger, and he decided to propose. However, Fedosia's parents had no wish to allow their daughter to marry a former servant, although she loved Shevchenko. She took her parents' refusal so much to heart that later, apparently, she lost her sanity.

Saddened, Shevchenko left Kerelivka and went to visit Lukianovych, who lived like a baron, held frequent receptions, and was an avid hunter. Perhaps through Lukianovych, Shevchenko met another Myrhorod landowner, Pavlo Shershevytsky, whose father had been a Decembrist. Shershevytsky lived a very simple life in Myrhorod, and Shevchenko often visited him. Shevchenko also painted portraits of Lukianovych's family and stayed with them in Mariinske until almost the middle of November. While there he made friends with several of Lukianovych's serfs. Later he also visited the landowner Arkadiy Rodzianko, who wrote bad poetry and who had known Pushkin personally. At the Rodzianko's estate in Vesely Podil, Shevchenko met the Czech composer Vjačeslav Jedlička, who was arranging some Ukrainian songs for the piano. He also met the family of the German physician Drexler, whom he liked very much and later used as prototypes of the doctor Anton Karlovich and his wife in the long story 'The Musician.' Shevchenko left Rodzianko's household quite abruptly after he saw an older servant flogging a younger one. Without even taking his manuscripts Shevchenko hurriedly fled, leaving a house where such violence could occur. Later he left the house of a Lubny landowner after seeing him waking his serf with blows to his body. He could not bear witnessing any injustice.

While fleeing from the Rodziankos Shevchenko caught a severe chill. He locked himself up at a friend's house, read the Bible, and wrote poetry. In spite of his sickness he felt a surge in his creative powers and within two weeks had written such great poems as 'The Heretic' ('Yeretyk'), 'The Blind Man' ('Slipy'), and 'The Great Vault' ('Velyky liokh').

Possibly what led him to Rodzianko was the desire to meet Jedlička, who had known Šafařik and Hanka personally and who was the only one who could tell Shevchenko the details of the story of John Huss, the hero of 'The Heretic.' The primary source for the poem was a book by the young Moscow scholar Palauzov, a pupil of Bodiansky. After reading this scholarly book, Shevchenko created his masterpiece 'in one breath,' as it were, and in the process made some minor factual errors. True, he created his own Huss, a fighter for freedom, who appeared in the poem as a vengeful revolutionary. Huss's prayer

> Consecrate
> For vengeance and for torture,
> Bless, O God, my hands,
> Which are not hard

was Shevchenko's own prayer, the prayer of a Ukrainian revolutionary who, while seeing events in the West, bore in mind his own country's dire situation:

> The robbers and cannibals
> Have vanquished truth,
> They have ridiculed thy glory,
> Thy power and will.
> The earth weeps in its chains
> Like a small child for his mother.
> There is no one to break the chains
> And resist.[1]

The final chord of this revolutionary music was the picture of the bloody warrior Žižka, menacing threateningly with his mace. This was Shevchenko's threat against the Ukrainian magnates 'who without a thought live in debauchery and feasting.'

At the end of October or in early November Shevchenko drove from Myrhorod to the Zakrevskys and, after meeting Chuzhbynsky at Pyriatyn, went to visit him in Iskovets. Just before that he had learnt of the tragic death of Yakiv de Balmen, who had been killed in battle in the Caucasus. Chuzhbynsky, who had recently been to the Caucasus himself, described the area to him. In November, as he had promised, the poet returned to Kozachkovsky in Pereiaslav. The small town of Myrhorod had no doctor

---

1 'Yeretyk,' ibid, 262–3

or pharmacy, and that might have made him, ill as he was, go to Pereiaslav. Kozachkovsky saw to it that Shevchenko received medical attention. Curiously enough, despite, or perhaps because of, his illness, Shevchenko wrote a great deal. In Pereiaslav, in a few days, the poems 'The Servant Girl' ('Naimychka') and 'The Caucasus' ('Kavkaz'), full of Promethean fire, were created. In the latter poem, dedicated to de Balmen, 'who shed his blood not for Ukraine but for her executioner,' Shevchenko poured out all his hatred of Russia and called on all the peoples subjugated by her 'to fight – and you will win!' Kozachkovsky recorded that Shevchenko wrote all this with 'extraordinary ease,' participating, as he was writing, in conversations with other guests.

In December he moved to the nearby *khutir* Viunyshcha, the property of Samoilov, a former Decembrist. He met Samoilov and his family through Kozachkovsky. It was in Viunyshcha, on 14 December, that he wrote what is generally regarded as a true work of genius, his 'Friendly Epistle to My Dead, Living, and Yet Unborn Countrymen' ('Druzhnieie poslaniie i mertvym i zhyvym i nenarodzhenym zemliakam'). After this he wrote 'Kholodny Yar,' verse paraphrases of ten psalms of David, and the poems 'To Little Mariana' ('Malenkii Mariani'), 'The Days Are Passing' ('Mynaiut dni'), and 'Three Years' ('Try lita'). On 22 December he was still there, but for Christmas he went back to Pereiaslav. His illness grew worse. Fearing that he might die, on 25 December he wrote his famous 'Testament' ('Zapovit'). The genesis of this poem was a presentiment that his health would deteriorate. In fact Shevchenko had fallen ill with typhus. Information on this critical period of illness is very scarce, and we do not know how he managed to survive. Later, he moved to Yahotyn.

On 22 December he summed up his tragic impressions of the previous three years. The cycle of poems written in 1843–45 he called 'The Three Years' and in the closing poem of the cycle he wrote:

> Three small years
> Have flown in vain,
> They cause tumult
> In my house.
> They have laid waste
> My poor, quiet heart,
> They ravaged all the good
> And set evil on fire.[2]

He wrote how he 'gradually became enlightened':

---

2 'Try lita,' ibid, 351

> I look closely –
> All around, wherever I look:
> Not men, but serpents...
> My tears dried up,
> My young tears.
> Now my broken heart
> I try to heal with venom –
> I do not cry, I do not sing,
> But howl like an owl.³

These 'enlightening' moments were terrible. He saw clearly that Ukraine was being tortured by her own sons, that she was helpless, unable to resist, that her entire elite had betrayed her. He was convinced that nearly all Ukrainian landowners were 'inhuman,' 'bandits and cannibals,' 'hungry ravens.' He saw how they

> Swap chains,
> Trade in truth,
> Defile God –
> And harness people
> To a heavy yoke.⁴

These 'renegades' rejected all their national traditions; the former 'good glory of Ukraine' was alien to them. They did not want to hear of it, smothered as they were 'with Muscovite henbane' in 'German hothouses.' Poisoned by foreign culture and foreign science, they could not understand that

> In a man's own home [is] a man's own truth,
> And power and freedom.

When, in the backwoods of the Pereiaslav region, he was writing his inspired 'epistle' to these Ukrainian landlords, he called on them to 'embrace the smallest brother' – the serf – beseeching them not to look to 'foreign fields' for answers but to love with all their hearts 'the great ruin.' A vision of a future bloody revolution rose before his eyes, and he implored and threatened these 'inhuman traitors':

> Come to your senses! Be human,
> Or woe will befall you:

---

3 Ibid, 352
4 'I mertvym i zhyvym,' ibid, 329

The Ukrainian Journeys 1843–47

> Soon the people's chains
> Will be broken,
> Judgment will come,
> The Dnieper and the mountains will speak!
> And a hundred streams will flood
> The blue sea with the blood
> Of your children – and no one
> Will help:
> Brother will renounce brother
> And the mother–her child;
> And smoke, like a cloud,
> Will obscure the sun before you,
> And you will be damned for ever
> By your own sons.[5]

This terrible vision alternated with a joyful one, when, on the day of revolution

> Punishment will rain down
> And a new fire will blow
> From the Kholodny Yar.[6]

Laid low by serious illness, thinking of his possible death, with an unsteady hand he wrote his testament, calling on those whose hearts were still living to start a revolution:

> Bury me and rise,
> Break your chains
> And with the foul blood of the foe
> Sprinkle your freedom!
> And in that great family,
> Now free and new
> Do not fail to mention me
> With a soft, kind word.[7]

In the face of death he called, once more, for the armed liberation of Ukraine from the chains of national and social bondage.

After six weeks of illness Shevchenko recovered and had to continue his work for the Archaeographic Commission. As early as 15 November he

5 Ibid, 330–1
6 'Kholodny yar,' ibid, 338
7 'Yak umru,' ibid, 354

had been officially confirmed in this position. He had already visited every corner of the Poltava region, and now he was ready to study the Chernihiv region. His modest annual salary was 150 roubles. While staying at various estates he also earned money by painting.

Shevchenko searched for a travelling companion and found one in Afanasev-Chuzhbynsky, who liked to travel and was a good reporter. Shevchenko called on him in the middle of February, before Lent. He wore a black velvet cap, for his head had been shaved during his illness. From Iskovets both men went to the fair at Lubny and thence, through Pryluky and Nizhyn, to Chernihiv. The fair at Lubny was crowded, and they did not stay long but went to Nizhyn, Gogol's alma mater, and a fine town it was. Several students from the Lyceum visited Shevchenko, and he also met Nikolay Gerbel, the future translator of his poems into Russian. He saw his old friend Soshenko, who was now teaching in Nizhyn. After a Saturday ball, on 23 February, they both left for Chernihiv. They attended a party on Sunday night at a local club, where Shevchenko, surrounded by a host of admirers, spent the last convivial evening before Lent.

With the coming of Lent Shevchenko worked more intensively, sketching various historic monuments in Chernihiv, some of them from Mazepa's time. The leaders of local society invited him to their homes, and the poet was well received everywhere, including the residence of the governor general.

Princess Repnina had long ago asked Shevchenko to visit Andriy Lyzohub, and now he decided to do so. He went to Lyzohub's estate in Sedniv, twenty-five *versts* from Chernihiv. Andriy Lyzohub was an old admirer of Shevchenko's poetry. He lived with his older brother Illia, a retired colonel of the Russian army, a musically gifted and interesting old gentleman. Andriy Lyzohub himself was a good pianist and a talented painter. At his estate he kept an artist's studio. Both brothers were very humane men and treated their serfs very well. Andriy carefully charted the growth of Ukrainian literature, was a connoisseur of Ukrainian folksongs, and corresponded with his neighbours in Ukrainian. Both Lyzohubs came to love Shevchenko 'as a person, a poet, and a highly qualified singer and interpreter of folksongs.' Shevchenko felt quite at home. After his illness and the accompanying creative tension, he relaxed here and recuperated under the very best conditions.

Spring came. The river Snov spread its quiet waters far and wide, and the poet, after a day's painting, feasted his eyes on glorious landscapes. Sometimes he would sing songs accompanied by Andriy Lyzohub; at other times he would sit and listen to old Illia Ivanovych play the cello or just reminisce. Illia was an old freemason, a participant in the Napoleonic wars who had lived in Western Europe for twenty years before retiring to his native Sedniv. Andriy was twenty years younger than his brother. He was the embodiment of human kindness, and his wife and children created a warm and cozy atmosphere in his home. During Lent Shevchenko left Sedniv for a week to visit Chuzhbynsky, who had fallen ill in Chernihiv. The first day of Easter, 7 April, was spent in Sedniv. In the middle of April Shevchenko left for Kiev, where he planned to continue sketching historic sites.

In Kiev Shevchenko stayed at first at an inn on Khreshchatyk, opposite Besarabka. A few days later he visited the young Ukrainian scholar Mykola Kostomarov, who had reviewed his poetry favourably. This meeting happened at the very end of April or early in May. Kostomarov's first impression of Shevchenko was very favourable. 'It was sufficient to talk for an hour to this man,' wrote Kostomarov, 'in order to get to know him and feel friendship for him.' Their second meeting took place in the orchard of the Sukhostavskys' house, which stood at the corner of Khreshchatyk and Besarabka, where Kostomarov lived. The cherry trees and plum trees were in bloom; the lilac was about to burst into blossom, and the birds were singing. In this romantic setting, blessed by a triumphant spring and screened by blossoming branches, Shevchenko recited to Kostomarov his poems from the cycle of 'Three Years.' Kostomarov was overwhelmed. Shevchenko left a copy of his poems with his friend and throughout the entire month of May visited the young scholar regularly.

Shevchenko's new poems captivated Kostomarov. He was the illegitimate child of a Ukrainian serf-woman and of a Russian father, a landowner whom his peasants had murdered. Kostomarov was a highly sensitive man. Brought up on Romantic philosophy and poetry, he was deeply religious, inclined to mysticism and strict moralism. He was enamoured of the people, and the source of his love for the *narod* (people) was Ukrainian folk poetry, which he had begun to study in his student days in Kharkiv. He took an active part in the Ukrainian literary movement, as both a poet and a critic. He praised the *Kobzar* and the 'Haidamaks' highly. Now the author of these poems appeared to him an angelic messenger who, with his fiery words, stirred his soul to the depths. Later in life, in his memoirs, he could still recall the impression that 'The Three Years' had made on him in Kiev:

Taras Hryhorovych read me his manuscript verses. Terror seized me ... I saw that Shevchenko's muse had torn asunder the curtain draped over the people's life. It was terrifying and sweet, painful and tempting, to look inside! Poetry always marches ahead, always dares some bold act: history, science, and practical work follow in its footsteps ... Taras's muse has broken some underground dam, closed by many locks for centuries, buried in the soil, deliberately ploughed and cultivated, so that the very memory of the place where this underground stream flows is hidden from younger generations. Taras's muse daringly entered this cleft with an inextinguishable torch and opened up the way for sunlight, fresh air, and human curiosity. It was easy to step into this subterranean place when air reached it. But what human power can withstand the ancient vapours, which in a trice kill all the forces of life, extinguishing all earthly fires! ... But poetry is not afraid of the deadly vapour, if it is true poetry. And no historical or moral carbonic acid will extinguish this torch, since this torch is aflame with an immortal fire – the fire of Prometheus.[8]

Kostomarov was not the only one to whom Shevchenko brought the 'fire of Prometheus.' It was from Kostomarov that Shevchenko learned of the existence, in Kiev, of the secret Ukrainian society – the Brotherhood of Sts Cyril and Methodius.[9] Early in January 1846 this society had been founded by Mykola Kostomarov, Mykola Hulak, a young scholar specializing in the history of Slavic law, and Vasyl Bilozersky, a student whom Shevchenko had already met. Hulak and Bilozersky managed to attract some new members, mostly students – Opanas Markovych, Oleksander Navrotsky, Yuriy Andruzsky, Ivan Posiada, and Dmytro Pylchykiv. The latter soon left to take up a teaching post in Poltava. Kostomarov himself at first planned it as a purely scholarly circle, a legal 'Slavic society,' but later, under the influence of his friends, he produced the most important ideological documents of the secret society – the constitution, the rules, the proclamations, and the programmatic work 'The Books of Genesis of the Ukrainian People' ('Knyhy bytiia ukrainskoho narodu'). It is impossible to maintain that all these documents existed before Kostomarov's meeting with Shevchenko. On the contrary, one can argue that the Ukrainian part of the 'Books of Genesis' was written after that meeting, since it bears traces of Shevchenko's Promethean ideas.

It is not known whether Kostomarov informed Shevchenko fully about

8 N.I. Kostomarov, 'Iz vospominanii o T.G. Shevchenko,' *Vospominaniia*, 151–2
9 For studies of the brotherhood see M. Vozniak, *Kyrylo-Metodiivske Bratstvo* (Lviv 1921); Z. Hurevych, *Moloda Ukraina* (Kiev 1928); J. Gołabek, *Bractwo Św. Cyryla i Metodego w Kijowie* (Warsaw 1936); P.A. Zaionchkovsky, *Kirilo-Mefodievskoe obshchestvo* (Moscow 1959); and H. Serhienko, *T.H. Shevchenko i kyrylo mefodievske tovarystvo* (Kiev 1983).

The Ukrainian Journeys 1843-47

the brotherhood. Its ideology was clearly spelt out in the documents described above. The statute contained six important points:

1 We hold that the spiritual and political union of the Slavs is the true destiny to which they should aspire.
2 We hold that at the time of their union each Slavic tribe should be independent, and we acknowledge these tribes to be: the South Russians [Ukrainians], the North Russians together with the Belorussians, the Poles, the Czechs with the Slovaks, the Lusatians, the Illiro-Serbians with the Croats, and the Bulgarians.
3 We hold that each tribe should be ruled by the people and should observe the complete equality of citizens according to their birth, Christian faith, and status.
4 We hold that the government, legislation, the right to private property and to education of all the Slavs should be based on the holy religion of our Lord, Jesus Christ.
5 We hold that in this condition of equality, education and pure morals should be a stipulation for participation in government.
6 We believe that a general Slavic council made up of the representatives of all the tribes should come into being.[10]

The chief rules, apart from organizational details, spelled out the brotherhood's goals. The first rule specified that the ideas of the brotherhood should be propagated by educating young people through literature and by enlarging the membership of the organization. Rule seven stressed complete religious tolerance, and rule eight called for the abolition of serfdom and better treatment of the lower classes. The ninth called on members to reconcile their activity with the biblical precepts of love, kindness, and suffering and rejected the idea that ends justify means.

In the proclamation to 'brother Ukrainians' Kostomarov wrote that the new Slavic union would have a parliament (*sejm* or *rada*) of elected deputies to decide on federal matters. At the same time each constituent union member would be a republic and would preserve its own language, literature, and social structure. Each republic was to be headed by a president and the union by a federal president. Deputies and officials should be chosen not according to birth or wealth but according to intelligence and education. The Christian religion was to be the foundation of the legal, social, and political system, based on equality and

---

10 M. Kostomarov, *Knyhy bytiia ukrainskoho narodu* (Augsburg 1947), 29-30

freedom. Social ranks were to be abolished. The proclamation to 'Brother Great Russians and Poles' read as follows:

This is addressed to you by Ukraine, your mendicant sister, whom you dismembered but who does not call attention to this evil, who feels for your misfortunes and is ready to shed the blood of her children for your freedom. Read this fraternal epistle; consider the grave matter of your salvation; rise from your sleep; cleanse from your hearts your hatred for one another, inflamed by tsars and lords to the detriment of your freedom; be mortified by the yoke that burdens your backs; be ashamed of you own depravity; curse the sacrilegious names of the tsars and the lords of this world; purge from your minds the spirit of unbelief, the legacy of German and Romance tribes, and the spirit of impenitence, inspired by the Tatars; clothe yourselves in that love of humanity peculiar to the Slavs, and also remember your brothers, languishing in silken German fetters and in Turkish claws, and let this be the goal of your life and activity: the Slavic Union, universal equality, brotherhood, peace, and the love of our Lord, Jesus Christ. Amen![11]

In the socio-political section of the 'Books of Genesis' the tsarist principles of 'autocracy, orthodoxy, and nationality' were countered by two new principles: the autocracy of God as 'the only Lord,' and a true Christian religion, with full political equality and freedom. The feudal landowners and despotic monarchy were to be replaced by a democratic, constitutional republic, with legislative power vested in a parliament where the government 'does not what it wishes, but what is legislated,' where 'officials and governors are subject to parliament,' where class and social distinctions have been abolished, and where there are neither 'slaves' nor 'magnates' nor 'the destitute.'

Kostomarov relates that when he told Shevchenko about the idea of a Slavic federation, the latter greeted it with enthusiasm. But on another occasion Kostomarov also said that Shevchenko reacted to some of the ideas of the brotherhood with 'great animosity and the utmost intolerance.' There must have been strong disagreements between them.

A great deal of what he heard about the brotherhood from Kostomarov was consonant with Shevchenko's own views. It is enough to read 'The Caucasus' and 'The Epistle,' permeated as they are with a Christian ethical outlook and ideas of national and political liberty, to recall his unhappiness about Slavic disunity in 'Nikita Gaidai,' 'The Haidamaks,' and the epistle to Šafařík, to know that his own ideas were not so very different from those of Kostomarov. If he disagreed with Kostomarov, it

11 Ibid, 27–8

was probably because the brotherhood's program paid little attention to the Ukrainian national cause, which was of prime concern to Shevchenko. Perhaps also the brotherhood's principles of 'love, kindness, and suffering' were unacceptable to him. In order to liberate the subjugated millions and create a 'new, free' family of nations, he thought it was legitimate to use the sword against the oppressors, who held these millions subject by force. He wrote openly about it in 'The Caucasus' and his 'Testament.' It was a voice from the deep, underground cavern of the Ukrainian nation, from 'the great vault, which Moscow could not find,' and towards which he was now leading his countrymen.

As early as May Shevchenko met Hulak, Markovych, and other 'brethren.' He certainly met regularly with Bilozersky. Further discussions had to be postponed until the fall. Shevchenko found himself a place to live, on Kozyne Boloto (later Khreshchatyk Crescent), where he shared rooms with the painter Mykhailo Sazhyn. Chuzhbynsky was his guest at the time. Shevchenko had met Sazhyn at the academy, and they both spent entire days sketching street scenes in Kiev, the interiors of churches, and interesting places. Shevchenko was fascinated by pilgrims and beggars at the famous Lavra monastery with its catacombs. In bad weather he stayed at home and read. 'There was nothing pleasanter,' reminisced Chuzhbynsky, 'than coming home tired in the evening, opening the windows, and sitting down to drink tea and talk about the wonderful impressions of the day.'

Sometimes Shevchenko would visit the homes of the aristocracy, where he was well received 'by haughty dandies and ladies,' with whom he felt ill at ease. He preferred the company of simple people, like Chuzhbynsky's relatives, with whom he consumed good Ukrainian food, or the old guildmasters of Kiev, who had now been deprived of the 'Magdeburg Law'[12] by the tsar. Occasionally he would disappear from his apartment for a couple of days, spending his time in agreeable but not 'lordly' company.

Among the noble families Shevchenko often visited were the Tarnovskys from Potoky, who had a house in Kiev, and their relative Mykhailo Yuzefovych, the assistant trustee of the Kiev school district. Underlining his loyalty to the serfs, Shevchenko often, when visiting these houses, talked to and visited the serfs. One of them, Vasyl, Yuzefovych's servant, became the poet's friend. Shevchenko would spent too much time talking to him in the antechamber before going into the family rooms.

---

12 Magdeburg Law, a form of urban self-government practised in Lithuania, Poland, and Ukraine. In 1831 it was abolished in all cities in Ukraine, and in 1835 in Kiev.

When he left his apartment Shevchenko never failed to take with him some money for the poor in the city streets. Once, when a beggar came up to his window, he gave him a golden half-rouble that was lying on the table. The beggar was astounded and refused the coin, simply because 'old beggars don't carry as much money as that.' Shevchenko had to give him a smaller coin. Sometimes his generosity led to his being swindled. His comment was invariably: 'I know, and it's better to be swindled three times, but the fourth time give money to someone without a piece of bread.' He could rarely refuse anyone who wanted to borrow money from him.

Shevchenko was very fond of small children. Chuzhbynsky has recorded that on their expeditions through the Puriatyn region Shevchenko would 'sit with a circle of children, tell them stories, and sing children's songs.' In Kiev, Chuzhbynsky witnessed a scene when Shevchenko, sketching the Golden Gate, left his work to take care of a small girl abandoned by a drunken nurse. He played with the child, made her a paper toy, and happily handed her back to her mother.

Shevchenko's love for all living things extended to animals. On several occasions he rescued cats and dogs from street urchins, and once he bought a caged bird and returned him to freedom. Once he had a nasty row with a dog-catcher who was beating a dog with a stick. Chuzhbynsky stopped the dog-catcher from beating Shevchenko instead. In his private life the revolutionary poet was always an enemy of the powerful, the 'insatiable tsars.'

In his personal relations Shevchenko often displayed a naïveté bordering on carelessness. After meeting the Russian journalist Askochensky, who later joined the ultra-reactionary camp, Shevchenko read his revolutionary poems to him in the journalist's apartment, even though his host warned him that verses like that might lead to prison. Shevchenko paid no attention and read him more and 'better ones.' It was to be expected, therefore, that because of this carelessness, rumours would begin to circulate about the 'dangerous' works of Shevchenko. His distant relative Varfolomey Shevchenko, who also came from Kerelivka, heard about them. This half-educated, practical-minded peasant, who had bought his own freedom, heard in the summer of 1846 about Shevchenko's 'illegal works' and that some people were warning him not to disseminate them. Hinting in his letter to Shevchenko that this type of activity could lead to exile, he wrote: 'They say that wise men like your works, but some say that they are not nice ... It is possible that they will force those who speak the truth into imprisonment ... When I heard that you had been warned not to broadcast your works among the people because of the sting they carry, I grew very sad.[13] Varfolomey liked Shevchenko's poems, especially 'The Haidamaks,' but was concerned about his safety, since he knew that some Polish students had been jailed for distributing revolutionary poems that were not even their own. Varfolomey's letter was written on 5 July, forty days after Shevchenko had read his poems to Askochensky, who was a tutor to Governor General Bibikov's nephew and lived in Bibikov's house. Shevchenko also read his 'Epistle' to the guests assembled at Tarnovsky's house. The hosts would never harm him, but the same could not be said about their guests. It was not even a question of malevolence towards the poet. A careless remark about his new poetry would be enough, if it were picked up by someone close to government circles, to land him in trouble. Possibly a rumour of that type was circulating about Shevchenko; how else would Varfolomey have heard it?

May and June passed while Shevchenko was busy sketching the magnificent Kievan antiquities. He fell in love with the ancient city. Often, instead of visiting someone, he would walk to the high banks of the Dnieper and sing some songs there while admiring the view. On these occasions he liked to be alone. He had, of course, his favourite places. One of them was the ravine beyond St Michael's monastery. One day Askochensky saw him there, sitting on the ground, his head resting on his hands; he was looking, 'as the Germans say, *dahin*, far into the distance.' The poet was so deep in thought that he did not notice any passers-by. Even more to his liking was the view from the porticos of the Kievan Caves Monastery. He wrote of the view from the famous Lavra: 'For a long time he was unable to forget this famous porch. One day, after attending a morning mass, he stepped out on to this porch: the morning was still and bright, while before his eyes there lay outstretched the entire province of Chernihiv and part of Poltavan too ... The entire picture evoked the mighty chords of Haydn.'[14] It is characteristic that strong aesthetic sentiments were always connected in him with holy, religious experiences.

The image of 'golden-domed Kiev, garlanded with orchards and poplars,' remained vivid in Shevchenko's mind for the rest of his life. In exile, in distant Asian deserts, the Ukrainian 'eternal city' rose in his imagination:

13 *Lysty do T.H. Shevchenka*, 50
14 'Bliznetsy,' *Povne*, IV, 126–7

> As if from heaven suspended
> Lies our great, sacred Kiev.
> Its holy temples shine translucently
> As if talking to God himself.[15]

The pure joy felt on these occasions at the 'immortal beauty of Kiev' was transformed into nostalgia. The poet was aware of the sad fate of Christianity in Ukraine, manipulated as it was by the state church. In the poet's imagination there arose an image of the legendary apostle (Andrew) who had brought the Christian faith to the hilly area of what is now Kiev. 'I see him,' wrote Shevchenko, 'a grey-haired, serious, and gentle old man with a book in his hands who preaches to the astonished barbarians.' But later generations put a 'suit of armour' on that gentle apostle, beginning with the Varangian period of ancient Rus history. Shevchenko was convinced that the first Slavic inhabitants of Kiev, the ancestors of the Ukrainians, were farmers who did not engage in war. Their social order was founded on an equality that Christianity could only reinforce.

As a participant in the work of the Archaeographic Commission Shevchenko met some local scholars, like Ivanishev and Selin, as well as important administrators like Yuzefovych and Governor Ivan Fundukley, the commissioner of local antiquities and the patron of artists as well as the owner of a fine art gallery. He also met many of the local intelligentsia, the military, and other citizens. While sketching the churches and monasteries he met the clergy and monks. Thus he entered into the very core of Kievan society. His study of historical Kiev paved the way to ancient Kiev. He remembered the scholars of the Mohyla Academy, the saintly monks of the Lavra, the generous benefactors of Ukrainian art and culture during the Cossack era, and viewed the old knights, the seminarians, and the burghers as if they were still alive. He recalled the role of the church brotherhoods in Ukraine and felt encouraged by the formation of the new Cyril and Methodius Brotherhood, which was trying to revive some of the old traditions of the nation to which he belonged. He met many of these new brethren, who, as Kulish wrote,

> were in advance of their age.
> And feeling the approaching dawn,
> Have opened a window on the world,
> So that the heavens may be visible.[16]

15 'Varnak,' ibid, II, 84
16 P. Kulish, 'Na nezabud roku 1847,' *Khutorna poeziia* (Lviv 1882); here quoted from Kulish, *Tvory* (Lviv 1908), I, 270

At times Shevchenko felt moments of childlike happiness, as when, on 4 June, meeting Kostomarov, who had just delivered his first lecture at the university, he started to sing in the street, oblivious to the passers-by, happy for his friend's success.

July was approaching, and during the vacation Shevchenko was asked to join Professor Ivanishev's archaeological expedition, which was to conduct excavations of the Scythian mound, known as Perepeta, in the region of Khvastiv. Apart from Shevchenko, two other illustrators, Senchylo-Stefanivsky and Prushynsky, were included in the expedition. Shevchenko sketched little and was more interested in collecting popular legends about the gravemounds of the era as well as folksongs, especially songs about Paliy and Mazepa. While walking through the area he visited Bila Tserkva. The region around Khvastiv and Bila Tserkva was the scene, from 1694 to 1714, of the last attempt by Right Bank Cossacks to defend their land from the Russians. This attempt proved unsuccessful because of the policies of Tsar Peter I, who was being assisted by the still-loyal hetman Mazepa. This tragic episode of Ukrainian history was deeply felt by Shevchenko. The material he collected and the thoughts and experiences he felt at that time gave rise to a historical poem, 'Irzhavets,' written a year later, beyond the Urals, in which these lines stress Ukraine's tragedy:

> If they only knew
> And would unite the hetman
> With the colonel of Khvastiv [Paliy].

The wide fields around Khvastiv belonged to the Kievan Catholic bishops. The remnants of Paliy's fortifications evoked in the poet feelings similar to those he experienced among the ruins of Chyhyryn:

> Fortresses stand in Ukraine –
> All – Paliy's, in Khvastiv land;
> In the valleys and swamps cannons lie.
> What for? No one needs them,
> The Jews alone own the Khvastiv hills
> While the people of 'Khvastiv slave for Polish priests.[17]

In Bila Tserkva Shevchenko visited a local ethnographer, the Polish

---

17 'Kniazhna,' *Povne*, II, 24–36. This is an early variant of the poem, written in 1847 in Orsk.

priest Izopolsky, and shared with him his collection of folksongs. He also saw the beautiful residence of the magnate Branicki, along with Aleksandria, one of the handsomest private parks in Europe, founded by Countess Aleksandra, sister of Shevchenko's old master, Vasiliy Engelhardt.

By the end of July Shevchenko was back in Kiev. On 25 July he wrote his poem 'Lily' ('Lileia'), and on 9 August the poem 'Mermaid' ('Rusalka') – both probably inspired by the folk ballads he collected in the Vasylkiv region. He also received a long letter from Kulish containing a thorough critical analysis of *Kobzar* and 'The Haidamaks.' Some of Kulish's criticisms were to the point; others were not. He suggested several emendations in the texts of 'The Haidamaks' and 'Catherine.' He also envisaged the publication of Shevchenko's works abroad in a German translation. Kulish's chief objection was that Shevchenko's poetry was too spontaneous and showed little craftsmanship. Only by applying himself more thoroughly to his craft, in Kulish's opinion, would Shevchenko reach the pinnacle of art, higher than that of Pushkin. Kulish deliberately chose a rigorous critical approach, sharply different from the adulatory reaction to Shevchenko of his countrymen. His letter contained the first insightful opinion of Shevchenko's *oeuvre*: 'Your works do not belong to you alone and to your own time; they belong to the whole of Ukraine, and they will speak for it for ever.'

On 9 August the poet was still in Kiev. Then he took a short trip to Slobidska Ukraine. We know little about it, except that on 14 August he visited Okhtyrka, the native town of the poet Shchoholiv. His reason for the visit might have been the cathedral in that town, built by Rastrelli and decorated with Italian paintings. He had wanted to visit Kharkiv for a long time. Why he did not go to Kharkiv from Okhtyrka we shall never know. Kharkiv was a prominent centre of Ukrainian cultural life in the 1820s and 1830s and was the site of the first university in Ukraine. However, by 21 September Governor General Bibikov ordered Shevchenko to travel to the provinces of Kiev, Podillia, and Volhynia. Up to now Shevchenko had visited most places in the area of the old hetman state, knew the eastern part of the Kiev region well, and had travelled through the Ukrainian steppes. Now he was to see the western part of the country – Volhynia and Podillia. He drove through picturesque Berdychiv and Zhytomyr to Kamianets Podilsky. The latter town is especially colourful during the fall. One can only guess at the enthusiasm with which Shevchenko greeted the golden appearance of the town which he reached early in October. He must have painted some landscapes at the time, but none has been preserved.

A friend of Kulish, P. Chuikevych, who was an amateur ethnographer, was a teacher in Kamianets Podilsky. He was very helpful to Shevchenko in his archaeological and ethnographic research. He knew the area extremely well and was hoping to go abroad with Kulish, who had a high opinion of him. It is likely that Shevchenko told Chuikevych about the secret Brotherhood of Sts Cyril and Methodius.

We do not know the exact itinerary of Shevchenko's travels from Podillia to Volhynia. On 20 October he reached Pochaiv, where he drew, from several angles, the famous Pochaiv Lavra monastery, as well as the interior of the Church of the Assumption. He visited Vyshnivka, Kremianets, and the battlefield of Berestechko. Before leaving Kiev he was briefed by Kostomarov on all the historic sites in the area. Shevchenko was close to the Austrian border and must have thought of the Ukrainian land of Galicia just beyond that border. He had heard a great deal about the young Galicians from Bodiansky and Lukashevych who had visited the country. 'Shevchenko knew some Galician songs, and now, so close to Galicia he could not help thinking about the Ukrainians in Austro-Hungary. He was at the very place where illegal anti-Russian Polish propaganda was smuggled into eastern Ukraine from the west, together with calls for the abolition of serfdom.

After making a few sketches of Pochaiv, which was on his official itinerary, he was to travel to Volhynia, Polissia, and to the Kovel region, to sketch the monuments of Prince Kurbsky. He must have passed through Dubno and Lutsk. During his trip he saw many ruined castles, which, for him, were a reminder of the oppression of the *narod*. From his later reminiscences we can see that the trip through Volhynia stirred up in the poet's mind thoughts similar to those he had had while visiting Chyhyryn and Khvastiv. The journey was exhausting but very rewarding, since he learned a great deal about the history and folklore of the region.

Returning to Kiev in November, Shevchenko decided to visit Yahotyn. He was going to ask a favour from the old Princess Repnina, whose sister was married to Count Uvarov, the minister of education. Shevchenko wanted her to intercede on his behalf since he was applying for a position as teacher of drawing at Kiev University. The position had recently become vacant. If there many applicants, his chances would be improved if he were to be recommended to Uvarov. He made his application to General Traskin and to Governor General Bibikov, who was also the head of the Archaeographic Commission for which Shevchenko was working. In his application to Bibikov the poet also offered his services to the lithographic division of the university. In the meantime he polished up his sketches from the Volhynian trip and, along with the songs, legends, and historical documents, presented them to Bibikov on 31 December.

During the period from the end of November to the beginning of January Shevchenko may have become acquainted with the members of the Brotherhood of Sts Cyril and Methodius. In the spring of 1846 he had only met Kostomarov, who left for Odessa in June for medical reasons. Hulak had also left Kiev. Bilozersky was preparing for his final exams at the university and had no time to meet Shevchenko, who was very busy himself. It was the long November and December evenings that were more conducive to meetings and discussions. Shevchenko probably got to know the younger members of the brotherhood better: Markovych, Navrotsky, Posiada, and Andruzsky. The latter even left a short poem addressed to Shevchenko. The brethren eagerly read and copied Shevchenko's poems from the cycle 'Three Years.' As they had been to Kostomarov and Hulak, these poems were to the young brethren a kind of heavenly revelation. The brethren had been brought up in a Christian spirit and had always attempted to do some good for serfs and for their unhappy native land. Shevchenko's poetry boldly proclaimed to them that

> Ukraine will rise,
> Will light the beacon of truth,
> And the slave children
> Will pray in freedom.[18]

Moreover, the 'new cannibals' – the Russians and their renegade Ukrainian friends – were threatened with a bloody revolution; the scales would fall from the eyes of the poet's countrymen, and they would realize the tragic consequences of the union of Ukraine and Muscovy at the time of Bohdan Khmelnytsky.

Kulish, who came back to Kiev for Christmas 1846, was surprised at the activities of his old friends, and Shevchenko's new poems made a deep impression on him. Writing later about those days in Kiev he could say:

Our youthful dreams, it seemed to me, have found a justification: the kingdom of higher wisdom, the kingdom of blessed intentions, was, as it were, at hand ... Our youthful dreams have found in Shevchenko their realization ... The Kievans were very happy and the happiest among them was Shevchenko. He, like the others, felt that, as a poet, he was fulfilling his highest hopes. His muse was protesting

---

18 'Stoit v seli Subotovi,' *Povne*, I, 307

The Ukrainian Journeys 1843-47

strongly against the evil of those in power ... If one can ever say truthfully that the heart came to life, the eyes grew bright, and over men's foreheads appeared flaming tongues, it was at that moment in Kiev ... Shevchenko himself was not the man I had known when I left Ukraine. He was no longer merely a minstrel, but a national prophet...The Kievan intelligentsia surrounded the Ukrainian poet with the deepest admiration ... They looked upon him as a light from heaven ... for me the radiance of his spirit was something supernatural.[19]

On the first day of Christmas Shevchenko, Kostomarov, Markovych, and others gathered to sing carols at Hulak's apartment. Among them was the landowner Mykola Savych, who had recently returned from Paris. They talked about a Slavic federation, the division of Russia into separate parts, the preparation for a popular uprising, and the possibility of a revolution. The discussions lasted till three o'clock in the morning. Next day Kulish arrived in Kiev and was met with great respect. All of them met again and wanted to make him the leader of their organization. The most urgent matter under discussion, this time at Kostomarov's apartment, was the publication of a journal in Ukrainian. Other matters were also hotly debated there. Kulish and Shevchenko defended the Ukrainian national cause. In supporting Kulish, Shevchenko 'expressed himself in unprintable terms about the existing order.' He recited his poems, among them his 'Epistle.' For him this Christmas was a true festival: the revolutionary spirit and the nationalism of his friends were intensified under the influence of his fiery poetry.

On 1 January 1847 Kulish left Kiev for Borzna, after inviting Shevchenko to his wedding. Kulish was going to marry the sister of Vasyl Bilozersky, Oleksandra. On 9 January Shevchenko and Hulak left Kiev individually. Hulak went to St Petersburg, Shevchenko to visit his friend Viktor Zabila, near Borzna. 'Kulish's wedding was held at the *khutir* Motronivka on 24 January. Nearly all the relatives of the bride were present. Vasyl Bilozersky had arrived from Poltava. Kulish had invited Kostomarov, telling him to come and see 'the representatives of the Ukrainian people.' Kostomarov was unable to come, but Shevchenko came and assumed the role of best man. The wedding was conducted with all the traditional ceremonies. Shevchenko was in an excellent mood. He liked the atmosphere in Bilozersky's home and praised the bride for her good Ukrainian. Certainly the bridegroom, his best man, and Vasyl Bilozersky were indeed true representatives of the young Ukrainian

---

19 P. Kulish, 'Istorychne opovidannia,' *Khutorna poeziia*; here quoted from Kulish, *Tvory*, I, 377-85

intelligentsia. Viktor Zabila, who was older, was an excellent raconteur and singer and got on well with the others. There was singing to the accompaniment of a piano or a *bandura*. Shevchenko was the chief soloist, singing his favourite, 'Starlet' ('Zironka'), to everybody's delight. Oleksandra Kulish was so enchanted by Shevchenko that she was ready to give her entire dowry (three thousand roubles) to the poet to enable him to travel abroad. Kulish, without disclosing the source of the funds to Shevchenko, persuaded him to accept the gift. Shevchenko was overjoyed, 'like a child.' At the same time Shevchenko thought of the journey abroad as something that would happen in the future. For the time being he was still anxious to obtain the position at Kiev University. In his enthusiastic dreams he was already planning a separate Ukrainian academy of fine arts.

From the end of January to March Shevchenko stayed with various friends in the Chernihiv region. He visited the newlyweds for a while, then visited Zabila and a new friend, Mykola Bilozersky, an amateur ethnographer, in Mykolaivka. He painted portraits and in his free moments sang for his hosts, the Bilozerskys and the Sredbolskys. He was an accomplished singer of Ukrainian folksongs. Vasyl Bilozersky later remembered how 'he sang, while walking across the room, his hands behind his back, his proud head bowed, a scarf tied around his neck, with a sad expression on his face, and in a thin, quiet voice.' Old Mrs. Bilozerska and the stern old Sredbolsky were unable to listen to these songs without tears.

In a letter written from Borzna to Kostomarov on 1 February Shevchenko inquired about his appointment at the university. He asked that a reply should be sent to Zabila's address in Borzna. In the same letter he wrote: 'I am not writing about the brotherhood since there is nothing to report. When we meet we'll cry together.' He told Kostomarov that he planned to be in Chernihiv. At the end of February, in a letter written to Chernihiv, Kostomarov told Shevchenko that he had been appointed to the university position and asked him to return to Kiev as soon as possible. In the meantime, after a short stay in Chernihiv, Shevchenko visited the Lyzohubs in Sedniv. He did not, therefore, receive Kostomarov's letter and did not return to Kiev. Easter that year was very early – 23 March. School vacations began on 16 March. Even had he received Kostomarov's letter, there would have been no point in hurrying to reach Kiev. Shevchenko decided to spend Easter in Sedniv, as he had the previous year.

In Sedniv Shevchenko painted and wrote a great deal. Four *versts* from there, in the village of Bihachi, there lived the landowner Prince

Keikuatov, a Georgian who had married a daughter of Platon Lukashevych, whom Shevchenko met in 1843 at the Repnins. Having been invited to paint a portrait of the princess, Shevchenko visited Bihachi, sometimes accompanied by Lyzohub. Whenever he had to spend a night there he inevitably preferred the company of the prince's servants. 'Shevchenko loved to talk to simple people and avoided the prince's company, though he was often invited to join him.'

In Sedniv he took walks to the village. In the evenings concerts were held at the Lyzohubs' home, and he often sang there. He stayed until 4 April. On 7 March he wrote the poem 'Aspen' ('Osyka'), which he later renamed 'The Witch' ('Vidma'). A day later he wrote a preface to the second edition of *Kobzar*, which was to include the ballads 'Lily' and 'Mermaid,' the poem 'Aspen' and other poems printed in 1841–43 in various almanacs, besides the poem 'Hamaliia.' Because of the censorship he could not include poems from the cycle 'Three Years' except for 'Servant Girl' ('Naimychka') and 'The Blind Man' ('Slipy'). The censor might possibly pass the 'Psalms of David.' Shevchenko's plan to publish a new collection of poems may have been discussed with Kulish at the latter's wedding in Motronivka. As we know, Kulish was interested in publishing Shevchenko's poems abroad, but this could not be easily accomplished, since the copyright was held by the bookseller Lisenkov. However, the idea of a new publication might have been a result of the meeting with Kulish.

Shevchenko's preface to the second *Kobzar* is a most important document that shows how deeply interested the poet was in Ukrainian literature and what firm views he held on that subject. It was a kind of manifesto addressed to Ukrainian writers. Finding that Ukrainian literary production was lagging badly while other Slavic literatures were developing, Shevchenko sharply condemned Kotliarevsky's imitators, who, in his view, identified the national with the vulgar. He pleaded for a serious grasp of national life and remarked ironically that it had been limited so far to Kotliarevsky's travesty of the *Aeneid* and to tavern anecdotes. He demanded that literature reflect the true life of the Ukrainian people and their view of the world. He indicated the gulf dividing those who wrote about the people from the people themselves. 'In order to know people,' he wrote, 'one must first of all *become human*' (italics in the original). He scornfully rejected all the opponents of a separate Ukrainian literature, who pointed to the fact that Gogol wrote in Russian and Walter Scott in English. He claimed that both these writers had received a foreign education, and in contrast to them he mentioned Robert Burns, 'a great poet of the people.' Some of Shevchenko's remarks were very insightful.

He called Kotliarevsky's great work 'a joke in the Muscovite vein,' blamed Kvitka for not 'listening properly to the speech of the people,' and scolded Hulak-Artemovsky for ceasing to write and becoming a 'lord' (*pan*). He ended his preface with an attack on two types of renegades: petty Russified officials, spineless and obsequious, and 'wise and scholarly men' who also exchanged Ukraine for Russia. At the end he showed a little regret for his censorious style. This literary epistle, direct and forthright, was the first open rejection of the 'common Russian' (*obshcherussky*) theory of language and literature. 'Pay no attention to the Russians,' he wrote; 'let them write in their way and we will write in our way. They have a *narod* and a literature, and we have a *narod* and a literature.' His last words were spoken with the zeal of an evangelist: 'Woe to us! But, brethren, do not lose heart, and work wisely in the name of our hapless mother Ukraine.'[20]

This was his last literary effort before the great change awaiting Shevchenko. His last artistic effort was the magnificent portrait of Princess Keikuatova. When it was finished Shevchenko remained in Sedniv for Easter, and early in April he made his way to Kiev. He was anxious to be in time for Kostomarov's wedding. He had been asked, again, to be the best man. At the Brovary station he changed into formal dress, but when the ferry reached the Kievan bank of the Dnieper, he was arrested by the police, who were awaiting his arrival. He was taken to Fundukley, the governor of Kiev, along with all his baggage, which contained his illegal poems.

20 For the complete text see *Povne*, VI, 312–15.

PART FOUR

Arrest and Exile

1847-57

VII

Shevchenko's arrest happened on 5 April 1847. An hour later Shevchenko was facing the governor, who joked about the poet's festive dress. When Shevchenko explained that he was on his way to be the best man at Kostomarov's wedding, Fundukley exclaimed 'Aha! Where the bridegroom is there should the best man be, too!' Kostomarov had been arrested on 26 March and had already been taken to the gaol in St Petersburg. In Shevchenko's bag the police found six portfolios containing sketches, many poems, letters, and other papers. After looking at these papers the governor wrote the next day to the Third Section of His Majesty's Own Chancery: 'Among the papers a book of [Shevchenko's] poems has been found, some of them rebellious and criminal.'[1] The papers, therefore, as incriminating evidence, were dispatched, along with their owner, to St Petersburg. On 6 April Shevchenko, escorted by police officer Grishkov, left Kiev after only one night in the local gaol. He could not help but realize the seriousness of the situation, but his spirits were good, and one stationmaster remarked on the way: 'Looking at you two, you can't tell who is under arrest and who is escorting whom.' Shevchenko seemed carefree; he joked and sang along the way. Eleven days later, on 17 April, the poet and his escort reached the notorious building of the Third Section in St Petersburg that also housed the gaol.

Shevchenko's arrest was the consequence of a denunciation by a student, Oleksiy Petrov, concerning the existence of a secret political society, the statute of which Petrov had earlier delivered to the curator of the Kiev educational district, General Traskin. Petrov, who had rented a room on 1 November 1846 in the same house as Hulak, overheard through

---

1 The Third Section of His Majesty's Own Chancery, formed by Nicholas I in 1826, performed the functions of a secret police. It was known for its repressive actions, and its head was assassinated in 1878. The Third Section was abolished in 1880, and its functions were transferred to the Ministry of the Interior.

the wall the conversations of Hulak's guests, the members of the Sts Cyril and Methodius Brotherhood. He met Hulak and, pretending to hold republican views, gained the latter's confidence. Hulak showed Petrov the statute and other literature dealing with the brotherhood and read him four poems by Shevchenko, which Petrov described in his denunciation as 'clearly expressing illegal sentiments.' During a brief interrogation by Yuzefovych, Petrov related the contents of Shevchenko's 'Dream' and 'Epistle,' adding that in the first poem Shevchenko 'vehemently expresses his hatred for the imperial family' and in the second 'he incites Ukrainians to an uprising.'

On 17 March, when the Third Section received information from Kiev about the secret 'Slavic society,' the chief, Count Alexey Orlov, ordered the arrest of Hulak, who was in St Petersburg. Among his papers the gendarmes found 'The Books of Genesis of the Ukrainian People,' a work 'of most criminal intent,' and some letters from Kulish, Markovych, Bilozersky, and other brethren. The police particularly noted a passage in Bilozersky's letter: 'What a genius we have in Taras Hryhorovych, for only a genius with his deep emotion can guess the true needs of the people, of the entire century, something which rational thought cannot give us without poetic and religious fire.'

Count Orlov dispatched orders to Ukraine to mount a search for the men mentioned in Hulak's correspondence and named in Petrov's denunciation, among them Shevchenko. Pisarev, the Kievan expert in ferreting out secret societies, was in St Petersburg with his superior Bibikov. He was not satisfied with Orlov's order and suggested that all the men be arrested immediately. On 23 March Orlov agreed with Pisarev and sent the appropriate order to Prince Dolgorukov, the governor general of Left Bank Ukraine, since Bilozersky and Shevchenko were believed to be in the Chernihiv region. Before Dolgorukov could request the governor of Chernihiv to carry out the order, Shevchenko, as we know, arrived in Kiev and fell into the hands of the police.

On 26 March, before Shevchenko's arrest, his poems 'The Dream,' 'The Epistle,' and a fragment from 'The Great Vault' were found during a search of Kostomarov's apartment. On 3 April the gendarmes took from Bilozersky in Warsaw an entire booklet containing Shevchenko's poems. During Shevchenko's arrest they confiscated the whole cycle 'The Three Years.' Many letters seized by the police at Kostomarov's apartment mentioned Shevchenko. The longer the inquiry into the brethren lasted, the more evident it became that they were all under Shevchenko's influence. The respect shown to him reached beyond the circle of the brotherhood. Artists (Bashylov, de Balmen) illustrated his works; scholars

(Metlynsky) worried about him; poets (Aleksandrov, Chuzhbynsky, Andruzsky) eulogized him. His name and his works were widely revered, and he was called father (*batko*) and leader (*otaman*).

The gendarmes took it upon themselves to study those of Shevchenko's works that they had confiscated. The assistant chief of police, General Dubelt, also read Shevchenko's printed works and was astonished to find that the censors had let through poems that, according to him, 'deplored the sufferings of Ukraine,' 'awakened hatred towards the Russians,' and 'remembering the ancient freedom, accused contemporary Ukrainians of indifference.' The police also commented on the poems found in Bilozersky's possession and described them as 'written in order to sow dissatisfaction among the people with the government.'

On 17 April police officer Grishkov brought Shevchenko before the Third Section. On the same day Shevchenko was questioned and was asked to answer several charges in writing. His behaviour was restrained and cautious. He categorically denied membership in the Brotherhood of Sts Cyril and Methodius and answered no to ten questions that concerned the brotherhood.[2] He answered only those charges that referred to him personally. As for his relations with Kostomarov, Hulak, and Kulish, he claimed that he met them infrequently and that he knew little about the other brethren. In his written testimony there was not one word that might compromise his friends. His answers were brief, almost laconic. Some of the questions were formulated very shrewdly. The investigators reminded him that his freedom had been purchased by the imperial family, a fact he could not deny. 'Which incidents,' the question continued, 'encouraged in you the impertinence and ingratitude of writing exceedingly insolent verses attacking the emperor ... and thus forgetting your personal benefactors?' Shevchenko's answer was very diplomatic. He said that while he was still in St Petersburg he had heard insults and complaints directed against the tsar and his government. Then, while travelling in Ukraine, he had heard more grievances and saw the oppression of the serfs by the landowners, and this led him to write the insolent verses attacking the tsar, for which he was sorry. For perhaps the first time in his life he restrained his emotion, since he realized that the most severe punishment awaited him as a result of the evidence that the police had in their hands. By feigning contrition he was safeguarding himself against further severe consequences. But he did voice openly his

---

2 The first and only complete transcript of the interrogation was published by M. Hrushevsky in 'Materialy do istorii Kyrylo-Metodiivskoho bratstva,' *Zbirnyk pamiaty Tarasa Shevchenka* (Kiev 1915); hereinafter referred to as *Materialy*.

observations on the oppression of the peasants 'in the name of the tsar and the government.' Two other questions deserve some attention. Question 15 read: 'What was your purpose in composing verses that may incite Ukrainians against the government? Why did you read them and other slanders at gatherings of your friends, and why did you allow them to be copied? Did you not compose these verses in order to propagate the idea of a secret society, and did you not hope to evoke an uprising in Ukraine?'[3] Shevchenko answered that Ukrainians liked his poems, which he had composed without ulterior motives, and that he did not allow them to be copied but was careless and did not hide them properly. Question 18 read: 'Why did your friends like your verses, although they contain no sense of beauty – were they not appreciated simply for their insolent and rebellious thoughts?' Shevchenko's answer was: 'My verses were possibly liked because they were written in Ukrainian.'

After this inquiry he was left alone for three weeks. The prison cell was clean; it was possible to look out through the bars into the street, and the food was passable. The police were even ready to indulge some inmates by buying cream, cigarettes, and cognac for them. Shevchenko had no complaints, but he felt isolated and had nothing to do. When he asked for books to read, he was given the Bible, which pleased him very much (his own copy, given to him by Varvara Repnina, had been left somewhere in Ukraine). He also asked for paper on which to draw. But most important, he started to write poetry, and before 19 May he had completed six short poems. On that day, looking through the window, he saw Kostomarov's mother come to visit her son. Seized with this image he wrote a poem dedicated to Kostomarov in which, apart from evoking a mother's tragedy, he expressed some thoughts of his own:

> The merry sun was hiding
> Among spring clouds,
> The chained guests
> Were given tea to drink
> While the blue-uniformed guards
> Were being changed.
> I have grown somewhat accustomed
> To the locked door
> And the prison grille ...
> I did not mourn
> The old, buried,
> Forgotten and bloody tears –

3 *Materialy*, 166

> And many of them were shed
> On an empty field ... Nothing,
> Not even rue did sprout!
> And I remembered my village.
> Whom did I leave there and when?
> My father and my mother lie in their graves ...
> My heart was wounded with grief
> For there is no one to remember me!
> I look: it is, my brother, your mother,
> Blacker than the earth,
> Walking, as if taken down from the cross ...
> I pray to God, I pray!
> I will not stop praising him,
> That I'll not share with anyone
> My prison and my chains.[4]

After writing some lyrical ballads and a historical ballad, 'Beyond the Wooded Valley' ('Za bairakom bairak'), about a romantic group of three hundred dead and damned Cossacks whom the earth would not receive because of their treason, Shevchenko composed a masterful poem, 'It Is All the Same to Me' ('Meni odnakovo'), the words of which, 'In our glorious Ukraine, / This land of ours that is not ours,' are often quoted today. The ending of that poem is very dramatic:

> But it is not all the same to me,
> When evil men lull Ukraine to sleep
> And will waken her afire
> And plundered.
> It is not all the same to me.[5]

All the poems Shevchenko wrote while he was under arrest are marked by great artistry. The spell was broken on 15 May, when he was called to a confrontation (*ochnaia stavka*) with Yuriy Andruzsky. He was the youngest (nineteen years old) of the brethren, and his testimony was rather voluble. Noticing his fear and lack of moral fibre, the gendarmes realized that he was ready to tell all. Not only did he tell them what he knew, but he embroidered a lot while describing the activities of each of the accused. Andruzsky's testimony was particularly damaging to Shevchenko. He

---

4 'M. Kostomarovu,' *Povne*, II, 14
5 'Meni odnakovo,' ibid, 9–10

called the poet the 'immoderate representative of a Ukrainian party, which was attempting to restore the hetman state', and claimed that he abused all monarchists, that his presence enlivened all the brethren, that he glorified Hetman Mazepa, and that during the evenings at Kostomarov's apartment he read his 'slanderous verses.' During the brief confrontation all these charges were read to Shevchenko, who denied them all and forced Andruzsky to admit that his testimony as to Shevchenko's membership in the organization was based only on the fact that Shevchenko knew all the accused. Shevchenko continued to deny membership in the brotherhood but admitted to writing 'insolent and rebellious' verses.

During Hulak's confrontation with Bilozersky and Kostomarov, the former maintained his ignorance of the brotherhood. This enraged Count Orlov, who began stamping his feet and shouting. Kostomarov, already ill and distraught, was very depressed by this scene. Shevchenko, while returning to his cell with Kostomarov, tried to cheer him up by saying 'Don't worry, Mykola, we will live together one day.' Answering a gendarme who said 'God is merciful, Taras Grigorievich, you will confess and your muse will sing again,' Shevchenko replied, jokingly, 'It is that devilish muse that has brought us all here.' The poet showed great courage and steadfastness and tried to encourage the others.

The inquiry finished at the end of May, and Count Orlov prepared a report for the tsar, in which punishment was suggested for each of the accused. He wrote of Shevchenko as follows:

Instead of being eternally grateful to the members of the august family, who bought him out of serfdom, this artist composed poems in Ukrainian that were most rebellious in content. He wept about the imagined oppression and misery of Ukraine, glorified the hetman government and the ancient liberties of the Cossacks, and then, with incredible effrontery, heaped slander and bile on the members of the imperial house, forgetting that they were his benefactors. Making allowance for the fact that young people and those of weak character are attracted to the forbidden, Shevchenko acquired among his friends the reputation of a brilliant Ukrainian writer, and so his poems are doubly harmful and dangerous. His favourite poems could be disseminated in Ukraine, inducing thoughts about the alleged happy times of the hetman era, the exigency of the return of those times, and the possibility of Ukraine's existence as a separate state.

Taking into account the extraordinary respect with which all Ukraino-Slavicists have treated Shevchenko and his works, it appeared at first that he might have been, if not an active conspirator, then an instrument that was used for their plans. All the same, their plans were not very important, and Shevchenko had started to write rebellious poems in 1837, when the Kievan scholars were not interested in Slavic ideas. The entire inquiry shows that Shevchenko did not belong to the Ukraino-Slavist Society and acted independently, wrapped up as he was in his own self-destruction. However, because of his insolence and his rebellious spirit, which are boundless, he must be regarded as one of the most important criminals.[6]

Considering Shevchenko's 'strong physique,' Orlov proposed that he be sent on military service to the distant Orenburg Corps. Nicholas I wrote in his own handwriting on Orlov's report: 'Under the strictest surveillance, prohibited from writing or painting.' On 30 May Count Orlov and General Dubelt announced the tsar's sentence to all the brethren, assembled together. The heaviest punishment was meted out by the tsar to Shevchenko. A slightly less severe sentence was given to Hulak, who had refused to say anything and did not implicate his friends. He was sentenced to solitary confinement for three years in the notorious Schlisselburg fortress. Kulish, Kostomarov, and Navrotsky were, after a term of imprisonment, to be exiled to distant places; Bilozersky was exiled to Petrozavodsk, and Andruzsky and Posiada were to be allowed to complete their studies at the University of Kazan. All were banned from returning to Ukraine. Kulish, Kostomarov and Hulak were forbidden to publish.

Shevchenko listened to his sentence 'with unperturbed calmness' and even asked Dubelt if he would be allowed to correspond with his friends, and a positive reply was given. The reading of the sentences came with a request from the gendarmes that the accused should admit their guilt and repent. After undergoing this moral humiliation, Shevchenko the same day wrote his poem 'He Walks over the Fields' ('Ponad polem ide'), a real *marche funèbre*, a hymn to invincible death. The sombre musical quality of this poem gives the best indication of his mood. Possibly on the same day he also wrote a poem addressed to his brethren:

> Shall we ever meet again?
> Or have we parted for ever?
> Bearing the words of truth and love
> Into the steppes and wastelands!
> Let it be! It was not our mother
> We had to honour!
> It is God's will! Obey it,

6 Here quoted from P. Zaionchkovsky, *Kirilo-Mefodievskoe*, 132

> Be humble, pray to God,
> And remember one another;
> Love your Ukraine,
> Adore her in the piercing times of evil,
> In the last terrible moment
> Pray to God for her.[7]

This was not an expression of resignation but rather an acknowledgment of a terrible defeat on a national scale. The sentence meant that the most prominent Ukrainian young people would be for ever denied the possibility of working for their country, for its cultural renewal, and for their ideas of 'brotherhood and love.' It was a catastrophe. A year and a half earlier the poet had called on all Ukrainians to 'embrace the smallest brother.' Later he came to believe that this was indeed possible. Now he realized that that path had been brutally blocked. He wondered if the brethren would ever be able to continue their work. At this saddest of moments in his personal life he thought not about himself but about the national cause and those friends who were dedicated to it.

These two poems were Shevchenko's answer to the edict forbidding him to write. He was sure that all these events were 'God's will,' and there is a note of final resignation in his lines about death:

> It will not pass me by,
> It will mow me down in a foreign land,
> Smother me behind a prison grille
> And none will erect a cross,
> None will remember me![8]

A few days earlier he had expressed a similar feeling:

> My heart grows cold when I think
> That they will not bury me in Ukraine,
> That I will no longer live in Ukraine
> And love men and God there.[9]

The separation from his native land might be a long one, perhaps for ever. That was his fate. The following day he was sent into exile.

---

7 'Chy my shche ziidemosia znovu,' *Povne*, II, 18
8 'Kosar,' ibid, 17
9 'V nevoli tiazhko,' ibid, 16

VIII

In order to understand more fully why the young Ukrainian intelligentsia of the 1840s followed Shevchenko with such enthusiasm and why he, as well as they, was attracted to pan-Slavism, it is necessary to study the intellectual climate of the time. The new ideas came from the West, but they assumed a new colouring in Ukraine, turning towards a national revival and a new social outlook. The most salient belief to which Shevchenko and his friends subscribed was known as Rousseauism, after Rousseau's doctrine of the innate goodness of man, corrupted by civilization. The second premise of the new outlook was the belief that each nation had its own destiny, its place in world history, a belief propounded by many German philosophers. Rousseau's theories spurred enormous interest in the life of the common people (*narod*) and in folklore. At the end of the eighteenth century Herder, the godfather of European Romanticism, turned his attention to the study of folk poetry and came to the conclusion that the folk poetry of the Slavic peoples, the least touched by civilization, was the richest and most artistic. He propounded a theory about the special world mission of the Slavic peoples.[1] The study by the Slavic scholars of the period of the native Slavic histories and folk literatures took for granted the common origin of all the Slavs and the existence of a proto-Slavic people. The study of Slavic languages supported this assumption. After linguistic research, the study of Slavic customs and social institutions followed. The results of these studies, not always very scholarly, created a very attractive picture of a distant Slavic past, in which the ancient Slavic herdsmen and ploughmen appeared as paragons of moral purity and their social organization as an ideal standing in sharp contrast to the contemporary despotic regimes in these countries.

---

1 For Ukraine, Herder reserved a special place. He wrote that 'Ukraine will become a new Greece: the beautiful sky, the gay spirit of the people, their natural musical gifts, and fertile land will awaken one day' (*Herders Sämtliche Werke* [Berlin 1878]. IV, 402).

The Turks, the Germans, and the Russians (the latter under Tatar influence), who then prevailed over all the Slavic nations, came to be regarded by the ideologues of the Slavic renaissance as the 'destroyers of the pure Slavic nature' for forcing the Slavs into foreign, repressive forms of government.

The first decades of the nineteenth century saw a great revival among the Slavic nations ruled by Turkey and Austria. The so-called Illyrian movement among the Serbs, which preached national liberation, and Czech efforts to throw off German domination, could not but affect the views of Ukrainian patriots. They conceived new Slavic ideas for their own struggle against the Austrians and the Russians. Their considerations were not only theoretical but practical. Austria, Prussia, and Russia, ruled by the Habsburg, Hohenzollern, and Romanov dynasties, were allies of the Holy Alliance of 1814. Could Ukraine, by herself, oppose these mighty states, which dominated Europe and threatened the Middle East? Since the answer was clearly in the negative, many Ukrainian activists, among them Shevchenko, began to believe that only through friendly contacts with other Slavs would opposition be possible. The Brotherhood of Sts Cyril and Methodius was founded on this premise, although the subsequent histories of the two chief allies of Ukraine, Poland and Russia, did not fulfil hopes that these countries would throw off their yokes and become members of a Slavic federation. However, the naïve political views of the future held by the Ukrainian pan-Slavists were totally justified as expressions of their religious and philosophical convictions. The belief that these Slavic nations, freed from their despotic regimes and alien forms of government, would form a happy, united family was understandably attractive to them.

The enthusiastic activists also believed that Christian teaching should form the foundation of any new political and social order. Vasyl Bilozersky wrote about it explicitly in his 'Note'[2]: 'Pan-Slavism is a union of all the Slavic nations into one family, which, through love of humanity, must develop Christian principles of living, apply them in the life of society, and thus provide a new impulse to universal activities.' These activities included the chief mission of any future Slavic union: to return lost Europe to religious foundations. 'As before,' Bilozersky went on, 'their task is to expand a peaceful agricultural civilization, and as in earlier times they had conciliated the warlike nations, so now they will bring harmony to troubled nations by offering social solutions based on the virtues promoted by the Saviour.'

---

2 See Zaionchkovsky, *Kirilo-Mefodievskoe*, 84.

This faith inspired 'Young Ukraine' to strive for the unity of all the liberated Slavic peoples. The separate existence of Ukraine 'amid foreign fires' was impossible. It would then suffer a worse fate than that which befell Poland. Ukraine's salvation lay in the union of Slavic peoples, which would 'defend them from all barbarians and respect their laws.' Five years before Bilozersky wrote these words, Shevchenko, in 'The Haidamaks,' deplored the fact that 'the children of the ancient Slavs were drunk with blood.' He blamed the Polish priests and the Jesuits for this fratricidal struggle, and, in *Nikita Gaiday*, the Polish magnates as well. All were the products of an alien, non-Slavic background. 'Are you always going to remain a toy in the hands of foreigners?' he asked the 'unfortunate Slavs.' The Ukrainians and the Poles were uselessly engaged in fratricidal war. Shevchenko, therefore, awaited a leader-prophet who would end this strife and unite all the Slavic tribes. He believed that 'all Slavs are the children of one mother.' Like Bilozersky, he believed that the united Slavs would promote peace, would clothe their lands 'with wheat, like gold.' He anticipated this union with great joy:

> And, oh wonders! Corpses rose
> And opened their eyes;
> And brother embraced brother,
> Speaking of quiet love,
> For ever and ever!
> And all the Slavic rivers
> Flowed into one sea![3]

Like the other brethren he believed in the peaceful mission of the Slavs in the world:

> So all Slavs become
> Good brothers
> And sons of truth's sun.[4]

They would offer 'peace to the world,' and the poet's final vision was ecstatic:

> The new, Slavic sea
> Will be unbounded.

---

3 'Yeretyk,' *Povne*, I, 261
4 Ibid, 262

> The boat will glide
> Under full sail
> And steady steering,
> It will glide on a liberated sea,
> On broad waves.[5]

The 'liberated sea' is, of course, the Slavic territory, freed from Russian, Austrian, and Turkish domination. 'Steady steering' is a metaphor for good national government.

Shevchenko also believed in Ukraine's special mission to arouse other nations and 'to light the beacon of truth.' What Shevchenko expressed in poetry, Kostomarov set out in his 'Books of the Genesis of the Ukrainian People': 'And Ukraine will rise from the grave and speak once more to her Slavic brethren, and they will hear her call and all the Slavs will rise ... And Ukraine will be an independent republic in the Slavic Union. Then all will say, pointing to the place occupied on the map by Ukraine, "Behold, here is the stone which the builders rejected; it has become the cornerstone."'[6]

As a historian Kostomarov sustained his faith in the future mission of the Slavs and the particular destiny of Ukraine through his historical research. The Slavic past, which was thought to be common to all the Slavic peoples, was idealized by the Polish ethnographer Zorian Dołęga-Chodakowski, who also pioneered the study of Ukrainian folklore, and by the Czech poet Kollar. In his 'Books of the Genesis of the Ukrainian People' Kostomarov emphasized everything in the history of the ancient Slavs that appeared to demonstrate their high moral and democratic qualities. According to him the ancestors of Ruś-Ukraine acknowledged neither lords nor tsars and paid tribute to only one God. Their princes and elders were elected by the people. Later, in Ukraine, church brotherhoods were organized for the defence of the Christian faith. 'Ukraine did not like either the tsar or lord, but created a true brotherhood of the Cossacks,' where all were equal, elected their officers, and served God faithfully. Shevchenko's ideas were similar: 'Our brotherly freedom, / Without servant or lord.'

Kostomarov searched in Ukrainian history for Christian altruism, the liberation of 'neighbours from slavery,' pointed to Hetman Svyhorsky's defence of the Vallachians and Hetman Sahaidachny's rescue of the prisoners in Kaffa. Similar motifs may be seen in Shevchenko's 'Hamaliia.'

---

5 Ibid, 261
6 M. Kostomarov, *Knyhy bytiia ukrainskoho narodu*, 24

The Cossack order, based on absolute equality, was to provide an example to other Slavic peoples. Moreover, Ukraine had always followed God's laws, while her neighbours did not. The Polish order was borrowed from the Germans, and Russian tsardom was a Tatar product. Both these countries had divided and oppressed Ukraine, which, however, refused to abandon its historic mission. Both the Polish constitution of 1791 and the Decembrist revolt in Russia were echoes of 'Ukraine's voice,' but both were crushed by German despots. Both Kostomarov and Shevchenko believed that, in the future, these Slavic nations would unite in freedom and harmony. Both defended this brand of Ukrainian pan-Slavism in contrast to Russian pan-Slavism, which saw Russia as the liberator of all the Slavs, and to Polish pan-Slavism, which reserved this role for Poland. Their almost mystical faith in a future Slavic Utopia sprang from a combination of Rousseauism and Christian evangelism, and neither could resist its charm.

The repercussions of the trial of Shevchenko and, as the gendarmes called it, the 'Ukrainian-Slavist society,' were fatal for the Ukrainian cause. Tsar Nicholas I and his government had to come face to face with the 'Ukrainian problem' at a time when most people in Russia thought that it had ceased to exist. They were convinced that there was a danger of Ukrainian separatism and that such ideas were finding some response. This realization prompted the government to take a series of steps designed to stop the movement and prevent it from flaring up again. Count Orlov, in his report to the tsar, said that disclosure of this affair 'will for decades strengthen peace in Ukraine, which might have been disturbed.'

The direction and nature of the steps taken by the government to secure this 'peace' may be seen from a separate document that Orlov prepared for the tsar's approval. The chief of the gendarmes correctly argued that the trial showed that ideas of *narodnost* and of a Slavic union were not solely the property of Ukrainian activists but constituted an important subject for Russian Slavophils, who wanted to use these ideas to strengthen Russia's prestige. While in Russia pan-Slavism became in fact pan-Russianism, in Ukraine it engendered dangerous thoughts about 'the return of the ancient freedoms of the hetman state.' Orlov's conclusion was that Russian pan-Slavists should be warned not to antagonize other Slavic nationalities. At the same time energetic measures had to be taken against the 'Ukrainophils,' since their ideas were likely to lead 'Ukrainians and other peoples subject to Russia to desire an independent existence.' Orlov outlined in detail how best to deal with this situation. The ministry of education, he suggested, should see to it that educators and writers did not express views contrary to government policies, that in Ukraine care should be taken to ensure that 'love of one's native land does not outweigh love for the imperial fatherland,' that no ideas should be spread about the contemporary poverty and the earlier happy state of the country, that all scholarly opinions should 'elevate not Ukraine, Poland, or other countries, but the Russian Empire as a whole,' and that the censors should take special care to ban any thoughts or opinions that might lead readers 'to think about the possibility of an existence independent' of Russia.

The government measures directed against the Ukrainian movement had repercussions for the whole empire. In Ukraine the measures taken were very severe. Not only were Shevchenko, Kulish, Kostomarov, and Hulak forbidden to engage in any literary activity, but their published works were confiscated and censors who had passed them received severe reprimands. New regulations practically paralysed all Ukrainian literary and cultural activity. Universities were placed under political control. Governors general were given control of all the schools in both Left and Right Bank Ukraine. They were instructed to watch for any clandestine circulation of Shevchenko's works and other 'seditious' literature. Both the Kiev and the Kharkiv governors general were asked 'to pay close attention to those who engage in the study of Ukrainian antiquities, history, and literature.' This was to be carried out unobtrusively, 'so as not to annoy the inhabitants of Ukraine.'

The news of the trial of Shevchenko and other brethren spread in St Petersburg, Moscow, throughout Ukraine, and among Polish émigrés and reached the foreign press and diplomatic circles. Some versions of the news assumed fantastic proportions. Count Orlov was of the opinion that the tsar's verdict should not be kept secret but should be published in order to frighten any possible opposition. The tsar did not follow this advice, and there was no official announcement. As a result, rumours began to circulate, arousing both sympathy for and revulsion against the accused. In many of the rumours Shevchenko figured as the chief conspirator and hero. It was rumoured that the conspirators wanted 'to provoke an uprising in Ukraine, to proclaim a hetman state and to separate from Russia.' Others maintained that the new hetman state would be created with the Emperor's permission, and still others believed that the whole affair was invented by Bibikov in order to win another medal. The first version was current in Ukraine, where Shevchenko's name was connected with a call to an uprising.

Public opinion in Russia was soon intrigued by the many administrative changes that occurred as a result of the Ukrainian conspiracy. The tsar dismissed the Kiev school curator, General Traskin. The Moscow curator,

Count Stroganov, received from the minister of education, Count Uvarov, a new program to foster an exclusively Russian *narodnost*, a purely Russian patriotism 'uninfluenced by contemporary political ideas,' as well as a personal letter from him containing advice on how to implement the new measures. Stroganov refused to follow these instructions, requested more information about the Cyril-Methodians, and ended his answer to Uvarov by reminding him that 'written orders and ministerial circulars are powerless to sway human thoughts.' As a result, Stroganov, a courageous statesman, was forced to resign after receiving a reprimand from the tsar. The new instructions were executed by his successor. While Stroganov's reaction was a liberal one, Prince Paskevich, the tsar's vicegerent in Poland, reacted to these events from a conservative point of view. He was well informed about the Cyril-Methodians and he severely criticized Uvarov's report on Slavic affairs. A strict adherent of the Holy Alliance, he accused Uvarov of flirting with the Western Slavs, an attitude reflected in the latter's promotion of Slavic studies in Russia and in the travels of scholars to other Slavic lands, especially Bohemia. Paskevich considered even literary relations with the Western Slavs to be an act disloyal to the German states. He maintained that Slavic studies in Russian universities tended to foster provincial separatism, as they had in the case of the Sts Cyril and Methodius Brotherhood.

The political repercussions of the Ukrainian trial became a favourite topic of conversation in the salons of Moscow and St Petersburg, where, in the absence of a free press, people loved to gossip. The reaction of the Russian intelligentsia was ambivalent. Shevchenko's chief enemy, Belinsky, in a private letter to Annenkov, wrote the following venomous denunciation:

I have heard about Shevchenko, and I am convinced that faith, outside of religion, is a worthless thing ... Faith created miracles; it makes men out of asses; that means it can make of Shevchenko a martyr for freedom. But common sense should see in Shevchenko only an ass, a fool, and a scoundrel, and a drinker besides, who is eager to imbibe his *khokhol* [Ukrainian] patriotism ... Shevchenko has been sent to the Caucasus as a soldier. I am not sorry for him; if I were his judge I would be no less severe. I feel a personal animosity towards this type of liberal. They are enemies of all progress. With their impudent stupidities they provoke the authorities and make them suspect a rebellion where none exists, and invite measures which are sharp and disastrous for literature and enlightenment ... This is what these beasts are doing, these brainless liberals. Oh, these *khokhols*! They are sheep, but they play at being liberals in the name of dumplings and pig fat.[7]

7 V. Belinsky, *Polnoe sobranie sochinenii* (Moscow 1956), XII, 441

Belinsky, the great 'Westerner,' spoke here in the true voice of a rabid Russian chauvinist. The Moscow Slavophils also reacted to the whole affair. Samarin warned them to be more careful when he learned about the arrests of Kulish, Savych, and the Slavophil Chizhov, who, by mistake, was also temporarily in police custody. The apolitical Konstantin Khomiakov wrote to Samarin that 'Ukrainians, it seems, have been seized by political folly.' Not realizing how serious were their 'mistakes,' Khomiakov complained about the Ukrainians' lack of wisdom, since 'the time for politics has passed.'

At the same time, there was a group of people in St Petersburg who greeted the news of Shevchenko's arrest sympathetically. This was the so-called circle of Butashevich-Petrashevsky, which was interested in social reconstruction. Two members of this circle, Mombelli and Schtrandman, knew Shevchenko. Mombelli wrote in his diary that Shevchenko had written a proclamation to the Ukrainians and that a Frenchman, Lesage, had been taking it abroad when he was arrested at the border.[8] Mombelli was of the opinion that the Ukrainians viewed Shevchenko's revolutionary plans favourably and that, 'once his countrymen are aroused, it will be difficult to pacify them until they reach their goal.' Butashevich-Petrashevsky had some reason to believe that the conspiracy 'had taken root' in Ukraine and that Shevchenko's works had evoked much unrest there.

There is no doubt that the sentencing of Shevchenko provoked much comment in Ukraine, where he was well known in those places he had visited. His printed works were celebrated, and he himself had allowed his unprinted poems to be copied by various hands. Kostomarov and Kulish were also well-known figures. Anyone interested in a Ukrainian revival could not but react to the imprisonment of these leaders. A few days after the arrest of Kostomarov and Shevchenko the Kiev police tore down a proclamation put up by some young Ukrainians. It read: 'Brothers! A great hour is approaching, an hour in which we can wash away the shame brought to our dead forefathers, our native Ukraine, by the despicable hand of our eternal enemies. Which of you will not raise an arm in this great cause? God and good people are on our side, the true sons of Ukraine, the enemies of the Russians [*katsapiv*].'[9]

After receiving a copy of this proclamation on 26 April 1847, the tsar wrote: 'An obvious product of propaganda from Paris. We did not believe it for a long time, but now there is no doubt about it, and, thank God, it

---

8 Obviously, a reference to Kulish
9 Serhienko, *T.H. Shevchenko i kyrylo*, 147

has been uncovered.' The tsar asked Bibikov, who was in St Petersburg at that time, to return immediately to Kiev 'to look everywhere with great watchfulness.' While the proclamation may be regarded as an outburst by some unknown young hotheads, very soon young Kievans had created a new secret political organization. The Polish revolutionary Zygmunt Miłkowski, known under his pseudonym Teodor Jeż, who was then a student at Kiev University, relates in his memoirs that the brotherhood affair assumed 'large proportions.' After the suppression of the brotherhood Ukrainian students felt humiliated, and they 'thought of improving matters, seeing a way to this through activities banned by authorities, activities which were secret and conspiratorial.'[10] However, the organizers were at a loss how to proceed. They decided to seek advice from their Polish friends, who had the reputation of being practised conspirators. And yet it turned out that most of the young Poles in Kiev, after the suppression of the 1831 uprising, were rather passive. The Ukrainian initiative stirred them up. During the summer holidays Polish students set up an underground organization and shared it with the Ukrainians. Thus two separate secret organizations were created, one Polish and the other Ukrainian, the two keeping in close touch. The police never discovered the men involved and little is known about their activities. One can assume that the Ukrainian conspirators continued some of the traditions of the brotherhood and kept the flame of resistance alive until, upon the death of Nicholas I, cultural and national development could be revived. Another, similar group existed in Kharkiv. It was ready to defend 'Shevchenko's cause.' One of the participants, Holovko, the holder of a master's degree awarded at Kharkiv University in 1847, committed suicide rather than be arrested; he had reported that 'over one thousand people' were ready to fight for Shevchenko's ideas. Even if the figure was exaggerated, there is no doubt that Shevchenko's imprisonment caused wide reaction in Ukraine.

The Polish press reported the trial. The *Dziennik Polski*, which was published in Lviv, wrote about Kulish's arrest. Another Lviv paper, *Postęp*, in the words of its correspondent Karol Paduch, foresaw 'a bloody outburst' among the Ukrainian population. He wrote at length about Shevchenko as 'a man of the people, born in Polish Ukraine,' who had been appointed to the staff of Kiev University. Shevchenko's poems, written in a living national language, proclaimed that 'a free, independent Ukraine' was his goal. Moreover, he foresaw bad economic and political consequences for Russia in the event of Ukraine's independence, since it

10 T. Jeż, *Od kolebki przez życie* (Kraków 1936), I, 236

would deprive Russia of Ukraine's agricultural riches and cut the links between Russia and the southern Slavs. 'The discovery of Shevchenko's and Kulish's intention,' Paduch continued, 'to separate Ukraine from Russia has terrified the tsar.' The article was obviously inspired by Polish sources in Kiev. Rumours were rife among the Poles in Ukraine that Shevchenko had intended to proclaim himself 'hetman of Ukraine' and that Ukraine's 'resurrection would lead to the resurrection of Poland.' In Mombelli's report of his conversations with the Ukrainians similar ideas were expressed about the effect of a Ukrainian uprising on Poland. 'Gradually, the entire southern and western parts of Russia would rise up in arms.'

Shevchenko's political poems must have been known to some young Poles. Franciszek Duchiński emigrated from Ukraine in 1846. He was a staunch supporter of Ukrainian independence, an idea he propagated among other Poles. Duchiński went to Paris, where he informed Prince Adam Czartoryski, the leader of the Polish émigrés, about the idea. He tried to persuade the prince that Ukrainian independence was in Poland's interest and that the Polish leader in exile should declare himself in favour of Ukraine. In his letters to Czartoryski, Duchiński referred several times to Shevchenko's works, and cited them and the existence of the Brotherhood of Sts Cyril and Methodius as proof that Ukraine was ripe for political independence. He regarded Shevchenko and his friends as the natural allies of Poland in her struggle against Russia. Duchiński's articles, published in Czartoryski's paper *Trzeci Maj*, reminded Europe of the existence of the 'Cossack nation' and glorified its fighters for freedom. In his other articles he quoted, from memory, from Shevchenko's 'Epistle.' That Prince Czartoryski formulated, in 1848, his so-called Ukrainian policy[11] shows how strong Duchiński's influence was. In his instructions to Polish political agents and in his insurrectionist activities Czartoryski underlined the 'Cossack military force' of Ukraine. Understanding of the Ukrainian cause could be found not only in the Polish press but in the concrete political plans of the Polish émigrés. In 1849 the Galician priest Volodymyr Terletsky, close to Czartoryski's circle, published in Paris a booklet called *The Word of a Ruthenian* (*Slovo Rusyna*) in which he reiterated the political program of the Cyril and Methodian Brotherhood, calling for an independent Ukraine in a Slavic federation. He correctly perceived that Russia discouraged pan-Slavism because pan-Slavic ideas in Ukraine and other Slavic countries had encouraged the ideas of national separat-

---

11 For more details see M. Handelsman, *Ukraińska polityka ks. Adama Czartoryskiego przed wojna krymska* (Warsaw 1937).

ism. Terletsky wrote openly about the harsh tsarist punishment of Shevchenko, Kulish, and others. The ideas expressed by Duchiński and Terletsky inspired a French journalist, Cyprien Robert, to foresee an important role for Ukraine in the struggle of the Slavic peoples against the states in the Holy Alliance.

Rumours about the brotherhood circulating in St Petersburg could not help but draw the attention of some foreign diplomats. No one has so far investigated the diplomatic archives of Austria, Prussia, France, and England, where undoubtedly reports of foreign envoys about the Ukrainian conspiracy might be found. The *Augsburger Zeitung* reflected the views of Bavarian politicians when it attacked Czech pan-Slavism for inciting the Kievan brethren. Austria and Prussia were afraid of all Slavic movements and looked with apprehension at the revival of a Slavic nation, which might endanger the Holy Alliance. Their negative attitude to 'Young Ukraine' was even stronger, since the latter had advanced a plan for Slavic liberation. The Austrian government in particular was having trouble with the subjugated Croatians, Czechs, Slovaks, Poles, and Ukrainians (in Galicia). This government readily deported to Russia a member of the brotherhood, Mykola Savych, who, on his way to Paris, had stopped in Prague. There was even a rumour that Shevchenko had escaped his captors and had been arrested by the Austrians in Galicia. In the meantime Shevchenko, ignorant of all the news and rumours of which he was the central figure, was preparing to serve his heavy sentence in a desolate part of the empire he hated so much. Defiant in the face of the tsarist prohibition against writing and sketching, he was ready to continue his work in exile.

IX

On 30 May 1847 a carriage drew up in front of the Third Section building. Shevchenko was placed in it to be transferred to the jurisdiction of the army. Kostomarov looked at the scene from the window of his cell. Shevchenko, who had grown a beard, saw his friend, took off his cap, smiled, and waved farewell. On that day General Adlerberg, chief of the inspection department of the army, reported to Count Orlov that orders had been issued to send Shevchenko, under courier escort, to the Orenburg Separate Corps. After spending one night in a military prison, probably in the Peter and Paul Fortress, Shevchenko left St Petersburg at midday on 31 May accompanied by his escort, Vidler. Orenburg was 2,110 *versts* from the capital. According to the prevailing rules, an officer escorting a criminal to his place of punishment was not allowed to interrupt his journey. Both Vidler and Shevchenko were very fit physically, and they covered the distance in eight and a half days. On the night of 8 June they reached the headquarters of the Orenburg Corps. Shevchenko remembered this trip all his life. Ten years later he wrote this ironic account of it in his diary: 'I was, I later learned, urgently needed in Orenburg, and therefore the escorting officer of the "enduring Obstacle" [*Tormoz*] did not sleep a wink. He brought me from St Petersburg to Orenburg in eight days, having murdered only one post-chaise horse.'[1] In the story 'The Twins,' written a little earlier, Shevchenko wrote that during the trip 'the entire landscape flashed before me and still flickers in my memory – I cannot seize on one single feature.' Had the escort not stopped at all they would have travelled almost 250 *versts* a day in a *tarantas* (a springless carriage) on bumpy roads. However, they must have stopped to eat and change horses, so the journey was actually even faster.

---

1 'Shchodennyk,' *Povne*, v, 123. Shevchenko borrowed the nickname 'Enduring Obstacle' for Nicholas I from Alexander Herzen.

It was a tortuous journey for eight days, particularly hard and dismal beyond the River Samara, across the flat steppe, without any vegetation.

Shevchenko was sent from headquarters to a transit barrack, where he and other convicts waited to be posted to individual army units. The letter brought by the escort from the minister of armed forces, together with the tsar's prohibitions against writing or sketching, made a deep impression even on the hardened Orenburg officials. The commanding officer, Colonel Pribitkov, said to Staff Officer K. Gern, who was to become a friend of the poet: 'Imagine, Karl Ivanovich, what a distinguished gentleman they have sent us today: He is forbidden to sing and talk and everything else! How can he live?' Fedir Lazarevsky, a Ukrainian who was an official at Orenburg in charge of Kirghiz affairs, learned of Shevchenko's arrival. His clerk, Halevynsky, came into his office with the words 'The gendarmes brought Shevchenko here at night. I heard it from an officer who is guarding him in a transit barrack.' Thanks to Lazarevsky's memoirs we can see, as if on a screen, the first day of Shevchenko's stay in Orenburg. Lazarevsky did not know the poet personally but had read his works. On hearing the news, he immediately left his office and rushed to the barracks:

The poet was lying on his back on a bunk, sunk in reading the Bible ... Forgetting the presence of the guards, I, in youthful enthusiasm, threw my arms around his neck. Unwillingly getting down from his bunk, Taras Hryhorovych began to talk to me, full of suspicion, and answered my questions abruptly ... Among other things I asked him if I could be of any service to him. He replied with some reserve: 'I do not need anyone's help – I'll help myself. I have been asked by the officer commanding the transit camp to teach his children.'[2]

Shevchenko escaped his depressing new surroundings by taking refuge in the words of the biblical prophets. His suspicion of Lazarevsky was understandable, and Lazarevsky took no offence. After leaving the barracks, Lazarevsky went to his superior, General Ladyzhensky, and asked him to help Shevchenko. But the general thought this intercession was tactless. Lazarevsky and another Ukrainian, Serhiy Levytsky, who worked in his office, went to see the influential Lieutenant-Colonel Matveev, who was the right-hand man of the governor general, Obruchev. Matveev, who was known for his kindness, came of Ural Cossack stock. He received them, and although he made no promises, he was

2 F.M. Lazarevsky, 'Iz vospominanii o Shevchenko,' *Vospominaniia*, 176

moved by what he heard about Shevchenko. As it turned out, although he had promised little, he did in fact help a great deal. Matveev became Shevchenko's main protector for years to come. The following day, after seeing Shevchenko, he granted him a pass allowing him to spend some time outside the barracks in the town of Orenburg. He must also have mentioned to Shevchenko his Ukrainian admirers, Lazarevsky and Levytsky, whom the poet decided to visit. This time their meeting was very friendly, and Shevchenko spent the night in their rooms. After a long talk they all lay down to sleep on the floor, but were unable to fall asleep. Shevchenko recited 'The Dream' and 'Caucasus' to them. Then he got up and sang his favourite song, 'Starlet' ('Zironka'), which he had sung so well at Kulish's wedding. Levytsky had a good tenor voice and sang along with him. They all sang and shed some tears together. The summer night was drawing to a close, and here, in the distant Orenburg steppes, a group of three Ukrainians had found friendship and peace.

Shevchenko captivated not only his fellow-countrymen but people like Matveev and other superior officers. When he was posted to the fortress of Orsk, letters were sent from Orenburg by Staff Captain Gern and General Fediaev to Captain Meshkov, the commander of the Fifth Battalion at Orsk, asking him to show consideration for Shevchenko. They did so, probably at Matveev's request. Lazarevsky also found another channel of assistance – he had a good friend at Orsk, an official, M. Aleksandreisky, to whom he recommended Shevchenko. In Orenburg Shevchenko met a classmate from the academy, the Ural Cossack Chernyshev, who, together with his family, received him very warmly. Here Shevchenko also met the Pole Węgrzynowski, a minor official, who was a member of the Polish colony in the town, consisting mostly of former political exiles. Węgrzynowski had been born in Ukraine and remained Shevchenko's friend for life. It was obvious that the inhuman verdict of the tsar was not being enforced by this official of the Orenburg Corps, who, like Shevckenko's own countrymen, felt great sympathy for the exiled poet.

On 18 June the 'former artist' Shevchenko, now a private of the Fifth Battalion of the Orenburg Corps, left Orenburg for his new posting at the fortress of Orsk, where his battalion was stationed. It was 280 kilometres from Orenburg to Orsk. Shevchenko had money and friends and hired a coachman for himself. The journey was much slower than the one from St Petersburg to Orenburg, and the poet could observe the countryside that had become for him 'an unlocked prison.' Later he recorded his impressions. During the journey he became interested in the country through which he was passing. He was overjoyed when he saw a unique 'village covered with green vegetation,' Ostrovna, which was inhabited by colonists from Ukraine. He was moved to tears by the appearance of this steppe settlement, 'which reminded him of his beautiful native land.' He stopped and talked to the villagers in Ukrainian. Further on, in Huberla, he admired the mountains that he had to cross before reaching the 'desert, which sent shivers down your spine.' It appeared to him like 'an open grave, ready to bury me alive.' Looking ahead at the 'sad panorama,' he saw 'a white dot, surrounded by reddish ribbon.' This was the fortress of Orsk. Drawing nearer he wondered 'if they sing songs in there and was ready to swear to God that they did not. The setting is only suitable for silence.' It turned out that the white dot was a small brick church on a hill, and the reddish ribbon the roofs of the office buildings and barracks. The fortress was surrounded on three sides by a canal and a fortified wall and on the fourth side by the Ural Mountains. The convicts were busy preparing a road for the arrival of the corps commandant, and the soldiers were exercising on the parade square. These were Shevchenko's impressions of Orsk, where scores of convicts from every part of the empire were serving their twenty-five-year terms in the army or were being used as forced labour in the mines.

Shevchenko arrived on 23 June and the same day was ordered by the commandant to join the Third Company. His army number was 191. He became one of those whom he described in his 'Dream' as

> wearing boots,
> Fettered by chains,
> They are drilled.[3]

Drill and the barracks were what he most hated, but now they dominated his daily routine. Like all new recruits he was given an instructor. His uniform was too tight for him, but every morning he had to put it on properly under the watchful eye of the instructor. Then he was ready for the drill. Captain Gern, from Orenburg, wishing to help Shevchenko, had written to Major Meshkov, the commandant at Orsk, asking him to 'show the exiled man some consideration,' but Meshkov understood the request in his own way and began to supervise Taras's drill personally. He was determined to teach him all there was to know to become a good soldier, and foot drill was the foundation for this. Meshkov was not a bad man, just a very limited officer of Nicholas I, who himself was a great drill master. His efforts in the case of Shevchenko proved to be wasted. No

---

3 'Son,' *Povne*, I, 243

matter how long he tormented the poet on the parade square, the latter would not or could not grasp the rudiments of military exercises. Those who saw the hapless poet on the square agreed that he was unfit to be a soldier. Yet Meshkov did not punish the poet for his clumsiness. He remembered the letter from Orenburg. Much worse was the officer commanding the Third Company, whose name was Globa and who was a Russified Ukrainian. He was very strict, brutal, and a drunkard to boot. When Shevchenko appeared before him for the first time, Globa threatened to have him flogged if his drill were unsatisfactory. He treated Shevchenko with contempt, especially during inspection, when the poet 'with trembling heart' had to show what he had learned. Shevchenko wrote of it 'that I had to hide in myself all human feeling, becoming a soulless automaton, listening in silence, without blushing or growing pale, to a lesson in morality from a thief and a bloodsucker.' The most difficult task for the poet was to suppress all human feeling, to submit to the military machine of the empire he hated so much. His inner torment was reflected in this passage from his diary:

When I was a child, as far back as I can remember, I showed no interest in soldiers, as is common with children. When I was growing up and grasping the rational order of things, I began to feel an innate irresistible dislike for 'Christ-loving warriors.'[4] My antipathy grew as I had a chance to meet these warriors. I do not know if it was accidental or whether it was really true, but even among the guardsmen I never met a man in uniform who was a decent human being. When they were sober they were ignorant and boastful, and when they had a spark of intelligence and enlightenment then they were also boastful and drunkards and debauchees to boot. My antipathy became revulsion. And yet my fate maliciously laughed at me when it pushed me into the thick of these most malodorous Christ-loving soldiers. Were I some monster or bloodsucker, my punishment could not be harsher than being sent as a private to the Orenburg Separate Corps. That is the cause of all my suffering.[5]

While every day the poet had to feign obedience and humility before his superiors, life in the barracks was torture for him. During the day, after parade hours, it was possible to take a walk to the River Ora or visit officers and officials he knew, but in the evening he was expected to be back in the barracks. The stench of human sweat and rotten tobacco, the

4 The official formula used for the army in church services
5 'Shchodennyk,' *Povne*, v, 22

noise and rowdiness could not be escaped after the signal to close the barracks for the night was sounded. At night he listened to filthy anecdotes or stories 'about those who had been flogged or were to be flogged.'

This stifling atmosphere did not, fortunately, last long. We do not know how and when, but Shevchenko succeeded, at the end of the summer or in early fall, in being transferred from the barracks. This might have coincided with the poet's new illness – rheumatism. He complained about it in a letter to Fedir Lazarevsky's brother Mykhailo: 'Apart from the fact that there is no one to exchange a few words with, apart from boredom, which like a viper sucks my heart, apart from everything which torments me, God has punished me with a physical illness.' And yet, he continued, he felt better now, because he was staying 'in a dingy, but free little house.'

Shevchenko's new friends did not forget him, and this made life easier for him. Mykhailo Lazarevsky came to visit him in Orsk in the summer. He was an outstanding person, dedicated to helping his fellow-men. He became one of Shevchenko's most faithful friends, and reported that the poet was still in good spirits. Another of the Lazarevsky brothers, Vasyl, sent Shevchenko some of his favourite cigars and fifty roubles. Chernyshev wrote from Orenburg, telling Shevchenko that his friend d'André was to visit Orsk in the fall. He recommended him as an artist and a man of culture. At the same time Chernyshev warned Shevchenko not to do any sketching, since he knew of an informer in Orsk who would report it to the authorities.

Shevchenko's local friendships grew stronger. This was partly due to a letter of introduction he had brought to a fellow-countryman, M. Aleksandreisky, who worked in the same office as Lazarevsky. Shevchenko became welcome a guest in the Aleksadreisky household. There he was received 'not as a soldier, but as a true friend, on the same level as the other guests.' He also met the battalion commander and other officers there, but as an invited guest of the host, not as soldier number 191. Shevchenko wrote to Princess Repnina that on social occasions his officers 'treated me, thank God, as a comrade.' At times, however, even the social occasions became unbearable because of the low cultural level of the guests who were, as the poet wrote to Repnina, 'worse than the barracks.' Most of the officers at Orsk were of rather low intelligence. They were often sent there because of a poor service record and unsatisfactory performance. Their superiors were of a slightly higher calibre because they had to look after a demoralized, half-educated band of officers and privates. The low morale even affected some of the good men with ideas, like the Polish exiles. And yet there were exceptions. Shevchenko became friendly with two officers – one a Ukrainian, Veryho, and the other a Pole, Mostowski, a participant in the 1831 uprising. Another Pole, Private Otto Fischer, introduced Shevchenko into the household of the commandant of the fortress, General Isaev. Two ladies, whose names we do not know, took care of Shevchenko and, in winter, procured a warm coat made of rabbit fur for him. The household of the army clerk Lavrentev was particularly hospitable. Shevchenko liked Lavrentev, a 'simple and humane' man, and spent long hours in his house, sometimes acting as tutor to his son. In the fall, when Shevchenko was allowed to leave the barracks, he even managed, through his connections, to acquire a servant, a Ukrainian private, Halushchenko. This concession was probably allowed because of the poet's rheumatism.

The reprieve from the barracks did not last long. No one wanted to take the responsibility of doing favours for Shevchenko, and his superiors were afraid that they might suffer the consequences if someone reported such favours, perhaps adding that not only did Shevchenko not live in the barracks but that he was believed to be sketching and writing again: It was very hard to return to the barracks, particularly since the winter was severe and it was very stuffy there. Shevchenko's mood worsened, and it was discovered that he was suffering from scurvy, caused by a lack of vitamins in his diet, since in this desert land there were no vegetables to be seen. Before Christmas, complaining of his hard life in the barracks, Shevchenko wrote to Lazarevsky: 'I have become a little accustomed to the pipe smoke, the stench, and the clamour, but now I have been struck down by severe scurvy and am like Job on the dungheap, with no visitors.' His spirits reached a new low as his gums began to rot and his teeth to loosen, and his body was covered with boils. Stuck in the harsh desert, among noisy and filthy soldiers, he was indeed like Job on a dungheap. Life in the barracks and his new illness drove the poet to a state of true depression. 'At first,' he wrote, 'I looked evil in the eye and thought that I had willpower enough, but no – this was my blind pride. I could not see the bottom of this deep hole into which I had fallen, and when indeed I saw it, my poor soul disintegrated like a speck of dust in the wind. This, my friend, is not very Christian, but what can I do?'[6] Facing the bottom of the hole was indeed terrible, but hope for a better life did not desert him. It was this 'hope of one day seeing my hapless native land' that kept him alive.

6 Ibid, VI, 45

So it was the Dnieper with its winding banks
And hope, my brother,
Which would not let me, in captivity,
Beg for death.[7]

He complained that 'yearning was oppressing my heart,' that he thought about death, but eventually his mind and will took the upper hand. He began planning systematically to improve his situation so that he could be creative again. He understood that in order to achieve this, two things were necessary: to leave the barracks, and to receive permission to sketch. The ban on literary activity did not surprise him. He did, after all, write revolutionary poetry, and the punishment was not unexpected. But he could not comprehend why he had been forbidden to sketch. He noted later, in his diary: 'I was forbidden to write for writing rebellious poems in Ukrainian, But even the Most Supreme Judge does not know why I was forbidden to sketch.' He decided to try everything to overturn this verdict. On 24 October he wrote to Chernyshev, who was on his way to St Petersburg, and asked him to intercede on his behalf with influential officials. According to Shevchenko's plan, Count Orlov had to be persuaded to talk to the tsar himself and explain to him that Shevchenko had never sketched anything criminal. Perhaps, during the trial, there had been some rumour that Shevchenko had drawn a caricature of the tsar. This false legend had to be set at rest. This could only be done by Count Orlov himself or by his assistant, General Dubelt. They had access to all the 'criminal' evidence, in which not a word had been said about Shevchenko's sketching. Some influential people had to be found who would put pressure on Orlov to speak to the tsar.

One of the most active tsarist politicans, especially in the East, where Russia controlled all the lands between the Urals and British India, was Count Perovsky. Formerly the governor general of Orenburg, he was now the minister of the interior. Despite the defeat, in 1839, of his military expedition against Khiva, he never gave up his interest in the conquest of Kokand, Khiva, and Bokhara, so as to reach the borders of Afghanistan in one direction and, in the other, to control the area around the Syr-Daria and the banks of the Sea of Aral into which it flowed. A fortress was being built at the mouth of Syr-Daria, and in the spring an expedition was planned to explore the Aral Sea. Perovsky was anxious to include in this expedition an artist who would illustrate objects, a task which today would be left to the photographer. Shevchenko's friend Schternberg was

7 Ibid

drafted into the expedition to Khiva, but withdrew since he was unable to stand the climate. Now an opportunity appeared for Shevchenko's friends to put his name forward to Perovsky, as a sketcher for the Aral Sea expedition. Chernyshev, who knew Perovsky very well, took it upon himself to do so. He asked that General Dubelt grant Shevchenko permission to draw landscapes and portraits. Perovsky himself was a lover of art and had heard a great deal about Shevchenko from Zhukovsky, Briullov, and the Repnins. However, Chernyshev, an insignificant person, carried little weight alone. So, knowing that Perovsky respected the writer V. Dal, Shevchenko, who also knew him, decided to ask him for help. He also dispatched a letter to Briullov asking him to intercede with Dubelt. Shevchenko's plan was well thought out: all the necessary letters were forwarded to Chernyshev, who was to take them to St Petersburg. But Cherhyshev delayed his departure till December. On 20 December Shevchenko wrote to M. Lazarevsky:

Please be kind enough to visit Chernyshev, who is now in St Petersburg ... When you see him, ask him if he has delivered all the letters I sent him and what response he received. Ask him from me to see Karl Pavlovich [Briullov] and Dubelt urgently. When you see Dal give him my greetings, and ask him to implore Perovsky to liberate me from barracks and allow me to sketch. Dal is a good man as well as wise and influential. He is aware of how wretchedly we live here, so his sin will be grave if he does not intercede on my behalf with a good word.[8]

Shevchenko also wanted to write to Zhukovsky, who was abroad, and asked Lazarevsky for his address. For three months (November 1847–January 1848) Shevchenko waited anxiously for the results of his scheme. His chief hope was that he would be allowed to sketch again. But events in St Petersburg moved very slowly. Chernyshev could not get an appointment with Dubelt and did not see Dal. In February Lazarevsky wrote that there was still no news and that 'Briullov merely shrugged his shoulders,' which must have hurt Shevchenko. Zhukovsky was travelling in the Rhineland and could not be reached. Lazarevsky's letter would have led Shevchenko to utter despair were it not for the fact that shortly before he received it he heard that Count Orlov had asked the governor general, Obruchev, to send him a report on Shevchenko's behaviour and inquired whether this behaviour warranted a relaxation on the prohibition to sketch. The battalion commander was asked by the Orenburg Corps Headquarters to supply the information, and on 10 March Major

8 Ibid

Meshkov sent Obruchev a very favourable report on Shevchenko, pointing out that because of his exemplary behaviour he deserved to be allowed to sketch. The proposal from Orenburg was forwarded to the Third Section in St Petersburg. It is clear that both in Orenburg and in Orsk, Orlov's request was interpreted as a willingness by the highest powers to receive some justification for withdrawing the ban on sketching. The favourable report upon Shevchenko must be seen as the result of the atmosphere his friends had created around him. He had been visited by men in high places who wanted to help him. In addition, his personality, intelligence, and charm had won him friends everywhere. Above all, officials at Orsk must have been impressed by the fact that prominent men in St Petersburg (Zhukovsky, Briullov) knew Shevchenko and that he corresponded with a princess. All these factors helped his cause enormously.

In the meantime Princess Repnina, having received a letter from Shevchenko in which he complained about not being able to paint ('to look and not to sketch is a torment which only an artist can understand'), decided to write to Orlov. On 18 February she wrote a letter, trying to convince the chief executioner that 'the task of virtue is to see that the law does not turn to cruelty.' In Shevchenko's case, she argued in French, his punishment amounted to *le cruel raffinement* because he was forbidden to sketch. Shevchenko, she pleaded, was *complètement orphelin dans ce monde*, and she felt it her duty to defend his rights. Despite compliments thrown in Orlov's direction, this letter was not very diplomatic. Although she did not know that the *cruel raffinement* came from the tsar himself, she must have annoyed Orlov by her frankness. In any case, there was no immediate reaction to her letter, since Orlov was waiting for a report from Orenburg. Even before it came, a new turn of events provided a solution for Shevchenko.

Very early in 1848 the news spread in the fortress of Orsk that part of the garrison would be sent into the Raim steppes, where a new fort was to be built not far from the Aral Sea. Shevchenko expected that he might be included in that expedition and wrote about it to Lyzohub on 1 February. On 25 February he wrote to Princess Repnina as if his departure were inevitable. He was afraid of becoming further isolated, of not receiving any mail, and of the possibility of further attacks of scurvy. Yet he ended his letter with the words 'let us exchange despair for hope and prayer.'

Corresponding with friends was now almost his only joy. He rarely received letters from Ukraine, which he appreciated the most, and only Andriy Lyzohub and Princess Repnina were regular correspondents. Lyzohub was the first to write to Shevchenko in exile. He himself was in deep mourning after the death of his young daughter. But as a true Christian he felt all the more for the poet's fate, and he tried to encourage him. He wrote to Shevchenko as if he were his spiritual son: 'God's punishment and trial are always good for us; they make us better, more merciful, and compassionate, and let us respect both ourselves and others more.' He quoted someone who thought that those who look evil in the eye will conquer it. These words must have been a solace to the poet. He, too, was in a religious mood and, as he wrote to Lazarevsky, tried to 'look with daring into evil's eyes.' What touched him most in Lyzohub's letter was the latter's offer to send him a box of water-colour paints, a few Parisian paintbrushes, a pad of English sketching paper, and even, if need be, some oil-paints. Perhaps Shevchenko had expressed a hope that he would be allowed to sketch again. At the end of the letter Lyzohub promised to do all he could. How pleased Shevchenko was to hear this may be seen from his reply. 'You have given me great joy with your Christian letter in this godless desert. I thank you warmly, my friend. Since the spring I have not heard one honest native word. God allowed you to be the first to dispel my heavy sorrow in this desert with heartfelt words.'[9]

Because Lyzohub lived in Odessa it took a month for his letters to reach the fortress of Orsk, but Shevchenko waited patiently for these glad tidings. Beginning in March Lyzohub, apart from his letters, also sent the poet parcels containing books, sketching pads, fine pencils, and, at last, a box of paints and brushes. Princess Repnina, who had received Shevchenko's letter (written in October) before Christmas, wrote to him regularly. Her letters, like those from Lyzohub, touched the poet deeply. The princess and the two 'Yahotyn anchoresses,' Hlafira and Oleksandra Psiol, wrote that they were continually praying for him and how glad they were to hear from him. In letters to them Shevchenko described his miserable life as a soldier. He wrote to Lyzohub, 'I am now a veritable *moskal*,'[10] and to Princess Varvara, 'You would burst out laughing if you saw me now. Imagine a clumsy garrison soldier, unkempt, unshaven, with a large mustache – that's me.' He even sent Lyzohub a caricature of himself doing drill exercises. His friends commiserated with him, and the princess answered that she would cry, not laugh, if she saw him. She advised him to pray and seek solace in the love of his fellow-men. The same sentiments were expressed in the letters of Hlafira Dunin-Borkowska.

Sometimes Shevchenko complained that his friends had forgotten him.

9 *Lysty do T.H. Shevchenka*, 69
10 'Moskal' – here, a soldier. It can also be used as a mild pejorative for a Russian.

In a letter to Lyzohub he wondered if 'they have died, God forbid? No, they are well; they have only forgotten their unlucky friend. If they only knew that one kind word is the greatest joy for me.' But kind words reached him frequently. He read his friends' letters many times over before answering them. On his birthday, 25 February (o.s.), he began writing a letter, continuing with it for five days. This letter was, in fact, a fragment from his diary. He told the princess that 'whenever I get a letter from someone who has not forgotten me, it is as if I wake from a bad dream ... I celebrate my birthday quietly but joyfully, as I never have before, and I am grateful to you and Hlafira Ivanovna for it.' On 28 February he described how prayer and holy communion had raised his spirits:

Yesterday I sat up [throughout the night] till morning and could not collect my thoughts in order to finish this letter. An indescribable feeling came over me ('Come unto me all ye that are heavy laden and I will give you rest'). Before I went to morning mass I remembered these words of the One who was crucified for us, and I, as it were, came to life. I went to mass and prayed more fervently than ever before. Today I received Holy Communion. I would like the whole of my life to be as pure and beautiful as this day.[11]

He further asked that the princess pray for him and send him *The Imitation of Christ* by Thomas à Kempis.

Correspondence with friends filled his life. Each letter he received evoked a new emotion in him. This was the case when he received a letter from Oleksandra Psiol, author of the poem 'Blessed Water.' It was with a quotation from this poem, before his arrest, that he had ended his preface to the second edition of *Kobzar*. Now, Oleksandra Psiol sent him a new poem, entitled 'A Prayer for Shevchenko':

> We pray to you, God of truth and mercy,
> Abandon not our brother, who is like an orphan
> In the desert steppes. Like his father, like his own mother,
> Speak to his heart, let him not languish.
> Gather, oh God, our tears into a small dark cloud
> And when his heart grows weary and hot
> Let the rain fall like a spring shower ...
> Create a miracle! The tears will turn to holy water
> Life-giving and healing – so that all his wounds will heal
> And his soul be bathed and satisfied.[12]

---

11 *Povne*, VI, 50
12 *Lysty do T.H. Shevchenka*, 71

These tearful poems did help the poet to forget his solitude. He knew that his friends had not abandoned him. That the poem was written by a woman also had a special meaning for Shevchenko, who once wrote that 'one tear from hazel eyes would make him feel like a lord.' Oleksandra Psiol also wrote: 'Your soul, once an altar for the creation of pure beauty, from which such solemn hymns could be heard, must not now turn into squalour and desolation. Do not be afraid, Taras Hryhorovych; your sisters are praying for you.' His despondency may be seen in his letter to Princess Repnina, in which he feared that he might lose his feeling for beauty: 'And I treasured it so highly. No! I must have sinned before God since I am being punished so much.'

While December and January were spent in the filthy barracks, his spirits at a low ebb, in February the poet's mood began to improve, and in the spring of 1848 there came some good news. Before Easter he received the poem from Psiol, and letters and parcels from Lyzohub. Apart from the paints and brushes Lyzohub sent him there were also two volumes of Shakespeare. Shevchenko thanked him on 7 March, describing his joy as that of 'an unfed child who sees his mother coming.' He kissed each gift, and was so excited he could not sleep a wink.

His friends from Yahotyn and Sedniv were now not the only ones to write to Shevchenko. Among the new correspondents were the brothers Lazarevsky, Mykhailo from St Petersburg, Fedir from Orenburg, and Vasyl from the Orenburg district, where he was fighting an outbreak of cholera. Vasyl, who did not know Shevchenko personally, wrote to him that 'perhaps your heart may feel easier if it knows that there is another human being worrying about your fate as if it were his own.' Fedir sent the poet some writing paper; Mykhailo and Vasyl dispatched books and the cigars which Shevchenko liked to smoke. Mykhailo, who had visited Ukraine, sent his greetings from compatriots in Konotop and told him how fondly he was remembered in Kiev by the university official Hlushanovsky. Mykhailo even complained that Shevchenko did not ask for more to be sent to him. He refused to take any money for the books he sent to the poet. As a matter of fact, Shevchenko was running out of money. He had brought with him to Orenburg 365 silver roubles, more than his annual salary in Kiev. However, he spent money freely, and by Christmas he was almost penniless. One reason for this was his readiness to lend money to anyone who asked for it. Thus he lent Lieutenant Barkhvitsev 65 roubles; not only was this loan not returned, but the lieutenant complained to the authorities when Shevchenko demanded its repayment. Shevchenko thus gratefully accepted the money his friends sent him. Vasyl Lazarevsky, his friend Yezuchevsky, and others were quite generous. When Lyzohub offered to send him some cash, Shevchenko replied that it was unnecessary and that he hoped to earn some money once he was allowed to paint again.

Conditions in the army improved a little. The brutal drunken Captain Globa had been replaced by Captain Stepanov, and Shevchenko stopped complaining about his superiors. Yet in spite of these improvements and the friendship shown to him by so many people, he still brooded over his fate. 'I feel almost like crying,' he wrote to Lazarevsky in April. 'Sometimes I am ashamed of myself. But there is nothing I can do to stop this cursed nostalgia.'

One of the ways to dispel it was to read, and Shevchenko read a great deal. When he first arrived in Orsk, he had complained to Lyzohub that there was nothing to read. This was an exaggeration, but what he meant was that he did not have enough to read. He read the books that were sent to him very quickly. Lazarevsky sent him several volumes of *Notes of the Fatherland* and Ustrialov's *History of Russia*. Gradually he built up a small library of authors whom he could read over and over again if need be. Among these were Shakespeare, Lermontov, Koltsov, Pushkin, Thomas à Kempis, and Gogol. The latter's *Selected Passages from Correspondence with Friends* was one of the books he read, as well as *Readings in the Moscow Society of History and Antiquities*, edited by Bodiansky, which contained Ukrainian chronicles. These works, along with the Bible, nourished his mind.

May was approaching, and the matter of the expedition to the Aral Sea was soon to be decided. The expedition was to start from the Orsk Fortress. It was to cover a difficult route and had to be guarded by the army. At the end of April Shevchenko still did not know whether he would be invited to join the expedition. He might have been tempted to try to avoid being included in the expedition in order to avoid fresh hardships. But he was inclined to favour participation in the expedition, perhaps hoping that the lifting of the ban on sketching would come sooner.

On 5 March 1848 Captain Butakov, an officer of the Black Sea fleet, came to Orenburg. He was a professional geographer and hydrologist who was to take charge of the expedition to explore the Aral Sea. While in St Petersburg discussing plans for the expedition, Butakov brought up the question of including some experts in various fields. Since two boats were to be used for the voyage, he was looking for additional hydrologists, topographers, and artists who could sketch. It is possible that Shevchenko's name was mentioned to Butakov in St Petersburg as a possible sketcher for the expedition, since the poet was already at Orsk, and few artists from St Petersburg would volunteer for such dangerous service. If we consider that Orlov's request to grant Shevchenko permission to draw may have come before Chernyshev could speak to Dubelt, then it is not impossible to assume that this request came as a result of Butakov's efforts to find a sketcher. Sketching done on a military expedition would be more likely to be approved by the tsar.

On 20 March a good report on Shevchenko was sent from Orenburg to St Petersburg. Now May was approaching, and, under Butakov's direction, a schooner, the *Constantine*, was being built, then disassembled and dispatched to the Aral Sea. The expedition was to start soon, but orders about Shevchenko's part in it were slow in coming. Butakov must have talked about it to Obruchev, who was waiting for orders. The expedition was to set sail on 11 May, and Butakov urgently needed a sketcher. Obruchev decided to act on his own initiative, and in expectation of receiving a favourable reply about Shevchenko he transferred him from the Fifth to the Fourth Battalion and, unofficially, included him in the expeditionary force. Without mentioning Shevchenko's new duties, Brigadier-General Fediaev ordered the commander of the Fifth Battalion to detail two hundred soldiers, including Shevchenko, to join the Fourth Battalion at the Raim Fortress. In this way all the formalities were adhered to, and Butakov got Shevchenko as a sketcher. A year later, in an official report, Butakov mentioned that the new sketcher was 'to draw views of the steppes and the Aral Sea.' On 9 May Shevchenko wrote to Lyzohub that 'permission to sketch has arrived' and that the expedition was to begin the next day. Yet he also voiced his uncertainty over 'whether I'll paint.' This hastily written letter reflects Shevchenko's own doubt: on the one hand he had been made a member of the expedition; on the other he knew that the order allowing him to sketch had not yet arrived. It is certain that by then he must have met Butakov and discussed the matter with him.

Soon after arriving at Orsk, Shevchenko disregarded the 'strictest ban on writing' and resumed writing poetry. The first work to be written in exile was the long Shakespearean poem 'The Princess' ('Kniazhna'). In the invocation to the poem Shevchenko stressed the imperative need to create, the inner compulsion to 'tell what is happening in Ukraine.' The invocation was his 'Tristia,' composed in distant Kirghizia, just as Ovid's work was written in exile, on the Black Sea. Having finished the poem, Shevchenko copied it into a miniature notebook that could be hidden in the top of his high soldier's boot. The first to be copied into this 'boot-leg' notebook was the introductory poem to the entire new cycle 'Thoughts of Mine' ('Dumy moi'). He asked them to fly to him

> From the wide Dnieper,
> To frolic in the steppes
> With the poor Kirghiz.[13]

Despite the prohibition against writing he was determined to continue. He hoped that songs from Ukraine

> Will fly to me, my dear ones,
> With soft words,
> And I will welcome you, like children,
> And weep with you.[14]

He was aware of the risks he was taking:

> Let them crucify me,
> I will not lie down without verse.

He wanted to preserve, in the notebook, some of his earlier works. The poems from 'The Three Years' cycle were safe, since some of his friends had copied them. He managed to preserve everything he had written during his arrest somehow, perhaps copied on to the margins of the Bible, and now he recopied it into the boot-leg notebook, following 'The Princess.' The short prison cycle he dedicated to the comrades who had been tried with him, and he ended this dedication with the following apostrophe:

> Remember, my brothers,
> (I hope those bad times will never return)
> How you and I humbly
> Looked through prison bars.[15]

What is of further interest in this poem is Shevchenko's realization that any Ukrainian activity had become impossible after the arrest and

---

13 'Dumy moi,' *Povne*, II, 22
14 Ibid
15 'Zhadaite,' ibid, II, 7

punishment of his associates. This tsarist blow had paralysed all effort for a long time to come:

> We shall trust in freedom a little
> And then begin to live
> Among other people, as they do.[16]

This realization was very painful. It meant that the message of all his creative work would only be revealed to future generations.

Among other earlier poems copied from memory into the notebook were 'Lily,' 'The Mermaid,' and 'The Aspen' (renamed 'The Witch'). Altogether he copied sixteen old poems and included seventeen new ones (among them 'The Princess,' 'Irzhavets,' 'The Monk,' and 'Moskal's Well').

Not only did Shevchenko write poetry in exile – he kept a diary. In a letter to Princess Repnina, written on 27 February 1848, he told her about it:

It is the quietest and most favourable time now – eleven o'clock at night. Everybody is asleep; the barrack is lit by one candle, in the light of which I am writing my clumsy letter. Isn't this a Rembrandtesque picture? But even the greatest poetic genius will not find in it anything encouraging for mankind ... From the day I arrived in Orsk Fortress I have kept a diary. I opened it today and thought I would copy at least one page from it for you – but I gave up. Everything in it is so monotonously sad that I myself took fright and ... burnt my diary in the flame of the candle, which was about ready to give out: I did the wrong thing, and later I missed my diary as a mother misses her child, monster though he be.[17]

Shevchenko, however, only burnt a small section of his diary then. When he left the Orsk Fortress, a thick notebook remained there containing his diary.

Shevchenko did not only write by candlelight in the middle of the night. More often he composed new poems during the holidays, while he was taking walks outside the fortress. Once more, as he had in childhood, he had to hide in order to create:

> Once again I had,
> In my old age, to hide with my verses,
> To embroider notebooks, to sing
> And cry among the weeds.[18]

16 Ibid
17 Ibid, VI, 50
18 Ibid, II, 63

Arrest and Exile 1847–57

He described his outings on holidays:

> Like a thief outside the walls
> On Sundays I make for the fields
> And come through the willows beyond the Urals,
> Into the wide steppes, as if I were free.
>
> And my aching heart
> Will revive
> Like a fish in water,
> Will smile gently
>
> And will fly like a dove
> Above the alien fields –
> And it is as if I come alive
> In these fields, in freedom.[19]

The vistas of the bare Asiatic steppes evoked for Shevchenko contrasting images of the lush Ukrainian landscape, and the feeling of relief was soon replaced by one of nostalgia.

> I walk on a high mountain
> And I gaze around,
> But I remember Ukraine
> And I fear remembering it, ...
> There are steppes there
> And there are steppes here,
> But here they are different –
> Russet and red –
> And there – blue,
> Green, embroidered
> With plants and meadows,
> With high gravemounds
> And dark fields,
> Here there are weeds, sand, and willows
> And rarely a gravemound,
> Whispering about the past ...
> As if no one lived here![20]

19 Ibid, 64
20 Ibid

This was only the beginning of a long exile. Sometimes, the mere thought that it might continue for decades provoked the poet into crying out:

> Oh, my fate! My country!
> When will I escape from this desert?
> Or perhaps, God forbid,
> I will perish here?[21]

Sundays and holidays offered some escape, but weekdays were much worse:

> And so, my friend, I celebrate
> Here the Holy Sunday!
> But on Monday, my friend,
> Night will come in a smelly hut,
> Dark thoughts will crowd in
> And smash a hundred times
> My heart and hope,
> And what I cannot express ...
> And they will drive out everything
> And slow the night. Hours will crawl
> Like years and flow like centuries,
> And I will sprinkle my bed many times
> With tears of blood.[22]

The poet was particularly afraid of the long nights in the barracks. 'They are terrible and long,' he complained in a letter to Lyzohub. However, the days were full of torment, too:

> I pray to God that it may dawn,
> I await the sunrise like freedom.
> But when the crickets cease and reveille is sounded
> I pray to God that dusk begin
> Because I, old fool, am driven
> To be drilled and humiliated.[23]

Whenever he was oppressed by dark thoughts he looked back at his life and searched for 'his sins' that had caused this misfortune. He asked himself:

21 Ibid, 65
22 Ibid
23 Ibid, 66

177   Arrest and Exile 1847–57

> Whom, where and when did I love?
> For whom did I do anything good?
> No one in the world.²⁴

This self-flagellation was hardly justified. His whole aim in life was precisely to 'do something good.' Perhaps his efforts were not intense enough? Perhaps he had wasted a good deal of time? Yet these moments of self-doubt passed quickly. Free of them, he once more became confident that what he had done was right and that he had an important mission to fulfil:

> Oh, my songs, my fatal fame!
> For you I waste in vain in a foreign land,
> I am punished, I suffer, but I have no regrets! ...
> I love my hapless Ukraine like a true spouse,
> Do what you like with my benighted self
> But do not leave me. I'll trudge with you to hell.²⁵

This 'fatal fame' was forever linked to 'hapless Ukraine' in his innermost being. Whatever he wrote here, in exile, was saturated with nostalgia for his country, which grew even more attractive and beautiful to him. When he thought that he possibly might die in exile, he asked:

> That the Russian soldiers
> Not make my coffin
> Of foreign timber.
> May a speck of earth
> From beyond my sacred Dnieper
> Be borne by holy winds.²⁶

Everything connected with Ukraine is 'sacred 'or 'holy.' The vision of the distant, beloved country sharpened his poetic style. Peasant huts are 'scattered ...like boxes by an old drunk'; a lonely house on the river-bank is 'like an orphan drowning in the deep and wide Dnieper'; a cluster of huts is 'like playful children in white shirts,' and churches 'with their green eyes look like corpses from the coffin.' This yearning for his native land had intensified his feelings, and he saw it as would a visionary in a trance.

24 Ibid
25 'O dumy moi,' ibid, 50
26 'Ne hrie sontse na chuzhyni,' ibid, 40

X

On the morning of 11 May 1848 the military detachment that was to guard and escort Captain Butakov's expedition left Orsk, making for the expedition's main encampment. After crossing the River Ora they halted for a brief prayer service, and then the whole convoy moved on to its distant destination. The entire force consisted of 2,500 carts and 3,500 camels. Apart from supplies and equipment, the carts carried the disassembled schooner *Constantine*, which was to be put together and made navigable. The force was commanded by General Schreiber and included two hundred infantrymen, two companies of Ural Cossacks, six hundred Bashkir cavalrymen, and an artillery detachment.

Although Shevchenko was a member of the Third Company and was to be seconded to Butakov later, right from the start of the expedition he was treated as one of the members, not as an ordinary soldier. He did not carry a rifle or backpack, nor did he wear a uniform, but a light overcoat. His task from the beginning was to sketch anything worthy of note. There was no wind, but the sun was scorching. At the end of the first day Shevchenko fainted. He was extremely tired after the farewells to his friends at Orsk and had been too excited to sleep. He was also meeting new friends in the expeditionary force. The head of the expedition, Butakov, was born in Mykolaiv, in Ukraine. He was an officer of the Black Sea fleet, well educated, and progressive in his outlook. His assistant, Staff Captain A. Maksheev, had only recently been posted to Orenburg from the capital and became friendly with Shevchenko on the very first day of the expedition, when he invited him to spend the night in his tent. Maksheev was closely associated with the Butashevich-Petrashevsky circle and knew Shevchenko's friend Mombelli. He welcomed Shevchenko as one who knew prominent people in St Petersburg and Kiev and might be good company during an arduous journey. Shevchenko rarely rode on horseback but walked most of the way. The transport moved very slowly and covered on average twenty kilometres a day. Although the terrain was very difficult and rocky, Shevchenko was beginning to enjoy the change.

At first, as he recalled later, 'he could not see anything because of the cloud of dust raised by the carts, the Bashkirs, the camels, and their half-naked Kirghiz drivers.' But the following day, at dawn, as the transport continued its journey, Shevchenko rode ahead with the Ural Cossacks and 'could give himself over entirely to quiet sorrow and the observation of nature.' They rode through a steppe as flat 'as if it were covered with a white table-cloth.' It was a sad but moving picture. There were no bushes or valleys, nothing apart from the tall steppe grass, which looked 'petrified' because it was motionless. No sounds of insects or birds could be heard; not even a lizard crossed the path.

Unexpectedly, Shevchenko one day saw a huge grass fire, which began as he was looking at a small white cloud on a horizon as wide as the ocean. The Cossacks explained that the Kirghiz had set the steppe on fire. Looking more closely, he realized that the white cloud was, in fact, smoke. At noon the wind brought the smell of fire. The transport had to halt on the banks of the River Ora. Shevchenko bathed in the river and felt refreshed. At this point the fire was distant, but after sunset Shevchenko feasted his eyes on an 'indescribable, magnificent picture of fire.' The sky glowed as the conflagration came nearer, with' 'red tongues licking the sky.' Everyone became quiet, as if expecting some wonder. General Schreiber himself asked Shevchenko to paint the terrible sight of the raging elements. Shevchenko obliged, and created one of his best water-colours. Afterwards he sat all night in Maksheev's tent, enjoying the sight of the distant flames. He also saw how 'along a curved line' against the fiery background there appeared a long row of camels, 'which disappeared, like Oriental shadows in the reddish mist.' His artistic imagination was sated, and when he fell asleep he dreamt about the fire, this time vivified by 'pictures of Sodom and Gomorrah, by the English painter Martin.' When he woke up he was startled to remember that he had seen a real fire before falling asleep.

So far, their itinerary allowed them to bivouac at night on the river-bank. One day Shevchenko noticed that some Bashkir members of the expedition, on horseback or on foot, were beginning to leave the ranks and travel in a certain direction by themselves. One Bashkir elder told the poet that they had gone to see the 'holy tree.' Curious, Shevchenko rode two *versts* in that direction and came to a huge old poplar, growing at the side of a well. This 'green giant' in the middle of the desert caught his imagination, and he painted it. The tree was surrounded by a crowd of worshippers bringing all kinds of sacrifices. The whole scene stunned the poet, and he 'halted his horse to look for the last time at the green giant of the desert.' The giant, moved by the wind, waved its branches, and Shevchenko said 'farewell' and returned to the transport. The episode later inspired Shevchenko to write the poem 'Behind the Door in God's Place an Axe Lay' ('U Boha za dvermy lezhala sokyra').

The well where the holy tree grew created a stream that flowed into the Kara-Butak River. The transport remained there for two days. A fort was being built and the priest from the expeditionary force consecrated the ground, while the engineer in charge of construction, whose name we do not know, invited the leaders of the expedition, including Shevchenko, to his quarters for a meal. He must have been an exceptionally intelligent military engineer because Shevchenko remembered that 'he was the only human being in this desolate land.' Shevchenko spent a long time in conversation with him, after which his host gave him a bottle of tarragon vinegar and a few lemons, a 'priceless gift in this desert.' Before the expedition reached the Irghiz River, two streams, the Yaman-Kairokta and the Yaksha-Kairokta, had to be crossed. The steppe, the poet wrote, 'continued to be joyless,' except that on the horizon some Kirghiz houses 'made of stone or clay could be seen.' The desert was full of quartz sand. Beyond the Irghiz River a tall mountain, Aulie-Tau, was visible. Some Kirghiz saints were buried there. Bypassing the mountain, the expedition again grew close to the Irghiz River and spent a night near the gravemound of the warrior Dustan. Shevchenko, who was such an avid collector of the antique remains in his own country, now began sketching the views and monuments of this eastern people.

Not far from Dustan's grave the expedition came across the corpses of the Russian patrol that had been routed there by the defenders of Khiva.[1] For the first time in his life Shevchenko saw mutilated, headless corpses 'strewn across the steppe.' He attended the mass burial. These experiences had a special significance for him. Only two and a half years earlier he had written his 'Caucasus,' in which he called on the native peoples to defend their freedom from the Russian invaders. Sarcastically he characterized Russian imperialist policy:

> We are Christians, we have shrines, schools,
> All the wealth, and God himself is with us!
> One thing disturbs us: your hut,
> Built without permission. Why don't we

---

1 After several military expeditions against it, the Khanate of Khiva was finally conquered by the Russians in 1873.

Arrest and Exile 1847–57

> Throw you your own crust, as if you were a dog?
> Why don't you pay us for the sun?[2]

Now Shevchenko could see how the native peoples of this Asian area defended their huts and crusts and their right to the sun. These thoughts were close to the poet's heart, and he repeated them at Orsk:

> Since time immemorial
> The desert has hidden from the people,
> But we have found it:
> We have built fortresses,
> And soon there will be graves –
> We shall achieve all this.[3]

Fifteen *versts* further on Shevchenko saw in the foothills another Russian fort which struck him as very 'desolate.' Four similar forts were passed before the expedition stopped for a longer rest on the banks of the swampy River Yaman-Okty. The rest was necessary because, during the next seven days, they had to cross the 'Kirghiz Sahara' – the terrible desert Karakumi (Black Sands), which had given rise to dreadful legends.

In order to avoid the heat General Schreiber commanded the transport to start moving before sunrise. Yet to everyone's surprise, that day a keen, cool northerly wind made them shiver. For three days it was cool, but when the expedition was still ten *versts* away from any water-wells, the weather changed and it grew very hot. Never in his life had Shevchenko experienced such a heat wave. When they finally reached water, they found it polluted and salty. The poet was saved by the lemons he had been given by the engineer in Kara-Butak. He boiled some water and had tea with lemon, which quenched his thirst. It would have been better to cross the Karakumi Desert at night, when it was not so hot, but then the horses and camels would get no rest, since at night they would be moving in harness and during the day the mosquitoes would give them no peace. The most difficult part of the journey followed. Before them there appeared a 'light-pink plain.' This was a dried-up lake, covered with a thin layer of white salt. Shevchenko was fascinated by the sight but was warned to close his eyes, which might be damaged by the fine dust. Many members of the expedition had to receive medical attention, and Shevchenko, too, was temporarily blinded.

2 'Kavkaz,' *Povne*, I, 326
3 'A.O. Kozachkovskomu,' ibid, II, 65

Beyond the blinding plain, strewn with sandhills, there opened up a flat land, which was 'marked with a white row of horses' and camels' skeletons.' Most of them had been abandoned after the unsuccessful expedition against Khiva by General Perovsky, in which, nine years earlier, hundreds of men and thousands of horses and camels had perished. Finally, after the transport crossed another river, 'a faint blue line' on the horizon could be seen. This was the Aral Sea. Shevchenko noted that everybody 'suddenly cheered up,' as if sensing 'fresh air and a bright breeze from the sea.' Next day Shevchenko and others bathed at Sari-Chaganaku, which was a bay of the Aral Sea. But this was not the end of the journey. Their destination, Raim, was still sixty kilometres away. The last lap was travelled mostly at night because the daytime temperature reached forty-five degrees and one could fry an egg in the blazing sun. At last the fort of Raim was reached. It had a rather dismal look – 'one long barrack, covered with reeds – that's all.' The expedition was met by the entire garrison from the fort. Shevchenko was frightened when he saw the pale, sad faces of the soldiers, who appeared more like prisoners. He would now be a member of that garrison. The fort stood on a hill between two lakes where, a hundred years earlier, the Kirghiz had built a memorial to their hero, Raim. Beyond the fort one could see the silvery band of the River Syr-Daria.

It was on 19 June that the expedition reached its base. Work on assembling the schooner *Constantine* took thirty days, until 20 July. It was to serve as the headquarters of Butakov's expedition to explore the Aral Sea. As he had during the journey, Shevchenko shared quarters with Maksheev in Raim. He had recovered his good spirits. During the trip he had sketched several landscapes, and now he was busy doing the same kind of work in Raim. Although he found it hard to bear the inconveniences of camp life, the great heat, the tarantulas and scorpions, he was glad to dispense with the daily drill. The people he met there treated him very well. His future superior, Butakov, became so friendly with him that Shevchenko, writing later to Princess Repnina, called him his 'comrade and friend.' With Butakov's deputy, Pospelov, Shevchenko was on familiar 'Thou' terms. The botanist and geologist, Tomasz Werner, was a Polish exile and soon found a common language with the poet. Apart from these men, all members of the expeditionary force, Shevchenko got to know, with the help of Fedir Lazarevsky, several of the local people, who protected him, helped him to send out mail, and shielded him from those who might not have liked the poet.

Finally, on 25 July everything was ready and the schooners *Constantine* and *Nicholas* sailed from Raim. The fort's commandant, Yerofeev, seconded to Butakov's expedition five non-commissioned officers, one medical orderly, and thirty-six privates, among them Shevchenko. Together with the officers, the entire crew of both vessels numbered fifty. The *Constantine*, which was the larger of the two, had a crew of twenty-seven men. It was commanded by Butakov, and the complement included Shevchenko. The boat had one large cabin where, apart from the officers (Butakov, Maksheev, and two topographers), there was also the medical orderly Istomin, the geologist Werner, and the sketcher Shevchenko. Both exiles were treated as equals by Butakov.

For six days they sailed through the mouth of Syr-Daria, and on 30 July they reached the open sea. The schooner *Nicholas*, commanded by Pospelov, was to explore the west shore of the Sea of Aral from the mouth of Syr-Daria to the cape of Kum-Su-Ata. The *Constantine*'s course was to the west, where she was to undertake a general exploration of the sea within the next two months.

The expedition started work from the eastern shore. Topographical measurements were taken, and a map of the shoreline was sketched. Butakov used the sextant, and whenever the schooner dropped anchor, Shevchenko sketched views of the shoreline. When they decided to land, Werner conducted botanical and geological research and Shevchenko painted landscapes. Sailing was very hard, for the heat was at its peak. The Aral Sea has a reputation for being very stormy, and the small schooner was ill equipped to withstand turbulence. The men were tired, worked very hard under the scorching sun, and were short of food. The food supplies, prepared in Orenburg, had gone bad – 'the dried bread became mouldy; the fat turned pink; butter was rancid and could not be used with *kasha*, and only the peas remained wholesome, but they were in short supply and were served once a week.' Terrible northwesterly and northeasterly winds caused great storms, and when the winds suddenly dropped, it took a long time for the boat to return to an even keel. Several times the schooner struck underwater rocks, which were frequent in the northwestern part of the sea. Another danger was the possibility of running aground. Sometimes storms would catch sailors in small boats outside the vessel and toss them about until they were exhausted. Yet, in spite of all the difficulties the energetic Butakov managed to survey the sea in thirty-eight days, and on 7 September he changed course for the north to reach the delta of Syr-Daria during high tide and land on the island of Kos-Aral, where there was a fortification that had been recently built. During the last stage of the voyage the members of the expedition discovered several hitherto unknown small islands. Butakov named the largest one after Nicholas I. A pleasant surprise awaited them on the island – hundreds of wild goats innocently approached the travellers, probably the first men they had ever seen. That night the hungry sailors ate goat meat for dinner.

On 23 September the *Constantine* was anchored near the desert island of Kos-Aral, which would be the expedition's home until the following spring. After two months of sailing without stop it was good to step on firm ground. Shevchenko was disappointed when, in the first batch of mail that reached the island, there were no letters for him. He tried to cheer himself up by comparing his fate with that of the others. Earlier in his exile he had written to Princess Repnina, comparing himself to Kulish and Kostomarov. He felt lucky, because the former had been unfortunate enough to cause suffering to his wife and the latter to his old mother. Now Shevchenko compared himself to Werner, who had a wife and children and who had not received mail either.

A funny episode occurred in Kos-Aral. Soldiers were not allowed to grow beards, but Shevchenko, during the voyage, was unable to shave and, like the other sailors, grew a beard. The garrison at Kos-Aral consisted of Ural Cossacks, many of whom were old believers.[4] Seeing a man with a long beard, they took Shevchenko to be a martyred priest. The commandant of the Cossacks came to Shevchenko, fell on his knees, and asked to be blessed. The poet was amused but also touched, and quickly made the sign of the cross over the pious old believer. In the evening the Cossacks honoured Shevchenko at a banquet that 'he could not have dreamt of.' The end of this episode came later, in Raim.

Soon the officers, the members of the expedition, rejoined their units. Maksheev returned to Orenburg, and Shevchenko went with him as far as Raim. Before leaving the Cossack leader again asked to be blessed and offered Shevchenko twenty-five roubles. Shevchenko refused the money and wanted to end this farcical mystification. Leaving Kos-Aral, having got to know the Ural Cossacks a little better, his opinion of them declined because of their 'superstition and backwardness.'

On arrival in Raim, Shevchenko found some mail – letters from Aleksandreisky and Lyzohub. They brought news of the European revolution, which gave rise to hopes 'for a better time.' Aleksandreisky wrote that 'this is an old song ... only now it is sung to the accompaniment of the twenty-four-pound calibre.' The Russian press did not adequately inform its readers about the revolutions of 1848 that swept across Western

---

4 Old believers, a religious sect that separated from the Russian Orthodox Church in the seventeenth century. They refused to acknowledge any departure from Muscovite religious customs and were persecuted for their beliefs.

Europe. Yet some of Shevchenko's friends might have received news of them through correspondence. Early in May, when the expedition started off from Orsk, the members could have had only the vaguest information about the European events of February 1848. In the middle of March the Russian press reported that Louis Philippe had voluntarily renounced his throne, and the radicals were blamed for creating ferment. On 14 March Nicholas I proclaimed that the rebellion (*miatezh*) was also threatening Russia. Both Maksheev and Werner could have had more detailed information about what was actually going on. The Poles in particular were well informed, since they participated in an uprising in Hungary and many of them had recently been exiled. This was welcome news to Shevchenko. Yet he received bad news from Lyzohub about the rapid spread of cholera in Ukraine. The disease, which could not be properly combated, had reached Odessa. The news of the cholera epidemic reached Orenburg and caused panic there. Senior officials, the clergy, and physicians were fleeing the city. The battalions stationed there lost hundreds of men to cholera. A prisoner arrived in Raim who had been exiled for not controlling the guards who had refused to bury the corpses. Under the influence of these stories Shevchenko later wrote his poem 'The Plague' ('Chuma').

Returning to Kos-Aral, the poet settled down in the wooden barracks. The boredom was unbearable. There was nothing to do in his spare time. The only occupation during his free time was to hunt the tiger that was attacking the camp. Butakov had organized an ambush, using half the men in his garrison, and the tiger was finally killed. Shevchenko painted the vanquished king of the desert. In one of his 'tristia' the poet expressed his mood at this time:

> Boredom and autumn
> Surround me in a foreign land.
> Dear God! Where shall I hide?
> What shall I do? I walk along the Aral
> And secretly write verses. I sin,
> And I recall other times
> In my soul and write about them.[5]

When the days were warm and windless it was possible to wander all over the island, viewing the monotonous but colourful seascapes. Then, on 22 October, winter struck with severe frosts. Bad weather began, and

5 'Mov za podushne,' *Povne*, II, 107

snowstorms were frequent. The days became even drearier. Shevchenko could not sketch or paint, so he wrote. Just as in Myrhorod and Pereiaslav, when he had written while he was very ill, so now he devoted his free time to writing. One-fourth of all his poetry in exile was written in Kos-Aral. Shevchenko had started a new notebook into which he copied some earlier poems and wrote down new ones, beginning with the lines 'Let us versify, again.' His creative imagination was unimpaired. Various genres intertwined: after a ballad came a serious poem, then a lyric, and after that a stylized folksong, followed by a grotesque poem. Christmas that year was a sad occasion. In his thoughts the poet was in Ukraine, and, on Christmas Eve, in a poem dedicated to F. Lazarevsky, he wrote:

> The Christmas Feast is drawing near ...
> It is difficult, dear friend and brother,
> To celebrate alone
> In the desert. Tomorrow morning
> Belfries will sound throughout Ukraine,
> Tomorrow morning the people will
> Go to church to pray. Tomorrow morning
> A hungry wolf will howl
> In this desert and a cold hurricane
> Will blow fiercely, covering
> With sand and snow my barracks.
> That is how I will celebrate
> This blessed Feast.[6]

Shevchenko spent four months, until the end of January 1849, in Kos-Aral, and then, together with Werner, went to Raim. The northern side of the Aral Sea froze in winter, and one could travel from Kos-Aral to the mainland across the ice. For the previous two years Shevchenko had been intermittently ill with scurvy. He also had frequent headaches. His feet were covered with boils that he had acquired during the long expedition. In Raim the barracks were infested with bedbugs. However, there were also two doctors whom Shevchenko knew and consulted. The new commandant of Fort Raim was Lieutenant-Colonel Matveev. His predecessor, Yerofeev, while completely drunk, had staged a fire raid against a Kirghiz settlement so that he could watch the flames. Matveev was good to Shevchenko and allowed him complete freedom. The poet still had a beard, wore a fur cap and an overcoat, and had no military

---

6 'Ne dodomu vnochi iduchy,' ibid, 184–5

duties. He lived in a hut with Werner. Brigadier-General Fediaev, while visiting Raim, brought Shevchenko a whole new box of paints. With these Shevchenko painted portraits of the officers, asking one rouble for each portrait. Now he could afford to buy his favourite bottle of rum.

The poet was mostly sad and withdrawn, but on occasion, especially after a few drinks, he grew livelier and more talkative. Then he amused everyone with his stories. Yet, as the group became tipsier, Shevchenko's jokes turned to sarcasm, even to tears. He cursed his fate, and one officer cadet remembered how the poet, in such a mood, called Matveev an 'executioner' and wished that he and the entire garrison would 'fall into a bottomless pit.' Life was hard, even for free men. Snowdrifts sometimes reached the rooftops, and 'for weeks one could not see God's world because of constant snowstorms.' Doctor Kilkevich, a friend of Shevchenko's, maintained that he had only a little more time to suffer the boredom and terrible living conditions. On 26 March Shevchenko wrote to Maksheev that there was absolutely nothing new to report from Raim. In order to kill boredom the officers in the garrison sometimes visited the Kirghiz elders. They took Shevchenko along with them. On one occasion they killed a big boar, and Shevchenko participated in a hunt for a tiger who fell into a trap set for him near the dead boar.

The only thing to look forward to was the mail, but it often disappointed the poet: 'Once again the mail / Brought me nothing from Ukraine', he wrote, and further complained that

> At one time they swore
> Eternal friendship with me,
> But now they have vanished
> Like a cloud, without a tear,
> This holy dew.
> Now, in my old age
> I must ... people.[7]

Yet he could not write the word 'curse' and continued, in a different mood:

> No, no!
> They are dead of cholera,
> Or they would send me
> Just a scrap of paper.[8]

7 'I znov meni,' ibid, 173
8 Ibid

He searched for solace in his work:

> People will talk, they will betray me,
> But it will cheer me
> And encourage me,
> As well as tell the truth.⁹

Nostalgia for his native land never left him, and in the next poem he described his loneliness:

> In bondage and solitude
> There is none
> To share the heart with ...
> ...
> And yet the heart must be consoled,
> It yearns, begging
> For a kind word. It listens in vain!
> It is as if the snow has laid
> My tepid corpse upon the plain.¹⁰

Often he wrote of 'anguish invading his lonely heart' like 'a thief.'

Raim was snowbound till the end of March. The ice broke on Syr-Daria in April. The expedition could not begin its work before the beginning of May. On 22 April Butakov sent letters to Orenburg asking General Obruchev to allow Shevchenko and Werner to be included in the expedition, especially since Shevchenko was needed to sketch 'hydrographic sites' on the maps. This also meant that Shevchenko would accompany Butakov on a visit to Orenburg, which would be a pleasant change. Yet the prospect of a new expedition of five, not just two, months' duration was not appealing. Terrible heat, constant thirst, and lack of fresh water could not be avoided. One improvement over the first expedition was that Butakov secured better food supplies.

On 5 May the expedition set out to sea. Pospelov, in the schooner *Nicholas*, sailed along the eastern shore of the Sea of Aral, while Butakov explored the western coast. At times it was very picturesque, because of the proximity of the Ust-Urt mountains. Wherever there was vegetation along the shore, drinking-water could also be found. Sometimes, however, it was hard to land a small boat because of the stormy waves. Only the southern shores of the Aral Sea are shallow and sandy. At one time,

---

9 Ibid, 174
10 'V nevoli,' ibid, 175

Fire in the steppes, 1848; watercolour

Moonlit night at Kos Aral, 1848; watercolour

Arrest and Exile 1847-57

during a lengthy storm, the schooner had to be anchored at sea for two weeks, and everyone was forced to drink sea-water. They all paid for this with stomach cramps, and two weeks later Shevchenko suffered from a terrible headache.

The long sea voyage and the difficult conditions it entailed drove the poet to despair. On one occasion, when a boat was sent to a small island, he went along and deliberately lost himself, not wanting to return. In the end he was found and brought back to the boat. Watching his friend Werner he learned a great deal about geology. Later he wrote that 'Murchison himself would have thanked him for his knowledge.'[11] One can assume that during this sea voyage Shevchenko's scientific knowledge, which he had first acquired at the academy, was considerably widened. Werner's collection of specimens of 150 different minerals and 75 examples of the local flora must have helped in this. There must have been a great deal of talk on board about scientific subjects. It was then that Shevchenko got to know the first two volumes of the famous encyclopaedia of the natural sciences, Humboldt's *Cosmos*. Butakov was a serious scientist and must have encouraged the poet to read and discuss various books and explorers. Some of the islands discovered during the voyage were named after famous explorers.

In spite of all the obstacles, the expedition succeeded, during the two months in 1848 and the five months in 1849, in exploring an area of 65,000 square kilometres of the sea. Shevchenko executed over two hundred sketches illustrating the work of this very important expedition. All this had to be done anonymously, for Shevchenko's name could not appear in the public annals of the expedition. It could even be said that, ironically enough, he perfomed this entire task illegally, for the formal revocation by the tsar of the ban on sketching never came.

The summer drew to an end and the expedition had to return to its base, via Aral to Raim and on to Orenburg, covering a distance of over one thousand kilometres through parched steppes and waterless desert. They had to reach Orenburg before the onset of the terrible snowstorms (*purgas*). They passed through Kos-Aral, where Butakov found a positive reply to his request to include Shevchenko and Werner in the expedition. Although this was to be expected, since a great deal of work still remained to be done, Shevchenko was glad to hear the news. Had the reply been negative he would have had to remain in the bug-infested barracks in Raim.

Once again, however, Shevchenko experienced disappointment when

---

11 Sir Roderick Murchison (1792-1871), famous geologist, co-author of *Russia and the Ural Mountains* (1845)

there was no mail waiting for him. In fact, this time he grew angry rather than depressed, and in a poem hurled bitter accusations against the Ukrainian public:

> It is almost ten years
> Since I gave my *Kobzar* to the people,
> And their mouths are sealed tight,
> None barks, or swears,
> As if I did not exist.[12]

The feeling of loneliness in a sea of national indifference must have been deep. This led him to believe that his torment and his love for his native land were in vain, unnecessary. He asked:

> For whom do I write? For what?
> Why do I love Ukraine?
> Does she deserve this sacred fire?[13]

He created his poems without any hope of publication, simply to 'relieve his bondage.' He followed an inner urge to create, without any need to justify it. This drive was irrational, a mysterious national feeling, which appeared in his imagination as

>   an old Cossack,
> Bewiskered, rides across my fancy
> Poor sinner that I am, free,
> Riding on a black horse!
> I know nothing else.[14]

The poet was powerless to explain this love which truly possessed him. All he knew was that it was invincible:

> And all the same, I love her,
> My vast Ukraine,
> Though I've roamed around her in loneliness.

The suffering was sometimes unbearable:

12 'Khiba samomu napysat,' *Povne*, II, 224
13 Ibid
14 Ibid, 225

Arrest and Exile 1847-57

> As a fierce serpent,
> Crushed, lies dying in the steppes
> Awaiting sunset,
> So I suffer now.[15]

He asked not for praise and admiration but for moral support. And when his countrymen remained silent, his inner voice told him:

> Steel yourself in patience,
> Pray quietly to God,
> And spit on the community;
> It's as stupid as a cabbage.[16]

The inner, instinctual voice prevailed, and the poet steeled himself and wrote on.

There were letters for him, but they were kept in Orenburg by Lazarevsky, who was expecting Shevchenko's arrival any day. These letters, of course, were not from 'the community' but from Princess Repnina and Lyzohub, both very faithful correspondents. But the hundreds of other fellow-countrymen who had greeted him with such enthusiasm during his Ukrainian travels remained silent.

After these stormy travails, the time came to depart. The poet marked the end of his stay with the expedition (which had lasted for one and a half years) in calm and collected fashion:

> All ready now! The sails have been unfurled;
> We glided over blue waves,
> Weed-strewn, to Syr-Daria,
> The boats and ship looming large.
> Farewell, poor Kos-Aral!
> You have amused me for two years
> In my cursed boredom!
> Thank you, my friend! Be proud
> That men have found you at last
> And understood you.
> Farewell, my friend! I grant
> Neither praise nor blame for your desert.
> Perhaps, in another land, I will recall
> My earlier boredom on your shores.[17]

15 Ibid
16 Ibid
17 'Hotovo, parus rozpustyly,' ibid, 232

Early in October the small flotilla reached Raim. On the fifth day of that month the fort commandant, Damich, issued an order detailing a military guard which was to leave Raim on 8 October to escort the following members of the expedition on their return journey to Orenburg: Captain Butakov, Lieutenant Pospelov, two topographers, Rybin and Khristoforov, the medical orderly, Istomin, and Privates Werner and Shevchenko. On 10 October they left Raim. The autumn sun was mild, and the return journey was bearable. Shevchenko has left no account of it. The only document to refer to it is his beautiful elegy, possibly written in Kara-Butak, addressed to an unknown local friend:

> You, my only precious friend,
> Woe to your spirit in a foreign land
> In loneliness!
> Who will speak to you,
> And greet you with a friendly glance?
> Around you, like a lifeless body,
> Stretches a wasted wilderness,
> Forsaken by God.[18]

He himself was familiar with the 'God-forsaken wilderness' and sympathized with a friend who had been left behind.

In some letters, written later, Shevchenko said that his journey 'was measured with his feet.' This must have been an exaggeration because it was impossible to cover the thousand kilometres from Raim to Orenburg on foot in three weeks. The poet and his fellow-travellers reached Orenburg on 1 November. Even if they all walked occasionally to give the horses a rest, they must have travelled in wagons.

---

18 'My voseny taky pokhozhi,' ibid, 234

XI

After two and a half years Shevchenko was back in Orenburg. He did not return to the barracks but settled in a private apartment. He had been released from the Fourth Battalion and seconded to Butakov's group until the work of the expedition finished. At first he even shared quarters with Butakov. Fedir Lazarevsky was away on a trip across the steppes, but Serhiy Levytsky, whom the poet knew well, was there. Captain Gern, whom he recalled from an earlier stay in Orenburg, also greeted him warmly. Shevchenko asked Lyzohub to address all his letters in care of Captain Gern. Butakov was busy completing the work of the expedition, and Shevchenko was fully occupied. As a draughtsman he had to sketch a map of the Aral Sea, prepared in pencil by topographers, and paint, in water-colour, the surroundings. Some of the work had to be copied since officials in St Petersburg as well as Butakov and Obruchev all needed copies. Shevchenko was given an assistant. He was Bronisław Zaleski, a Polish exile and amateur painter who, on 5 November, began to work for Shevchenko, who took a great liking to him. Zaleski was very modest, a dreamer, generous, and with wide artistic interests. Soon he became a second Schternberg for Shevchenko, bringing into the poet's life a calming and steadying influence.

Shevchenko's main worry was still his uncertainty whether he would officially be allowed to sketch and paint. Twenty months had passed since Orlov had asked the commandant of the Orenburg Corps for his verdict, and so far there had been no official answer. To be sure, Shevchenko had sketched for Butakov's expedition, but was his work never to be acknowledged? Were all the sufferings he had undergone in vain? And what would the poet's future be if he were to be treated with such indifference by the officials in St Petersburg? Soon after settling down in Orenburg he wrote to Lyzohub, asking him to let Varvara Repnina know that 'even if I am not very happy, I am at least cheerful.' On 14 November he wrote to the princess, telling her that he often thought of Yahotyn. He claimed that he had changed: 'Now I experience neither joy nor sorrow. Instead my spirit is at peace ... almost cold. The future does not exist for me. Can constant misfortune cause such an unpleasant change in a human being? And yet it is so. Now I am only a shadow of the old Shevchenko and I thank God for it.'[1]

It would be wrong to interpret this as a sign of the poet's resignation. It was only a passing mood. His entire spirit was rebelling once again. Obruchev, after consulting with Butakov, on 20 November sent a request to Count Orlov asking if Shevchenko might be permitted to paint under 'the supervision of his superiors,' without, of course, mentioning that he had been sketching and painting for the past year and a half. While all this was in progress, Shevchenko became very depressed and started drinking. This lasted for some time and led to a serious illness. On 28 November Zaleski wrote to Arkady Węgrzynowski that Shevchenko was very ill, and he blamed his drinking for it. Zaleski expressed the hope that Christian feelings of contrition would help the poet to recover. It was not surprising that he was taken ill. Shevchenko's body had been seriously undermined during the expeditions and could not tolerate large doses of alcohol. Very soon after he became ill, his friends rallied around and did their utmost to help and encourage him. Fortunately, there were many friends, almost as many as he had had during his student days in St Petersburg. On 14 November Lazarevsky returned from a field trip and took care of the poet. He and the others saw to it that Shevchenko had enough money, though later he began to earn some by painting portraits. On his return to Orenburg, Lazarevsky discovered in his apartment (apart from Shevchenko and Levytsky) the naval officer Pospelov, whom Shevchenko had got to know very well in Kos-Aral. All four lived together in great comradeship, sharing everything between them. Lazarevsky even loaned Shevchenko some of his clothing, because 'by that time he almost never wore his uniform.' This close-knit group was joined occasionally by Captain Gern, by Butakov, and by Colonel Matveev, who had shown so much regard for Shevchenko when he was his superior officer in Raim. Shevchenko was at the heart of this group. Often they talked well into the night, occasionally till the early hours of the morning. During these improvised discussions Shevchenko and Levytsky entertained the others by singing. Whenever there were ladies present, 'Shevchenko's constant companion was a Tatar woman, Zabarzhada, who was extremely beautiful.' She inspired some lines in Shevchenko's poem, written in 1850 in Orenburg:

1 Ibid, VI, 58

195   Arrest and Exile 1847-57

> On your supple form and beauty
> So innocent and young
> I feast my eyes.[2]

The merry social circle broke up early in January 1850, when Lazarevsky had to leave for the Caspian Sea and Levytsky for St Petersburg, where Butakov also had to go to present the final report on his expedition to the authorities. The disconsolate Shevchenko wrote:

> We sang together and parted
> Without tears, without much talk,
> Shall we ever meet again,
> Will we sing together once more?[3]

Shevchenko began his fourth year of exile with a poem entitled 'I count my exiled days and nights' ('Lichu v nevoli dni i nochi'), and he ended with the lines

> Even if I were crucified,
> I'd still embroider
> Quietly white sheets of paper.[4]

He was now reading Lermontov with great pleasure and was greatly encouraged by him. After Lazarevsky's and Levytsky's departure he moved to Gern's apartment in the Nova Slobodka suburb of Orenburg. He made many new friends among the Polish exiles there. There were over two thousand of them in the province of Orenburg, and after the European upheavals of 1849-50 their number had steadily increased. Gern's sister was married to Kirsha, an official in Orenburg. Zaleski was a frequent guest at the Kirshas'. Apart from this old friend, Shevchenko met Staniewicz, Serednicki, Turno, Father Michał Zielonka, and Arkady Węgrzynowski – all Polish exiles. He also knew the Polish pharmacist in Orenburg, Zeisyk. The Poles knew a great deal about events in Europe, and they were well organized. One Polish group held a banquet in Shevchenko's honour. He had earlier written a poem 'To the Poles' ('Poliakam'), dedicated to Bronisław Zaleski.

Shevchenko's friendships were not limited to an intimate circle of

---

2 'I stanom hnuchkym,' ibid, II, 259
3 'My zaspivaly,' ibid, 240
4 'Lichu v nevoli,' ibid, 237

friends or to Polish exiles. Lazarevsky wrote that in general Orenburg had extended a warm welcome to the poet. He was well received in the upper circles of society, too. Occasionally he was invited to receptions given by the governor general, Obruchev. There not everyone was to his liking, but of some he was fond. One of them was Baron Meidel, the senior medical officer in Orenburg. Shevchenko also painted a portrait of the wife of the quartermaster general, Colonel Blaramberg, who was also conducting research in the Caspian area and in Persia. Doctor Meidel showed true heroism during the outbreak of cholera in 1848, when he alone remained at his post while others fled the city. These men attracted Shevchenko, and they also found him likeable. Lazarevsky reports that while visiting Meidel, Shevchenko acted with 'great restraint' and 'great dignity.' The wife of the governor general, Matilda Obruchev, was one of Orenburg's great hostesses. Someone suggested that he should commission Shevchenko to paint her portrait, which she did. Shevchenko obliged and, ironically enough, was paid by Obruchev, one of the faithful servants of Nicholas I, who had forbidden the artist to paint. Butakov also presented Obruchev with a deluxe album of water-colour sketches by Shevchenko painted during the Aral Sea expedition. With friends in such high places Shevchenko felt better. He behaved as if he were a free man, walking through the town in civilian clothes without fear. It was thus all the more disappointing when, on 20 November, a reply was received from St Petersburg to Obruchev's request that Shevchenko should be allowed to paint. The answer from the tsar was a firm no.

This occurred before Butakov's and Levytsky's departures for St. Petersburg. Shevchenko was also informed that he must rejoin his company in Raim. Fortunately, this could only happen in the spring, since no one could travel from Orenburg to the Aral Sea in the winter. Shevchenko, for the time being, was spared returning to the army. He continued living at Gern's apartment, trembling at the thought of returning to Raim the following May. He still had time to try once more to obtain a reprieve, and he wrote letters to Zhukovsky and to Count Orlov. He pleaded with the latter: 'I ask only one favour – permission to paint. Throughout my whole life I have never painted anything criminal – I swear before Almighty God! You will open my blind eyes and enliven my dead soul.'[5] In both letters he complained about his health, undermined by military service, and cited Butakov as a witness to his good behaviour. In other letters written at that time to Lyzohub, Bodiansky, and Repnina he complained about his fate. He asked the princess to intercede for him

---

5 P. Zaitsev, ed., *Povne vydannia tvoriv Tarasa Shevchenka* (Warsaw 1935), XI, 66

with Zhukovsky and Gogol, and asked for the latter's address so that he could write to him himself. Hope was failing him, and 'only Christian philosophy can struggle with it.' The poet was becoming desperate and, at times, despondent, but he also asked his friends to send him books and begged them not to abandon him. He had little hope that the tsar would show mercy, but perhaps he might at least allow him to paint. After all, his 'crime' was only literary.

As it happened, Shevchenko's fear of returning to Raim soon dissipated. Obruchev was planning another expedition, this time a geological one, into the mountains of Kara-Tau. Deposits of coal had been discovered there, and Werner was to be the chief geologist in this new expedition. Shevchenko's friends did not find it hard to persuade Obruchev to include the poet as Werner's assistant. The route to be taken went to the Mangyshlak peninsula, up to the Kara-Tau Mountains, then along the Ural River as far as Guriev. The route was much shorter than the one to the Aral Sea. The journey included a three-day voyage across the Caspian Sea to the fortress of Novopetrovsk. Altogether it was a much pleasanter route than the exhausting trek across the desert. On 22 January Obruchev ordered the commandant of the Twenty-third Division, General Tolmachov, to include Werner and Shevchenko in the expedition. This time the poet had a new role – that of geologist.

Early in March Obruchev received a letter from General Dubelt, notifying him that Count Orlov did not wish to ask the tsar to rescind Shevchenko's prohibition from painting because the tsar had turned down an ealier request in December. This was the final negative answer in response to the intercessions of Shevchenko's friends.

With the coming of spring Lazarevsky returned to Orenburg from his field-trip. Shevchenko was secretly painting in Gern's apartment, where he was living. In April he began to paint a portrait of Gern and his wife. The spring was unusually warm, and Shevchenko wore a light overcoat. Because the expedition was delayed, he had not been summoned to go. Just before 20 March he received a letter from Serhiy Levytsky in St Petersburg. The letter raised some hopes, but it must have been written before Dubelt's letter. Apart from news about efforts to help the poet, the letter contained some information about Shevchenko's old friends and an interesting passage about a young scholar from Kharkiv, Mykola Holovko, who apparently said that 'almost one thousand men are ready to stand up for what you said' and were not afraid of the tsar himself. Shevchenko might have interpreted this news as evidence of the existence of a revolutionary organization supporting his ideas.

In the meantime the poet became the victim of his own decency. Gern's wife was having an affair with a young officer, Isaev. Full of gratitude to Gern for his help, Shevchenko could not stand idly by while his friend's wife was betraying him. Lazarevsky tried, in vain, to warn Shevchenko not to interfere in other people's affairs. But the poet was furious, and on Good Friday, 25 April, he spotted the lovers together and brought the deceived husband to the scene. Isaev did not challenge Gern to a duel, but the following day he reported to Obruchev in writing that Private Shevchenko was wearing civilian clothes and, contrary to the tsar's orders, was writing poetry and painting. Obruchev was astounded. He could not ignore the matter, since he was afraid that Isaev would denounce him. He acted slowly, and Gern managed to warn Shevchenko that his room would be searched. Shevchenko and Lazarevsky tried to get rid of any incriminating evidence but did such a bad job that the police found Shevchenko's civilian clothes, a box of paints, and a whole pile of letters addressed to him. All these materials were sent to Obruchev, who after reading some of the letters, was beside himself. At an Easter reception in his residence Obruchev was very complimentary to Isaev and lambasted Shevchenko. On the same day he gave orders to arrest the poet. Two weeks later, on 12 May, Shevchenko was ordered to rejoin the Fifth Battalion at the fortress of Orsk, where three years earlier he had started his military service. It was back to the barracks, military drill, and all the other hated duties. Commandant Meshkov received orders from Orenburg to keep the poet under strict surveillance.

For some time Obruchev did nothing with the materials seized in Shevchenko's room. He was uncertain what to do. A whole month elapsed before, on 23 May, he sent a report to the army minister, Prince Chernyshev, about Shevchenko's civilian clothes, his writing, and his painting. He forwarded the relevant materials and singled out the letters that Shevchenko had received from Serhiy Levytsky and the Lazarevsky brothers. In his report Obruchev did not mention how Shevchenko came to be in Orenburg. The army minister had Shevchenko listed as a private in the Fifth Battalion of the Orenburg Corps. No one had notified the ministry that this private had been transferred to the Fourth Battalion in the spring of 1848. The army minister referred the matter for further investigation by the Third Section and gave the information to the commandant of the Fifth Battalion, who for the previous two years had had no knowledge of Shevchenko.

In accordance with the tsar's orders two investigations were started: one in St Petersburg, where, on the basis of Levytsky's letter to Shevchenko, the existence of a possible Ukrainian secret society was suspected; the other in Orenburg and in the fortress of Orsk, to find out who had allowed Shevchenko to write and to paint. As far as the second inquiry was concerned, it was obvious that Obruchev himself was guilty, since at Butakov's request he had allowed Shevchenko to sketch. But he had to find a scapegoat. Shevchenko was re-arrested and placed in gaol in the fortress of Orsk. This occurred on 28 June, when the commandant, Colonel Chigir, arrived at Orsk to take charge of the investigation. Shevchenko was interrogated, and answered questions in writing. His replies were straightforward, but when asked about writing poetry he did not tell the truth but maintained that he had merely copied verses written before his arrest in 1847. He also claimed that some of these poems were in fact transcriptions of Ukrainian folksongs that he had collected in his travels. Colonel Chigir, who did not see the poems, since they had been sent to St Petersburg, accepted this explanation. As for his sketching and painting, Shevchenko told the truth: that he had been asked to do so by Captain Butakov. In summing up, Shevchenko declared that he had not broken the tsarist prohibition and reiterated that the original sentence did not forbid him to correspond with friends. In any case, in his letters he had not expressed any disloyal opinions. While writing his testimony the poet became worried that he might be forbidden to write letters.

In the meantime, the investigation of Levytsky and Holovko was in full swing. The official file of the case was entitled 'The Case of Private Shevchenko, Collegiate Secretary Levytsky, and Master of Arts Holovko.' Count Orlov, after casually looking through the evidence, exaggerated its importance, and the gendarmes began to worry. The passage in Levytsky's letter to Shevchenko saying that there were one thousand men ready to support Shevchenko's ideas drew Orlov's attention, and on 13 June he wrote to the tsar telling him that he suspected the loyalty of both Levytsky and Holovko. The tsar ordered their arrest and a search of their homes. Levytsky was arrested on 15 June after an unsuccessful attempt to drown himself in a river. Holovko shot himself as soon as the police entered his apartment. The search revealed nothing sensational, except that Holovko was a liberal and had contacts with socialists and with Mombelli, who knew Shevchenko personally. After a thorough investigation of Levytsky the gendarmes failed to find anything incriminating and decided that he did not belong to any secret society. General Dubelt aptly summed up the interrogation by saying that 'the thousand Shevchenkos existed only in [Holovko's] imagination.' Orlov himself cross-examined Levytsky and found him innocent.

On 24 June the tsar confirmed Orlov's report dismissing the case as having in it 'nothing political.' The letters seized from Shevchenko demonstrated, however, that there were some people determined to alleviate his fate (Chernyshev, Butakov, Princess Repnina). They had used legal means to do so. The tsar ordered Levytsky to be kept under police surveillance, wrote, at Orlov's suggestion, to Princess Repnina, advising her 'to take less interest in the affairs of Little Russia,' and pronounced sentence on Shevchenko, instructing the ministry of armed forces to 'keep the aforesaid private under arrest' and empowering his superior officers to see that orders were carried out and Shevchenko closely watched. The tsar, relying on Orlov, believed that Shevchenko's superiors were more to blame than he was, and on 27 June he ordered that those who were guilty be punished. On 30 June the ministry of the army informed Obruchev of the tsar's orders, pointing out that the seized documents proved that Shevchenko still 'held to his earlier convictions, and was writing and sketching on slanderous topics.'

Obruchev received these instructions on 10 July, but even earlier, on the basis of Chigir's investigation, he had ordered the re-arrest of Shevchenko. Chigir blamed Major Meshkov for not informing the commandant of the Fourth Battalion, to which Shevchenko had been transferred, about the ban on writing and sketching. The ministry of the army was informed of all this, but since the investigation had brought to light no new facts about Shevchenko, it was decided, on 9 August, in accordance with the tsar's orders, to consider the arrest to be Shevchenko's punishment and, while repeating the ban on writing and sketching, to transfer the poet to a distant battalion, under strict supervision. Major Meshkov was given a severe reprimand. The commandant of the fortress of Orsk, Nedobrov, continued to cross-examine Shevchenko on the matter of his civilian clothes. The poet declared that he had worn them only at Gern's house. Pospelov also became involved in the investigation, since it was to his command that Butakov transferred Shevchenko. Pospelov denied ever seeing Shevchenko in civilian clothes. In the end Obruchev decided to put the blame on Butakov, but by that time Butakov was back in the navy and escaped punishment. The investigation failed to follow up Isaev's leads about Shevchenko's painting of portraits and writing new verse. Fortunately, before the search Shevchenko had managed to pass his 'boot-leg' booklets to Gern for safe keeping.

Even before the last traces of the investigation had died down Shevchenko was assigned to a new battalion. He had spent two and a half months, not in a military prison but in gaol, in the fortress of Orsk. On 8 October he was finally released and escorted by a non-commissioned officer, Bulatov, to the newly built fort of Novopetrovsk on the Caspian Sea. The battalion headquarters was in the city of Uralsk. Bulatov and Shevchenko stayed there for a day. Shevchenko rested in the private apartment of a Polish exile known by his pseudonym, Jakub Gordon, who was impressed by what the poet told him. In a later memoir the Pole wrote that 'an independent Ukraine was the object of [Shevchenko's] dreams.' Afterwards Shevchenko was taken by boat to Guriev, and on 14 October the local commandant dispatched him, again by sea, to his new destination.

XII

After a three-day voyage on the Caspian Sea, on 17 October 1850 the mailboat carrying Shevchenko and his escort Bulatov reached the fortress of Novopetrovsk on the sandy and rocky peninsula of Mangyshlak. It was the last voyage on that route before the start of the hurricane season. Bulatov, who delivered Shevchenko to the commandant of the fortress, was forced to spend the winter there. He brought two letters with him: one to the commandant of the fort, the other to the officer commanding two of the companies stationed at Novopetrovsk. The first letter contained an order in which private Shevchenko, a 'political criminal,' was assigned to serve in the companies of the First Battalion in Novopetrovsk, under 'the command of Staff Captain Potapov,' who was instructed to see that Shevchenko neither wrote nor painted, nor even 'had instruments for writing and painting.' This had the effect of surrounding Shevchenko with an aura of mystery. Captain Kosarev, in his memoirs, records that everyone was trying to guess who Shevchenko was and why a writer and painter should be punished in this way.

For two and a half years Shevchenko had done no military drill and had, in fact, been free from all military discipline. His situation was now far worse than at Orsk, where he had known people who were ready to protect him. He was quite defenceless and had no hope that his condition would ever improve. Now he was even forbidden to write letters, a right of which even the worst criminals were not deprived. Staff Captain Potapov turned out to be 'uneducated and heartless,' a man hated by everyone for his severity and cruelty. He detailed one soldier to keep an eye on Shevchenko, and he himself 'often tormented the man, who was already full of suffering,' as Kosarev relates. The poet's pockets were often searched to check whether he had hidden some of his writing. Worst of all, he was continually humiliated on the parade square, where he was unable to drill as he was ordered. The situation became so bad that other officers, seeing Shevchenko's suffering, interceded with Potapov, who refused to relent. In addition to the drill, he ordered Shevchenko to perform heavy physical labour, which he was unable to do. The situation was becoming desperate, and the desolate natural environment depressed the poet even further.

It is doubtful whether Shevchenko could have survived for long under these conditions. Once more it was his warm-hearted personality and charm that saved him. More and more officers objected to Potapov's treatment of the poet, who had won them over to his side. At Christmas 1850, in an empty barrack, an amateur theatrical performance was staged of Ostrovsky's play *A Family Affair* (*Svoi liudi sochtemsia*). Shevchenko took part in the production as set-designer and actor. It is not impossible that, as an enthusiast for the theatre, he could have been the inspirer and producer of the play. In any case, his appearance on stage was a huge success. In the life of the desolate fortress this was a real event. The performance was repeated, and Shevchenko drew the greatest applause. At the end of the last act he danced, to everyone's delight, a Ukrainian *hopak*. The influence of this performance was lasting. The soldiers of the garrison persuaded him later to stage two vaudevilles. After the first performance of Ostrovsky's play a reception and ball were arranged in honour of the actors by the commandant of the fortress, Major Anton Maevsky. He congratulated Shevchenko, and before offering a toast to him, he expressed sympathy with the poet's fate, saying that God had given Shevchenko a great artistic talent. Maevsky ended his toast with the words 'God is not without mercy and a Cossack not without fortune.'

In November Shevchenko managed to smuggle out a letter to Repnina via Colonel Matveev and Captain Gern. After Shevchenko's great theatrical success, Major Maevsky agreed that all the poet's correspondence should go to Maevsky's address. Shevchenko was very pleased to be able to write letters again, something he probably did in Maevsky's own house, since he did not want to be seen writing. Another close friend of the poet was Captain Khairov, a Bashkir. He and the army doctor, Nikolsky, were the only two men in the fortress with a university education. They also subscribed to literary journals, which arrived at irregular intervals. In his letters to Repnina Shevchenko complained that he had nothing to read. Mail arrived in Novopetrovsk once a month, and the poet pinned all his hopes on that day. He was often disappointed, since few letters arrived.

In view of the sympathy with which the others surrounded Shevchenko, Potapov relented his rigorous discipline. Still, the hated drill had to be done, and after the lights-out signal Shevchenko could not leave the barracks, which, although cleaner than those at Orsk, were very smelly.

Sometimes he was posted as a sentry, a duty which he liked because from the high upland he could contemplate the ever-changing sea. For a long time no letters came from the Lazarevsky brothers, Lyzohub, or Varvara Repnina. The reason for their silence was unknown to the poet. Fedir Lazarevsky was reprimanded for his contacts with the poet and warned against being friendly with him. Count Orlov, in the name of the tsar himself, sternly warned Princess Repnina not to show sympathy to Shevchenko or for Ukraine. As for Lyzohub, he was, on orders from Orlov, given a reprimand and a warning by Governor Hesse. Their silence was, therefore, understandable, but for Shevchenko, hard to accept.

With the coming of spring there was some improvement in the general atmosphere. Early in May 1851 a geological expedition arrived in Novopetrovsk on its way to Mangyshlak. This was the expedition in which Obruchev had promised to include Shevchenko before the poet was re-arrested. Among the members of the expedition were Shevchenko's Polish friends Bronisław Zaleski and Ludwig Turno, who brought him news from Orenburg as well as books and journals. The poet was overjoyed. The purpose of the expedition was to explore the coal deposits in the mountains of Kara-Tau. Zaleski was to be a sketcher. Commandant Maevsky detailed a detachment of soldiers from his garrison to escort the expedition. The detachment, which included some mounted Ural Cossacks, was commanded by Antipov. Soon the expedition left for the mountains in the vicinity of the fort. Unaccountably, Shevchenko was included in the detachment of escorting soldiers. Maevsky probably did this in answer to the pleas of the poet's friends. He was taking a considerable risk in allowing Shevchenko to join the unit, where strict supervision was difficult. It is not clear just when the poet joined the expedition, since Zaleski fell ill and spent the month of May in Novopetrovsk. Perhaps Shevchenko waited until Zaleski recovered. In any case, at the beginning of June Shevchenko, Zaleski, and Turno were together, sharing a tent in a Kara-Tau valley, near the Apazir well.

As a sketcher Zaleski had a great deal of freedom of movement. He was not tied to the geologists, and roamed on horseback through the mountains. Soon Shevchenko began to accompany him and, since no one was watching, started to sketch and to paint. He would return before nightfall not to the main camp but to Zaleski's tent. His sketches would be placed in Zaleski's portfolio. Good fortune once again smiled on him, and during the next two months he satisfied his hunger for painting and sketching, a basic necessity for an artist.

Two mountain chains, Kara-Tau and Ak-Tau, extended along the Mangyshlak peninsula. They were not very high (up to 780 metres) but displayed a stern and mysterious beauty. In places there were enormous stone boulders hanging over a sandy desert, like Cyclops. At night, in the moonlight, they looked like stage sets – an enchanted, sleeping kingdom, disturbed only by the howling of jackals, hyenas, and wolves and the screeching of predatory birds. This landscape provided unique nourishment for the poet's romantic imagination, and he ably re-created moods of melancholy and terror in his paintings. The pictures speak more eloquently than his letters of the poet's isolation in this mysterious, ominous Eastern desert.

The track to the area where the geologists were to begin their work lay through deserted valleys. The expedition moved slowly, at the most covering twenty-five *versts* a day. It is not certain whether Shevchenko, like Zaleski and Turno, had a horse, but somehow they all forged ahead. Zaleski wrote to Węgrzynowski from Apazir that all three of them were sharing one hooded cart (*kibitka*). To Sierakowski, who had been exiled to Novopetrovsk, Zaleski wrote that the steppe was one vast 'waste' with very little grass, where, from between the stones, occasional trees grew. The *kibitka* served as the only place where sketches made in the daytime could be finished. The three worked at a small folding table, shielding it from the sand constantly whipped up by the wind. Shevchenko completed some fine compositions here, especially *The Gypsy*. He also drew sketches of his friends and how they lived. Altogether, the expedition was a godsend to the poet and the artist. He sketched a great deal, in his free time read Humboldt, Georges Sand, and Mickiewicz, and remarked that Commandant Antipov was a 'decent man.' Later Shevchenko wrote that 'Kara-Tau will always remain in my memory.' But good times could not last. By October they were all back in Novopetrovsk. The respite from the daily drill was over. Now, Shevchenko had to shave off the beard he had grown in Kara-Tau and become a soldier again.

After tasting relative freedom in Kara-Tau, Shevchenko found the return to barracks very difficult. There is little information on his life for the rest of 1851 and the whole of 1852. We know that Zaleski's arrival was a joyful event. Zaleski became a go-between for the poet and his friends and performed this function in a truly conspiratorial manner. He also managed to sell Shevchenko's sketch *The Gypsy*, and the money was very useful. In the summer of 1852 the poet unexpectedly received a letter and twenty roubles from his old friend Semen Hulak-Artemovsky. He was overjoyed to acknowledge these tokens of friendship and wrote back, recalling the 'Bohemian Sich' of 1842. Describing the landscape around him he wrote: 'You look and look and such boredom overcomes you that you feel like hanging yourself, but there is nothing to hang yourself with ... I was born and grew up in bondage and now it looks as if I'll die a soldier. I wish the end would come soon.'[1]

The poet suffered another blow at the end of 1852 – the decent commandant, Maevsky, died. At about the same time Shevchenko was glad to see the brutal Potapov leave Novopetrovsk, while Captain Kosarev, a much more decent man, was put in command of his company. Since 1851 the Orenburg and Caspian lands had been placed under the governor generalship of Count Vasiliy Perovsky instead of Obruchev. He appointed Major Irakliy Uskov to be the new commandant of Novopetrovsk. Early in 1853 Uskov took up his new duties. His arrival in Novopetrovsk marked a turning-point in Shevchenko's life in exile. It is possible that Shevchenko's friends in Orenburg told Uskov about the poet and his difficult life. The new commandant was a kind and decent man. He had a young wife and a three-year-old son who liked to play 'with bald uncle Taras.' Tragically, the little boy soon died, and his parents were heartbroken. Shevchenko, who by then had become a friend of the family, designed and built a monument for the child's grave and often placed flowers on it.

Uskov was unable to change the poet's military routine, but he offered him the run of his house during the poet's free hours and Sundays. Shevchenko now had a hospitable home, where he could rest, write letters, and even paint. Near the fort Shevchenko found some clay and alabaster and began to sculpt, and Uskov told him to go ahead since sculpting was not forbidden. At the same time Shevchenko took up writing again, not poetry but stories in Russian prose. At Christmas 1853 he read to Uskov passages from his long story (*povest*) 'The Servant Girl' ('Naimychka'), which he deliberately misdated as Pereiaslav 1845.

Sculpting and writing helped to kill boredom and were a welcome change after military drill. Shevchenko was now able to receive mail and money addressed to Uskov. During 1853–54 he received money from Hulak-Artemovsky, M. Lazarevsky, and Kozachkovsky. Letters came infrequently. He was particularly anxious to correspond with Zaleski, with whom he could discuss art. Apart from Uskov his friends in Novopetrovsk were few in number. There were few books to read, although Nikolsky, the physician, subscribed to literary journals. Shevchenko asked Bodiansky, Kozachkovsky, Pleshcheev, Kukharenko, Ivanishev, and Zaleski to send him books. Zaleski was the only one to respond. Shevchenko wanted to read in Ukrainian and asked Bodiansky

1 *Povne*, VI, 85

to send him the *History of the Rus People* (*Istoriia Rusov*) and Velychko's chronicle. He wrote little poetry, but in 1853 he wanted to translate into modern Ukrainian *The Lay of Ihor's Armament* (*Slovo o polku Ihorevi*) and asked Bodiansky to send him the text. But again there was no response. Only later did he discover that two of his best correspondents, Repnina and Lyzohub, had been warned by the authorities not to write to him.

Zaleski and Węgrzynowski tried to sell Taras's paintings, which were produced in secret. In his correspondence he referred to his paintings cryptically as 'pieces of cloth.' Sometimes a sale brought him some money. In 1854 Shevchenko made an attempt to legalize his painting activities. The interior of a church in Novopetrovsk was to be painted. Shevchenko applied, with Uskov's help, to obtain permission from Perovsky to paint the central picture – of the Resurrection – above the altar. A request to that effect left Novopetrovsk on 7 January 1854. Both Shevchenko and Uskov hoped that Perovsky would be unable to refuse the request and that he would either grant permission personally or forward the request to St Petersburg. However, Perovsky refused to grant the request. As for asking the authorities in St Petersburg, Perovsky recalled that earlier he had been to see General Dubelt to intercede on Shevchenko's behalf and that this had proved unsuccessful. In 1851 he had told Captain Gern of the failure of his mission and now, as a faithful servant of the empire, he was not ready to ask favours for a man who had insulted the tsar. When Shevchenko learned of the refusal he was discouraged and wrote to Zaleski: 'It is sad, unbelievably sad! Such setbacks would dishearten any poet, and I, miserable as I am, may have to close my eyes to any better future.'

At the end of 1854 new hope arose of improving Shevchenko's military status. General Freiman, who was inspecting the fortress, asked Perovsky on 28 October to raise Shevchenko's rank to that of non-commissioned officer. No doubt Uskov had requested this of the general, and he even dared to accept a gift from Shevchenko, his water-colour *The Night*. Perovsky, before granting the request, asked the battalion commander, Major Lvov, for his opinion. Lvov, who often visited Novopetrovsk, replied that Shevchenko's conduct was good but that his military record was poor and he did not deserve the promotion. As if this were not sufficient humiliation, in the spring of 1855 Lvov asked Shevchenko to practise additional drill so that he could be promoted. Finally, on 7 July Lvov recommended his promotion to NCO. All this spelled greater hardship for Shevchenko, and in the spring of 1855 he wrote to Pleshcheev that he had been 'tormented for eight hours every day.' He also asked Zaleski why a major's recommendation against promotion should be given preference over a general's request. Time passed, and Lvov's final recommendation for promotion remained unanswered.

In the meantime, despite his torment on the parade square, Shevchenko experienced an upsurge in his creative powers. In his free time he sculpted, read a great deal, wrote letters, painted, and above all wrote several long stories in Russian. In the end, seven of them were composed during that period. Intensive creative work was his only defence against total despair, and he refused to allow despair to drive him to a breakdown. For him real holidays were those times when interesting people visited Novopetrovsk. That happened rarely, but when it did Shevchenko seized every opportunity to talk to them. This represented his only chance to learn what was going on in the world. At the end of 1852 the fortress was visited by Golovachov, the natural scientist, and in 1853–54 by a scientific expedition led by academician von Ber. Golovachov knew Bodiansky and took Shevchenko's letter to him. One of the members of von Ber's expedition was a well-known economist and writer, Nikolay Danilevsky,[2] with whom Shevchenko had interesting discussions and whom he mentioned warmly in his later letters and diary. For the visitors a meeting with Shevchenko was also quite an event, as the memoirs of the novelist Alexander Pisemsky, who also visited Novopetrovsk a little later, attest.

Shevchenko's ability, even under conditions of utter deprivation, to create a congenial atmosphere, to meet new friends, and even to indulge in romantic dreams never left him. In Novopetrovsk he engaged in a long platonic love affair with Uskov's wife, Agatha. This attractive woman took a great liking to the rapidly aging convict. In her company Shevchenko found peace and consolation in a deep romantic affection and attachment. In the fall of 1854 he wrote to Zaleski of his friendship with Agatha: 'This most beautiful of women is for me a truly divine fulfilment. She is the only living creature to inspire me to write poetry. I am more or less happy – one can say that I am completely happy.'[3] Almost every night he dined with the Uskovs, and he became used to the constant company of Agatha, whom he took for long walks outside the fortress. 'What a strange, enchanting creature is this immaculate woman! She is a shining jewel in the crown of creation. If it were not for her I would not know what to do with myself. I love her with a pure and noble love, with

---

2 Nikolay Danilevsky (1822–85), a Panslavist thinker and a scientist. In his book *Russia and Europe* (1871) he was the first to expound a philosophy of history as a series of civilizations, with the Slavs triumphing over the West.
3 *Povne*, VI, 105

all my heart and grateful soul. Do not suspect, my friend, anything impure in this immaculate love of mine.'[4]

This platonic love for a woman whose presence made the poet forget the miseries of barrack life was also a tonic for his tormented heart. 'Do you know,' he wrote to Zaleski, 'that I sometimes think that my bones will lie here. Sometimes I am beside myself with pain and bitter agony, so great that I cannot find a place for myself, and the longer I stay here the worse my terrible illness becomes. Moreover, to see over and over again these stupid drunken faces – it would drive a more balanced man than I am crazy! Sometimes I really lose hope of seeing any end to my terrible trials.'[5] In these dark moods it is no wonder that he idealized his relationship to Uskova, the desperate need of a tormented soul. It certainly helped in the resurgence of his creative energy.

The year 1855 was a time of great events in Russia. The country's might, founded on militarism and the tyranny of Nicholas I, crumbled with his death. The tsar's death became a stern warning to reactionary government circles and to everyone else a cause for celebration after the military defeat of the empire. Shevchenko could now realistically hope for a change in his condition. He lived in a state of great expectation from the moment he heard of the tsar's death and the new tsar's manifesto. Everyone was waiting for concessions and reforms from the new tsar, Alexander II. Nicholas I died on 19 February (o.s.) 1855, just when Shevchenko's promotion was being discussed. In April Shevchenko decided to write letters to influential men in St Petersburg to ask them for their support. He wrote to the vice-president of the Academy of Fine Arts, Count Fiodor Tolstoy, and to Shevchenko's former protector, the secretary of the academy, Hryhorovych. He asked them to intervene with the governor general, Perovsky. Though his letters were couched in diplomatic language, he described his real situation to Hryhorovych openly: 'For eight years I have suffered in silence ... I thought that my suffering would be victorious ... My physical strength has abandoned me and rheumatism racks my body. But even worse is the loss of hope. This is a terrible condition.'[6] These letters brought some response. In May the poet received a letter from his fellow painter Osipov, who at Tolstoy's request told him that the first steps towards improving Shevchenko's lot had been taken. Another ten months passed before Taras received further encour-

4 Ibid
5 Ibid, 109
6 Ibid, 115

aging news. On 15 April 1856 Countess Anastasia Tolstoy wrote to him asking him to 'open his soul to hope,' and to 'believe in a better future.' Shevchenko was heartened by this letter and expected his name to be included in the list of those pardoned. He replied to the countess, repeating his grievances, especially the ban on sketching, and asking her to 'rescue me, or I will perish here in another year.' He redoubled his efforts in asking his friends to influence Perovsky, whose recommendation for possible amnesty was crucial. Some of the Polish exiles had been amnestied and were leaving Orenburg. Among them was Bronisław Zaleski, who, in a farewell letter to Shevchenko, mentioned that Countess Alexandra Tolstoy was asking Perovsky about Shevchenko. Perovsky apparently promised to help, and the countess hoped that by the time of the new tsar's coronation the poet's 'bitter fate' would change. Another amnestied Pole, Sierakowski, wrote to Shevchenko that 'your case is the first on the agenda.'

The coronation drew near. A week beforehand M. Lazarevsky sent Shevchenko some money and assured him that, apart from Count Tolstoy, there were other influential people interceding for him and that they had been given an assurance 'which will soon be realized.' The Tolstoy family did a great deal to help the poet. Count Fiodor Tolstoy was much respected by the Grand Duchess Maria, and Countess Alexandra Tolstoy, from a different branch of the family, was a 'maid of honour,' while Count Alexey Tolstoy, the poet, was an admirer of Shevchenko's poetry. They did everything possible to expedite Shevchenko's amnesty. Yet when the Grand Duchess Maria Nikolaevna asked the tsar to pardon him, the tsar refused, struck the name of Shevchenko from the amnesty register, and reportedly said, 'I cannot forgive him; he insulted my mother.' This setback was not reported to Shevchenko by his friends, and he continued to hope for amnesty. November passed, and the poet was still waiting. The latter half of 1856 was the hardest time for him – 'quite agonizing.' In the meantime, despite the tsar's refusal, Shevchenko's friends in St Petersburg did not cease their efforts to free him. They persuaded the Grand Duchess Maria to reopen the case, and she decided to wait until the tsar's mother had gone abroad. There was new hope that matters would be more successful this time, and Shevchenko was told of this at the very end of 1856. Uskov, who had received the news, kept it secret until 1 January as a surprise New Year's present for Shevchenko.

Replying to the good news, Shevchenko described all sorts of fantasies of what he would do when he was free again. He dreamt of going back to St Petersburg and then to Ukraine to settle down on a *khutir*. 'Like a babe after a bath,' he wrote, 'I am now leaving this dark purgatory behind.' A month later he wrote to Zaleski, still in an exalted mood. He promised to visit his friend in Raczkiewicze, and then, together, they would both go to Vilno. He even dreamt of returning to work at the Academy of Fine Arts. At times, however, he realized that these were only 'beautiful, shining castles in the air.'

The previous year he had completed his autobiographical story 'The Artist' ('Khudozhnik'). Against a background of student life at the academy in St. Petersburg he painted the tragedy of an artist who fell in love with a bourgeois woman, unsympathetic to his artistic aspirations. This theme was inspired by an unexpected turn of events in Shevchenko's relationship with Agatha Uskov. At first he had idealized her in the extreme, but later he came to see her as a 'soulless coquette,' and a card-player to boot. This happened when the physician Nikolsky started teasing Agatha about her long walks with Shevchenko. She stopped going out with him and Shevchenko turned sour, regarding it as a 'betrayal.' Once he came to the Uskovs' house a little tipsy, and Agatha reprimanded him. The poet reacted sharply, and his platonic love affair came to an abrupt end.

Hopes of freedom remained with the poet, and with renewed vigour he continued writing, this time completing his long story 'The Sailor' ('Matros'), which, in the spring of 1857, he sent to M. Lazarevsky. It was Lazarevsky who told him, at Easter, the precious news that the tsar had agreed to release Shevchenko from military service and that the necessary orders were being dispatched by the ministry of armed forces. Along with this welcome letter Lazarevsky sent a box of cigars and some paint – *sepia di Roma*. Other friends hastened to send greetings to Shevchenko. Kukharenko sent a letter and twenty-five roubles. Andriy Markevych, the historian's son, sent sixteen roubles collected by Ukrainian young people, and Panteleimon Kulish sent the first volume of his *Notes on Southern Rus* (*Zapiski o yuzhnoi Rusi*). Shevchenko was jubilant. He answered his well-wishers promptly. He promised Kukharenko a visit to the Black Sea country and, in addition, sent him a self-portrait. He thanked Kulish for his splendid volume, the first Ukrainian achievement after a decade of silence. He hoped that the *Notes* would become a periodical publication.

The letter from Kukharenko had a curious effect. Kukharenko had asked Shevchenko to send him some of his recent poetry. In reply, on 22 April Shevchenko wrote that now, 'in his old age,' he would probably continue to write prose rather than poetry. But a little later he took another look at 'Moskal's Well,' finished in 1847, and in a few weeks he reworked the poem, improving it enormously. He then wrote to Kukharenko that he had not grown cold as a poet in exile and thanked him for rekindling 'the sacred fire.' The flame of poetry was once more beginning to burn brightly, fanned by the hopeful winds of freedom.

Months passed, and the impatient poet was still waiting for the offical orders from Orenburg, which did not come. On 12 May he received another letter from Lazarevsky which confirmed that in April the wheels of the official bureaucracy had begun slowly moving. Then, a month later, Lazarevsky informed him that at the end of April orders for Shevchenko's release had been sent from St Petersburg to Orenburg. Tension rose. Each mail delivery could bring the release. Lazarevsky sent the poet seventy-five roubles to cover the cost of travel and jokingly added in a note to Uskov – 'get rid of him soon!'

In order to kill time Shevchenko, on 12 June 1857, began to keep a diary, which later became known as his *Journal* (*Zhurnal*). He recorded daily events but also reminisced about his earlier life before and during exile, scattered interesting thoughts and reflections about art, and, above all, depicted very vividly the life around him. He described, for example, the flogging of soldiers and convicts, illustrated by a sketch. In fact life in the barracks became a little easier for him, since he no longer had to go on sentry duty. After Easter he was relieved from the daily drill since his company commander, Kosarev, knew that this private would soon be released. In return Shevchenko painted Kosarev's portrait. The poet spent most of his free time in the commandant's garden, where trees planted by Uskov in 1853 grew. An even older tree was a willow the poet had planted soon after his arrival at the fortress. He also cared for it, watering it frequently. He often sat in the small shadow of the willow, drinking tea and even sleeping.

June and July passed and no word came from Orenburg. Orders for Shevchenko's release had to be passed down from corps to division to brigade and finally to battalion level. Nobody was in a hurry, except the poet, who anxiously awaited every mail delivery, which came by sea. At long last, at eleven o'clock on the morning of 21 July, Officer Bazhanov informed him that the orders had arrived and that Shevchenko was a free man.

XIII

The order for release came from the battalion commander, who instructed Captain Kosarev to free Shevchenko and dispatch him to the battalion headquarters in Uralsk. Kosarev asked Uskov to send Shevchenko and four freed Polish exiles by boat to Guriev and to supply them with adequate rations. When Shevchenko learned of this plan, he asked Uskov not to send him to Uralsk but by a more direct route to Astrakhan and St Petersburg. The boat to Guriev was to leave on 8 August, but on 31 July Uskov unexpectedly decided to grant Shevchenko's request to take the shorter, more direct route. The poet said goodbye to his friends, and on 2 August he left on a fishing boat for Astrakhan. Four days later the boat docked at Astrakhan, and Shevchenko, unshaven, wearing an old cap, a white soldier's coat, worn army boots and carrying a Turkoman bag, stepped on land.

He had very few roubles in his pocket. Walking along the streets of this large port he decided that this 'southeastern Venice' of the Russian empire was more like 'a large pile of refuse,' although it was crowned by the white walls of a Kremlin and a seventeenth-century cathedral. He searched in vain for a place to stay overnight, and in a restaurant he could not even get ordinary soup. He was surprised at the poverty of the town, which 'feeds sturgeon to half the Russian empire.' Fortunately he had the address of a former resident of Novopetrovsk, Burtsev, and at last found food and shelter there. He learned that the boat to Nizhny Novgorod along the Volga would leave in two weeks and he was condemned to stay in 'this dirty city' until then. A few days later Shevchenko had to leave Burtsev's apartment because the latter was getting married. He rented a room for twenty kopecks a day and spent his time strolling along the streets, visiting the library, and observing the Kalmyks.

On 15 August a Ukrainian doctor, Muravsky, learnt that Shevchenko was in town and alerted the local Ukrainians. Ivan Klopotovsky, a former student at Kiev University, where he had met the poet, was the first to greet Shevchenko. There was a large group of former Kievans here and all knew of the Brotherhood of Sts Cyril and Methodius and admired Shevchenko's poetry. A year earlier the Russian novelist Pisemsky had written to Shevchenko from Astrakhan that he had met a group of the poet's admirers in that city. Now they had an opportunity to greet the liberated poet. They received him very warmly, and after a banquet in his honour Shevchenko noted in his diary: 'Thank you, my selfless friends! You have granted me so much happiness that I can scarcely find room for it in my heart.' The poet's financial situation also improved rapidly. The rich Sapozhnikov offered Shevchenko a separate cabin on the boat *Prince Pozharsky*, which he had chartered for his family and friends to sail to Nizhny Novgorod. Shevchenko gave his old ticket to five poor men who were unable to afford the trip.

On 23 August the *Prince Pozharsky* sailed up the Volga heading for Nizhny Novgorod. Shevchenko, as a privileged passenger, admired everything on board and wrote about it in his diary. He was enchanted by the river, the moonlit nights, and the distant river-banks. Three nights in a row he listened to Aleksey Panov, a former serf, now a deck-hand and waiter, play the violin. It sounded 'like the sighs from an abused serf's heart, merging into one, long, dismal, deep groan from millions of serfs.' Under the magic influence of the violin and the sound of the boat engine Shevchenko wrote the following meditation on revolution: 'Great Fulton and Watt! Your young child, growing by leaps and bounds, will soon devour the knouts, the thrones, and crowns swallowing up diplomats and landowners, playing with them like a schoolboy with candy. What the encyclopaedists started in France will be fulfilled throughout the entire planet by your gigantic child of genius. I prophesy this without a tremor.'[1]

The friendly behaviour of the people on board was very moving to the poet. 'From excessive enthusiasm' he did not know 'what to do with himself.' He ran about the deck 'like a schoolboy at the end of the school year.' In his journal he wrote that 'only now have I completely understood how my spirits have been permeated for ten years by all the humiliating experiences of the barracks.' The contrast between his army life and free people seemed to him almost unbelievable. He talked to his fellow passengers and listened to their tales about Stepan Razin, who once threatened the tsar of Russia and the shah of Persia in these parts.

On 31 August the boat docked at Saratov. Shevchenko had learned that Kostomarov had been exiled to that town and that his mother still lived there. He visited her and she greeted him with tears. She showed him a

---

1 'Shchodennyk,' ibid, v, 109

letter from her son, who was on a visit to Stockholm. When they recalled May of 1847 they both 'cried like children.' Shevchenko left her a poem that he had written in St Petersburg ten years earlier and had dedicated to Kostomarov and his mother. Next day a new surprise awaited the poet when a Ukrainian admirer, Maria Solonyna, visited him.

The next stop for the *Prince Pozharsky* was Samara and then Kazan. On board there were banquets and celebrations. Shevchenko was invited to attend by various millionaires, and he enjoyed himself hugely. Apart from these festivities he liked talking to Captain Kishkin, whose cabin he shared. Literary readings were also held on board, where the poet heard some poems that had been banned by the censor. In Kazan, Shevchenko asked after Posiada and Andruzsky, who were exiled there, but no one had heard of them. Along the way he sketched the various sights and drew portraits of his fellow travellers. Finally, after an exciting voyage lasting almost one month, the boat reached Nizhny Novgorod. Here a new blow awaited him. Soon after he arrived he learned that the police were looking for him. The next day he was told by the police that he had to return to Orenburg.

Before Shevchenko's arrival in Nizhny Novgorod a letter had arrived from Uskov asking the local police to return Shevchenko to Orenburg. Apparently the release orders for Shevchenko stated that he was forbidden to live in Moscow or St Petersburg and that he would have to remain in Orenburg until 'the time of final liberation.' Uskov learned this after Shevchenko's departure, and he was anxious to correct an error that threatened to have unpleasant consequences. In addition, Uskov had yielded to Shevchenko's plea that he should not be sent to Uralsk and was now trying to extricate himself from all the bureaucratic bungling.

Shevchenko was naturally upset. He noted in his diary that he was 'very dismayed by this bolt from the blue.' He had dreamt about being in St Petersburg soon and seeing his old friends again, and now he railed against 'the corps commanders and all my tormentors.' His chief tormentors this time were in the Third Section in St Petersburg: they had barred him from returning to the capital. Fortunately for Shevchenko his new friends (Sapozhnikov, Brylkin, and Ovsiannikov), whom he had met on board the *Prince Pozharsky*, had good connections with the administrators in Nizhny Novgorod. They advised Shevchenko to feign illness, and the police doctor was bribed to issue a certificate claiming the poet's 'prolonged illness.' Orenburg and Novopetrovsk were notified that Shevchenko had to rest and was unable to travel.

This new comedy, orchestrated by Shevchenko's friends in order to save him from returning to the hated Orenburg, lasted for some time.

Shevchenko was living in the house of a fellow Ukrainian, Ovsiannikov, and was 'lying low,' mostly reading. There was a great deal of interesting material to read in Nizhny Novgorod, a city with a strong liberal tradition. Shevchenko read Alexander Herzen's journal the *Bell* (*Kolokol*), published in London, as well as other publications by Herzen. His friendship with all sorts of liberals grew apace, and he continued to sketch and paint. On 22 October he began to revise his long poem 'The Sailor.'

Simultaneously, he bombarded his old friends in St Petersburg with letters, imploring them to intervene, once more, with the authorities. On their advice he wrote, on 14 November, to Count Fiodor Tolstoy. While efforts were being made in St Petersburg (again involving the Grand Duchess Maria) to allow the poet to return there, he had to remain in Nizhny Novgorod. He was out of uniform, and his financial situation had much improved, since he was receiving money from friends. Zaleski sent him 150 roubles, proceeds of the sale of four of Shevchenko's pictures, and Kulish sent 250 roubles for a series of sketches and water-colours purchased by Tarnovsky and Halahan. Lazarevsky wrote that he was holding 36 roubles for Shevchenko, in addition to 175 roubles from another admirer, Lev Zhemchuzhnikov's brother Aleksey. Shevchenko also earned money by painting portraits. Yet any money he acquired he spent quickly. In spite of the fact that he did not have to pay for board and lodging, he soon managed to dispose of large sums of money. Lazarevsky was wise to withhold some funds for future use. Another 500 roubles, collected for Shevchenko in St Petersburg after a theatrical performance in his honour, was kept in the capital to await his arrival.

Shevchenko's friends in Nizhny Novgorod were from all walks of life. He met the musicologist Ulybyshev; the virtuoso pianist Tatarinov; the writer Dal, who was in government service there; the young historian Varentsov; the Decembrist Annenkov; as well as actors and actresses from the local theatre. He was also well received by Prince Golitsyn and by the wife of the governor general of Nizhny Novgorod, Muravev. Many Ukrainians passing through the town brought him greetings and news. Shevchenko also corresponded with Kulish, Kostomarov, and Maksymovych. They all wished him well and were eagerly awaiting his new works. Kulish, particularly, felt that 'your fame is now at its zenith,' but he was also anxious to edit Shevchenko's new poems so that they would appear polished and not 'dishevelled.' This irked Shevchenko a little, but at the same time he was grateful to Kulish for his *Primer* (*Hramatka*), the first Ukrainian text for elementary schools, and for Marko Vovchok's short stories, which Kulish had helped to publish.

Despite his arrogant nature Kulish gave high praise to Shevchenko's poetry. Maksymovych, after reading Shevchenko's 'Monk,' 'Evening,' and 'The Well,' wrote of the deep impression they had made on him and called Shevchenko another Boian.[2] Kostomarov was involved with his plan to publish popular books for the peasants, and Kulish urged the poet to prepare another series of historical drawings. All these new contacts reinvigorated Shevchenko, and, hoping that Shchepkin, Kulish and M. Lazarevsky would visit him in Nizhny Novgorod at Christmas, he began writing a new long poem, 'The Neophytes' ('Neofity'). He dedicated it to Shchepkin. Although the poem was set in a period 'when Russia was not yet in the world,' the reader could easily see that behind the Roman caesar stood Tsar Nicholas I. Recovering his earlier poetic powers, so expressive in 'The Epistle,' 'The Caucasus' and 'Kholodny Yar,' he once more castigated the oppressor and prayed to the Virgin Mary to

>   send
> And give the poor soul the strength
> To inflame words,
> To melt the human heart
> And spread across Ukraine
> This word, God's incense,
> The incense of truth.[3]

He called on his muse to 'thunder from the walls of the dark dungeon.' Though he had suffered so much, he was neither chastened nor altered, but returned in spirit to those days in Myrhorod and Pereiaslav in 1845. The main thrust of his poetry remained unaltered.

Shchepkin, now seventy years old, arrived in Nizhny Novgorod on Christmas Eve, and Shevchenko was overjoyed. 'This is the feast of feasts,' he wrote in his diary. For six days the two friends talked and relaxed. Shchepkin took part in several plays performed in Nizhny Novgorod, among them Gogol's *The Inspector General* and Kotliarevsky's *Moskal the Sorcerer*. After his departure Shevchenko wrote to his friends describing the visit in detail.

Shchepkin's visit had another, unexpected result. His partner in Kotliarevsky's play, playing the role of Tetiana, was a young fifteen-year-old actress, Katia Piunova. Shchepkin was delighted with young Katia's acting, and she received an ovation from the public. On stage she wore

2 Boian, the legendary minstrel of Kievan Rus in the late eleventh century, mentioned in the *Lay of Ihor's Armament*
3 'Neofity,' *Povne*, II, 281

Ukrainian costume and obviously attracted Shevchenko to the point where he once more began 'building castles in the air' and fell in love with the girl. He prophesied a brilliant acting career for her and was determined to obtain a place for her in one of the best theatres in the country. On 21 January Shevchenko wrote a review of the benefit performance in which Piunova took part, in which he praised her but also gave her some advice. The young actress was deeply offended and returned to Shevchenko books he had lent her, without reading them. To counter her bad humour the poet unexpectedly proposed to her, and made a formal offer of marriage to her parents. In his diary he wrote: 'I am totally unsuited for the role of lover. She probably takes me for a madman, a drunkard, or a ne'er-do-well.' After two days Shevchenko was told by her father that Katia 'considered his proposal to be sheer theatre.' Katia's father expressed no opinion, and the naïve poet dared to hope that he would be accepted.

In reality, Katia had not the slightest intention of marrying Shevchenko, and her parents supported her. She was barely fifteen, and the poet, who was forty-four, with a bald head and greyish beard, looked closer to fifty. In any case Katia already had a sweetheart, the pharmacist Fuss. If Katia's parents did not directly refuse the offer, they did not because they were waiting for a reply from a theatre director in Kharkiv to whom Shevchenko had recommended the young actress. Finally the letter came, with an offer for Katia. She used this to obtain a better offer from the theatre in Nizhny Novgorod. This was the end, and Shevchenko, totally disappointed, complained in his diary about moral decadence and swore that 'Miss Piunova is despicable from head to foot.' Once more his naïve idealization of a woman had led to the collapse of his hopes.

During the 'romance' with Piunova, Shevchenko wrote some very good poetry. Apart from finishing 'The Sailor' he composed, in one day, on 9 February, 1858, a triptych: 'Fate' ('Dolia'), 'Muse' ('Muza'), and 'Glory' ('Slava'). The central figure was the Muse, which was both his fate and his glory. In a flash of poetic insight he called on his fate or destiny:

> Let us go on, my fate,
> Most humble, unpretentious friend,
> Let us go on: for there the glory lies,
> And glory is my final prize.[4]

He remembered how

---

4 'Dolia,' ibid, 299

Arrest and Exile 1847–57

> Out of the filthy barracks
> Like a pure and holy
> Bird you flew[5]

in order to

> Hover around me teaching me
> To tell the truth with lips untainted.
> Help me make my life
> A prayer to the end.[6]

The poet once more became conscious of his destiny.

His circle of correspondents grew, the latest being Sergey Aksakov. He was also most interested in the work of Marko Vovchok. On his name-day, 25 February, he received a letter from Mykhailo Lazarevsky, giving the good news that he was to be allowed to return to St Petersburg. Apparently in response to his sister's pleas, Tsar Alexander II had given permission for the poet to return to the capital, provided he lived there under strict police surveillance, supervised by the Academy of Fine Arts, so that he did not 'misuse his talent.'

While the official papers were on their way from the new chief of the Third Section, Prince Dolgorukov, to the authorities in Nizhny Novgorod, the poet was waiting for permission to travel. Captain Gern had sent the 'boot-leg' notebooks from Orenburg, and Shevchenko was busy revising some of his poems. On 6 February he wrote in his journal: 'How will my fellow-countrymen greet my captive Muse?' After saying goodbye to his friends, he left Nizhny Novgorod on 8 March, after spending five and a half months there. He left many friends and memories behind. In one of the last new poems he wrote there, 'God's Fool' ('Yurodyvy'), he once more attacked' the tsarist régime and wondered

> when
> We shall get ourselves a Washington,
> With a new and just law?
> Some day we must surely find the man.[7]

On this note of optimism Shevchenko's exile virtually came to an end.

---

5 'Muza,' ibid, 300
6 Ibid, 301
7 'Yurodyvy,' ibid, 296

PART FIVE

Back to Freedom

1858-61

XIV

Shortly before midnight on 10 March 1858 Shevchenko arrived in Moscow. On his way, at Vladimir, he had an unexpected and joyful meeting with his 'friend, comrade, and commander' Captain Butakov, who was travelling back to Syr-Daria with his wife. 'The very mention,' wrote Shevchenko in his diary, 'of that desert sends shivers through my heart, but he appeared to be ready to stay there for ever.' In Moscow the poet lodged at a cheap hotel, and the next day he found the place where his friend Shchepkin lived, near the little church of 'old Pimen.' On the way to Moscow Shevchenko had complained of a slight inflammation in his left eye and an itchy forehead, and in Moscow his eye began to swell, while his forehead was covered with a rash. Shchepkin called Doctor Van Puteren to attend to his friend. Shevchenko had known the physician in Nizhny Novgorod. The doctor ordered rest and a diet, and gave him some medication. Instead of sightseeing, the poet was forced to stay indoors and admire, through the window, the church of old Pimen. However, Shchepkin spread the news of Shevchenko's arrival, and friends and admirers soon came to see him. Ukrainians were the first to come: Maksymovych came three times, bringing with him the son of the historian Markevych. The Moscow scholars, writers, and actors followed. Van Puteren had to return to Nizhny Novgorod and was replaced by Doctor Min, a translator of Dante. 'A poet and physician,' wrote Shevchenko in his diary, 'a beautiful disharmony.' Shchepkin did everything to comfort his sick visitor and 'cared for him like a spoilt child.' Shevchenko's condition improved, and on 16 March he drew a pencil portrait of Shchepkin. The next day, in spite of his doctor's orders, he went out and 'in the evening visited a friend whom [he] had not seen for a long time – Princess Varvara Nikolaevna Repnina.'

Perhaps there was no one whom Shevchenko was so anxious to meet. It was not only memories of Yahotyn but gratitude for her steadfast help and correspondence during his exile that made the poet eager to meet her. Yet the meeting took place in an atmosphere neither had envisaged. They failed to find the right words or strike the proper chord. The princess thought the poet had grown old and was 'extinguished.' In his diary the poet noted that the princess 'had changed for the better. She is prettier and younger and full of sanctimoniousness. Has she, perhaps, met a good confessor in Moscow?' The last sentence jars unpleasantly, but perhaps the princess, always inclined to moralize, had offered a little too much advice at their meeting. The impression that the poet made on the princess is also understandable. With his greying beard he looked ten years older; his eye was bandaged, and he might indeed have appeared to her, as he once wrote from exile, 'like a shadow of the old Shevchenko.'

On 18 March Shevchenko went to visit Maksymovych, Mokrytsky, and Bodiansky. Three days earlier Shchepkin had asked a half-Ukrainian woman, Grekova, to come and entertain Shevchenko with Ukrainian songs. Shevchenko did not care for her singing, but after meeting Maksymovych's young wife he was captivated by the latter's 'pure type' of Ukrainian beauty and her skill as a pianist. 'Where did that old antiquarian [Maksymovych] find such fresh, pure gold? I am both saddened and jealous,' the poet noted wistfully. For three days Maria Maksymovych charmed him by singing Ukrainian songs. The happy poet imagined himself 'on the banks of the wide Dnieper.' He ended an entry in his diary with the words: 'Marvellous songs, marvellous singer!'

Holy Week was passing as Easter approached. Shevchenko's health improved, and with it his humour and gaiety. He visited friends, both old and new, and inspected the architecture of Moscow. His mood was buoyed by the admiration he received from many prominent Muscovites. He confided in his diary that 'it was a sin to grumble about the delay in returning to St Petersburg.' On Holy Saturday, 22 March, he made the acquaintance of Sergey Aksakov, with whom he had corresponded. Although the famous old Russian writer was ill, disregarding doctors' orders he had invited Shevchenko to visit him. The brief meeting was one of the poet's 'brightest memories.'

Easter came. Before the early mass Shevchenko went to see the Kremlin but was unimpressed by the procession there. 'There is little light and a great deal of bell ringing,' he wrote; 'there is a lack of harmony and not a scrap of beauty.' He did not like the way the Muscovites celebrated Easter. The following day he went to visit the Aksakovs and Princess Repnina and in the evening was a guest at a banquet for literary and scholarly luminaries given by Shchepkin's son, who was about to open a bookstore. All liberal and radical literary Moscow was present. On 25 March, during the third day of Easter, Maksymovych hosted a dinner in

Shevchenko's honour. Apart from the Ukrainians Shchepkin and Halahan, Maksymovych also invited two prominent Moscow scholars, Shevyrev and Pogodin. His intentions were good, but Shevchenko felt uncomfortable with these pillars of the establishment. Maksymovych went to great lengths to please his guest of honour and recited some poems dedicated to him. Everyone was moved. Hryhoriy Halahan, describing the dinner in a letter to his wife, wrote that 'Shevchenko has changed a great deal, has grown old, his broad forehead crowned with baldness, and he has a greyish beard that makes him look like one of our wise old colonels, to whom people come for advice.' After dinner Shevchenko, who was in a good mood, sang Ukrainian songs with Maksymovych's wife. Afterwards the poet drove to say goodbye to Aksakov, where he was once more entertained with Ukrainian songs, sung by the youthful Nadia Aksakov. The final memorable evening in Moscow ended with a visit to the Slavophil Koshelev, where Shevchenko met Khomiakov and the Decembrist Prince Sergey Volkonsky, brother of the late Prince Repnin. Prince Sergey 'gently and without any bitterness' recounted episodes of his thirty-year-long exile in Siberia.

On the morning of 26 March Shevchenko left Moscow for St Petersburg, travelling for the first time on a newly built train. The next day, at eight o'clock in the evening, he was in St Petersburg and was warmly welcomed by Mykhailo Lazarevsky, who took him to his apartment on Great Morska Street. The following day the poet 'needlessly walked on foot through half the town,' although heavy snow was falling. He longed to see every familiar corner in the city. So much reminded him of his student days in 'this sinful paradise.' At three o'clock in the afternoon he returned and found a visitor – Semen Hulak-Artemovsky. Hours of meeting old friends passed quickly, like minutes. In the evening, accompanied by Lazarevsky, he went to see the Tolstoys.

The young Katerina Tolstoy recalled the joyful moment very distinctly: 'They have arrived, someone called out. Before we could go to meet them Taras Hryhorovych entered the room. Of medium height, not thin but rather plump, with a long beard and eyes full of tears, he stretched out his hands to embrace us. We were all overwhelmed by this joyful event. Everyone was embracing one another, laughing and crying, and he only repeated, 'My dear ones, my friends.'[1] Everyone was very moved here, in the home of this old Voltairean artist, who remained faithful all his life to the eighteenth-century ideas of enlightenment. Fiodor Tolstoy's house had been the real headquarters for all the efforts that had been made to

1 E.F. Tolstaia-Yunge, 'Vospominaniia o Shevchenko,' *Vospominaniia*, 277

free Shevchenko. Now the poet was able to thank his benefactors. On returning home, he wrote in his diary: 'No one has greeted me more warmly and I have met no one with more gratitude than I felt for Count Fiodor Petrovich and the Countess Anastasia. Our meeting was warmer than any family gathering.' They all drank champagne to celebrate Shevchenko's return.

Neither Kostomarov nor Kulish was in St Petersburg, so Shevchenko hurried to visit Bilozersky, who was married and allowed to live in the capital. The happy reunion with his 'ally of 1847' was unexpectedly made even happier by the presence at the Bilozerskys' of Shevchenko's former fellow convicts Sierakowski and Staniewicz, as well as of the poet Sowa-Zeligowski. They were all rejoicing in their new-found freedom and, of course, sang Ukrainian songs.

St Petersburg bestowed on Shevchenko its warmest embrace. A veritable human flood engulfed him and was ready to swallow him up. Old and new friends, fellow-countrymen and Russians, all representing the upper reaches of literary and scholarly society, as well as artists, actors, composers, former political prisoners and exiles, society beauties, titled and untitled officials, and university students – all flocked to Shevchenko and invited him to their homes. The poet had neither rest nor time to himself but was continually being asked out to dinner, where he was fêted in extravagant fashion. After one such evening at the Tolstoys,' where he was greeted 'as a long-awaited guest,' Shevchenko wrote in his diary: 'I was afraid that I might become a popular figure in St Petersburg and now it has happened!' Maksheev wrote that the poet was 'almost carried shoulder-high by the people.' The Ukrainians particularly (and some of them were quite rich) invited the poet to banquets in his honour and at fashionable restaurants plied him with food and wine as if they were trying to make up for their previous neglect and silence during the years of exile, when he waited in vain for some friendly words. All the Dziubyns, Soshalskis, Tupytsias, and Trotsyns, who had been his friends but had forgotten about him during his exile, were now out in full force, surrounding him with lavish hospitality.

At first Shevchenko found it difficult to refuse invitations, but he soon grew tired and tried to decline them by claiming illness. Sometimes he sought out people he enjoyed, especially old friends from his student days. He was also anxious to catch up on the plays and operas he had missed. At the opera he listened to two prominent singers of the time, both Ukrainians, Hulak-Artemovsky and Petrov. His friends, knowing how fond he was of music, invited him to musical evenings at their homes. Countess Anastasia Tolstoy asked him to listen to the piano virtuoso A.

Kontsky, Alexandra Gulakov played the harp for him, and Miss Grinberg captivated him with her singing. At the theatre he admired Shchepkin and Sadovsky, and he attended a reading of a new play by Zeligowski. Once again he went to see the riches of the Hermitage art gallery – sculpture, classical art, Western European painting, and, finally, a special exhibit of flowers, where he was 'renewed by the fresh beauty of nature.' He noticed 'the variegated greenery, masses of beautiful fresh flowers, music, and, to crown it all, a host of fresh flower-like young women.' This surfeit of aesthetic impressions did not tire him, though it consumed all his nervous energy. He could no longer complain of a dearth of people or good conversation. Satisfying his hunger, he discussed aesthetics and became involved in the latest intellectual problems. He attended public lectures and engaged in conversation with the most prominent scholars like Kavelin, with whom he argued about 'the past and future of the Slavs' until three o'clock in the morning.

Neither his busy social life nor the aesthetic and intellectual diversions that preoccupied him prevented Shevchenko from thinking about his own writing and painting. A week after his arrival in the capital he was already wondering 'how to gain access to the censors,' planning a new edition of his old poems, and advising Kamenetsky, the manager of Kulish's printing shop, to republish *Kobzar* and 'The Haidamaks' as well as the first volume of *The Poems of Taras Shevchenko*. He had with him almost everything he had written before his arrest, with the exception of 'The Heretic' and some shorter poems. Kulish had collected all these for Shevchenko, after transcribing everything in his own handwriting. Shevchenko also began a new work, 'Lunacy' ('Lunatyka'), which has been lost. He was longing to get back to painting and etching, too. His first idea was to make an etching of Murillo's *The Holy Family*. He appeared to have lost interest in darker subjects, such as his *Prodigal Son*, a series of sketches done in exile, and he wanted to return to nobler themes. With this in mind he visited the old masters of engraving and etching, Jordan, Klodt, Sluzhynsky, and Utkin, and asked them for advice.

Summer was approaching, and it was hoped that social activities in St Petersburg would wind down. That would be the time to escape from the hospitable embrace of friends and return to work. Shchepkin, for one, urged the poet to concentrate on his work. When he visited St Petersburg in May, he found Shevchenko enjoying himself with Hulak-Artemovsky and Soshalsky. On his return to Moscow, Shchepkin wrote, begging Shevchenko, 'To work, to work! Do not let inactivity dominate you.' The warning was timely but unnecessary. Shevchenko was soon busy etching, and after finishing the copy of Murillo, he started, on 15 July, to etch Rembrandt's *Parables of the Vintner*. Shevchenko sent his first completed work after exile to Aksakov, proud that his technique was truly a pioneering effort in this field. Etching now absorbed him entirely. He studied the technique with the connoisseur Marin, who owned a huge collection of etchings and engravings.

Instead of resting during the summer, the poet worked hard, but when the fall came, with its social diversions, he joined the festivities without hesitation. On 9 October he wrote to Lazarevsky's mother: 'After long and difficult trials ... I have still not grown used to the joys of freedom and have not returned to a normal way of life. I always seem to be attending a reception and so do no work.' This 'do no work' was an exaggeration, but Shevchenko longed to work more systematically.

For the first two months in St Petersburg Shevchenko was financially secure. He lived at the Lazarevskys, and Countess Anastasia Tolstoy gave him five hundred roubles, which had been collected for him at a benefit performance. Yet the money was quickly spent. In November Shevchenko complained to Shchepkin that he was penniless. He could not afford to see his favourite opera. His etchings were few, and they did not sell well. He had hoped that the republication of his works would bring in royalties, but the censor refused to grant permission to an author who had been previously banned. A new application was necessary, and Shevchenko complied on 27 October by writing to Prince Dolgorukov. He asked for permission to publish his poetry and, in the hope of a favourable reply, sold the rights to the publisher Kozhanchikov for two thousand roubles. However, Dolgorukov refused permission. He had studied Shevchenko's file in the Third Section carefully and remembered Dubelt's pronouncement that the poet 'wanted to provoke hatred for Russian domination.' Dolgorukov also knew of the unfavourable views of Shevchenko held by the tsar and his mother.

Dolgorukov's refusal was the first blow to Shevchenko's hopes after his liberation. His friends advised him to try to approach the new liberal minister of education, Yevgraf Kovalevsky. This he did, and, as a result, on 4 December, the ministry of education took under advisement the matter of Shevchenko's new publication. Progress was slow and on 28 January 1859 Dolgorukov informed Kovalevsky that he had decided to allow the republication of *Kobzar*, provided that 'special attention' was paid to it by the censor.

The effect of these dealings with the ministry and the Third Section, although they were successful in the end, was depressing for Shevchenko. Like many under the regime of Alexander II, he was hoping for radical change, but he saw that the old bureaucracy remained unmoved. This was also evident in progress of the central political issue of the time: the liberation of the serfs. The long-hoped-for reform became bogged down in various government committees. Liberal hopes that the government would show a decisive attitude in this matter and would speed up the process remained unfulfilled. The local liberal committees encountered great hostility to the proposal from reactionary landowners, while the government was indecisive and cautious. Peasant rebellions, which flared up in every part of the country, did not help matters, since the reactionary elements pointed to them as inevitable results of the expected reforms. Shevchenko's attitude to all this was uncompromising. For him, a former serf, the abolition of serfdom was of paramount importance. A month after his arrival in St Petersburg he wrote in his diary that the discussions he had heard about the emancipation of the peasantry 'were endless, empty talk.' In his view this Gordian knot had to be cut. The liberation of the serfs was a precondition for any further progress by the Ukrainian people on the road to complete national liberation. All the delays depressed him still further and shattered his earlier illusions. The hopes with which he had returned to the capital were now dashed. He poured out his disappointment in his new poems.

The woman serf in the poem 'The Dream' ('Son') falls asleep in the fields near her baby son and dreams that her

> Ivan [is]
> Handsome and rich,
> Already betrothed, even married,
> To a free woman; no longer a serf
> But a free man;
> In their own happy fields
> Together they reap their own wheat,
> Their children bringing them lunch.[2]

Yet the idyll is shattered when she wakes:

> Suddenly she woke – there was nothing,
> She looked at her Ivan, picked him up
> And gently swaddled him.
> She hurried off to reap her sixty sheaves
> Before the steward appeared.[3]

2 'Son,' *Povne*, II, 318
3 Ibid

This rude awakening was the poet's realization that things continued to be as bad as ever. In November Shevchenko wrote:

> Anticipate no good,
> Do not wait for expected freedom –
> It is asleep, Tsar Nicholas
> Has lulled it to sleep. But
> To wake this sickly freedom,
> We must, all as one,
> Temper the axe well,
> Sharpen its edge,
> And try to rouse this freedom,
> Or it will go on sleeping,
> The wretched creature, till the Last Judgment.[4]

The poet once more directed his anger towards the landowners, who, he felt, would lull this freedom to sleep,

> Building more churches and palaces
> To adore their drunken tsar
> And praise Byzantine-style servility.[5]

It is clear that, at that moment, the poet believed that only an armed struggle would liberate his people.

While still in Nizhny Novgorod, Shevchenko had admired the short stories of Marko Vovchok, published by Kulish. Believing in literature as a guide to the moral regeneration of mankind, he was pleased to find that the works of this young woman writer defended human rights and protested against serfdom. In St Petersburg he arranged for a collection to be taken up among his fellow Ukrainians and with the proceeds bought a golden bracelet, which he sent to the writer. Marko Vovchok's husband, one of the former 'brethren,' Opanas Markovych, wrote to Shevchenko thanking him both for the bracelet and for dedicating 'The Dream' to his wife. In January 1859 both of the Markovyches visited the capital, and to commemorate his meeting with Marko Vovchok, Shevchenko wrote a poem about her. Entitled 'To Marko Vovchok,' it praised the humanity and social awareness in her work:

---

4 'Ya ne nezduzhaiu,' ibid, 320
5 Ibid

> The Lord has sent us
> You, a gentle prophet
> And the exposer of cruel,
> Insatiable men.[6]

In this exalted mood he was ready to regard her as one to continue his mission.

> And all my unshackled poetry, my love,
> Our prophet and my darling daughter,
> I will proclaim as yours![7]

Revived by a revolutionary spirit and disgusted with Russian politics, Shevchenko sought congenial themes in the works of the biblical prophets. In the 'Imitation of Psalm xi' he wrote:

> 'I shall rise,' our Lord will cry –
> 'I shall rise this day, for the sake
> Of my people who are in chains,
> The humble and the poor. I shall extol
> These small, dumb slaves
> And set my Word on guard.'[8]

Imitating the prophet Isaiah, he saw a vision of his country:

> The steppes, the lakes will all revive,
> And sacred roads, their miles unmarked,
> But free and wide,
> Will spread afar.
> These highways will be hidden from the masters,
> But will be trodden by the slaves
> Without hue or cry;
> They will join together
> In merriment and rest,
> While the desert will be ruled
> By happy villages.[9]

6 'Marku Vovchku,' ibid, 323
7 Ibid
8 'Podrazhanie 11 Psalmu,' ibid, 321
9 'Isaiia. Hlava 35,' ibid, 325

After these prophetic visions it was all the harder to return to a reality that could only bring disappointment. The censors delayed passing his works, already once censored, for publication. Lack of money and his precarious existence in the capital began to depress the poet. True, since June 1858 he had had a small apartment in the building of the Academy of Fine Arts, secured for him by Count Tolstoy. The Russian writer Leskov, who visited Shechenko there, has left a detailed description of it. It

consisted of one very narrow room, with a window, which Shevchenko faced as he worked behind an easel. Apart from a table piled with books and a small sofa covered with chequered oilcloth, two very simple chairs, and a modest screen dividing the room from the door, there was no other furniture. Behind the screen there was also another small door that led to a narrow staircase and another room, the same as the one below, with one square window, which reached the floor. This was Shevchenko's bedroom and study. The furniture in this room was even more dilapidated. To the right, in a corner, was a small table, at which Shevchenko usually wrote, a bed with very unpretentious bedding, and at the foot of the bed another little table with a carafe of water, a wash-stand, and a tea set.[10]

The winter of 1858–59 brought Shevchenko some earnings from his artwork. P. Kochubey requested a portrait of his notorious ancestor, who had denounced Mazepa to Peter I. Shevchenko did other work for Kochubey and sold him a series of his Novopetrovsk and Kara-Tau sketches. A wealthy Ukrainian landowner, Sukhanova-Podkolzyna, apprenticed her teenaged son to Shevchenko and paid him very well. The preparation of his etchings, which was very costly, was financed by various connoisseurs. Count Alexander Uvarov, the son of the former minister of education and a distant relative of the Repnins, bought the Murillo etching, while a wealthy merchant, Soldatenkov, probably purchased the etching of Rembrandt's *Parables*. Shevchenko's friends, particularly Lazarevsky and Shchepkin, made great efforts to see that the title 'Academician of Engraving' would be awarded to him. Meanwhile, Shevchenko worked very hard and enjoyed a growing reputation. Many an outstanding Russian artist came to visit his tiny workshop. From the summer of 1858 to the spring of 1859 ten etchings were produced there. Anyone who realizes the amount of labour required to produce this type of artwork will understand that Shevchenko must have devoted a great deal of his time to it outside his busy social life.

10 N.S. Leskov, 'Posledniaia vstrecha i posledniaia razluka s Shevchenko,' *Sobranie sochinenii* (Moscow 1958), x, 7–8

His day usually began early, and, as was his custom, he worked best before noon. He lunched with Lazarevsky, who now lived on the fifth line of Vasilevsky Island, opposite the left wing of the academy. Before lunch Shevchenko liked to drink a glass of *horilka*. He also liked to joke with Lazarevsky's younger brothers, Oleksander, who was starting his career as a historian, and Ivan, a university student. Through the prism of his own romanticism and idealism he loved to observe the younger generation's interest in the natural sciences. Sometimes, listening to their talk, he would smile ironically. To him, who could 'see almighty God in the smallest leaf,' the new materialist philosophy was rather foreign, and he teased his young friends by saying that Humboldt was 'only a court flatterer.' The younger Lazarevskys would protest, and Shevchenko was pleased with their enthusiasm. He liked young people and children, was very fond of his fifteen-year-old pupil, Sukhanov, and the young Katia Tolstoy. Many young artists came to him for advice.

He was equally interested in Ukrainian cultural developments. While he was still in Nizhny Novgorod he had enthusiastically received Kulish's *Notes on Southern Rus*, which also contained his long poem 'The Servant Girl' ('Naimychka'), and welcomed the appearance in print of Marko Vovchok's work. He was pleased to see Kulish's 'Primer' ('Hramatka') and was contributing to the latter's new almanac, the *Home* ('Khata'). He hoped that it would become a periodical publication. Other Ukrainian writers honoured him as their mentor. The elderly Maksymovych asked him to review his translations of the Psalms, and Opanas Markovych asked him to polish his wife's stories.

Shevchenko was generally regarded as an arbiter in the use of language and as a fine literary critic. The only exception among his own critics was Kulish, who, although under the spell of Shevchenko's poetry, remained full of criticism and advice. It was hard for the ambitious Kulish to acknowledge Shevchenko's superiority as a poet. After Taras's return from exile, Kulish attempted to assume the role of mentor and editor. While Shevchenko was in Nizhny Novgorod, Kulish had criticized him for writing 'The Neophytes,' since the poem could not be published without offending the new tsar, of whom Kulish had high hopes. After returning from abroad in the summer of 1858, Kulish gave further extensive advice to Shevchenko on his poems, and Shevchenko grew to resent this constant paternalism. In the fall of 1858 Kulish returned to St Petersburg, and on one occasion, after reading Shevchenko's poem 'To the Poles,' he attacked it so harshly that the next day he was afraid that he had gone too far in his criticism. For his part Shevchenko made it clear that he would no longer listen to his friend's advice. This made Kulish bitter, and he complained that Shevchenko was preventing him from editing the works of Marko Vovchok. Yet during the winter of 1858–59 they saw each other frequently, until Kulish, having fallen in love with Marko Vovchok, followed her abroad, after being rebuffed, behaved very strangely to all his friends. Unlike most of them, who turned against Kulish, Shevchenko felt some sympathy for the man and perhaps prevented a rift between Kulish and the Ukrainian community, which did, however, appear later. At the same time Shevchenko, while feeling sorry for Kulish, deplored the latter's behaviour and was sad to see all these quarrels among the Ukrainian intellectual elite.

In August 1858 Shevchenko re-established contact with Kostomarov, who, on his way from abroad had stopped to do some research in the capital. Kostomarov unexpectedly visited Shevchenko, and after an interval of eleven years the poet was unable to recognize the scholar, his old friend. The meeting was very moving for both of them, and for two weeks they met regularly at Palkin's restaurant. Kostomarov then left for Saratov, where he spent an entire working year as the local secretary of a committee on peasant reform.

Among Shevchenko's friends there were many prominent Russian writers. The poet knew Vasiliy and Nikolay Kurochkin, met Chernyshevsky and his family, and on several occasions saw Turgenev. He also frequently met the poets Polonsky and Shcherbina, the brothers Aleksey and Lev Zhemchuzhnikov, their cousin the poet Count Aleksey Tolstoy, and the young novelist Leskov. Nikolay Kurochkin and the Zhemchuzhnikov brothers became close friends because of their deep Ukrainophilism. The friendly home of Count Tolstoy and his wife Anastasia soon received, besides Shevchenko, his Ukrainian friends Kulish, Hulak-Artemovsky, and Kostomarov. The upper-class salons of Natalia Sukhanova-Podkolzyna and Varvara Kartashevska, both wealthy Ukrainian landowners, were always open to him. At Kartashevska's salon Ukrainian literary evenings were held, attended from time to time by Marko Vovchok, Vasyl Bilozersky, and Turgenev. Polonsky, Apollon Maikov, Shcherbina, Turgenev, the painters Aivazovsky, Sokolov, and Pimenov gathered at Sukhanova-Podkolzyna's salon. Sukhanova's son and Shevchenko's pupil, Borys, later recalled how Shevchenko, 'with his simplicity, sincerity, and his appearance alone, captivated both young and old.' The poet was admired for his 'clumsy but not at all vulgar manners, his simple language, and genial, wise smile.' Tolstoy's daughter Katia also confirmed the appeal of Shevchenko's personality. 'He was very gentle, soft and naïvely trusting, finding something good in everyone, even those who were unworthy of it. He had a strong influence on others, including the servants.' Servants, particularly, loved Shevchenko and 'tried to please him.' At the Sukhanovs' the servants learned by heart Shevchenko's poems from the first edition of *Kobzar*, owned by the butler Pyvovarenko. When he left his apartment Shevchenko used to write in chalk on the door the address where he might be found. Guests who visited him during his absence also wrote messages on the door. Sometimes, when he returned home, the poet found the door covered with Ukrainian verse.

Before Christmas 1858 St Petersburg was visited by the famous black American actor Ira Aldridge, who was known for his performance of the role of Othello. Shevchenko liked his performance enormously and soon afterwards met Aldridge at the Tolstoys'. Young Katia acted as an interpreter, since Aldridge spoke only English. She has left an account of the meeting. 'Shevchenko could not help liking him – they both had much in common. Both were honest men and real artists; both had suffered deprivation in their youth. The one, in order to gain entry to the theatre, became an actor's servant; the other was flogged for painting by candlelight.'[11] The artist Mikeshin witnessed an episode, following a performance of *King Lear*, with Aldridge in the title role, when Shevchenko raced to the latter's dressing-room and kissed his black friend's face and hands, thanking him profusely. Aldridge liked the Ukrainian songs that Shevchenko sang to him, and he reciprocated by singing some spirituals. Shevchenko painted Aldridge's portrait, and both listened, at Tolstoy's, to Kontsky playing Mozart and Chopin.

It appeared as though, surrounded by human kindness, Shevchenko was living without many cares. But the intellectual climate was not good. The liberal policies of the new regime failed to materialize, and there was no change in the attitude of the Russian public to Ukrainian aspirations. Occasionally, Shevchenko had to react strongly to Russian chauvinism. This happened in 1858, when Ivan Aksakov began to publish a new journal, called the *Sail* (*Parus*), in which he wanted to involve Maksymovych and Shevchenko. It became obvious that in Aksakov's view Ukrainian cultural aspirations consisted merely of singing songs and writing verse. When Maksymovych agreed to collaborate on the new journal, an incensed Shevchenko wrote to him: 'The *Sail*, in its editorial, mentioned all the Slavs, but failed to mention us ... I do not wish to send any of my poems there, and in addition the *Sail* is promoted by the illustrious prince,

11 E.F. Tolstaia-Yunge, 'Vospominaniia o Shevchenko,' *Vospominaniia*, 278

who is a believer in corporal punishment.' The reference was to an article by the so-called liberal Prince Cherkasky, who advocated the flogging of peasants.

Unlike some Ukrainian intellectuals (Kulish, Maksymovych), Shevchenko very quickly came to distrust the liberalism of the new tsar. He saw little change in government policy in Ukraine, and his hatred of Russia intensified. A young painter, Chestakhivsky, records that Shevchenko often talked to him about the Ukrainian people 'in bondage, tormented by serfdom, but still alive, warm, and religious.' The poet believed that the 'glorious Cossack people have drunk a cup of bitterness, but have not lost heart. The evil *moskal* trod on them with his dirty boots, ignorant of the good he was destroying.' For Shevchenko, who had always appreciated Russian literature and welcomed social progress in Russia, to have used an image such as 'dirty boots' meant that he was giving up any hope of progress. Everything Russian annoyed him. When Kukharenko used a Russian word in one of his letters, Shevchenko upbraided him for it, saying that he 'was forgetting our Christian tongue.' When he was showing friends his sketch of an episode in Mazepa's life, Shevchenko improvised a debate between Mazepa and Voinarovsky on the one hand and the Cossacks supporting Moscow on the other. At one point Voinarovsky accuses the Cossacks of voluntarily accepting the Russian yoke. 'Wait till the *moskals* have harnessed you,' he says; 'then they will drive you, and you will do whatever they tell you.'

Perhaps these anti-Russian sentiments prompted the poet to plan a journey to Ukraine, which he had not seen for twelve years. A hope he often entertained in exile – of building his own small house in Ukraine – now merged with another idea: that of marrying a Ukrainian girl. Before Christmas of 1858 he wrote to Maria Maksymovych, who was then living in Ukraine: 'Be kind enough to let me get married; otherwise I shall perish like a vagabond in a foreign land ... Next summer, God willing, I'll be in Kiev and in [your *khutir*], Mykhailova Hora. There, under a maple or a willow you will place a princess in a wreath of flowers, and I'll meet her. We shall fall in love and get married. You see, how simple and enchanting!'[12] This vision was enchanting indeed, but could it be realized? In her reply Maria Maksymovych promised to find a suitable girl – 'beautiful and lively.' Shevchenko wrote again, in 1859, that he hoped to settle the matter with the censor soon, to stuff his pockets 'full of money,' and then visit the Maksymovyches. Once again he wrote of marrying because he 'was tired of a vagabond existence.' May passed,

12 *Povne*, VI, 224

and the censor had not let the poetry 'out of his claws.' There was also another difficulty preventing travel to Ukraine: he was under police surveillance. In order to travel he had to obtain permission from the chief of gendarmes and from the president of the academy. Shevchenko applied for a permit, but the answer was not forthcoming. On 10 May he wrote to Maria Maksymovych, doubting whether he would ever receive it. Once more he was plunged into despair: 'At first they would not let me into the capital, and now they won't let me out of this stinking place. How long will they go on humiliating me? I do not know what to do ... Perhaps I should flee to you and, having married someone, hide there? Perhaps I'll do this. I shall wait for my passport till 15 May, and then what will be, will be.'[13] He ended his letter humorously: 'In the meantime, I am sending you my portrait. Be kind enough not to show it to the girls, because they will be frightened and think that I am some *haidamak* leader. None of them will want to marry such a cutthroat. But, all the same, you choose the prettiest and tell her quietly to get ready.'[14]

The travel pass was to be issued by the academy. The application had gone to the imperial court, since Grand Duchess Maria was the president of the academy. In the application Shevchenko asked permission to travel to the Kiev, Chernihiv, and Poltava regions for 'five months to improve his health and sketch landscapes.' Tolstoy testified that Shevchenko had made no political errors since he came back to St Petersburg. Yet the answer was slow in coming. Shevchenko became impatient and depressed. He had a prospective fellow-traveller, the Kharkiv landowner Khrushchev, who promised to accompany him on a trip from Moscow to Ukraine. The poet begged him to wait. On 25 May he wrote to Maria Maksymovych: 'I am still here. They won't let me go home. They are also refusing my publication. I do not know what to do. Should I not hang myself? No, I'll not hang myself, but run off to Ukraine, get married, and return to the capital.'[15] If there had been further delays perhaps Shevchenko would have done something desperate. But suddenly the police received the consent of the Third Section to issue Shevchenko with a travel pass. This happened on 25 May, and the poet hastened to leave the city.

13 Ibid, 230
14 Ibid 231
15 Ibid

XV

After arriving in Moscow by train, Shevchenko and Khrushchev in late May or early June set out by coach for Ukraine. Khrushchev had estates in the Sumy and Lebedyn districts and invited Shevchenko to stay with him. On the way they stopped at Orel, where Shevchenko visited his friend Fedir Lazarevsky. They reached Ukraine via the Kursk region, probably through the city of Putyvl, which was mentioned in the *Lay of Ihor's Armament*. On 5 June they were in Sumy, on the picturesque banks of the River Psiol. The area is one of the most beautiful parts of Ukraine. The River Psiol with its tributaries bisects the rich meadows and winds through wooded hills and copses. The vegetation is lush, the soil the very best *chornozem*. Shevchenko sketched one of the most picturesque places – Stinka, where the road to Lebedyn runs through the uplands beside the meandering Psiol. On 7 June the poet arrived at Khrushchev's estate, Lykhvyn. Here he rested for three days. The Khrushchevs and other Ukrainians from Lebedyn received Shevchenko very warmly. He felt relaxed and gave Mrs Khrushchev his sketch *A Spring Evening*. On 9 June, at Nov, the *khutir* of the Khrushchevs on the banks of the Psiol, a traditional tasting of *varenukha* (brandy with honey, spices and berries) was held, while the guests ate *kasha* prepared in the open over a blazing fire.

Before visiting the Maksymovyches Shevchenko took a series of side-trips, since Khrushchev lent him some good horses and a coachman. On 10 June he was in Pyriatyn, and then went on to revisit places he had known in his youth: Yahotyn (the Repnins now lived in Moscow), Berezova Rudka, and Pereiaslav, where he visited an old friend, Kozachkovsky. He stopped at the place where, in 1845, he had experienced such elation, the old Cossack settlement Monastyryshche, on the banks of the Dnieper. Seven years earlier, in exile, he had vividly remembered that moment and wrote to Kozachkovsky: 'Do you recall our trip ... to Monastyryshche on the hill? Remember that enchanting evening, the wide panorama, in the middle a wide mauve ridge and beyond it Pereiaslav cathedral, as if it were made of pure gold. What a marvellous, solemn silence. Do you remember? For a long time we could not say a word, until we heard a marvellous song coming out of nowhere. An enchanting evening, an enchanting land and strange songs!'[1] In the neighbourhood of Pereiaslav, Shevchenko had written his 'Testament,' 'The Caucasus,' and 'Epistle.' Now, after fourteen years of separation he was overcome with emotion, and on 12 June, the day of the local fair, he silently greeted these sites. After attending the fair, he expressed a desire to see the famous panorama at sunset, to look once more at the hills, where his heart, tormented in exile, wanted to find permanent rest.

Without waiting for the horses to be harnessed, the poet went ahead. In the cool of the evening people were fishing in the Dnieper. Looking around and taking in the abundant beauty of the countryside, Taras thought how happily he could live there 'if a poet could be only a poet, not a citizen.' The contrast between natural beauty and political reality troubled him deeply. He often expressed this in his poetry, especially when his thoughts veered towards this enchanted spot: 'Everything here gladdens the eye / But my heart is weeping; it does not want to look.' Sometimes, he regretted that his life had separated him from nature and thrust him into the struggle that had brought so many injuries:

> Why has the Lord not allowed
> Me to live my life in this paradise?
> I would die ploughing the field,
> Would know nothing,
> Would not be God's fool in this world,
> And curse both man and God![2]

He blamed those who 'taught me to write bad verse.' Now, on a moonlit night on the Dnieper, these thoughts kept nagging the poet. Would not this simple existence be the best? Often in exile he had wished 'to die on a hill near the Dnieper,' to find a wife there and 'beside her gaze from a hill at the wide Dnieper and the wide-skirted wheatlands.' Could not this dream be realized? As he stood there, he was overwhelmed by the force of his desire for peace and family happiness.

The next day, 13 June, he sailed in a small oaken boat on the Dnieper to nearby Prokhorivka, past the hilly banks on which, after his death, his

---

[1] Ibid, 76
[2] 'Meni trynadtsiaty mynalo,' ibid, II, 39

body would be laid to rest. The Maksymovyches awaited him with impatience and open arms. He stayed with them for two weeks. The small cottage in which they lived, high on a hill, had a veranda looking out on to the Dnieper. The hill was heavily wooded, and Shevchenko took walks in the vicinity, looking at the 'blue mountains beyond the Dnieper' between Pekary and Kaniv and sketching all the time. Often he came back just before nightfall. He also met and talked with the peasants, who offered him drinks.

At the end of June the poet crossed to the right bank of the Dnieper to visit his native Kerelivka. On the way he stopped at Horodyshche to see the sugar-beet factory of the former serfs Yakhnenko and Symyrenko. These were the Ukrainian capitalists he wanted to meet, since a great deal was known about their enterprise. After becoming millionaires they had not exploited their workers but, on the contrary, helped to raise the standard of living and culture of the local population from which they sprang. Shevchenko was greeted with great warmth and respect. The owners and their manager, O. Khropal, were enlightened Ukrainians. 'A few minutes after his arrival Shevchenko felt at home.' He was given the red-carpet treatment. The poet was in a good mood and recited the poems he had written in exile. He was also genuinely impressed with what he saw. The old Yakhnenko and his son-in-law, Fedir Symyrenko, were regarded as 'Ukrainian Fords,' and their giant plants were known throughout Russia. They employed free labour and paid their workers well, in stark contrast to other industrial enterprises, where serf labour was used. In addition, Horodyshche had well-equipped living quarters for the workers, steam-baths, a hospital and a pharmacy, a church, a library, and a school. Shevchenko was so pleased to see all this that, with tears in his eyes, he embraced and kissed Yakhnenko, saying, 'Father, what have you done here!' The poet's belief in the possibility of free, creative labour was strongly reinforced.

He visited Kerelivka to see his brothers and sisters still 'slaving in serfdom, with their children following them.' As he came close to his old house, from which his stepmother had chased him, he met and embraced Mykyta's wife, Palazhka, who was alone in the house. He was moved to tears. The old house had sunk to one side, and the orchard around it, which he had remembered so warmly in exile, had been cut down. His sister-in-law told him grim tales about her life. He then went to see his sister Yaryna. Like Palazhka, Yaryna was embarrassed by his sudden visit. Later she said: 'I do not remember what happened to me. We sat on the *pryzba* [a bank of earth against the outside wall of the house] and he placed his head on my knees and kept asking me to tell him about my hard life.' Her life was hard, and she cried as she talked, till she told him the latest news about the death of her husband, who had been a drunkard and whom Taras used to warn about his drinking. At least now she was free of him. The next day the poet went to the church, where he used to read the psalter over those who died. After the service his old schoolfriends came to Mykyta's house. They all asked him 'if freedom would come soon.' Shevchenko did not know the answer.

Shevchenko's brother Yosyp was married to Motria, who had a brother, Varfolomey, a manager on the estate of Prince Lopukhin. Taras remembered the latter's warning about not talking honestly. Now he went to visit him at Korsun, which was not far from Kerelivka. Perhaps Shevchenko wanted to meet this former serf, or to see, on the way, the picturesque environs of the River Ros, but probably he wanted to seek advice in the matter of purchasing some land. He had his eye on some property near Prokhorivka. At Korsun Shevchenko met Varfolomey and his family and stayed with them for ten days. He admired and sketched the magnificent park on the estate, and noted down some new folksongs. On 5 July he went to see the landowner Parchevsky in Mezhyrichchia to discuss the purchase of a small piece of land between Pekary and Kaniv. It was on a hill and was suitable for a small cottage. Shevchenko was shown the land by Parchevsky's manager, Volsky. As they proceeded to measure the lot, they were unexpectedly joined by the surveyor's cousin, Kozlovsky, who was dressed in his best and looked ridiculous in the open fields. Shevchenko made a remark about it, and Kozlovsky took offence. The poet apologized, and they all stayed and ate and drank together. This seemingly innocent episode later led to Shevchenko's arrest on 13 July, on charges of blasphemy.

The real reasons for the arrest become clearer when we realize that as soon as Shevchenko was given permission to travel to Ukraine, strict instructions were issued by the Third Section to the gendarmes in the Kiev, Poltava and Chernihiv regions to watch the poet very closely. The police were put on the alert, the governor general of Kiev asked for strict surveillance of Shevchenko wherever he went. Up to this point the poet had eluded the police by not travelling by stagecoach and taking little-known roads on his way to the Maksymovyches'. But when he appeared in Korsun and stayed with Varfolomey, the news reached the police station at Kaniv, and strict surveillance of his movements began. When Shevchenko reached Mezhyrichchia and began to negotiate the purchase of land, the police were on his heels. It is very likely, therefore, that cousin Kozlovsky was a police agent sent to provoke Shevchenko to make some irreverent statements.

After surveying the land Shevchenko returned to Kerelivka. Then, on 13 July, as he was crossing the Dnieper on his way to the Maksymovyches', a policeman, Dobzhansky, placed him under arrest and took him to the police station in Moshny. The next day the poet was interrogated by the district police officer Tabashnikov and the officer Kzhyvytsky. They already had in front of them the testimonies of Volsky, Kozlovsky, and Molendsky, as well as of the peasant Sadovy, who had been present at the land survey. Kozlovsky must have given the police most of the details of the meeting with Shevchenko. However, Kozlovsky's testimony was given with some verbal restraint since he did not want to implicate Volsky, who was a good friend of Varfolomey. The peasant Sadovy testified that Shevchenko's talk was blasphemous.

The next day the district police officer Tabashnikov sent a report to the governor general of Kiev. Citing Sadovy's testimony about Shevchenko's blasphemy, Tabashnikov wrote that, according to Sadovy, Shevchenko was also drunk, and that Volsky and Kozlovsky maintained that the poet was drunk and 'not in his right mind' because, whenever they could not understand what he was saying, he would immediately swear. Volsky also testified that the poet had narrated something from one of his works, which was unintelligible. Moreover, Tabashnikov reported that there were rumours among the people that, apart from blasphemy, Shevchenko had also told some men that 'there is no need for a tsar, landlords, or priests.' Finally, Tabashnikov recommended that Shevchenko be returned to St Petersburg.

Shevchenko testified that 'as far as he could remember, he did not say anything bad' and that he would not dare to do so since 'he is very well aware of his relationship with the government and that he is being watched.' The whole matter ended up in the hands of the governor general, Prince Vasilchikov. Fortunately, the prince referred the case to one of his officials, Marko Andrievsky, who was Ukrainian. Andrievsky, having studied the testimony, proposed two possible procedures in dealing with Shevchenko. One would be to return him to St Petersburg, the other to bring Shevchenko to Kiev. There is reason to believe that Andrievsky persuaded Vasilchikov to follow the second procedure.

From 13 to 18 July Shevchenko was under house arrest in Moshny, accompanied by the policeman Dobzhansky. From 18 to 21 July he was in Cherkasy, and then, until 27 July, back in Moshny. He could move about, visit people, and take walks, all under Dobzhansky's surveillance. Symyrenko tried to help the poet by interceding ,with Colonel Yagnitsky, the manager of Prince Vorontsov's estate at Moshny, but nothing came of his efforts. On 27 July Shevchenko was dispatched to Kiev, and four days later Vasilchikov asked Andrievsky to 'cross-examine Shevchenko thoroughly' and ascertain what was his thinking (*obraz myslei*). On 6 August Shevchenko wrote his testimony and Andrievsky passed it on to Prince Vasilchikov, enclosing his own favourable comment on the poet. As a result Vasilchikov advised Shevchenko to leave Ukraine and, at the same time, forwarded to the chief of gendarmes in St Petersburg a report based on the poet's own testimony. He wrote:

Soon after Shevchenko's arrival [in Ukraine] I received information that he intended to build a house for himself in the village of Pekary, Cherkasy district, and that having selected the spot he offered drinks to the officials and conducted an irreverent conversation in which he allegedly rejected the existence of God and the sanctity of the Holy Virgin.

Because such a conversation might have had repercussions, I asked to have Shevchenko brought to Kiev and entrusted one of my officials to cross-examine Shevchenko.

In his explanation Shevchenko said that, wishing to purchase ... a piece of land from the landowner, Parchevsky, in order to settle there permanently, he and the surveyor wanted to survey the land. While they were working, a certain Kozlovsky, wearing strange clothes, came to join them, and Shevchenko began to make fun of him. While they were eating, Kozlovsky started a theological conversation. In order to stop this conversation Shevchenko said that theology without a living God cannot create even one living leaf. Later, Kozlovsky asked Shevchenko what he thought about the mother of Jesus Christ, to which Shevchenko replied: We ought to revere the mother of him who suffered and died for us on the cross, because if she had not borne God, she would be an ordinary woman. The official who took down the testimony testifies that Shevchenko, as far as it is possible to ascertain his views, is unquestionably devoted to his ancestors' faith and that he shows a distaste for everything Latin and Polish.

In evaluating Shevchenko's testimony I conclude that the accusation against him might have arisen out of a misunderstanding of his conversation by other people, or was even caused by the resentment that was aroused in Kozlovsky by [Shevchenko's] ridicule and his answers to theological argument. Therefore I do not attach much importance to this matter, do not plan to pursue it further, and am allowing Shevchenko to return to St Petersburg in accordance with his wishes.[3]

3 *Taras Shevchenko: dokumenty i materialy* (Kiev 1963), 92–3. In the recent biography of Shevchenko by Yevhen Kyryliuk (Kiev 1964), more evidence is given about the alleged blasphemy of the poet (476). Taking into account that Shevchenko might have been tipsy at the time and that he held an unorthodox view of the virgin birth (see his poem 'Mariia,' 1859), it is not impossible that he did, indeed, express views that might have been considered blasphemous.

In the final paragraph the Kiev governor general expressed objection to the possibility of Shevchenko settling in Ukraine, but the entire tone of his report exonerated the poet.

Shevchenko was in Kiev for over two weeks. Although under police surveillance, he moved about freely and visited many friends. He was delighted to see his old friend Soshenko, at whose place he met his future biographer, M. Chaly. For a while Shevchenko stayed with his friend from the academy Hudovsky, who was now a professional photographer. While visiting Father Botvynovsky Shevchenko once again grew suspicious of the presence there of Askochensky, who, before 1847, had prophesied that Shevchenko would end up as a soldier. Perhaps in order to avoid constant invitations, Shevchenko decided to move to the outskirts of Kiev. He found a landlady in Prevarka, just outside the city, who was prepared to give him board and lodging free of charge, since the poet pleaded poverty. He was very happy staying at her peasant cottage, playing with children, and enjoying himself hugely. At last he received some money from St Petersburg. Soon after this, permission to return to St Petersburg came from Prince Vasilchikov. This permit was tantamount to an order to leave Ukraine. Instead of staying for five months, Shevchenko remained in his native country for only two months and ten days. He was deeply disappointed that all his plans to settle down and get married had come to nought. This time, however, he blamed himself for being so talkative and unnecessarily involving himself with strangers. His old inability to hold his tongue while he was drinking had caught up with him. In a way, he was lucky to be released so quickly.

On 13 August he said goodbye to his Kiev friends. The farewell reception for him was given by Kulish's friends the Kraskovskys. Early on 14 August he left Prevarka, after settling accounts with his landlady. He did not go straight to Moscow but returned once more to Pereiaslav, where he observed the religious festivities on 15 August. The contrast between the colourful mass of people and the grey remnants of the city where, in 1654, Bohdan Khmelnytsky had made the infamous agreement with Moscow made him write a short poem in which he vented his anger against the hetman:

> If, drunk Bohdan,
> You could now look
> At Pereiaslav and your castle
> ...
> If indeed you had never been born,

> I would not bathe you in a gutter now,
> You, the most celebrated one! Amen.[4]

The poet's anger was all the more understandable in view of his humiliating experiences with the Russian gendarmes in Ukraine.

From Pereiaslav he went to Pryluky and then to Hustyn, as if delaying his departure from Ukraine. At the Hustyn monastery old Prince Repnin and Mazepa's Colonel Horlenko were buried. From there Shevchenko wrote to Varfolomey, once more expressing his strong desire to purchase the land that he had liked so much. The poet did not know that Vasilchikov, in sending him back to St Petersburg, had recommended that he should never return to Ukraine. Travelling along the roads which he remembered so well, Shevchenko decided to visit the Tarnovskys at Kachanivka. He approached the palace from a side entrance. He was wearing a summer coat and straw hat and when he climbed up the stairs, the old servants recognized him. The elder Tarnovskys were away, but he was warmly welcomed by the young Vasyl Tarnovsky, who also lent him some money. In the guest album at Kachanivka Shevchenko wrote two lines from an old poem of his: 'And the path where you walked, / Is overgrown with prickly thorn.' We do not know who the woman was whom he was remembering here.

From Kachanivka he went to Hyriavka to visit the mother of the six Lazarevsky brothers. He found her with her son Fedir, who was on a visit there. In their secluded *khutir* he spent three very pleasant days. As a token of his gratitude he left Afanasia Lazarevska his favourite *Spring Evening*, as well as a portrait of her that he had sketched. Early on 25 August Shevchenko left Hyriavka with Fedir Lazarevsky. They spent the next night in Krolevets, with Fedir's sister, and on 27 August they parted at Sevsk. The route to Moscow was the same one he had taken in 1847, then escorted by Officer Grishkov. This time he was travelling alone.

---

4 'Yak by to ty Bohdane piany,' *Povne*, II, 349

XVI

After stopping for a few days in Moscow Shevchenko went by train to St Petersburg. On his arrival he was pleased to learn that the academy had awarded him the title of 'Academician of Engraving.' Three objectives were now on his agenda: to publish his works, to acquire a permanent home on the banks of the Dnieper, and to get married. He learned that the censor Palauzov had passed for publication not only the *Kobzar*, the 'Haidamaks,' and 'Hamaliia', but also 'The Servant Girl' and 'The Captive.' He immediately wrote about it to Varfolomey. However, a second censor, Troinitsky, had to approve the publication, and this could mean further delay. Obviously, the warning by the Third Section had had its effect, and the bureaucrats were being very cautious in dealing with Shevchenko. The poet was summoned to the Third Section and given a severe reprimand for his behaviour in Ukraine and a warning 'to conduct himself properly; if the order were contravened he should not be surprised about the consequences that might befall him.'

With impressions of his homeland fresh in his mind the poet could think of nothing but how to acquire the cottage on the Dnieper. He kept writing to Varfolomey, giving him instructions where to buy the lumber for the cottage. Yet no progress was possible. The landowner, Parchevsky, refused to sell his land to a 'blasphemer.' Desperate, Shevchenko wrote to Varfolomey that settling in Ukraine had become a matter of life and death to him. If he stayed any longer in Russia, he was certain he would be sent once more to Siberia. 'One way or another I must get married, or this cursed boredom will be the end of me,' he wrote to Varfolomey, and suggested that he would like to marry Varfolomey's servant Kharytia Dovhopolenko. During his visit he had seen her briefly, and now, forestalling her objections, he pleaded: 'Perhaps Kharytia will say that she is poor, an orphan, a servant, and I am rich and proud. Then tell her that I lack things, sometimes even a clean shirt ... Tell her that she will not be unhappy with me.'[1]

To Varfolomey this proposal came like a bolt from the blue. He tried in vain to dissuade the poet from proposing to Kharytia. 'You are an educated man,' he wrote to Taras; 'living alone with your wife on the Dnieper, you will need to tell her that you think this and that, that you have written something, and you may even want to read it to her. And what will she say? ... Your boredom will become all the greater, so that you will cry.'[2] Taras angrily protested: 'Have you forgotten that in my flesh and blood I am the son and brother of our hapless people?' He asked his sister Yaryna and Varfolomey's wife to try and influence Kharytia. From September 1859 to June 1860 in every letter he asked about Kharytia. Varfolomey wrote back saying that Kharytia considered Shevchenko to be a lord (*pan*) and that she was flirting with the village clerk. Eventually, Shevchenko had to give up any hope of winning Kharytia, who married the clerk. In the meantime Shevchenko was still hoping to purchase the land. On 4 December Varfolomey told him that Parchevsky definitely would not sell, and suggested other possibilities of acquiring a cottage. None of them materialized.

The fall of 1859 was taken up with publishing matters. Censorship became more difficult when it was discovered that during that year someone, without Shevchenko's permission, had published some of his revolutionary poems of 1843-45 in Leipzig. Finally, at the end of November, permission to publish his poems was granted, but the censors 'cleaned' Shevchenko's works so thoroughly that 'he hardly recognized his children.' The publisher Kozhanchikov, who a year earlier had been ready to pay the author 2,000 roubles, was now only willing to pay him one-half of the promised royalties. At the same time Shevchenko was guaranteed financial support by Symyrenko, who offered him 1,100 roubles. The poet decided to have 5,800 copies printed (in the end 6,050 copies appeared), and the whole month of December was spent reading proofs. He managed to save some uncensored copies, which he sent to his closest friends. At the end of January 1860 he was dispatching copies to Ukraine. The book appeared under the old title, *Kobzar*, and not, as the author had wanted, as *The Poems of T. Shevchenko*. In spite of the censor's cuts the new publication, which included 'The Servant Girl' and other earlier works, pleased Shevchenko. The book sold well and brought in

---

1 Ibid, VI, 239
2 *Lysty do T.H. Shevchenka*, 170

some money. On 1 February 1860 the poet wrote to Varfolomey that *Kobzar* was helping to pay the rent. He was anxious to see reviews and especially the response of readers in Ukraine.

Throughout the winter of 1859–60 Shevchenko regularly met Kostomarov, who, having secured a university chair in Russian history, lived in St Petersburg. Occasionally the poet liked to tease his scholarly friend. Kostomarov lived in a hotel, and his room was next to a restaurant. Once, having learned that Kostomarov was busy preparing his lectures, Shevchenko went to the restaurant and asked to play the player-piano. The endless arias so infuriated Kostomarov that he dashed into the restaurant and begged Shevchenko 'in the name of humanity' to stop tormenting him. But the poet kept saying 'No, no! Go on playing the tunes from *Il Trovatore, Rigoletto, La Traviata*. I like them very much!' Yet these incidents did not spoil their friendship. How close it was may be seen from an account by Shevchenko himself that describes how he once visited Kostomarov and the latter said that he was too busy to see him. Shevchenko, nonplussed, answered that he had come to visit his mother, not the great scholar. They often talked and argued till past midnight, and Shevchenko read his unpublished works to him. In the spring of 1860 Kostomarov moved to Vasilevsky Island and Shevchenko visited him every Tuesday, the day set aside for receiving guests.

The year 1860 saw Shevchenko's reputation soar. *Kobzar* appeared in January, and on 13 February the well-known journal *Popular Reading* (*Narodnoe chtenie*) published his autobiography in the form of a letter to the editor. The letter had been very well edited by Kulish. The sad story of Shevchenko's life ended with the words 'My brothers and sisters, of whom it is hard to speak here, are still serfs. Yes, mister editor, they are still serfs.' The autobiography was reprinted by other Russian and Polish journals. In the summer Shevchenko published his letter to the landowner Florkovsky. This was in response to Florkovsky's refusal, in response to the request of the 'Literary Fund,' to release Shevchenko's brothers and sister and to give them some land. Florkovsky published his correspondence with the 'Literary Fund' and argued that the serfs described in Shevchenko's autobiography lived well. Shevchenko's reply was full of sarcasm, and it evoked a wide and favourable response among those readers who favoured the emancipation of the peasantry. Florkovsky did not abandon his stand, but the moral victory belonged to Shevchenko.

The year 1860 was also a period of lively activity among the Ukrainians in St Petersburg. A cultural circle known as 'Community' ('Hromada') was organized; meetings were held in the apartment of Fedir Chernenko and were attended by Shevchenko. Steps were being taken to establish a

Ukrainian journal, the *Foundation* (*Osnova*). Kulish's almanac *Home* (*Khata*) was published, and it included some new poems by Shevchenko. The Russian critics began to pay attention to Shevchenko. The *Contemporary* printed a favourable review by Dobroliubov of the new edition of *Kobzar*. Dobroliubov wrote that Shevchenko was 'a poet of the people, a figure we cannot point to in our midst.' The poet Mikhailov wrote a favourable review in the *Russian Word* (*Russkoe slovo*). Both reviews emphasized the national character of Shevchenko's works, the very point which had not been conceded by Belinsky in the 1840s. A Russian translation of *Kobzar* appeared. It was prepared by M. Gerbel, and included among the translators N. Kurochkin, A. Pleshcheev, L. Mey, V. Krestovsky, and M. Mikhailov.

The publication in Paris of a Polish article in *Przegląd rzeczy polskich*, edited by General Mierosławski, was a disappointment for Shevchenko. The article attacked the poet for his 'cynicism and demagoguery' during his 1859 visit to Ukraine. It alleged that Shevchenko was a rabble-rouser, calling for a bloody rebellion. It also referred to his blasphemy. Interestingly enough, this almost slanderous attack did not attract the attention of the tsarist police.

In spite of his social and literary preoccupations Shevchenko was still thinking about marriage. His poems of that period paint an idyllic picture of marital bliss. After giving up his plan to win Kharytia, he wrote to Khtodot Tkachenko in Poltava, asking him to keep an eye out for a pretty girl. Before he could receive an answer, he found one himself in St Petersburg.

The mother of the Nizhyn landowner, Mykola Makarov, and of his sister, Varvara Kartashevska, had brought to St. Petersburg in 1859 a servant-girl, a serf, Lykera Polusmakivna. For a while she was a servant at the Kartashevskys', where Shevchenko could not help noticing her. Now that his plan to marry Kharytia had fallen through, he began to pay more attention to Lykera. For a while she was lent to Oleksandra Kulish, who had been temporarily abandoned by her husband, and her sister Nadia Zabila, who were living on a *dacha* in Strelno, near St Petersburg. Shevchenko was a frequent visitor at Strelno, and suddenly, on 27 July, he proposed to Lykera and told both the sisters and Vasyl Bilozersky, who was staying with them, about it. Lykera was not a great beauty but was well built and attractive. A description of her has been left by Turgenev: 'Young and fresh, a little uncouth, not very pretty, but in her own way attractive, with beautiful auburn hair and with a proud and quiet carriage that is characteristic of her tribe.' Lykera was lively and intelligent, which could have attracted Shevchenko. But she also had a darker side of which he was not aware. Realizing this, the Bilozersky sisters had decided to send her back to her old masters.

The history of Shevchenko's final romance is well documented in his and Lykera's letters and in many eyewitness accounts. In fact this tragic incident is the best-documented episode in Shevchenko's entire life. Yet it is still hard to arrive at the truth of what actually happened. The events connected with this romance, which took place between 27 July and 10 September 1860, definitely contributed to Shevchenko's untimely death.

On 27 July the feast-day of St Panteleimon, Kulish's patron saint, guests gathered at Strelno. Among them were Vasyl Bilozersky and the Ukrainian ethnographer Nomys. Shevchenko appeared after lunch, and while he was walking in the garden with the mistress of the house, Oleksandra Kulish, he told her that a few moments earlier he had proposed to Lykera. Oleksandra was shocked, not so much because Lykera was a servant-girl as because her moral conduct left much to be desired. Kulish's wife decided to be frank with the man who had been the best man at her wedding and told Shevchenko that Lykera was a slut, often appearing unwashed and dishevelled, that she was lazy, a habitual liar, fond of money, and licentious. Her only virtues were her sewing and embroidering skills. After listening to all this Shevchenko asked his hostess if she were not exaggerating, and she answered that she did not want to hide anything from him and that he could ask other people about Lykera. Shevchenko thanked her for her openness, and next day he asked the opinion of Vasyl Bilozersky, who confirmed what his sister had told the poet. Yet Bilozersky sympathized with Shevchenko's desire to marry 'a simple girl'. That evening a meeting was held at Strelno, with Shevchenko and the Bilozerskys present, at which Lykera declared her willingness to marry Shevchenko if her master, Makarov, agreed. Makarov was abroad, in Germany, and Oleksandra Kulish took it upon herself to write and ask for his consent. However, on second thought she decided to delay the matter, hoping that in the meantime the poet would get to know Lykera better and discover her darker side for himself. The Bilozerskys regarded Shevchenko's step as 'desperate' and hoped that he would change his mind.

For a while Shevchenko hesitated. He could not completely ignore the Bilozerskys' warning. At the same time he wrote a letter, which he never mailed, to another woman, offering his friendship, perhaps at some point when he had doubts of Lykera. In any case, the moment of hesitation passed, and the poet asked Kulish's wife to pass on to Lykera a little cross and Kulish's *Primer*. He also told her that Lykera's weaknesses were probably the result of her poverty, and in marrying her he would rescue and improve her. When Oleksandra Kulish gave Lykera the poet's gifts, the girl was not impressed and was disappointed to learn that the cross was not made of gold. On the next day, 30 July, the poet himself arrived at Strelno with a bouquet of wild flowers, which did not please Lykera. During a walk with her in the garden the poet grew thoughtful and a little sad, but 'did not change his mind.' While this assignation was taking place, the other servants gathered outside and laughed, while Mrs Kulish's 'heart broke into pieces.' The entire neighbourhood heard from Lykera about her elderly suitor and made fun of the situation. In the meantime Shevchenko tried to explain his plans for the future to Lykera. He had sent one thousand roubles to Varfolomey to acquire a cottage on the Dnieper. There he would settle with his bride in idyllic peace and happiness. He explained to her why he had sent her the cross and the *Primer*. He would try to educate her and improve her morally. He reiterated that since both of them were serfs, they could easily find common ground.

The content of Shevchenko's conversation may be gauged from Lykera's response, which she disclosed to Mrs Kulish. Apparently she was not interested in Shevchenko's ideas:; 'she wanted to become a lady, while he sought simplicity and native worth.' She was unhappy to learn that Shevchenko's sister wore peasant dress and asked Mrs Kulish if Shevchenko were well off. 'He is old and tight-fisted,' she said. 'I am very unwilling to become his wife.' In a few days, however, she changed her mind and said that she was ready to marry him 'just to show the other servants.' Vasyl Bilozersky wrote to Makarov that 'she sees in Taras Hryhorovych an old man who will take her where she does not want to go ... She is an egotist who will never appreciate him ... a woman who wants to live well and have a good time.' Bilozersky wrote that Shevchenko admitted that he had been hasty and might be disappointed, but still he did not want to change his mind. Mrs Kulish complained: 'He is blinded ... He has created an ideal for himself and does not see her as she really is.' On 30 July Shevchenko himself wrote a letter to Makarov asking him to give his 'blessing to Lykera and Taras.' The Bilozerskys urged Makarov not to give his consent but to delay a decision until his return to Russia. In the meantime the poet visited Strelno regularly and brought all sorts of presents for Lykera, from shoes and stockings to beads and a Bible.

After a while a reply came from Makarov. He wrote separately to Shevchenko and Lykera, assuring them that he did not want to stand in their way but asking them to await his return. Lykera understood this to be her master's consent to her marriage. She reacted strangely, for instead of behaving with greater restraint, she began to hold wild parties with the servants. Shevchenko, too, started to prepare himself for the wedding. He wrote to Varfolomey begging him to rent a house for him and his future bride. Lykera followed her mistress when the latter returned to St Petersburg, and saw Shevchenko every day. The future bridegroom was showering her with gifts. In one day alone, on 3 September, he spent 180 roubles on her. He also attempted to teach her housekeeping duties, giving her a notebook in which to enter various expenses. Lykera, as Shevchenko's fiancée, started to visit his friends and moved, at his expense, to a room in the apartment of an elderly lady. Lykera expected to be waited on by the lady's servants, but Shevchenko would not agree to this. Soon, Lykera and Taras began to quarrel, especially when he begged her to keep her room tidy. On those occasions when he took her out to a restaurant she tried to behave like a great lady and humiliated him. Finally, one day when Shevchenko came to visit her, he found her *in flagrante* in the embrace of the butler. No explanation was necessary, but Lykera later wrote Taras a vituperative letter, full of obscenities. The last great romance of the aging poet had come to an end.

Despite his daily involvement with Lykera Shevchenko did not abandon his art. Early in September, following the award of the title Academician of Engraving, an exhibition was held at the academy, at which a new self-portrait of Shevchenko in oils was shown. In the picture the poet, wearing a fur cap, with his Zaporozhian moustache, appeared a veritable symbol of the intractable Ukrainian spirit, a vengeful tribune of the people. The portrait caused a sensation and some controversy. It was purchased by the Grand Duchess Elena Pavlovna, widow of the tsar's uncle, the Grand Duke Mikhail Pavlovich. She came from the Wurtemberg royal family and had been educated in Paris. Known for her liberal views, she was a patron of the arts and took an active part in the campaign for the emancipation of the serfs. In 1859 she herself released all her serfs from bondage at her Ukrainian estate of Karlivka in the Poltava region. She knew some of Shevchenko's friends very well – the Tolstoys and the Tarnovskys. There is little doubt that by purchasing the portrait the grand duchess wanted to draw attention to the emancipation of the serfs. After buying the portrait she gave it to Tolstoy, Shevchenko's old benefactor. At the same time the portrait drew the ire of the reactionary press. The *Northern Bee* published a review that, while admitting the artistic merit of the picture, claimed that Shevchenko looked 'like a hetman' in it. The critic sensed the national and revolutionary symbolism of the work. Shevchenko was tempted to reply but decided not to do so, since public attention had in any case been aroused.

When Fedir Chernenko, the organizer of *Hromada*, visited Shevchenko on 26 September, he found the poet in a sad mood. He told Chernenko that he was still planning to settle in Ukraine and to publish there a series of cheap etchings on Ukrainian topics to counteract the flood of Russian popular art. During the conversation the mailman brought Shevchenko a letter from his old friend Khtodot Tkachenko, in which the latter informed the poet that he had found a girl for him, the daughter of the Ukrainian writer Vytavsky. Holding this letter in front of the easel, on which a portrait of Lykera was propped, Shevchenko grabbed the portrait and threw it to the floor. Turning to the startled Chernenko, he said: 'Fedir, what do you think? Should I try one last time? I have been unlucky with a serf girl; perhaps I'll be more successful with this *pannochka*?' He was overcome with sorrow and cursed his solitude. The next day he wrote to Tkachenko, asking him to send the girl's photograph.

Although he felt deeply insulted by Lykera, he was unable to abandon his dream of marriage. On 27 September he dedicated this short poem to the ideal Lykera:

> I'll build myself a one-room house,
> And plant a garden-paradise around.
> I'll sit and wander
> In this tiny heaven
> And will rest alone
> In the garden.
> I'll dream of little children
> And their happy mother,
> A bright dream of long ago
> Will come to me ... and you!
> No, I shall not rest,
> For you will enter in my dream,
> Stealing softly into my little Eden,
> Will create havoc ...
> And set aflame my little paradise.[3]

However determined he was to preserve a poetic vision of the beautiful bride, though, Shevchenko in real life realized what had happened. Early in October he met Kostomarov at a performance of his favourite opera,

---

3 'L.,' *Povne*, II, 401

William Tell, by Rossini. When Kostomarov asked him about the marriage, Shevchenko replied that they would both remain unmarried 'vagabonds.' During the second intermission he described his relationship to Lykera as that of Don Quixote to Dulcinea.

For two months Shevchenko demanded that Lykera return all the 'dowry' he had given her in the form of many gifts. Lykera wanted to keep some of them for herself. Shevchenko insisted that if she sold any of his gifts, the proceeds should go to finance Sunday schools in Chernihiv and thus redeem her bad reputation. In the end Lykera returned almost everything. The poet grew depressed and lonely, and described his state in this short poem, written on 4 November:

> If only I had someone
> To sit down with to a meal
> And exchange a word or two,
> I would be able to live
> Somehow in this world.
> But no! There is no one,
> The world is wide,
> And there are many people
> On this earth.
> Yet I alone am condemned
> To dwell in a crooked house,
> Or stretch out under a hedge.
> Or ... No, I must get married.
> Even with the devil's own sister!
> Because otherwise I'll go mad
> With loneliness.[4]

Some of the proceeds from the sale of *Kobzar* also went towards Sunday schools. Shevchenko became very interested in education in Ukrainian and was preparing a school primer. He paid particular attention to pre-school education. He was in sympathy with the well-known progressive theories of education held by Pirogov, Redkin, and Ushinsky, the two latter being Ukrainians. Training of the moral character had to go hand in hand with education in the national spirit. For him, Christian morality was the foundation of everything, and half of his Primer was devoted to religious texts. Apart from prayers, he included his translations of some of the Psalms and the texts of those Ukrainian *dumy* he

---

4 'Yakby z kym sisty,' ibid, 412

considered to be Christian in spirit. Busy with the preparation of the primer and still etching, he seldom left the house, except for dinner, which he ate at Lazarevsky's apartment, just across the street.

Empress Alexandra Fiodorovna, the widow of Nicholas I and the mother of Tsar Alexander II died on 19 October. Her death brought back memories of Shevchenko's grotesque description of her in 'The Dream' and of the legend created by the gendarmes that he had insulted his benefactress. Certainly, the empress was one of those who had bought lottery tickets for Briullov's portrait of Zhukovsky, the sale of which bought Shevchenko's freedom. But did she buy the tickets to free a serf or to acquire a portrait of her son's tutor? In any case, emperors and empresses were always regarded by Shevchenko as despots. Now, hearing of Empress Alexandra's death, he responded with a fierce apostrophe:

> Although one should not castigate the dead,
> A wicked soul cannot rest in peace ...
> Thus you, oh bitch, we'll curse,
> We and our grandchildren
> And the entire nation!
> Nay, not curse, but spit
> On your weaned pups.
> O grief, my grief! O my sorrow!
> Will you depart one day?
> Or will the tsars with slavish ministers
> Hound you to death?
> They will not! And the people
> Will quietly, without fuss,
> Lead the tsar to the gallows.[5]

One day Shevchenko visited the studio of the sculptor Mikeshin, who was then working on a monument to 'Russia's millennium.' Apart from Mikeshin, the writers Polonsky and Pomialovsky, as well as Fedir Chernenko, were present. After fortifying himself with a glass of rum and pacing up and down the studio, Shevchenko suddenly stopped in front of the figure of Peter I, which dominated the monument. He began to curse the tsar and later turned his venom against Catherine II whom he berated for the destruction of the Sich and the enserfment of Ukraine. He raved for some time, then recited the short poem he had written on the death of

5 'Khocha lezhachoho ne biut,' ibid, 409

Empress Alexandra, which the stunned visitors considered to be an attack on Catherine II. Mikeshin later wrote that 'the gigantic statue of Peter I, like a spectre, overwhelmed and annoyed Taras,' and Chernenko reported that he had never seen Shevchenko 'so enraged. His eyes fulminated and he resembled a prophet.' Anything in praise of the tsars provoked a sharp reaction from him. When he saw orphan girls from an orphanage parading early in the morning in front of the remains of the empress, he wrote:

> What do you want tsars for?
> Why do you need dog-keepers?
> You are, after all, people, not dogs![6]

His outbursts of rage apart, it became clear, as Chernenko reported October 1860, that Shevchenko was very ill. The poet did not want to talk about his illness and tried to continue his work. He intervened personally with the Orthodox Metropolitan to obtain permission for the publication of the primer. In the course of the preparation of this book Shevchenko once more clashed with Kulish, who objected to some aspects of the publication. At last, on 23 November, having met a physician, Dr Bari, at Lazarevsky's apartment, the poet confessed that he was feeling ill. He complained of a pain in his chest. Dr Bari gave him a thorough examination and told him to take care of himself and remain indoors. The painter Lev Zhemchuzhnikov, who had returned from Paris in the fall, felt that Shevchenko should be placed in a hospital, where he would receive regular medical care. But the poet would not hear of it. However, he listened to his doctor's advice and stayed indoors.

With more time to write Shevchenko composed, on 26 November, his last political poem about Ukraine's liberation from tsarist rule. The tone, this time, was optimistic: the downfall of tyranny was inevitable, and the Ukrainian 'oak was putting forth new green shoots.' After a two-week quarantine he felt a little better and told Chernenko that he wanted to go out. When his friends begged him to stay indoors during the winter, Shevchenko protested and said that at Christmas he wanted to go carolling. He actually kept this promise and went carolling to Kostomarov's house with the Decembrist Yakushkin. Both were quite tipsy. Kostomarov later reported that this was the only occasion on which he saw Shevchenko drunk and that the poet, who was very fond of rum, usually showed none of the effects of drink. Soon afterwards, on 2

---

6 'O liudy, liudy,' ibid, 411

January 1861, Shevchenko was unable to attend the meeting of the editorial board of the *Foundation*. He was ill again, and his doctor diagnosed it as dropsy (a morbid accumulation of watery fluid in the serous cavities or the connective tissue of the body) and forbade him to drink. The poet complied and did everything he was told. Unfortunately, his illness was well advanced, and his condition did not improve.

Official documents, as well as the testimony of those who knew Shevchenko well, indicate that he was of 'strong build.' This was confirmed by Count Orlov, who, in his report to the tsar, pointed to Shevchenko's strong physique as a reason for sentencing him to military service. The poet's friend Mombelli noted that Taras was 'of medium height, broad-shouldered and generally of strong build. His waist was large because of his bone structure, but he was not fat.' We have no medical history prepared by a doctor or any physician's account of his illnesses. Thus his medical history must be reconstructed from his biography. Taras's grandfather Ivan lived to be 107, but he did not pass on his good health and longevity to his son Hryhoriy. Taras's father died at the age of 47, and his mother at the age of 37. One of Taras's sisters was born blind. After he became an orphan Taras's diet was probably deficient. He was a sensitive boy who was often beaten and humiliated, and this increased his nervous condition. His first serious illness occurred in St Petersburg before he was freed in 1838. He spent eight days unconscious in the hospital of Mary Magdalene and had a high fever for two weeks. We do not know the nature of this illness. In 1842, during the sea voyage to Denmark and Sweden, he fell ill, and his condition was critical when he reached Revel. His recovery in St Petersburg took a long time, and he felt that he might die. In the fall of 1843, while in Yahotyn, he had carbuncles, which were treated by Doctor Fischer. In 1845 the poet fell ill in Pereiaslav and was looked after by Kozachkovsky. Immediately afterwards he had typhus. In exile, at Orsk, Shevchenko suffered from scurvy in 1848. This was caused by the lack of vitamins in his diet. He wrote that both his teeth and eyes ached a great deal. The expedition to the Aral Sea (1848–49) further undermined his health. He often went hungry and, on one occasion, had to drink sea-water, which affected his stomach. While he was there he was infected with boils. In Novopetrovsk he suffered from scrofula. On his way back from exile he once again suffered from boils and, in addition, rheumatism. All this must have weakened him considerably.

The general conditions of Shevchenko's life were not conducive to good health. He lived as a free man for only twelve and a half years. Tragic experiences, humiliations, insults, and traumas were common in his life and would have broken a weaker man. However, Shevchenko emerged from his suffering psychologically unbroken, despite several bouts of depression. His physical health was severely undermined.

Shevchenko cared little for his physical well-being. During the years of freedom his daily routine was irregular. As a student his way of life was truly bohemian. He was attractive to many people, and as a popular young man attended many drinking parties. His drinking, heavy at times, never reduced his ability to work hard. During the last two years of exile he sought refuge in alcohol when he was twice bypassed for an amnesty. Once he was freed, his life became one long banquet. Most of his friends, both old and new, received him so generously that they contributed to the deterioration of his health. Constant wining and dining were not good for him. The painful and tragic journey to Ukraine in 1859 had also affected his nervous system. On returning to St Petersburg he had experienced a real psychological blow as a result of his romance with Lykera. All his friends agreed that he needed rest, but instead he sought to forget his misery by working hard or by indulging in drink. Hard work, which he never gave up, was also a factor in his poor health. During his relatively short life Shevchenko created a great mass of literary works, hundreds of paintings and water-colours, thirty etchings and over one thousand sketches. All this required great nervous and intellectual energy as well as sheer physical labour. While writing poetry came easily to him, he worked hard at revision. As an artist he was passionately fond of drawing and painting, and lived his life to the full. This passion for creation dominated his entire personality and drove him occasionally to complete exhaustion. He was a truly 'possessed' genius, directed by a 'divine madness,' subject to a constant tension between art and life.

By the end of December 1860 the poet was quite ill. On doctor's orders he remained at home, and reconciled himself to his 'imprisonment.' He wrote to Varfolomey that he had a bad cough, and on 29 January he confessed: 'I was so weak that I could hardly hold a pen.' Yet he continued working and corresponding. He was promoting the sale of his *Primer* (*Bukvar*), which appeared in print early in January. He asked some of his friends to try to influence the Kievan Metropolitan, Arseniy, to endorse the book, but met with little success. The primer was to be followed by the publication of a text on Ukrainian history. Shevchenko had not forgotten the cottage on the Dnieper and urged Varfolomey to buy some land on Chernecha Hora, near Kaniv, which later became his final resting-place after his death. With renewed energy he worked on yet another self-portrait, to be sold by lottery in aid of Sunday schools. This time the portrait, foreshadowing the end, showed a sick man.

Back to Freedom 1858–61

On 14 February Shevchenko paid the printer for the primer and on the same day wrote his last, one of his best, poems. There, for the last time, he talks to his muse, a faithful consort who had never betrayed him. The poem was written as he lay in bed. The poet knew that his end was near. Here the entire poem is reproduced in a translation by Vera Rich:

> Should we not then cease, my friend,
> My poor dear neighbour, make an end
> Of versifying useless rhymes?
> Prepare our wagons for the time
> When we that longest road must wend?
> Into the other world, my friend,
> To God we'll hasten to our rest ...
> We have grown weary, utter-tired,
> A little wisdom we've acquired,
> It should suffice! To sleep is best,
> Let us now go home to rest ...
> A home of gladness, you may know!
>
> No, let us not depart, nor go, –
> It is early still,
> We shall yet take walks together,
> Sit, and gaze our fill,
> Gaze upon the world, my fortune,
> See how wide it spreads,
> Wide and joyful, it is both
> Bright, and of great depth!
> We shall yet take walks, my star,
> On a hill climb high,
> And take our rest together ... And
> Your sister-stars, meanwhile,
> The ageless ones, will start to shine,
> Through the heavens glide ...
> Let us linger then, my sister,
> Thou, my holy bride,
> And with lips unsullied we shall
> Make our prayer to God,
> And then set out quietly
> On that longest road,
> Over Lethe's plumbless depths,
> Waters dark and swarthy,
> Grant me then thy blessing, friend,

With thy holy glory.
While this and that and all such wear on,
Straight let us go, as the crow flies,
To Aesculapeus for advice,
If we can outwit old Charon
And spinning Fate ... And then, as long as
The old sage would change his purpose,
we would create, reclining there,
An epic, soaring everywhere
Above the earth, hexameters
We'd twine, and up the attic stairs
Take them for mice to gnaw. Then we
Would sing prose, yet with harmony
And not haphazard.
                Holy friend,
Companion to my journey's end,
Before the fire has ceased to glow,
Let us to Charon, rather, go!
Over Lethe's plumbless depths,
Water dark and swarthy,
Let us sail, let us bear
With us holy glory,
Ageless, young for evermore ...
Or – friend, let it be!
I will do without the glory,
If they grant it me,
There on the banks of Phlegethon,
Or beside the Styx, in heaven,
As if by the broad Dnipro, there
In a grove, a grove primeval,
A little house I'll build, and make
An orchard all around it growing,
And you will fly to me in the shades,
There, like a beauty, I'll enthrone you;
Dnipro and Ukraina we
Shall recollect, gay villages
In woodlands, gravehills in the steppes,
And we shall sing right merrily.[7]

---

7 'Chy ne pokynut nam,' ibid, 422–4

This is a poetic account of the poet's struggle with his deteriorating body faced with approaching death.

Although he felt very ill, the poet continued to welcome visitors. The Russian writer Leskov, who came from Kiev, found him in great pain. He was unable to leave his small bedroom. 'His whole being,' wrote Leskov later, 'was terribly sick.' Shevchenko complained of pain in his chest and heavy coughing. 'I shall perish,' he said to Leskov, 'but enough of that – tell me what's going on in Ukraine.' He was still talking of going there, 'for I'll perish if I stay here.' On Sunday, 19 February, the invalid was visited by Chernenko. This was the sixth anniversary of the accession to the throne of Alexander II. Everyone was expecting an announcement of the abolition of serfdom. When Chernenko entered the room Shevchenko stood beneath the window, leaning on the table. His sick body was exhausted by the long waiting. Instead of greeting Chernenko, the poet's first words were: 'What? There is? Is there a manifesto? Freedom?' But in Chernenko's eyes he could see a negative answer. Sighing deeply, the poet groaned – 'When – 'When will it come?' Then he fell on his bed and, covering his face with his hands, started crying. Chernenko tried to console him, saying that the manifesto had been signed but the proclamation had been delayed until March, during Lent, so 'that the people will celebrate it in church, not in taverns.' Shevchenko remained bitter.

On Friday, 24 February, Taras was visited by Kostomarov. Shevchenko, feeling a little better, was sitting at the table. He showed Kostomarov his new gold watch and promised, if he were up to it, to call on Kostomarov the following Tuesday. That day Shevchenko felt well enough to write a letter to Tavolha-Mokrytsky, greeting him on his name-day. The last sentence read: 'I have been ill for two months. They won't let me out into the corridor, let alone outdoors.' These were the last words the poet wrote.

Saturday, 25 February, was both Shevchenko's birthday and his name-day. Mykhailo Lazarevsky was the first of the well-wishers to arrive, early in the morning. He found Shevchenko in great pain: he had not slept the entire night, and because of chest pains he was unable to lie down. Now he was sitting up in bed, leaning on the mattress with his hands and breathing heavily. He asked Lazarevsky to notify Varfolomey of his condition. Soon Dr Bari appeared. He examined the poet and told Lazarevsky that there was no hope left: fluid had entered the lungs. At that time medical science was helpless in a case like this. Lev Zhemchuzhnikov, who arrived later, said that the poet found it difficult to talk. 'In order to say a word he had to gather all his strength ... but he did not groan.' The doctor ordered a device for drawing away the fluid to be placed on the poet's chest and thus reduce the pain. This was effective for a while. A telegram arrived from Petro Trunov of Kharkiv, conveying his best wishes. Shevchenko could barely say 'thank you.' Then he asked that the room be aired, drank a glass of lemon water, and lay down. The visitors left the bedroom and went down to the studio. New callers came, and everyone waited in silence downstairs. At three o'clock the visitors went upstairs quietly and saw the poet sitting up in bed and asking for a doctor. He wanted to ask him for some opium so that he could sleep. Every five minutes the poet was asking for the doctor.

The guests left, except for Lazarevsky, who stayed with the poet. Shevchenko felt a little better and talked about going to Ukraine in the spring. Lazarevsky promised to accompany him. Taras was glad to hear it and said that the air in Ukraine would strengthen him. He said that he did not want to die and that 'at home I will get better.' When, finally, Dr Bari arrived, the poet felt a little better. He was told to continue taking the prescribed medication. At six o'clock a Polish doctor, Kruniewicz, came. He had known Shevchenko in exile. This excellent physician was unable to help the poet, whose condition had again deteriorated. He found it difficult to speak. At nine o'clock the two doctors held a consultation but could not think of any remedy. Fluid was flooding the lungs. A telegram arrived from Poltava. When it was read to Shevchenko, he expressed his thanks to its authors for remembering him so warmly. The physicians departed. Shevchenko asked that the lamp be taken away, hoping that he would fall asleep in the dark. Five minutes later he felt an attack approaching and called for Dr. Bari. When Lazarevsky came back to see the poet at half past ten, his condition was grave. The poet wanted to but could not speak. He was left alone.

Lazarevsky's servant was left for the night downstairs, in the studio. Taras could not lie down. He sat up in bed, first lighting, then extinguishing the candle. The night passed agonizingly slowly. At five in the morning Taras called the servant and asked for a cup of tea with milk. After drinking it he said to the servant: 'Freshen up my bed and I'll walk downstairs.' On the stairs, he fell. His last hour had come and his heart stopped beating. The twenty-sixth of February became a day of national mourning in Ukraine.

The news of Shevchenko's death spread like lightning in St Petersburg. By wire it reached Ukraine and Galicia. In the evening Shevchenko's body was carried to the academy's chapel nearby. The coffin was placed in front of the pulpit on a black bier. It was decorated in white. Through the windows, framed by rose curtains, a pinkish glow spread over the poet's face. Leskov reported that 'his face reflected the noble thoughts that had never left him throughout his life.' The chapel was visited by scores of people. Artists sketched the coffin and the body, and a death-mask was taken. During the funeral, on Tuesday, 28 February, the chapel and all the corridors were full of people. Apart from a host of the poet's friends, representatives of the St Petersburg intelligentsia and of the student body were all present. Leading Russian writers of the day, Nekrasov, Dostoevsky, and Saltykov-Shchedrin were among them. Many members of the Ukrainian colony, representing *Hromada* and *Osnova*, were also there. Polish friends of the poet also attended. Among those closest to the coffin were the former 'brethren' of 1847, Kulish, Kostomarov, and Bilozersky.

'The last farewell was difficult, incredibly difficult,' wrote Zhemchuzhnikov of this moment later in the *Foundation*. 'Veneration for the deceased and an unbroken silence reigned everywhere.' After the requiem mass and the ceremonial 'last kiss,' the funeral procession moved to Smolensk cemetery, where Shevchenko used to sketch and where he had a favourite spot. There he was laid to rest. The coffin, borne by students, was lowered into the ground. During the final stages of the funeral ten eulogies were given in memory of the deceased. Among the Ukrainian speakers were Kulish, Bilozersky, Kostomarov, Tavolha-Mokrytsky, Afanasev-Chuzhbynsky, Chubynsky, and Khartakhay; among the Russians, Kurochkin and Yuzhakov. The Polish eulogist was the student Choroszewski.

The most memorable eulogy was given by Kulish: 'There is no one among us worthy of speaking in Ukrainian over Shevchenko's grave. All the power and beauty of our language was revealed to him alone.' It ended with this assurance: 'You can be certain, Taras, that we shall observe your testament and will not deviate from the path that you laid out for us. When we shall have no more strength to follow your path, when we shall be unable to proclaim, like you, the holy truth, then we had better keep silent.'[8] Bilozersky stressed the presence at the funeral of the sons of 'many fathers and many languages.' Kostomarov was so moved that after a few words he started to weep and was unable to continue. The most interesting was the Polish eulogy by Choroszewski, who declared that Ukrainian-Polish hostility of the past should cease. 'The sons are not responsible,' he said, 'for their fathers' mistakes.' He felt that old animosities would have to recede and that Shevchenko's call to love and brotherhood would prevail.

The funeral lasted till five o'clock in the evening. Fresh flowers covered

8 *Svitova velych Shevchenka* (Kiev 1964), I, 89–90

the poet's grave. The Russian writer Terpigorev, in his memoirs written twenty-five years after Shevchenko's death, recalled the poet's funeral: 'Of all the funerals I have seen since then, not one was marked by such simplicity and sincerity as Shevchenko's funeral ... [It] was free from any marketplace comedy, since there were no laurel wreaths or other theatrical trappings.' Ukrainians in St Petersburg, especially Lazarevsky, were credited with the good organization of the funeral.

Among the resolutions passed by the *Hromada* on the day of Shevchenko's death was one calling for the transfer of his last remains to Ukraine, in accordance with his own wishes. This resolution was supported by everyone. Shevchenko's body remained at the Smolensk cemetery for two months. Every Sunday a short requiem mass was celebrated at his grave. In March and April there were widespread reports in the Russian press of Shevchenko's death and funeral. The March issue of the *Foundation* was dedicated to the poet. Only one Polish newspaper, *Kurjer wilenski*, carried a report of his death. Abroad, the German *Glocke* carried a long article; Herzen's *Bell* published a notice, and in England Charles Dickens, Shevchenko's favourite novelist, wrote about the poet's death. The best appreciation of the dead poet came from the pen of the Russian critic Apollon Grigoriev. He wrote:

As far as the sheer beauty of his poetry is concerned Shevchenko is often placed beside Pushkin and Mickiewicz. I will go further: The naked beauty of folk poetry sparkles in Shevchenko's work, while in Pushkin and Mickiewicz it only appears here and there. Shevchenko's nature is more brilliant, simple, and sincere than Gogol's nature. [Gogol] placed himself in a false position – as the poet of Russian life, a niche quite alien to him ... Shevchenko was the last minstrel and the first great poet of a new literature.[9]

This view of Shevchenko was more profound than that offered the critics of the left, Dobroliubov and Chernyshevsky.

After many efforts by Ukrainian community leaders in St Petersburg, the date of the exhumation of Shevchenko's body was set for 26 April. The coffin was to be escorted by two young members of *Hromada*, the painter Hryhoriy Chestakhivsky and the student Oleksander Lazarevsky. Shevchenko had loved both of them, and they revered the poet. A special carriage was ordered to take the poet's remains from Moscow to Ukraine. Between St Petersburg and Moscow the coffin was to be transported by rail.

9 *Vremia*, Apr. 1861; reprinted in *Svitova velych Shevchenka*, 1, 107–8

Early on the morning of 26 April a large crowd gathered at the cemetery. The coffin was raised and placed inside a new metal one. Kulish spoke a few words of final farewell, and the coffin, at his request, was covered with red taffeta (*kytaika*), a traditional Cossack drapery for the departed. Kulish ended his speech with these words: 'Appear, our father, in our native land, under the red taffeta, and gather around you the blind, the deaf, and the tongueless: let them hear your immortal word from your dead lips, and let them speak in their own inimitable tongue. You are ours, and we, the people, are yours and will breathe your spirit for ever.'

The funeral cortège moved along Vasilievsky Island, Admiralty Square, and Nevsky Prospect to the station. On 27 April the coffin reached Moscow, where it was borne to a church for a requiem mass. On 2 May the last remains of the poet reached Orel, where another requiem mass was celebrated, attended by the staff and students of the Orel *gymnasia*. Fedir Lazarevsky, who lived in Orel, was also present. He paid his last respects to the poet, whom he had helped so much when he was in exile. The priest and most of the crowd remained close until the cortège reached the city limits. Then one of the wreaths was taken apart and flowers from it were distributed to the people.

After reaching Ukraine, the funeral procession was met at Nizhyn and then, on 5 May, at the Brovary railway station, near Kiev. Lazarevsky and Chestakhivsky decided to contact the poet's family, who were gathered in Kiev. At that time there was no organized body of Ukrainians in the city, apart from the student *Hromada*. The place of burial had not yet been chosen. Discussions took place between Ukrainians in St Petersburg and in Kiev as to a possible location, but no decision was taken. Several proposals were put forward: that Shevchenko be buried at Askold's Grave (Askoldova mohyla), at the cemetery in the Vydubytsky monastery, or at a cliff, Shchekavytsia, on the Dnieper. The latter site was the most spectacular and would have accommodated Shevchenko's wish to be buried on the Dnieper. When Lazarevsky and Chestakhivsky reached Kiev, great pressure was put upon them to select Shchekavytsia as the site. Yet they resisted and argued that instead the poet should be buried on Chernecha Hora, near Kaniv, where he had wished to buy a cottage on the banks of the Dnieper. A real controversy erupted, with the students from Kiev insisting that the poet should be buried near the Ukrainian capital. The argument was finally settled when Chestakhivsky declared that Chernecha Hora near Kaniv was Shevchenko's own choice before he died. Everyone agreed on Chernecha Hora, though Chestakhivsky had not been present during the final days of Shevchenko's life and could have invented the story. It was decided that the coffin should be taken to

Kaniv, but first the Kiev Ukrainians gathered for a final farewell in the city.

They encountered some difficulties in doing so. A Ukrainian delegation was sent to the governor general, Prince Vasilchikov, to request permission to place Shevchenko's coffin in one of the churches. Father Lebedyntsev and Varfolomey Shevchenko were members of the delegation, which was headed by the school inspector Chaly, Shevchenko's future biographer. The delegation consisted of men totally loyal to the regime and did not include the radical students. Prince Vasilchikov consented to their request and asked Metropolitan Arseniy to designate the church. The Metropolitan chose the small Church of the Nativity, near the Dnieper. Vasilchikov prohibited speeches inside the church. While these negotiations were in progress, a crowd of people gathered around the coffin. Among them were men and women of all ranks, from the wealthy to impecunious students. Some pilgrims also joined the crowd. The students wore national costume. Shevchenko's relatives, fourteen in number, were also present. The coffin was in Mykilska Slobidka, to which it had been brought from Brovary. The students grew impatient, and wanted to carry the coffin through the city streets to the university. They began doing so, until they were stopped by Chaly and persuaded to wait. Yet the procession continued, with many public speeches and recitations on the way. It looked like a public demonstration. When word came that permission had been granted to take the coffin to the Church of the Nativity, the students carrying the coffin surged in that direction. More speeches were made, not only in Ukrainian but some in Russian and one in Serbian by a Serbian theological student representing the Balkan Slavs. One speaker, Sheikovsky, compared Shevchenko to the prophet Jeremiah. At last the coffin reached the church, where a requiem mass was celebrated.

The following day, Sunday, 7 May, despite the rain a large crowd assembled in and around the church. The service was celebrated by Father Lebedyntsev. There were no speeches, but when the requiem mass began, a woman dressed in black placed a wreath of thorns on the coffin. When the funeral cortège moved from the church to the Dnieper, the scenes of the previous day were repeated. The procession had to stop frequently while speeches were delivered. Chaly maintained that the best speeches were given by the students – Oleksander Stoianov, Volodymyr Antonovych, and Mykhailo Drahomanov. Unfortunately, texts of the speeches by these future prominent Ukranian leaders have not been preserved. The boat was waiting near the bridge. The last farewell address was delivered by Chaly. Although it had been censored beforehand, it contained some daring thoughts about the Ukrainian national cause. Chaly was a school inspector, but a Ukrainian patriot as well. He declared that Shevchenko's muse 'has raised the people's self-esteem' and that 'it has gained for them the right of literary citizenship ... in the family of Slavs.' The last farewell to Shevchenko in Kiev took place on the spot where, in 1847, the police had arrested him.

Others followed Shevchenko's relatives and Lazarevsky and Chestakhivsky to escort the coffin on to the boat. Among them were Soshenko, Chaly with his wife, a group of Kievan students, and Viktor Zabila, who had travelled from his *khutir* near Borzna. The boat reached Kaniv the following day. It was met by a crowd of people, led by the clergy. Flooding made it difficult to transport the coffin to the river-bank in a small boat. A special carriage was brought alongside the boat to bear the coffin to the bank through the shallow waters. The procession moved to Kaniv, where the coffin was placed in a church and a requiem mass was celebrated. A solemn church service and the burial on Chernecha Hora were to be held on Sunday, 10 May. In the meantime a grave was being dug on the hill, over which a tall gravemound was to be raised. The digging was done mostly by students. This was because the regular gravediggers, under pressure from a Pole, refused to dig.

News of the funeral spread, and thousands hastened to attend. The church was besieged, and people listened attentively to the sermon preached by Father Matskevych. He ended his patriotic eulogy with these words: 'Here, on one of the tallest hills on the Dnieper, Shevchenko's ashes will be laid to rest and, as on Golgotha, which may be seen throughout Jerusalem and Judea, and like our Saviour's crucifix, a cross will be raised here and will be seen on both sides of our glorious Dnieper.'

After the service, thousands of peasants, some of them serfs, spread out in a colourful human avalanche from hill to riverside. The spring sun shone on this moving farewell of the Ukrainian people to their prophet. Towards evening a tall gravemound rose over Shevchenko's 'home – my coffin' (*khata-domovyna*). It was covered with hundreds of wreaths placed there by young Ukrainian women. A simple oak cross was placed on the top of the gravemound.

In the mid-1880s an iron cross bearing a bronze likeness of the poet replaced the wooden cross. After their occupation of Ukraine the Soviet authorities removed the cross, replacing it, in 1931, with a clumsy obelisk. In 1939 a large monument to Shevchenko was built there, with the bronze figure of the poet high on a pedestal. The gravemound and the park, covered with trees, may be seen from a distance, from the left bank of the

Dnieper. It is visible to all those travelling along the Dnieper near Kaniv. Millions of Ukrainians come here from both west and east. They come by boat, rail, and on foot. They take part in an eternal pilgrimage to a holy national shrine, where the poet rests in that beautiful spot on the Dnieper. For more than a century he has surveyed from his vantage-point the whole of Ukraine, for which he sacrificed his entire life. 'Everything passes,' he once wrote. Yet, as long as Ukraine remains a country, he will be immortal. He had told his countrymen everything they needed to know to 'reach the circle of the free,' to achieve full independence. His testament has not yet been fulfilled. In the meantime, he towers over the Dnieper and the 'wide-skirted wheatlands,' awaiting the time when his people will be free, that time when

>the foemen's blood
>will flow in rivers
>to the blue sea.

Glossary

bandura a stringed instrument
batko father
chornozem black earth
desiatina a measure of land (2.7 acres)
dumka a little song; a short poem
dumy lyric-epic poems about the Cossacks
hetman elected head of the Cossack state
horilka Ukrainian vodka
hromada community
khutir individual farm, homestead
kobza a stringed instrument
kobzar kobza player; minstrel
narod peasants; nation
narodnost national spirit
otaman Cossack chieftain
verst 3,500 feet

Selected Bibliography of Biographical Studies

Extensive biographies

Borodin, V., Ye. Kyryliuk, V. Smilianska, Ye. Shabliovsky, and V. Shubravsky. *T.H. Shevchenko; Biohrafiia*. Kiev 1984
Chaly, Mikhail. *Zhizn i proizvedeniia Tarasa Shevchenko*. Kiev 1882
Konysky, Oleksander. *Taras Shevchenko-Hrushivsky – khronika yoho zhyttia*, I–II. Lviv 1898–1901
Konyssky, Aleksandr. *Zhizn ukrainskogo poeta Tarasa Grigorievicha Shevchenko*. Odessa 1898
Kyryliuk, Yevhen. *T.H. Shevchenko: zhyttia i tvorchist*. Kiev 1959
Kyryliuk, Yevhen, Yevhen Shabliovsky, and Vasyl Shubravsky. *T.H. Shevchenko: Biohrafiia*. Kiev 1964
Zaitsev, Pavlo. *Zhyttia Tarasa Shevchenka*. Paris, New York, Munich 1955

Compilations and studies of memoirs

Biohrafiia T.H. Shevchenka za spohadamy suchasnykiv. Kiev 1958
Kostenko, Anatoliy. *Shevchenko v memuarakh*. Kiev 1965
Shevchenkivsky slovnyk u dvokh tomakh. Kiev 1976
T.G. Shevchenko v vospominaniiakh sovremennikov. Moscow 1962
Taras Shevchenko; dokumenty i materialy. Kiev 1963

Memoirs by Shevchenko's contemporaries

Chestakhovsky, G. 'Epizod na mogile Tarasa Shevchenka.' *Kievskaia starina* LII, no 2 (1896)
Chuzhbinsky, A. 'Vospominaniia o T.G. Shevchenke.' *Russkoe slovo*, no 5 (1861)
Kostomarov, Nikolay. 'Vospominaniia o dvukh maliarakh.' *Osnova*, no 4 (1861)
Kozachkovsky, A. 'Iz vospominanii o T.G. Shevchenko.' *Kievsky telegraf*, 26 Feb. 1875
Kulish, Panteleimon. *Khutorna poeziia*. Lviv 1882

Lazarevsky, A. 'Detstvo T.G. Shevchenka.' *Osnova*, no 3 (1862)
Maksheev, A. 'Vospominanii o. T.G. Shevchenko.' *Russkaia starina*, no 5 (1914)
Repnina, Varvara. 'Iz avtobiograficheskikh zapisok.' *Russky arkhiv* VII (1897)
Storozhenko, N. 'Pervye chetyre goda ssylki Shevchenka.' *Kievskaia starina* XXIII, no 10 (1888)
Sukhanov-Podkolzin, B. 'Vospominanie o T.G. Shevchenke.' *Kievskaia starina* XI, no 2 (1885)
Yunge, E.F. *Vospominaniia*. St Petersburg 1913
Zhemchuzhnikov, Lev. 'Vospominanie o Shevchenko; yego smert i pogrebenie.' *Osnova*, no 3 (1861)

For complete holdings of biographical studies consult *T.H. Shevchenko, bibliohrafiia literatury pro zhyttia i tvorchist*, I–II (Kiev 1963).

Works in English containing biographical data

Kyryliuk, Yevhen. 'The Bard of Ukraine,' in T. Shevchenko, *Selected Works*. Moscow 1964
Luckyj, George S.N. *Between Gogol and Ševčenko*. Munich 1971
Manning, C.A. *Taras Shevchenko*. Jersey City 1945
Shabliovsky, Yevhen. *The Humanism of Shevchenko and Our Time*. Kiev 1971

Complete works of Shevchenko indispensable for the study of his biography

Kobzar. Ed. L. Biletsky. 4 vols. Winnipeg 1952–54
Povne vydannia tvoriv. Ed. B. Lepky. 5 vols. Leipzig 1919–20
Povne vydannia tvoriv Tarasa Shevchenka. Ed. P. Zaitsev. Vols. 2–15. Warsaw 1934–38. Reprinted in 14 vols., Chicago 1961–63
Povne vydannia tvoriv v desiaty tomakh. Kiev 1939–63

Index

Adlerberg, General 158
Afanasiev-Chuzhbynsky, Oleksander 81, 82, 116, 120, 121, 125, 126, 141, 263
Afghanistan 165
Aivazovsky, Ivan 234
Aksakov, Ivan 235
Aksakov, Nadia 225
Aksakov, Sergey 219, 224, 228
Ak-Tau 204
Aldridge, Ira 235
Alexander II 209, 219, 228, 255, 261
Alexander, Tsarevich 37
Alexandra Fiodorovna, Tsarina 37, 255, 256
Aleksandreisky, Mykhailo 160, 163, 184, 185
Aleksandrov 141
Andrievsky, Marko 242, 243
Andruzsky, Yuriy 122, 132, 141, 143–5, 215
Annenkov, Ivan 216
Annenkov, Pavel 153
Antipov, Alexander 204, 205
Antonovych, Volodymyr 266
Apazir 204, 205
Aprelev, Vasiliy 54
Arago, Jacques 44
Arakcheev, Aleksey 11
Aral Sea 74, 165, 167, 171, 172, 182, 183, 186, 188, 196, 257

Arseniy, Metropolitan 258, 266
Askochensky, Viktor 126, 127, 244
Astrakhan 213, 214
Aulie-Tau 180
Austro-Hungary 131, 157

Bantysh-Kamensky, Dmytro 33, 52
Baranov, Yuliia 37
Baratynsky 90, 95
Bari, Eduard 256, 261, 262
Barkhvitsev 170
Barthelemy, Jean Jacques 30, 44
Bashylov, Mikhail 100, 140
Baturyn 105
Bazhanov, Nikolay 212
Belinsky, Vissarion 56, 61–4, 67, 68, 70, 73, 153, 154, 249
Benediktov, Vladimir 56
Ber, Karl 208
Berdychiv 130
Berestechko 131
Berezan 83, 84, 88, 97
Berezova Rudka 83, 98, 238
Bibikov, Dmitriy 108, 127, 130, 131–2, 155
Bihachi 134, 135
Bila Tserkva 3, 129
Bilozersky, Mykola 134
Bilozersky, Vasyl 101, 122, 125, 132–4, 140, 144, 145, 148, 149, 226, 234, 249–51, 263

Index

Black Sea 74, 171, 172, 178, 211
Blaramberg, Ivan 196
Bodiansky, Osyp 33, 83, 102, 104, 106, 107, 114, 116, 131, 171, 196, 206, 208, 224
Bohorsky, Petro 11, 14, 15, 17
Bohuslav 16, 31, 45
Boian 217
Boiko, Kateryna 4
Bokhara 165
Bonaparte, Napoleon 83, 121
Borovykovsky, Lev 33, 48
Boryshpolets, Platon 56, 73
Borzna 79, 133, 134, 267
Botvynovsky, Yukhym 244
Branicki, Alexandra 3, 9, 130
Branicki, Ksawery 3, 9
Briullov, Karl 34–8, 41–3, 45, 47, 56, 57, 166, 167, 255
Brovary 136, 265, 266
Brylkin, Nikolay 215
Budkov 107
Budyshcha 11
Buerger, Gottfried 48
Bulatov, Timofey 200, 202
Bulgarin, Faddey 58
Burachek, Stepan 68
Burns, Robert 135
Burtsev, Lev 213
Burty 16
Butakov, Aleksey 171, 172, 178, 182, 183, 185, 188, 189, 192, 194–6, 199, 200, 223
Butashevich-Petrashevsky, Mikhail 154, 178
Byron, George 44

Caspian Sea 197, 200
Catherine II 3, 8, 255, 256
Caucasus 99, 101, 153
Chaly, Mykhailo 244, 266, 267

Chaly, Sava 105
Chateaubriand, François René de 44
Cherkasky, Vladimir 236
Cherkasy 242, 243
Chernenko, Fedir 248, 253, 255, 256, 261
Chernihiv 4, 20, 79, 101, 108, 120, 121, 134, 140, 237, 241
Chernyshev, Alexander 160, 163, 165, 166, 172, 200
Chernyshevsky, Nikolay 234, 264
Chestakhivsky, Hryhoriy 236, 264, 265, 267
Chigir, Grogoriy 199, 200
Chizhov 19, 20
Chizhov, Fiodor 154
Chopin, Frederick 235
Chroszewski, Wladyslaw 263
Chubynsky, Pavlo 263
Chuikevych, Petro 131
Chyhyryn 3, 83–6, 89, 105, 129, 131
Copenhagen 73
Cornelius, Peter 34
Cyril, Saint 122, 148, 153, 156, 214
Czajkowski, Michał 44
Czartoryski, Adam 156

Dal, Vladimir 56, 166, 216
Damich, Commandant 192
Danilevsky, Nikolay 208
Dante, Alighieri 44, 102, 109, 223
David, Psalms of 21
de Balmen, Yakiv 82, 100, 101, 116, 117, 140
Defoe, Daniel 44
Dekhtiari 113
Demidov, Denis 54
Demski, Leonard 52, 53
Denmark 73, 257
Derzhavin, Gavrila 44
Dickens, Charles 42, 44, 264

Index

Dmytrenko, Danylo 19
Dnieper 64, 75, 80, 84, 114, 119, 127, 136, 165, 173, 177, 238–40, 242, 246, 251, 260, 265–8
Dobroliubov, Nikolay 249, 264
Dobzhansky, Franz 242
Dołega-Chodakowski, Zorian 150
Dolgorukov, Nikolay 107, 108, 140
Dolgorukov, Vasiliy 219, 228
Doroshenko, Petro 85
Dostoevsky, Fiodor 263
Dovhopolenko, Kharytia 246, 247, 249
Drahomanov, Mykhailo 266
Drexler, Joseph 115
Dubelt, Leontiy 141, 145, 165, 166, 172, 197, 199, 207, 228
Dubno 131
Duchiński, Franciszek 156, 157
Dumont d'Urville, Jules 44
Dustan 180
Dymowski, Jan 19, 20
Dziubyn 56, 226

Einar, Charles 89
Elena, Grand Duchess 252
Elkan, Alexander 72
Engelhardt, Andrey 18, 27
Engelhardt, Pavel 16–20, 22–8, 31, 34–7
Engelhardt, Sophia 27
Engelhardt, Vasiliy (father) 3, 4, 18, 130
Engelhardt, Vasiliy (son) 27
England 157

Fediaev, Logvin 160, 172, 187
Fischer, Ferdinand 98
Fischer, Otto 164, 257
Florkovsky, Valeriy 248
Fourier, François 53, 98
France 157

Frederick of Prussia 83
Freiman, Gustav 207
Fulton, Robert 214
Fundukley, Ivan 128, 136, 139

Galicia 83, 84, 131, 157, 262
Garibaldi, Giuseppe 53
Gedymin 107
Gerbel, Nikolay 120, 249
Gern, Karl 159–61, 193–8, 200, 203, 207, 219
Gibbon, Edward 52
Gillies, John 44
Glinka, Mikhail 43, 71, 79
Globa, Captain 162, 171
Goethe, Johann Wolfgang 44
Gogol, Nikolay 32, 33, 46, 62, 98, 110, 111, 113, 114, 120, 135, 171, 197, 217
Goldsmith, Oliver 44
Golitsyn, Vladimir 216
Golovachov, Andrian 208
Gordon, Jakub 201
Goszczyński, Seweryn 44
Grabowski, Michał 107
Grech, Nikolay 58
Grekova, Irina 224
Griboedov, Alexander 46
Grigoriev, Apollon 264
Grigorovich, Dmitriy 56
Grinberg, Izabella 227
Grishkov, Officer 139, 141, 245
Guarengi 20
Gulakov, Alexandra 227
Guriev 197, 201, 213

Halahan, Hryhoriy 104, 113, 225
Halahan, Petro 113, 216
Halevynsky 159
Halushchenko 164
Haluzevsky, Basyl 56
Hanka, Vaclav 116

Haydn, Franz Joseph 127
Heine, Heinrich 44
Herder, Johann Gottfried 147
Herzen, Alexander 216, 264
Hesse, Pavel 204
Hlushanovsky, Anton 170
Holovaty, Antin 51
Holovko, Mykola 155, 197, 199
Honcharenko, Taras 15
Honta, Ivan 8
Horlenko, Dmytro 245
Hornung, Joseph 83, 101
Horodyshche 240
Hrebinka, Yevhen 32, 33, 43, 47, 49, 52, 55, 56, 58, 61, 62, 79, 81
Hryhorovych, Vasyl 33, 35, 36, 41, 55, 60, 62, 100, 101, 104, 209
Huberla 161
Hudovsky, Ivan 244
Hugo, Victor 44
Hulak, Mykola 122, 125, 132, 133, 140, 141, 144, 152
Hulak-Artemovsky, Petro 33, 67, 71, 136
Hulak-Artemovsky, Semen 71, 72, 205, 206, 225-7, 234
Huliay-Pole 11
Humboldt, Alexander 189, 205, 233
Husikowska, Dunia 23, 24
Huss, John 116
Hustyn 112, 113, 245
Hyriavka 245

India 165
Irghiz 180
Irving, Washington 44
Irzhavets 113
Isaev, Dmitriy 164
Isaev, Nikolay 198
Isakov 73
Iskovets 116, 120
Istomin, Alexander 192
Italy 75, 111
Ivanishev, Mykola 128, 129, 206
Izopolsky 130

Jabłonowski, Princess 3
Jedlička, Vjačeslav 115, 116
Jez, Teodor 155
Joachim, Karl 45, 46
Jordan, Fiodor 227
Jurgens, Madame 57

Kachanivka 44, 46, 79, 84, 88, 101, 113, 245
Kaffa 150
Kamenetsky, Danylo 227
Kamianets Podilsky 130, 131
Kandyba 56
Kaniv 3, 240, 241, 258, 265-8
Kapnist, Oleksa 83, 96, 97, 99, 101, 103
Kapnist, Vasyl 83
Kara-Butak 180, 181, 192
Karakumi 181
Kara-Tau 197, 204, 205, 232
Karlivka 252
Karpo, Mykhailo 104
Kartashevska, Varvara 234, 249
Kartashov, Piotr 31
Katerynoslav 4
Kavelin, Konstantin 227
Kavos, Albert 31
Kazan 145, 215
Keikuatov, Nikolay 135
Keikuatova, Elizaveta 95, 136
Kerelivka 3-5, 7, 8, 11, 12, 15, 26, 27, 30, 31, 84, 87, 88, 108, 114, 115, 126, 240-2
Khairov, Ahmet 203
Kharkiv 60, 66, 67, 105, 114, 121, 130, 152, 155, 197, 218, 237, 262
Khartakhay, Feoktyst 263

Kherson 4
Khiva 44, 165, 166, 180, 182
Khlypnivka 19
Khmelnytsky, Bohdan 69, 85, 86, 105, 132, 244
Khomiakov, Aleksey 225
Khomiakov, Konstantin 154
Khorol 113
Khortytsia 84, 87
Khristoforov 192
Khropal, Oleksiy 240
Khrushchev, Dmytro 237, 238
Khvastiv 129, 131
Khyvrych 104
Kiev 3, 5, 12, 16, 17, 21, 22, 73, 75, 79–81, 91, 102, 107, 108, 113, 121, 125–8, 130, 131–4, 136, 139, 140, 152, 154–6, 170, 178, 236, 237, 241, 242, 244, 261, 265–7
Kikin, P. 41
Kilkevich, Sylbester 187
Kireevsky, Ivan 102
Kirghizia 172
Kirsha, Alfons-Karl 195
Kishkin, Vladimir 215
Kley 56
Klodt, Piotr 53, 106, 227
Klopotovsky, Ivan 213
Kochubey, Petro 232
Kock, Charles Paul de 52
Kokand 165
Kollar, Jan 150
Koltsov, Aleksey 171
Konotop 170
Kontsky, Anton 227, 235
Konysky, Oleksander 23
Korolev, Pylyp 73, 74
Korsakov, Piotr 54, 59
Korsun 241
Korsun, Oleksander 60, 66, 112
Kos-Aral 183–6, 189, 191, 194

Kosarev, Yegor 202, 206, 212, 213
Koshelev, Alexander 225
Koshyts, Fedosia 16, 115
Koshyts, Hryhoriy 16, 30, 115
Koshyts, Yas 16
Kostomarov, Mykola 25, 60, 73, 105, 121–4, 129, 131–4, 139, 140–2, 144, 145, 150, 152, 154, 158, 184, 214, 216, 217, 226, 234, 248, 253, 256, 261, 263
Kostroma 28
Kotliarevsky, Ivan 33, 49, 59, 62, 99, 110, 113, 135, 136, 217
Kovalenko, Oksana 6, 18, 66, 87, 88, 91
Kovalevsky, Yevgraf 228
Kovalivka 82, 83
Kovel 131
Kozachkovsky, Andriy 17, 114, 116, 117, 206, 238, 257
Kozhanchikov, Dmitriy 228, 247
Kozlovsky, Adalbert 241–3
Kraevsky, Andrey 49, 61
Krasiński, Zygmunt 44
Kraskovsky 244
Krasovsky, Andrey 59
Kremianets 131
Krestovsky, Vsevolod 249
Krolevets 245
Kronstadt 73
Kruniewicz, Paweł 262
Kukharenko, Yakiv 69, 71–3, 75, 87, 109, 110, 206, 211, 236
Kukolnik, Nestor 43, 46, 55, 56, 70
Kulish, Oleksandra 133, 134, 249–51
Kulish, Panteleimon 22, 23, 28, 79–81, 83, 103, 107, 128, 130–5, 140, 141, 145, 152, 154–7, 160, 184, 211, 216, 217, 226, 227, 230, 233, 234, 236, 244, 248, 249, 250, 256, 263, 265
Kum-Su-Ata 183

278   Index

Kurbsky, Prince 131
Kurochkin, Nikolay 234, 249, 263
Kurochkin, Vasiliy 234
Kursk 238
Kutorga 52
Kvitka-Osnovianenko, Hryhoriy 33, 47, 49, 51, 60, 62, 66–8, 70, 110
Kytchenko, Fedir 68
Kzhyvytsky 242

Ladyzhensky, General 159
Lamennais, Hugues 53
Lampi, Franz 24, 25, 27, 30
Lavrentev, Pavel 164
Lazarevska, Afanasia 245
Lazarevsky, Fedir 159, 160, 163, 164, 166, 168, 170, 171, 182, 186, 191, 193–8, 204, 212, 216, 228, 232, 238, 245, 254, 255, 265
Lazarevsky, Ivan 233
Lazarevsky, Mykhailo 163, 170, 204, 206, 210, 211, 217, 219, 225, 233, 261, 262, 264
Lazarevsky, Oleksander 233, 264, 265
Lazarevsky, Vasyl 163, 170, 204
Lebedyn 82, 238
Lebedyntsev, Petro 17, 266
Leipzig 247
Lelewel, Joachim 53
Lermontov, Mikhail 171, 195
Lesage 154
Leskov, Nikolay 232, 234, 261, 263
Levytsky, Serhiy 159, 160, 193–200
Lialychi 20
Lisenkov, Ivan 74, 75, 135
Lomonosov, Mikhail 44
London 216
Lopukhin 241
Louis Philippe 185
Lubny 113, 115, 120
Lukashevych, Platon 83, 84, 88, 95, 97, 100, 131, 135
Lukashevych, Vasyl 83
Lukianovych, Oleksander 112, 115
Lukomsky, R. 101
Lutsk 131
Lviv 155
Lvov, Gerontiy 207, 208
Lymar, Yona 15
Lynovtsi 82
Lysianka 15, 29
Lytvyniv, Mykhailo 104
Lyzohub, Andriy 120, 134, 135, 167–72, 176, 184, 185, 191, 193, 196, 204, 207
Lyzohub, Illia 120

Macpherson, James 44, 50
Maevska 101
Maevsky, Anton 203, 204, 206
Maikov, Apollon 234
Makarov, Mykola 249–51
Maksheev, Aleksey 178, 179, 182, 183, 185, 187, 226
Maksymovych, Maria 236, 237
Maksymovych, Mykhailo 48, 81, 83, 216, 217, 223–5, 233, 235, 236, 238, 240–2
Mangyshlak 202, 204
Maria, Grand Duchess 210, 216, 237
Mariinske 112, 115
Marin 228
Markevych, Andriy 211, 223
Markevych, Mykola 52, 55, 56, 100, 101
Markovych, Opanas 122, 125, 132, 133, 140, 230, 233
Martin, John 179
Martos, Ivan 33
Martos, Petro 54, 55
Matskevych, Father 267
Matveev, Yukhym 159, 160, 186, 187,

194, 203
Mazepa, Ivan 99–101, 120, 129, 144, 232, 236, 245
Mazzini, Giuseppe 53
Meidel, Piotr 196
Meshkov, Dmitriy 161, 162, 167, 198, 200
Methodius, Saint 122, 148, 153, 156, 214
Metlynsky, Amvrosiy 141
Mey, Lev 249
Mezhyrichchia 241
Michaud, Joseph 44
Mickiewicz, Adam 44, 53, 61, 109, 205
Mierosławski 249
Mikeshin, Mikhail 235, 255
Mikhail, Grand Duke 252
Mikhailov, Grigoriy 56
Mikhailov, Mikhail 249
Milan 71
Miłkowski, Zygmunt 155
Min, Dmitriy 223
Moisivka 81, 82
Mokrytsky, Apollon 32, 56, 75, 224
Molendsky 242
Mombelli, Nikolay 154, 156, 178, 199, 257
Monastyryshche 114, 238
Moryntsi 4
Moscow 75, 86, 100, 102, 125, 152, 153, 215, 223–5, 227, 244–6, 264
Moshny 242
Mostowski, Maciej 164
Moszczynski 24
Mozart, Wolfgang Amadeus 235
Muravev, Alexander 216
Muravsky, Hnat 213
Murchison, Roderick 189
Murillo, Bartolome 227, 228, 232
Mykilska Slobidka 266
Mykolaiv 178

Mykolaivka 134
Myrhorod 112, 113, 115, 116, 186, 217

Navrotsky, Oleksander 122, 132, 145
Nechyporenko, Ivan 29, 31, 45
Nedobrov, Yevgraf 200
Nekrasov, Nikolay 263
Neva 26, 56
Nicholas I 25, 42, 47, 70, 99, 108, 109, 145, 151, 155, 161, 183, 185, 196, 209, 217, 230, 255
Nikitenko, Aleksander 58, 59, 62
Nikolsky, Sergey 203, 206
Nizhny Novgorod 213–19, 223, 230, 233
Nizhyn 120, 265
Nomys, Matviy 250
Novomyrhorod 11
Novopetrovsk 197, 200, 202–8, 213, 215, 232

Obruchev, Matilda 196
Obruchev, Vladimir 159, 166, 167, 172, 188, 193, 194, 196–200, 204, 206
Odessa 5, 132, 168, 185
Odoevsky, Vladimir 56
Odran 30
Okhtyrka 130
Oleksiev, A. 83
Ora 162, 178, 179
Orel 238, 265
Orenburg 145, 158, 160–72, 183, 185, 187, 189, 191–5, 198, 206, 210, 212, 215, 219
Orlov, Aleksey 140, 144, 145, 151, 152, 158, 165–7, 172, 193, 194, 196, 197, 199, 200, 204, 257
Orsk 160, 161, 163, 167, 168, 171, 172, 174, 178, 181, 185, 198–203, 257
Osipov, Nikolay 209
Ostrovna 161

280   Index

Ostrovsky, Alexander 203
Ovid 172
Ovsiannikov, Pavlo 215, 216

Paduch, Karol 155
Paisiy, Archimandrite 113
Palauzov, Spiridon 116, 246
Paliy, Semen 105, 129
Palkin 234
Panaev, Ivan 56
Panov, Aleksey 214
Parchevsky, Nikodym 241, 243, 246, 247
Paris 133, 154, 157, 252, 256
Paskevich, Ivan 153
Pechersk 90
Pedynivka 11
Pekary 240, 241, 243
Pereiaslav 52, 112, 114, 116, 117, 186, 217, 238, 239, 244, 245, 257
Perovsky, Vasiliy 45, 165, 166, 182, 206–10
Persia 214
Peter I 70, 73, 100, 129, 232, 255, 256
Petrov, Oleksiy 139, 140
Petrov, Yosyp 226
Petrovsky, Petro 56
Petrozavodsk 145
Pidkova, Ivan 52, 60, 105
Pimenov, Nikolay 234
Pirogov 254
Pisarev, Nikolay 140
Pisemsky, Alexander 208, 214
Piunova, Katia 217, 218
Pleshcheev, Aleksey 206, 207, 249
Pletnev, Piotr 58
Plutarch 44
Pochaiv 131
Podberezki, Romuald 107
Podillia 130, 131
Pogodin, Mikhail 68, 225

Polevoy, Nikolay 46, 63, 70
Polissia 131
Polonsky, Yakov 234, 255
Poltava 81, 98, 108, 112, 113, 120, 122, 133, 237, 241, 249, 252, 262
Polubotok, Pavlo 105
Polusmakivna, Lykera 249, 250–4, 258
Pomialovsky, Nikolay 255
Ponomarev, Fiodor 56
Posiada, Ivan 122, 132, 145, 215
Pospelov, Ksenofont 182, 188, 192, 194, 200
Potapov, Merkul 202, 203, 206
Potemkin, Grigoriy 3, 4
Potoky 113–15, 125
Poussin, Nicolas 30
Prague 157
Prechtel, Stefan 20, 33
Prevarka 244
Prevlotsky, S. 31
Prianishnikov, F. 41
Pribitkov, Colonel 159
Prokhorivka 239, 241
Prometheus 122
Prushynsky 129
Prussia 157
Pryluky 101, 112, 113, 245
Psiol 238
Psiol, Hlafira 91–3, 98, 168, 169
Psiol, Oleksandra 91, 168–70
Pushkin, Alexander 27, 30, 33, 42, 50, 58, 90, 100, 130, 171
Puteren, Dmitri Van 223
Putyvl 238
Pylchykiv, Dmytro 122
Pyriatyn 32, 33, 101, 112, 113, 116, 238
Pyvovarenko 235

Raczkiewicze 211
Radziwiłł, Barbara 23
Raim 167, 172, 182, 184–9, 192, 194,

196, 197
Raphael, Sanzio 30
Rastrelli, Bartolomeo 130
Razin, Stepan 214
Redkin 254
Rembrandt van Rijn 106, 174, 228, 232
Repnin, Nikolay 83, 91, 101, 102, 108, 166, 225, 245
Repnin, Varvara Alexeyevna 91
Repnin, Vasiliy 88, 94, 97
Repnina, Varvara 88–99, 103–6, 112, 120, 131, 142, 163, 167, 168, 170, 174, 182, 184, 191, 193, 196, 200, 203, 204, 207, 223, 224
Reshetylivka 113
Revel 73, 257
Rhineland 166
Rich, Vera 259
Richardson, Samuel 44, 92
Robert, Cyprien 157
Rodzianko, Arkadiy 115
Rome 75
Romny 113
Ros 241
Rosen, Yegor 46, 70
Rossini, Gioachino 254
Rousseau, Jean Jacques 44, 147
Rozumovsky, Kyrylo 89, 90, 99
Rustem, Jan 23, 24
Rybin, Kuzma 192
Ryleev, Kondratiy 50, 99

Sadovsky, Prov 227
Sadovy, Tymofiy 242
Šafářik, Pavel 116, 124
Sahaidachny, Petro 150
St Petersburg 20, 26–34, 42–5, 47, 49, 52, 55, 71–3, 79, 81, 82, 84, 87, 102, 104, 105, 109, 112, 114, 133, 139, 140, 141, 152–8, 165–7, 170–2, 178, 193–9, 207, 210, 212, 213, 215, 216, 219, 224, 225, 227–30, 233, 235, 237, 242–9, 252, 257, 258, 262–4
Saint-Simon, Claude 98
Saltykov-Shchedrin, Mikhail 263
Samara 159, 215
Samarin, Yuriy 109, 154
Samoilov, Stepan 117
Sand, Georges 205
Sapozhnikov 41
Sapozhnikov, Alexander 106, 214, 215
Saratov 214, 234
Sari-Chaganaku 182
Savych, Mykola 133, 154, 157
Saxony 98
Sazhyn, Mykhailo 125
Schiller, Friedrich 44
Schmidt, Alexander 45, 46
Schreiber, Ivan 178, 181
Schternberg, Wilhelm 44–7, 52, 53, 56, 57, 75, 165, 193
Schtrandmann, Roman 98, 154
Scott, Sir Walter 34, 42, 44, 50, 135
Sedniv 120, 121, 134–6, 170
Seletska, Maria 104
Seletsky, Petro 99, 100
Selin 128
Semenenko-Kramarenko, Valerian 72
Senchylo-Stefanivsky, Oleksiy 129
Senkovsky, Osip 58, 59, 62
Serednicki, Eustachy 195
Serpiaha, Ivan 52
Sevsk 245
Shakespeare, William 44, 170–2
Shashkevych, Markian 84
Shchepkin, Mykhailo 102, 109, 110, 217, 223–8, 232
Shchepkin, Petro 224
Shcherbina, Nikolay 234
Shchoholiv, Yakiv 130
Sheikovsky 266

Shershevytsky, Pavlo 115
Shevchenko, Hryhoriy 4, 5, 12, 257
Shevchenko, Ivan 4, 7, 10, 13, 257
Shevchenko, Kateryna (mother) 4, 5, 10
Shevchenko, Kateryna (sister) 5, 6, 10, 12, 13, 16
Shevchenko, Maria 5, 6, 10, 12, 14
Shevchenko, Mykyta 5, 10–12, 16, 44, 55, 87, 240, 241
Shevchenko, Taras: childhood 4–15; youth 16–28; in St Petersburg 29–75; Ukrainian journeys 76–136; arrest 139–46; exile 147–212; return to St Petersburg 213–26; last years of freedom 227–62; last visit to Ukraine 238–45; death 262; funeral 263–8
Shevchenko, Varfolomey 126, 127, 241, 245–8, 252, 258, 266
Shevchenko, Yaryna 10, 13, 19, 240, 247
Shevchenko, Yosyp 5, 88
Shevyrev, Stepan 225
Shiriaev, Vasiliy 28–31, 35, 36, 38, 42, 44, 48, 57
Shpola 16
Siberia 99, 105
Sierakowski, Zygmunt 205, 210, 226
Skovoroda, Hryhoriy 15, 21
Sluzhynsky 227
Smirdin, Alexander 42
Smolensk 4, 19
Snov 120
Sokolov, Ivan 234
Soldatenkov, Kuzma 232
Solenyk, Karpo 113
Sologub, Count 56
Solonyna, Maria 215
Soshalsky 56, 226, 227
Soshenko, Ivan 23–6, 31–7, 42–7, 52, 120, 244, 267

Sovhyr 9, 11, 14
Sredbolsky, Yuliia 134
Sreznevsky, Izmail 52, 83
Staniewicz, Jan 195, 226
Stepanov, Aleksey 171
Stieglitz, Count 87
Stinka 238
Stockholm 73, 215
Stoianov, Oleksander 266
Storozhenko, Oleksa 107
Strelno 249–51
Stroganov, Count S. 153
Strugovshchikov, Alexander 56
Subotiv 85, 86, 105
Sue, Eugene 44
Sukhanov-Podkolzyn, Borys 232–4
Sukhanova-Podkolzyna, Natalia 232, 234
Sukhostavsky 121
Sumy 238
Svichka, Lev 113
Svyhorsky, Hetman 150
Sweden 73, 257
Symyrenko, Fedir 240, 242, 247
Symyrenko, Platon 240
Syr-Daria 165, 182, 183, 188, 191, 223

Tabashnikov, Vasiliy 242
Taglioni, Maria 45
Tahanrih 112
Tarasivka 11, 12, 16
Targowica 4
Tarnovsky, Hryhoriy 44, 46, 55, 56, 66, 69, 71, 74, 79, 83, 101, 113, 216, 252
Tarnovsky, Maria 114
Tarnovsky, Nadia 114
Tarnovsky, Vasyl 113–15, 125, 245
Tarnovsky, Yakiv 113–15
Tatarinov, Sergey 216
Tavolha-Mokrytsky, Petro 261, 263
Tereshchenko, Oksana 10

Tereshchenko, Stepan 10, 13
Terletsky, Volodymyr 156, 157
Terpigorev, Sergey 264
Thomas à Kempis 169, 171
Timm, Emilia 47
Tkachenko, Khtodot 29, 30, 45, 71, 72, 249, 253
Tolmachov, Afanasiy 197
Tolstoy, Aleksey 210, 234
Tolstoy, Alexandra 210
Tolstoy, Anastasia 210, 226, 228, 234
Tolstoy, Fiodor 209, 210, 216, 225, 226, 232, 234, 237, 252
Tolstoy, Katerina 225, 233–5
Trakhtemyriv 114
Traskin, Alexander 108, 131, 139, 152
Trediakovsky, Vasiliy 44
Troinitsky, Alexander 246
Trotsyna, Konstiantyn 56, 226
Trunov, Petro 262
Tsertelev, Nikolay 48, 107
Tupytsia, Trokhym 226
Turgenev, Ivan 234, 249
Turkey 74
Turno, Ludwig 195, 204, 205
Tykhorsky, Mykola 68, 70, 72
Tykych 15

Ulybyshev, Alexander 216
Uman 3
Ural 197
Urals 161, 165, 175
Uralsk 200, 213, 215
Ushinsky, Konstiantyn 254
Uskov, Agatha 208, 209, 211
Uskov, Irakliy 206, 207, 210, 212, 213, 215
Ustrialov, Nikolay 171
Ust-Urt 188
Utkin, Nikolay 227
Uvarov, Alexander 232

Uvarov, Sergey 131, 153

Vahylevych, Ivan 84
Varentsov, Viktor 216
Vasari, Giorgio 44
Vasilchikov, Ilarion 242–5, 266
Vasylivka 113
Vasylkiv 130
Velgorsky, Mikhail 35, 36, 38, 56
Velychko, Samiilo 207
Venetsianov, Aleksey 33, 35, 36, 41
Veryho 164
Vidler 158
Vilkhivska, Tetiana 81
Vilno (Vilnius) 21–4, 27, 211
Vilshana 4, 19, 20, 31
Vitzthum, Alexander 45, 46, 52
Vladimir 223
Vladislavlev, Vladimir 56
Voinarovsky, Andriy 236
Volga 213, 214
Volhynia 130-2
Volkonsky, Sergey 99, 225
Volsky, Witołd 241, 242
Voronizh 79
Vorontsov 242
Vovchok, Marko 74, 216, 219, 230, 233, 234
Vyshnivka 131
Vytavsky 253

Warsaw 21–30, 100, 140
Watt, James 214
Węgrzynowski, Arkady 160, 194, 195, 205, 207
Werner, Tomasz 182–4, 187, 189, 192, 197
Worcell, Stanisław 53
Wurtemberg, Alexander 27

Yagnitsky 242

Yahotyn 83, 89–91, 93, 97–9, 102, 112, 117, 168, 170, 193, 238, 257
Yakhnenko, Kindrat 240
Yaksha-Kairokta 180
Yakushkin, Pavel 256
Yaman-Kairokta 180
Yaman-Okty 181
Yaroslav 4
Yegorov, Aleksey 34
Yelysavet 11, 22
Yerofeev, Stepan 182, 186
Yershov, Piotr 56
Yezhov, Kindrat 71, 72
Yezuchevsky, Vasyl 56, 170
Yuzefovych, Mykhailo 106, 113, 125, 128, 140
Yuzhakov 263

Zabarzhada 194
Zabila, Nadia 249
Zabila, Viktor 25, 26, 79, 83, 102, 103, 133, 134, 267
Zaitsev, Ivan 30
Zakrevska, Hanna 82, 98
Zakrevska, Maria 82, 98
Zakrevska, Sophia 81, 98
Zakrevsky, Platon 82, 98, 101, 102, 112, 116
Zakrevsky, Viktor 82, 98, 101
Zaleski, Bohdan 44
Zaleski, Bronisław 23, 193–5, 204–11, 216
Zaleski, Wacław 84
Zalizniak, Maksym 8
Zaporozhian Sich 8, 9, 65, 72, 84, 86
Zavadovsky, Petro 20
Zeisyk, Michal 195
Zelena Dibrova 10, 17
Zeligowski, Edward Sowa 226, 227
Zhelekh 14

Zhemchuzhnikov, Aleksey 216, 234
Zhemchuzhnikov, Lev 216, 234, 256, 261, 263
Zhukovsky, Vasiliy 30, 33–8, 42, 48, 166, 167, 196, 197, 255
Zhytomyr 130
Zielonka, Michał 195
Žižka, Jan 116
Zvenyhorod 3, 19

www.ingramcontent.com/pod-product-compliance
Lightning Source LLC
Chambersburg PA
CBHW020356080526
44584CB00014B/1037